William Brown and Co.

The Liquor Prohibition Appeal, 1895

An appeal from the Supreme Court of Canada to Her Majesty the Queen in Council

William Brown and Co.

The Liquor Prohibition Appeal, 1895
An appeal from the Supreme Court of Canada to Her Majesty the Queen in Council

ISBN/EAN: 9783743423589

Manufactured in Europe, USA, Canada, Australia, Japa

Cover: Foto ©Suzi / pixelio.de

Manufactured and distributed by brebook publishing software (www.brebook.com)

William Brown and Co.

The Liquor Prohibition Appeal, 1895

THE
LIQUOR PROHIBITION APPEAL,
1895.

AN APPEAL

FROM

THE SUPREME COURT OF CANADA

TO

HER MAJESTY
THE QUEEN IN COUNCIL.

London :
PRINTED BY WILLIAM BROWN & CO. LIMITED,
36-42, ST. MARY AXE, AND 40-41, OLD BROAD STREET, E.C.
1895.

TABLE OF CONTENTS.

In the Privy Council.

FROM THE SUPREME COURT OF CANADA.

BETWEEN THE ATTORNEY-GENERAL FOR ONTARIO *Appellant*

AND

(1) THE ATTORNEY-GENERAL FOR THE DOMINION OF CANADA, and (2) THE DISTILLERS' AND BREWERS' ASSOCIATION OF ONTARIO - - - *Respondents.*

In the Matter of certain Questions referred to the Supreme Court of Canada by His EXCELLENCY THE GOVERNOR-GENERAL OF CANADA.

SUBJECT :

PROVINCIAL JURISDICTION,
PROHIBITORY LIQUOR LAWS.

Appellant's Case.

1. This is an appeal brought by special leave of Her Majesty in Council against the judgment of the Supreme Court of Canada given on the 15th January 1895, in the matter of certain questions referred to that Court by His Excellency the Governor-General of Canada.

2. Under the provisions of the Act of the Parliament of Canada 54-55 Victoria, chapter 25, section 4, His Excellency the Governor-General of Canada, by Order in Council passed on the 26th October 1893, submitted to the Supreme Court of Canada for hearing and consideration the following questions, namely :—

(1) Has a Provincial Legislature jurisdiction to

prohibit the sale within the Province of spirituous,
fermented, or other intoxicating liquors?

(2) Or has the Legislature such jurisdiction regarding such portions of the Province as to which the
Canada Temperance Act is not in operation?

(3) Has a Provincial Legislature jurisdiction to
prohibit the manufacture of such liquors within the
Province?

(4) Has a Provincial Legislature jurisdiction to
prohibit the importation of such liquors into the Province?

(5) If a Provincial Legislature has not jurisdiction
to prohibit sales of such liquors, irrespective of quantity,
has such Legislature jurisdiction to prohibit the sale, by
retail, according to the definition of a sale by retail,
either in statutes in force in the Province at the time of
confederation, or any other definition thereof?

(6) If a Provincial Legislature has a limited jurisdiction only as regards the prohibition of sales, has the
Legislature jurisdiction to prohibit sales subject to the
limits provided by the several sub-sections of the 99th
section of "The Canada Temperance Act" or any of
them (Revised Statutes of Canada, chapter 106 section 99)?

(7) Has the Ontario Legislature jurisdiction to
enact the 18th section of the Act passed by the Legislature of Ontario in the 53rd year of Her Majesty's reign,
and intituled "An Act to improve the Liquor License
Acts," as said section is explained by the Act passed by
the said Legislature in the 54th year of Her Majesty's
reign, and intituled "An Act respecting Local Option in
the matter of Liquor selling"?

3. The said 18th section of the Act of the Legislature
of Ontario, 53rd Victoria, chapter 56, referred to in the last
of the said questions, is as follows:—

"18. Whereas the following provision of this
" section was at the date of confederation in force as a
" part of the Consolidated Municipal Act (29th and 30th
" Victoria, chapter 51, section 249, sub-section 9), and
" was afterwards re-enacted as sub-section 7 of section 6

" of 32nd Victoria, chapter 32, being the Tavern and
" Shop License Act of 1868, but was afterwards omitted
" in subsequent consolidations of the Municipal and
" The Liquor License Acts, similar provisions as to local
" prohibition being contained in the Temperance Act of
" 1864, 27th and 28th Victoria, chapter 18 ; and the
" said last-mentioned Act having been repealed in
" municipalities where not in force by the Canada
" Temperance Act, it is expedient that municipalities
" should have the powers by them formerly possessed ;
" it is hereby enacted as follows :—

" The council of every township, city, town, and
" incorporated village may pass by-laws for prohibiting
" the sale by retail of spirituous, fermented, or other
" manufactured liquors in any tavern, inn, or other
" house or place of public entertainment, and for pro-
" hibiting altogether the sale thereof in shops and places
" other than houses of public entertainment. Provided
" that the by-law before the final passing thereof has
" been duly approved of by the electors of the munici-
" pality in the manner provided by the sections in that
" behalf of the Municipal Act. Provided further that
" nothing in this section contained shall be construed
" into an exercise of jurisdiction by the Legislature of
" the Province of Ontario beyond the revival of pro-
" visions of law which were in force at the date of the
" passing of the British North America Act, and which
" the subsequent legislation of this Province purported
" to repeal."

4. The Act of the Legislature of Ontario, 54 Victoria,
chapter 46, also referred to in the said seventh question, is
as follows :—

" 1. It is hereby declared that the Legislature of
" this Province, by enacting section 18 of the Act to im-
" prove the Liquor License Laws, passed in the 53rd
" year of Her Majesty's reign, chaptered 56, for the re-
" vival of provisions of law which were in force at the
" date of the British North America Act 1867, did not
" intend to affect the provisions of section 252 of the
" Consolidated Municipal Act, being chapter 51 of the

" Acts passed in the 29th and 30th years of her Majesty's
" reign by the late Parliament of Canada, which enacted
" that ' No tavern or shop license shall be necessary for
" ' selling any liquors in the original packages in which
" ' the same have been received from the importer or
" ' manufacturer, provided such packages contain re-
" ' spectively not less than five gallons or one dozen
" ' bottles,' save in so far as the said section 252 may
" have been affected by the 9th sub-section of section 249
" of the same Act, and save in so far as licenses for sales
" in such quantities are required by the Liquor License
" Act : and the said section 18 and all by-laws which
" have heretofore been made or shall hereafter be made
" under the said section 18, and purporting to prohibit
" the sale by retail of spirituous, fermented, or other
" manufactured liquors in any tavern, inn, or other house
" or place of public entertainment, and prohibiting alto-
" gether the sale thereof in shops and places other than
" houses of public entertainment, are to be construed as
" not purporting or intended to affect the provisions con-
" tained in the said section 252, save as aforesaid and as
" if the said section 18 and the said by-laws had expressly
" so declared."

5. The said Court at the said hearing was composed of
five judges, and the said questions were on the 15th January,
1895, all answered in the negative by three of the said judges,
the other two judges being of the opinion that all the said
questions should be answered in the affirmative except questions three and four.

6. Previous to the passing of the British North America
Act, 1867, the Legislatures of the several Provinces which
were formed into the Dominion of Canada had conferred upon
the municipalities within the respective Provinces large prohibitory powers with respect to the traffic in intoxicating
liquors, and ever since the said date the said traffic had been
prohibited in a large portion of the Dominion under and by
virtue of such legislation, and of similar legislation by the
several Provincial Legislatures.

7. The Appellant humbly submits that the present ap-

peal should be allowed, and the said questions answered in
the affirmative for, among others, the following

REASON.

Because the matters mentioned in the said questions
come within the classes of subjects enumerated in
section 92 of the British North America Act,
1867, and more particularly sub-sections 8, 9, 13
and 16 of the said section, and do not come within any of the classes of subjects enumerated in
section 91 of the said Act.

JOHN J. MACLAREN.

J. R. CARTWRIGHT.

Case of the Dominion of Canada,

ONE OF THE RESPONDENTS.

1.   This is an Appeal from the judgment of the Supreme Court of Canada, rendered on the 15th day of January 1895, upon certain questions referred by the Governor-General in Council to the Supreme Court of Canada for hearing and consideration, pursuant to "The Supreme and Exchequer Courts Act," (Revised Statutes of Canada, Chap. 135) as amended by an Act of the Parliament of Canada passed in 1891 (54-55 Vic., Chap. 25, Sec. 4).

2.   The questions referred are as follows :—

(1) Has a Provincial Legislature jurisdiction to prohibit the sale within the Province of spirituous, fermented or other intoxicating liquors ?

(2) Or has the Legislature such jurisdiction regarding such portions of the Province as to which the Canada Temperance Act is not in operation ?

(3) Has a Provincial Legislature jurisdiction to prohibit the manufacture of such liquors within the Province ?

(4) Has a Provincial Legislature jurisdiction to prohibit the importation of such liquors into the Province ?

(5) If a Provincial Legislature has not jurisdiction to prohibit sales of such liquors, irrespective of quantity, has such Legislature jurisdiction to prohibit the sale by retail, according to the definition of a sale by retail, either in Statutes in force in the Province at the time of Confederation, or any other definition thereof ?

(6) If a Provincial Legislature has a limited jurisdiction only as regards the prohibition of sales, has the Legislature jurisdiction to prohibit sales subject to the

limits provided by the several sub-sections of the 99th Section of "The Canada Temperance Act" or any of them (Revised Statutes of Canada, Chap. 106, Sec. 99) ?

(7) Had the Ontario Legislature jurisdiction to enact the 18th Section of the Act passed by the Legislature of Ontario in the 53rd year of Her Majesty's reign, and intituled "An Act to improve the Liquor License Acts," as said section is explained by the Act passed by the said Legislature in the 54th year of Her Majesty's reign, and intituled "An Act respecting Local Option in the matter of liquor selling ?

3.   At the hearing of the Case before the Supreme Court of Canada, constituted of the Chief Justice Sir Henry Strong, and Justices Fournier, Gwynne, Sedgwick and King, Counsel appeared for the Dominion and for the respective Provinces of Ontario, Quebec and Manitoba.   Counsel also appeared on behalf of The Distillers' and Brewers' Association of Ontario, that Association being represented under the authority of Sub-Sec. 4 of Sec. 37 of the Supreme and Exchequer Courts' Act.   Afterwards written opinions were delivered by each of the five Judges who heard the Case, in the result of which questions numbered 3 and 4 were unanimously answered in the negative, while as to each of the remaining questions, a majority of the Judges gave a negative answer, the Chief Justice and Mr. Justice Fournier holding, however, that they should be answered in the affirmative.

4.   From this decision the Attorney-General of Ontario obtained special leave to appeal.   The Respondents on the Appeal are The Dominion of Canada and The Distillers and Brewers' Association of Ontario.

5.   It is submitted on behalf of the Dominion that a Provincial Legislature has no authority to prohibit the sale, manufacture or importation of spirituous, fermented or other intoxicating liquors, and that it has no authority to prohibit the sale of such liquors either by wholesale or retail or subject to the exemptions established by the 99th Section of the Canada Temperance Act, and that the several questions contained in the Case submitted have therefore been properly answered in the negative. In support of this view the

Dominion will rely upon the grounds stated in the opinions of the Judges of the Supreme Court, and upon the following among other—

REASONS.

1. Because the subject of prohibition of the liquor traffic, either as to manufacture, importation or sale does not fall within any of the matters for Provincial Legislation enumerated in Section 92 of "The British North America Act, 1867."

2. Because the exclusive power of the Legislatures with regard to municipal institutions only enables the Legislature to establish regulations for the carrying on within their respective Provinces of such institutions, and any authority which the Legislatures may validly confer upon them must be derived through or have relation to the other subjects enumerated in Section 92. These do not include power to prohibit.

3. Because, whilst the Legislatures may have power under the Article " Municipal Institutions " or as part of the police power to make regulations for the carrying on within the respective Provinces of any lawful trade, they have no power to declare any trade unlawful or to prohibit the carrying on of the same, or to enact prohibitory laws containing as to their respective Provinces provisions similar to those of " The Canada Temperance Act."

4. Because to enable a Province to pass a prohibitory law for itself by reason of the authority of class No. 16 of Sec. 92, it would be necessary to construe the words "local or private" as including provincial, which construction is negatived upon a consideration of all the provisions of Section 92. Prohibition for the Province would be rather a public and provincial or public and general matter, than merely local or private. The expression "merely local or private matters in the Province " is intended to describe something less than a matter of equal and general application and interest to the entire Province.

5. Because the subject of prohibition strictly relates to matters within the exclusive authority of the Parliament of Canada, under Section 91 of " The British North America Act."

(*a*) It affects the peace, order and good government of Canada in relation to matters not coming within the classes of subjects assigned exclusively to the Legislatures of the Provinces.

(*b*) It necessarily comes within the scope of Dominion authority in the regulation of trade and commerce. The Supreme Court of Canada so held in the case of *Fredericton* v. *The Queen*, 3 Supreme Court of Canada Reports, 505, from which *Russell* v. *The Queen* was in effect an Appeal.

(*c*) It affects and has direct relation to Criminal law, which is one of the enumerated classes of subjects assigned exclusively to the Parliament of Canada.

6. Because trade and commerce would be affected by legislation restraining importation and manufacture. As a matter of trade and commerce the right to sell is inseparably connected with the law permitting importation, to which, with equal force, may be added *manufacture.*

7. Because before, at the time, and ever since the Union, a considerable portion of the public revenue has been derived from the customs and excise duties upon alcoholic liquors. The Dominion, under the terms of Union, assumed the public debt and the principal expense of the public service, besides undertaking to pay large subsidies to the Provinces, and became entitled to levy customs and excise duties, which had always been principal sources of revenue.

8. Because the field of legislation with regard to prohibition has been occupied by the enactment of the Canada Temperance Act, which still remains in force, and there is therefore no room for a Provincial Law.

9. Because Parliament having declared that it is desirable that there should be uniform legislation in all the Provinces respecting the traffic in intoxicating liquors, and that it is expedient for the peace, order and good government of Canada that the voters in every County or City in Canada should have the right to elect whether or not prohibition, as defined by the Canada Temperance Act, shall come into effect in such County or City, has given effect to the voluntary principle. If the Provincial Legislatures may, nevertheless, enact a compulsory system, the power of Parliament, which has been hitherto upheld, is denied.

10. Because there is no legal or absolute destinction between wholesale and retail trade, and the distinction between them whatever it may be, cannot be made a dividing line of prohibitive authority as between Parliament and the Legislatures.

11. Because definitions of sale by retail in Provincial Statutes at Confederation cannot affect the construction of the Union Act, which makes no reference to retail, nor other reference which renders it necessary to look for a definition of the word. Besides upon the Provincial legislation existing at the Union it appears that there was no uniformity of statutory definition.

12. Because Parliament and the Provincial Legislatures have under the British North America Act no concurrent authority except as to agriculture and immigration, under the provisions of Section 95.

13. Because the fact that particular enactments were in force at the Union cannot enlarge the powers of the Legislature of Ontario under the British North America Act.

14. Because Section 18 of the Ontario Act is inconsistent with and in conflict with the provisions of the Canada Temperance Act.

E. L. NEWCOMBE,

H. W. LOEHNIS.

Case for the Respondents,

THE DISTILLERS' & BREWERS' ASSOCIATION OF ONTARIO.

1.   This is an Appeal from a decision of the Supreme Court of Canada, upon a reference to that Court by His Excellency the Governor-General of Canada, for hearing and consideration of the following questions :—

2.   (1) Has a Provincial Legislature jurisdiction to prohibit the sale within the province of spirituous fermented or other intoxicating liquors ?

(2) Or has the Legislature such jurisdiction regarding such portions of the province as to which the Canada Temperance Act is not in operation ?

(3) Has a Provincial Legislature jurisdiction to prohibit the manufacture of such liquors within the province ?

(4) Has a Provincial Legislature jurisdiction to prohibit the importation of such liquors into the province ?

(5) If a Provincial Legislature has not Jurisdiction to prohibit sales of such liquors, irrespective of quantity, has such Legislature jurisdiction to prohibit the sale by retail according to the definition of a sale by retail, either in Statutes in force in the Province at the time of confederation. or any other definition thereof ?

(6) If a Provincial Legislature has a limited jurisdiction only as regards the prohibition of sales, has the Legislature jurisdiction to prohibit sales subject to the limits provided by the several sub-sections of the 99th section of "The Canada Temperance Act" or any of them (Revised Statutes of Canada. Chapter 106, Section 99).

(7) Had the Ontario Legislature jurisdiction to enact

the 18th Section of the Act passed by the Legislature of Ontario in the fifty-third year of Her Majesty's reign and intituled "An Act to improve the Liquor License Acts" as said section is explained by the Act passed by the said Legislature in the fifty-fourth year of Her Majesty's reign and intituled "An Act respecting Local Option in the matter of Liquor selling"?

For convenience of reference the enactments referred to in questions (6) and (7) are appended to this case.

3.   Pursuant to leave given by the Supreme Court under the statute in that behalf the Distillers' and Brewers' Association of Ontario (hereinafter called "the Association") were represented at the hearing before that Court.

4.   At such hearing were also represented the Attorneys-General of Canada, Ontario, Quebec, and Manitoba.

5.   In the result the Court answered all the questions in the negative in accordance with the contentions of the Association, the answers being unanimous as to questions (*iii*) and (*iv*), and by a majority as to the other questions.

6.   From this decision the Attorney-General of Ontario obtained leave to appeal, and on that appeal the Respondents are the Attorney-General of Canada and the Association.

7.   The Association submits that the decision of the Supreme Court was right and should be confirmed for the reasons stated in the judgments of the majority of the Supreme Court and on the grounds following.

REASONS.

1. Upon the true construction of the British North America Act as settled by decision of the Privy Council the Provinces have no legislative authority on any matter unless it is comprised within some of the subjects enumerated in Sec. 92 of the Act.

2. Upon such construction as so settled, the Provinces have no such authority (even if the matter might otherwise be so comprised), in any case wherein, or

to any extent whereby, the exercise of such authority
would interfere with the exercise by Canada of any
authority comprised within any of the articles of
Sec. 91 of the Act.

3. Upon such construction as so settled, the subject of
the prohibition of the trade of selling intoxicating
liquors, even by retail, in Canada, is not comprised
within Sec. 92.

4. It is submitted that *a fortiori* the prohibition of the
wholesale trade in liquors, or of the business of
manufacturing or importing liquors is not comprised
within Sec. 92.

5. Upon such construction as so settled, each of these
subjects not being comprised within Sec. 92, is
within the authority of the Parliament of Canada,
under its general powers conferred by Sec. 91
" to make laws for the peace, order and good
government of Canada, in relation to all matters not
coming within the classes of subjects assigned
exclusively to the Legislatures of the Provinces."

6. Among the subjects placed by Sec. 91 within the
exclusive authority of Canada are the regulation of
trade and commerce, the public debt, the raising of
money by any mode or system of taxation, and the
borrowing of money on the public credit.

By the Act, Canada became bound to pay the heavy
provincial debts, and to provide for the Provinces
large annual subsidies.

One of the main objects of the Act was to place the
trade and commerce of the various Provinces under
the general control of the central authority, and thus
to promote the removal, and to prevent the creation
of artificial barriers and diversities in this regard
between the Provinces.

The whole system of taxation by the Provinces before
Confederation was, and that of Canada since has
been and must long continue, indirect and large
sums had before and have since been yearly levied
by duties of Customs and Excise in order to meet

c

the public obligations and to maintain the public
services.

The ability of Canada to accomplish these and other
national objects was and is plainly dependent on
her possession of exclusive powers over trade and
commerce which she would not enjoy were it within
the legislative authority of the Provinces to prohibit
the manufacture, importation, or sale of goods, and
thus while creating artificial and prejudicial barriers
to trade and diversities of trade conditions to prevent
Canada from obtaining the duties of Customs and
Excise on which she must necessarily depend for
the performance of her national obligations.

The Customs and Excise duties on liquor, like those
on tobacco were before confederation as they have
ever since continued a substantial and necessary
part of the fiscal resources of Canada, and an
intolerable condition might be produced if each of
the Provinces had power to cut off from Canada her
receipts from these duties within the limits of such
Provinces.

It is obvious that the same Legislature which has
pcwer over these subjects in their trade and revenue
aspects should also control them in any other aspects
as to which the existence of a control elsewhere
might be fatal to the execution of the powers
conferred for trade and revenue purposes.

It is submitted that on the true construction of the
Act, the Parliament of Canada has been granted the
exclusive Legislative Authority over the subjects, as
part of "the regulation of Trade and Commerce,"
and that thus, even if apart from such grant they
or some of them might have been comprised within
the assignment to the Provinces, they are yet by
virtue of the grant vested in Canada.

7. Upon the true construction of the British North
America Act as established by decision of the Privy
Council there exists a broad distinction between an
authority to prohibit trades as unlawful and an

authority to prescribe conditions on which lawful
trades may be conducted.

And such latter authority may, within certain limitations, be vested in the Provincial Legislatures, under
the Article "Municipal Institutions," as part of the
police power, or under some other Article of Sec. 92,
quite consistently with the exclusive vesting in
Canada of the authority to prohibit.

8. There is here no concurrent jurisdiction; nor are
there two different aspects in which the subject can
be viewed so as to bring it in one aspect within
Canadian, and in the other within Provincial
Legislative power. It is the same subject under the
same aspect.

9. There is here no room for the contention that there
may exist a Provincial Jurisdiction unless and until
the Parliament of Canada occupies the field.

10. But if this were otherwise, yet the Parliament of
Canada has already occupied the field, by legislation
which provides certain conditions and limitations
under and to the extent of which sales are prohibited
all over Canada, and has thus in effect legislatively
decided that, save under and to the extent of these
conditions and limitations, sales shall not be prohibited anywhere in Canada.

11. On the true construction of the British North America
Act, as settled by decision of the Privy Council,
there is in this connexion no distinction favorable to
the Provinces as between wholesale and retail dealing.

12. There is no definition of retail and wholesale dealing
available for the suggested purpose, and the only
defining power that can be reasonably suggested is
the Parliament of Canada, which would thus
practically retain in its hands the control of the
subject.

13. The attempt to sustain the 18th Section of the
Ontario Act on the ground that it is a revival of the
analogous section of the preconfederation law must
fail, because the subject of that section, as already

c 2

shown, fell, after confederation, within the exclusive authority of the Parliament of Canada, by which alone it could be as it has been since affected.

14. The attempt to include the subject of that section within Provincial legislative power under the head of " Municipal Institutions " because it happened shortly before confederation to be embraced in a municipal Act by one Province must fail.

At the time of that legislation each Province had full legislative authority, and the mode of exercising such authority, whether direct or by reference to municipal bodies, was optional and changeable at pleasure. The experiment, for such it was, of entrusting municipal bodies with certain powers of prohibition had been entered on in the late Province of Canada shortly before confederation. That experiment had not been attempted in either Nova Scotia or New Brunswick.

Neither in the practice of the four Provinces nor in the nature of the subject nor in the methods of the United Kingdom is to be found any consensus of views or any established meaning which can be successfully invoked to show that the subject is in the British North America Act comprised within " Municipal Institutions."

It would be wrong to use the accident of the partial legislation referred to as ground for enlarging the phrase "Municipal Institutions," so as to vest in all the " Provincial legislatures," to be exercised at the option of each Province either directly or through the municipalities, a power so extensive and so inconsistent with the general scheme of the Act.

15. It is not to be overlooked that in an important particular, namely, with reference to cities, this 18th section conflicts in terms with the Canada Temperance Act.

16. On the whole, it is submitted that the answers of the Supreme Court should be approved and that the appeal should be dismissed.

EDWARD BLAKE.

APPENDIX

CASE FOR THE DISTILLERS' AND BREWERS' ASSOCIATION OF ONTARIO.

(I.)

Section 99 of the Canada Temperance Act, Revised Statutes of Canada, 1886, cap. 106, referred to in the Question Number 6 is as follows:—

"99. From the day on which this part of this Act comes into force and takes effect in any County or City, and for so long thereafter as the same continues in force therein, no person shall within such County or City, by himself, his clerk, servant or agent, expose or keep for sale or directly or indirectly on any pretence or upon any device, sell or barter or in consideration of the purchase of any other property, give to any other person any intoxicating liquor.

"2. No act done in violation of this section shall be rendered lawful by reason of

(*a*) Any license issued to any distiller or brewer; or

(*b*) Any license for retailing on board any steamboat or other vessel, brandy, rum, whiskey or other spirituous liquors, wine, ale, beer, porter, cider or other vinous or fermented liquors; or

(*c*) Any license for retailing on board any steamboat or other vessel, wine, ale, beer, porter, cider or other vinous or fermented liquors but not brandy, rum, whiskey or other spirituous liquors; or

(*d*) Any license of any other description whatsoever ;

" 3. Provided always that the sale of wine for exclusively sacramental purposes may, on the certificate of a clergyman affirming that the wine is required for sacramental purposes be made by druggists and vendors thereto specially licensed by the Lieutenant-Governor in each Province ; but the number of such licensed druggists and vendors shall not exceed one in each Township or Parish or two in each Town, or one for every four thousand inhabitants in each City.

" 4. Provided also that the sale of intoxicating liquor for exclusively medicinal purposes or for *bonâ fide* use in some art, trade or manufacture, may be made by such licensed druggists and vendors ; but such sale when for medicinal purposes shall be in quantities of not less than one pint, to be removed from the premises, and shall be made only on the certificate of a medical man having no interest in the sale, affirming that such liquor has been prescribed for the person named therein ; and when such sale is for its use in some art, trade or manufacture, the same shall be made only on the certificate signed by two Justices of the Peace, of the good faith of the application, accompanied by the affirmation of the applicant that the liquor is to be used only for the particular purposes set forth in the affirmation ; and such druggist or vendor shall file the certificates and keep a register of all such sales indicating the name of the purchaser and the quantity sold, and shall make an annual return of all such sales, on the Thirty-first day of December in every year, to the collector of Inland Revenue within whose revenue division the County or City is situated :

" 5. Provided also, that any producer of cider in the County may, at his premises, and any licensed distiller or brewer, having his distillery or brewery within any County or City, may, at such distillery or brewery, expose

and keep for sale such liquor as he manufactures thereat,
and no other ; and may sell the same thereat but only in
quantities not less than ten gallons, or in the case of ale
or beer, not less than eight gallons at any one time, and
only to druggists and vendors licensed as aforesaid, or to
such persons as he has good reason to believe will forthwith carry the same beyond the limits of the County or
City, and of any adjoining County or City in which this
part of this Act is then in force, and to be wholly
removed or taken away in quantities not less than ten
gallons, or in the case of ale or beer, not less than eight
gallons at a time.

" 6. Provided also, that any incorporated Company
authorised by law to carry on the business of cultivating
and growing vines and of making and selling wine and
other liquors produced from grapes, having their manufactory within such County or City, may thereat expose
and keep for sale such liquor as they manufacture thereat
and no other ; and may sell the same thereat, but only
in quantities not less than ten gallons at any one time,
and only to druggists and vendors licensed as aforesaid
or to such persons as they have good reason to believe
will forthwith carry the same beyond the limits of the
County or City and of any adjoining County or City in
which this part of this Act is then in force and to be
wholly removed and taken away in quantities not less
than ten gallons at a time.

" 7. Provided also, that manufacturers of pure
native wines made from grapes grown and produced by
them in Canada, may when authorised so to do, by
license from the Municipal Council, or other authority
having jurisdiction where such manufacture is carried
on, sell such wines at the place of manufacture in
quantities of not less than ten gallons at one time except
when sold for sacramental or medicinal purposes when
any number of gallons from one to ten may be sold.

" 8. Provided also, that any merchant or trader,
exclusively in wholesale trade and duly licensed to sell
liquor by wholesale, having his store or place for sale of
goods within such County or City, may thereat keep for

sale and sell intoxicating liquor but only in quantities not less than ten gallons at any one time, and only to druggists and vendors licensed as aforesaid, or to such persons as he has good reason to believe will forthwith carry the same beyond the limits of the County or City and of any adjoining County or City in which this part of this Act is then in force, to be wholly removed and taken away in quantities not less than ten gallons at a time.

" 9. In any prosecution against a producer, distiller, brewer, manufacturer, merchant, or trader under this section it shall lie upon the defendant to furnish satisfactory evidence of having good reason for believing that such liquor would be forthwith removed beyond the limits of the County or City, and of any adjoining County or City in which this part of this Act is then in force, for consumption outside the same."—41 Vic. c. 16, s. 99.

(II.)

Section 18 of the Statute passed by the legislature of Ontario in the 53rd year of Her Majesty's reign, chap. 56, referred to in Question Number 7 is as follows :

" 18. Whereas the following provision of this section was at the date of Confederation in force as a part of The Consolidated Municipal Act (29 and 30 Vic., cap. 51, sec. 249, sub-sec. 9), and was afterwards re-enacted as sub-sec. 7 of sec. 6 of 32 Vic., cap. 32, being The Tavern and Shops' License Act of 1868, but was afterwards omitted in subsequent consolidations of The Municipal and the Liquor License Acts, similar provisions as to local prohibition being contained in the Temperance Act of 1864 (27 and 28 Vic., cap. 18), and the said last-mentioned Act having been repealed in Municipalities where not in force by The Canada Temperance Act, it is expedient that Municipalities should have the powers by them formerly possessed; it is hereby enacted as follows :—

"The Council of every Township, City, Town and incorporated Village may pass by-laws for prohibiting the sale by retail of spirituous, fermented, or other manufactured liquors in any tavern, inn, or other house or place cf public entertainment, and for prohibiting altogether the sale thereof in shops and places other than houses of public entertainment : Provided that the by-law before the final passing thereof has been duly approved of by the Electors of the Municipality in the manner provided by the sections in that behalf of the Municipal Act : Provided further that nothing in this section contained shall be construed into an exercise of jurisdiction by the Legislature of the Province of Ontario beyond the revival of provisions of law which were in force at the date of the passing of The British North America Act, and which the subsequent legislation of this Province purported to repeal."

The explanatory Act of Ontario passed in the 54th year of Her Majesty's reign, chap. 46, also referred to in Question Number 7 is as follows :—

"Her Majesty by and with the advice and consent of the Legislative Assembly of the Province of Ontario enacts as follows :—

"1. It is hereby declared that the Legislature of this Province by enacting Section 18 of the Act to improve the Liquor License Laws, passed in the 53rd year of Her Majesty's reign, chapter 56, for the revival of provisions of law which were in force at the date of the British North America Act, 1867, did not intend to affect the provisions of Section 252 of the Consolidated Municipal Act, being chapter 51 of the Acts passed in the 29th and 30th years of Her Majesty's reign by the late Parliament of Canada, which enacted that ' No tavern or shop license shall be necessary for selling any liquors in the original packages in which the same have been received from the importer or manufacturer ; provided such packages contain respectively not less than five gallons or one dozen bottles,' save in so far as the said Section 252 may have been affected by the 9th Sub-section of Section 249 of the same Act, and save in so far as licenses for sales in such quantities are required by the Liquor License Act; and the said Section 18 and all By-Laws which have heretofore been made or shall hereafter be made under the said Section 18 and purporting to prohibit the sale by retail of spirituous, fermented or other manufactured liquors, in any tavern, inn, or other house or place of public entertainment, and prohibiting altogether the sale thereof in shops and places other than houses of public entertainment, are to be construed as not purporting or intended to affect the provisions contained in the said Section 252, save as aforesaid, and as if the said section 18 and the said by-laws had expressly so declared.

" 2. Whereas doubts have arisen as to the power of this Legislature to enact the provisions of the said Section 18 or of the said section as explained by this Act, and it is expedient to avoid a multiplicity of appeals involving the said question, the Lieutenant-Governor in Council is to refer to the Court of Appeal for Ontario under authority of the Act for expediting the decision of Constitutional and other provincial questions, the question of the constitutional validity of the said Section 18 and its true construction, effect and application.

" 3. The reference under this Act to the Court of Appeal by the Lieutenant-Governor in Council is to be heard in priority to any other cause or matter in said Court, unless the Court otherwise orders.

" 4. In case any by-law passed under said Section '8 is quashed before the passing of this Act the applica-.ion may be reheard by the High Court of Justice, at the instance of the Municipality which passed said by-law by motion on ten days' notice served on the relator, or within such further time as may be allowed by a judge of the High Court and the Court shall make such order for the rescission of the order to quash and as to costs as to the Court shall seem meet.

" 5. The limit as to the time for appealing from the judgment or order of any Court, in the case of quashing a by-law, or any other judgment, shall not apply to an appeal against a judgment or order quashing a by-law passed under the said section 18.

" 6. Where any such by-law has been quashed or has been passed and shall not be quashed before the determination of the questions referred under this Act, by the Lieutenant Governor in Council, to the Court of Appeal, the License Commissioners, under the Liquor License Acts, are not to grant licenses to any new applicants, and may only extend the duration of any existing license, from time to time, for any specified period of the year, not exceeding three months at any one time in their discretion, upon payment of a sum not exceeding the proportionate part of the duty payable for such license for a year.

" 7. All proceedings to quash by-laws passed under the authority of said section 18, or the enforcement of orders for the payment of costs thereon shall be suspended, and no proceedings to quash other such by-laws shall be instituted until after the final determination of the questions to be referred as hereinbefore provided."

In the Privy Council.

COUNCIL CHAMBER, WHITEHALL,
Thursday, *August 1st*, 1895.

Present—

THE RIGHT HON. THE LORD CHANCELLOR
(LORD HALSBURY.)
THE RIGHT HON. LORD HERSCHELL.
THE RIGHT HON. LORD WATSON.
THE RIGHT HON. LORD MORRIS.
THE RIGHT HON. LORD DAVEY.
THE RIGHT HON. SIR RICHARD COUCH.

THE ATTORNEY-GENERAL OF ONTARIO ... ... *Appellant.*

v.

(1) THE ATTORNEY-GENERAL FOR THE DOMINION
OF CANADA AND (2) THE DISTILLERS' AND
BREWERS' ASSOCIATION OF ONTARIO ... *Respondents.*

Counsel for the Appellant, Mr. J. J. MACLAREN, Q.C. (of the Canadian Bar), and Mr. R. B. HALDANE, Q.C., M.P. instructed by Messrs. Freshfields and Williams.

Counsel for the Respondent, the Attorney-General for the Dominion of Canada, Mr. NEWCOMBE, Q.C. (of the Canadian Bar), and Mr. LOEHNIS instructed by Messrs. Bompas, Bischoff, Dodgson, Coxe & Bompas.

Counsel for the Respondents, the Distillers' and Brewers' Association of Ontario, The Honorable E. BLAKE, Q.C., M.P., and Mr. WALLACE NESBITT (both of the Canadian Bar), instructed by Messrs. Linklater, Hackwood, Addison & Brown.

FIRST DAY.

Mr. MACLAREN—My Lords, in this case I appear with my learned friend Mr. Haldane on behalf of the Attorney-General of Ontario, who appeals to your Lordships from a Judgment, or Answers, given by the Supreme Court of Canada to certain questions which were submitted by His Excellency the Governor-General under an Order in Council under a Statute of the Dominion of Canada, for the submission of such questions to the Supreme Court of Canada with a further appeal, by the permission of Her Majesty, to your Lordships.

The questions are seven in number, and were submitted
under an Order in Council passed on the 26th October 1893.
They are as follows :—

" (1) Has a Provincial Legislature jurisdiction to
" prohibit the sale within the Province of spirituous,
" fermented, or other intoxicating liquors ?

" (2) Or has the Legislature such jurisdiction
" regarding such portions of the Province as to which
" the Canada Temperance Act is not in operation ?

" (3) Has a Provincial Legislature jurisdiction to
" prohibit the manufacture of such liquors within the
" Province ?

" (4) Has a Provincial Legislature jurisdiction to
" prohibit the importation of such liquors into the Pro-
" vince ?

" (5) If a Provincial Legislature has not juris-
" diction to prohibit sales of such liquors irrespective of
" quantity, has such Legislature jurisdiction to prohibit
" the sale, by retail, according to the definition of a sale
" by retail either in Statutes in force in the Province at
" the time of confederation, or any other definition
" thereof ?

" (6) If a Provincial Legislature has a limited
" jurisdiction only as regards the prohibition of sales,
" has the Legislature jurisdiction to prohibit sales subject
" to the limits provided by the several subsections of
" the 99th section of ' The Canada Temperance Act,' or
" any of them (Revised Statutes of Canada, chapter 106,
" section 99) ?

" (7) Had the Ontario Legislature jurisdiction to
" enact the 18th section of the Act passed by the Legis-
" lature of Ontario in the 53rd year of Her Majesty's
" reign, and intituled ' An Act to improve the ' Liquor
" License Acts,' as said section is explained by the Act
" by the said Legislature in the 54th year of Her
" Majesty's reign, and intituled ' An Act respecting
" ' Local Option in the matter of Liquor Selling ? ' "

When these questions were submitted to the Supreme
Court in accordance with the powers given them by the
Statute under which the questions were submitted and which

is referred to in the Case, the Supreme Court directed the Attorney-Generals of the various Provinces of the Dominion of Canada to be notified. In answer to this call three Provinces appeared before the Supreme Court at the argument: the Province of Ontario, the Province of Quebec, and the Province of Manitoba. The same Statute gives authority to the Court to allow any interested persons to appear if they think fit. Under this provision the Distillers' and Brewers' Association of Ontario applied for and obtained leave to become parties to the Case. After argument the questions were all answered in the negative by three of the five Judges who sat upon the Case. The two other Judges, the Chief Justice and Mr. Justice Fournier have answered five of the questions in the affirmative but the third and fourth in the negative.

Lord HERSCHELL—That is the prohibition of manufacture and importation ?

Mr. MACLAREN—Yes. The answer "No" to the questions 3 and 4 were unanimous by the Court.

Lord WATSON—Are you challenging those two answers ?

Mr. MACLAREN—We are challenging all. We ask for an affirmative answer to the 7 questions.

The questions 1, 2, 5, 6, and 7 received an affirmative answer therefore from two of the Judges. Your Lordships will observe that the first six questions are general, and in one sense theoretical, and do not refer to any existing legislation. The 7th question is in a different category and refers to an Act which has been passed by the Province of Ontario or to a section of an Act—the 18th section of the Act passed in the 53rd Victoria. I may say, however, that that section 18 which is quoted and which your Lordships will find in the Appellant's Case on page 2 and elsewhere in the Record, although it is section 18 of an Act it is an independent piece of legislation by itself and has no connection with the preceding 17 sections. It is independent legislation though forming only one section of an Act. So that it is not necessary really to refer to the other part of that Statute in order to ascertain the purport of this legislation. As already appears from the Petition which was presented to your Lordships for special leave to

appeal and from the Order in Council in this matter, there
was also before the Supreme Court a case involving the
validity of this 18th section of the 53rd Victoria, namely,
the case of *Huson* v. *South Norwich.* That was between
private parties and had been argued in the Supreme Court
before the submission of the special questions by His
Excellency the Governor-General and stood for judgment.
Judgment was given the same day as the questions were
answered. The Court was differently constituted. It was constituted of five Judges, but one of the Judges who had heard
Huson v. *South Norwich*, Mr. Justice Taschereau, did not sit
when the questions were argued, Mr. Justice King who did
not sit in *Huson* v. *South Norwich* having been subsequently
appointed to the Court sat in the case of the questions that
were submitted by the Governor-General. As a result of the
two arguments there was this anomaly as far as regards this
Act of 1890, that in *Huson* v. *South Norwich* the Court by a
majority of three, composed of the Chief Justice, Mr. Justice
Fournier and Mr. Justice Taschereau held the Ontario Act to
be valid.

Lord WATSON—They must have been right once.

Mr. MACLAREN—They were on the same side both times
but the majority was differently constituted.

Lord WATSON—The Court was differently constituted.

Mr. MACLAREN—Immediately after the rendering of that
Judgment they gave the answers to the questions submitted
by the Governor-General, Mr. Justice Taschereau not sitting
and being replaced by Mr. Justice King. The result
was the opposite so far as this question 7 is concerned—
the minority became the majority and the majority became
the minority. Mr. Justice King answered the questions and
joined the former minority and so in answer to the questions
the Court were 3 against 2. The result is that the Supreme
Court composed of 6 Judges were really equally divided
as to question 7, at least 3 of them being of opinion
that the Act was *ultra vires* and 3 of them being of opinion
that it was within the power of the Provincial Legislature.

Of those who were parties in the Court below the present
Appeal is brought by the Attorney-General of Ontario. The

Province of Quebec was also represented as I mentioned in
the Supreme Court, but I believe does not take any part in
this Appeal. The Province of Manitoba was represented at
the hearing in Ottawa by the same Counsel as Ontario, and I
am instructed by the Attorney-General of Manitoba to say
that he is not a party formally to this Appeal on account of
his concurrence with the position taken by the Province of
Ontario. The other two parties, the Attorney-General of the
Dominion and the Distillers' and Brewers' Association of
Ontario who were parties in the Court below are the
Respondents before your Lordships.

As the Attorney-General for Ontario whom we represent
is specially interested in the Act which was passed and which
is put in question No. 7, I think for that reason and because
historically this really forms a connecting link between the
anterior legislation on this subject and those theoretical
questions that are embraced in the first 6 questions that are
submitted, it would shorten the argument of the case and be
more convenient if your Lordships would allow me to consider the 7th question first. That is concrete legislation—a
special Act of the Legislature of Ontario—and the Attorney-
General for Ontario naturally feels a special interest in that
as legislation which has been declared invalid. In considering the question under the Rules that have been laid
down by your Lordships for the construction of the British
North America Act. it is incumbent on us to show that it
comes within one of the subsections of section 92 of the
British North America Act. In the case of the *Citizens
Insurance Company* v. *Parsons* * your Lordships, I think, for the
first time in a formal way, laid down the Rule for the construction of the British North America Act, and then decided
that the proper test when an Act of a Provincial Legislature
was being considered was whether it came within section 92
of the British North America Act. I will read the passage from
the *Citizens Insurance Company* v. *Parsons* from Cartwright's
Collection of Cases on the British North America Act.

The LORD CHANCELLOR—That was the Fire Insurance
case?

Mr. MACLAREN—The Insurance Case. At page 273 of
the first volume of Cartwright's Collection of Cases on the

* L. R. 7 Ap. Cas. 96.—1 Cart. 265.

British North America Act, your Lordships laid down the
rule as follows, and it has been several times followed :

> " The first question to be decided is whether the Act impeached
> in the present Appeals falls within any of the classes of subjects
> enumerated in section 92 and assigned exclusively to the Legislatures
> of the Provinces, for if it does not, it can be of no validity and no
> other question would then arise. It is only when an Act of Provincial
> Legislature *prima facie* falls within one of these classes of subjects
> that the further questions arise, viz., whether notwithstanding this is
> so, the subject of the Act does not also fall within one of the
> enumerated classes of subjects in section 91, and whether the power of
> the Provincial Legislature is or is not thereby over-borne"

That is the rule by which we are bound here. It is incumbent on the Appellant in this case to show in the first place
that this legislation which is in question before your Lordships, does come within one of the classes of subjects
mentioned in section 92, and that it is not taken out of
section 92 by being included within any of the enumerated
subjects in section 91.

Lord WATSON—Unless it is taken out by the last clause
of section 91 in general terms.

Mr. MACLAREN—There are I think *dicta* of your Lordship's which would go to show that it is only the enumerated
subjects in section 91 that are taken out.

Lord WATSON—That is so.

Mr. MACLAREN—That the general clause at the beginning
in the parenthesis " Notwithstanding anything in this Act,"
and the general clause at the end of section 91, do not override the enumerated subjects in section 92, but that it is only
the enumerated subjects in section 91, which can override
section 92.

Lord HERSCHELL—The general words in section 91
include what you do not find in section 92, but if you find
something in section 92, nevertheless the power in relation
to it may be restricted by the special provisions of section 91.

Mr. MACLAREN—It opens in this way :

> " It shall be lawful for the Queen, by and with the advice and
> consent of the Senate and House of Commons, to make laws for the

peace, order and good government of Canada in relation to all matters not coming within the classes of subjects by this Act assigned exclusively to the Legislatures of the Provinces."

Lord WATSON—We are very familiar with these clauses at the present moment. The result of them is that there may be legislation expressly given to the Dominion Legislature by section 91, which of necessity trenches upon some of the clauses embraced in section 92, some incidentally, others more directly; and when that is the case the Dominion Legislation must override that.

Mr. MACLAREN—Yes, my Lord. Now, with regard to this Act of 1890, which is referred to in question 7, our claim is that it is comprised within the term "municipal institutions," sub-section 8 of section 92. In construing that Act I would respectfully submit to your Lordships that we are to interpret the British North America Act, not exclusively by Imperial Legislation. Though it is in form an Imperial Act, yet it was based upon the Resolutions—almost exclusively upon the Resolutions which had been submitted to the Canadian Provinces. The preamble of the Act sets this out.

Lord WATSON—By being embodied in the Act they acquired the force of an Imperial Statute.

Mr. MACLAREN—But I am going to suggest, that in interpreting particular expressions which are embodied in the Act, and which came textually from the Quebec Resolutions, as they are called, Canadian Legislation is useful in deciding what these particular expressions mean.

Lord HERSCHELL—By giving power to the Provincial Legislature to legislate as to municipal institutions, can they give a municipality power to do all the things mentioned in section 91?

Mr. MACLAREN—Not at all.

Lord HERSCHELL—Or any of them; because that is what puzzles me?

Mr. MACLAREN—Probably I should answer that diffidently, because I think that none of the enumerated subjects in section 91 could be given by a local Legislature to a municipal institution.

Lord HERSCHELL—Take almost any of them. They might give them the power of dealing with "Beacons and Buoys" in some of the Provinces, and they might give them power of dealing with the Postal Service and Weights and Measures.

Mr. MACLAREN—Our argument is this : that the term "municipal institutions" is used in the Act in the sense in which "municipal institutions" were well understood in Canadian legislation at the time of the passing of the British North America Act.

Lord HERSCHELL—You mean that it includes everything that municipalities had been empowered to do, even although they had been empowered to do some of the things in section 91 ?

Mr. MACLAREN—I would say this : that out of Municipal Institutions as they existed at the time of confederation must be taken those subjects allotted to the Dominion by section 91. A local legislature could not legislate itself with regard to, and could not give to a municipality control of any of the subjects enumerated in section 91. Whether the Dominion could or not give it to a Provincial body would be another matter.

Lord HERSCHELL—Could they give anything except what is enumerated in section 92, because their powers were limited to matters enumerated in section 92 ?

Mr. MACLAREN—I would say this, that "Municipal Institutions" is one of the subjects given by section 92——

Lord WATSON—Municipal Institutions, of course, would involve, if it were not a restricted power of legislation, a great many powers that are usually or might be conferred upon and used by a Municipal Institution. It involves all that.

Lord HERSCHELL—Of course "Municipal Institutions" deals with two things, the constitution of municipalities or municipal bodies and their functions. As for the first, they

can constitute them if they please; as to their functions, so
far as that is included in " Municipal Institutions " can they
give them power to do anything which is not a power
conferred on the Provincial Legislature ? Can they delegate
to a municipality or modify the constitution of a municipality
in its functions to give it power to do something besides
the things they have power to do ?

Mr. MACLAREN—One of the enumerated things is
" Municipal Institutions," and my argument is that
" Municipal Institutions " involves not only the right to
create these corporations, but to give them such powers as
were understood to be comprised within the meaning of the
phrase " Municipal Institutions."

Lord WATSON—At the time before the Act passed, the
Provincial Legislature could have given them all the powers
which the Dominion Legislature subsequently had conferred
upon them.   Do you mean that because the phrase
" Municipal Institutions " is used in general terms in sub-
section 8 of section 92, that therefore the Province have
power to continue to create those institutions and to endow
them with powers which they themselves as a Legislature
were not possessed of ?

Mr. MACLAREN—Not at all. My argument is, that out
of the powers which had been conferred upon Municipal
Institutions previous to confederation must be taken out, so
far as local legislation is concerned, all the subjects which
have been assigned to the Dominion.

Lord WATSON—That goes very much back to the question,
do not you think, of what powers in the subsequent Act are
competent to the Provincial and what powers are competent
to the Dominion Legislature ?

Lord HERSCHELL—Of course so far as the Legislature
did so before that law no doubt remains, but the question is
whether the new law can be enforced under any of the
subjects which are enumerated in section 92. I do not see
how they can give the Municipality power to legislate, because
that is what it comes to.

Mr. MACLAREN—My argument would be respectfully

this : that the word " Municipal Institutions " is used in a general sense, and as I hope to be able to show your Lordships, in a sense very well understood in Canadian Legislation, and that when the framers of the Quebec Resolutions which are embodied in the British North America Act, put in Resolution No. 43, the words " Municipal Institutions," and gave the local Legislature authority to pass laws respecting Municipal Institutions, they meant such legislation as had been theretofore enacted in Canada from time to time ; and subjects which were not expressly assigned to the Dominion by section 91. I admit that there are some subjects in section 91 which——

Lord WATSON—Supposing there were a municipality on the sea coast which had charge of buoys and various other subjects given to the Dominion Parliament, you would not say that subsequently the Provincial Legislature could give them any new rights ?

Mr. MACLAREN—Not at all. My argument is that they would not have that power.

Lord HERSCHELL—Your argument is that everything they had done theretofore as Municipal Institutions they may legislate about afterwards ?

Mr. MACLAREN—Not at all, my Lord, because the buoys mentioned by his Lordship are expressly taken out and assigned to the Dominion.

Lord WATSON—I notice you use the words " expressly taken out," but are not there also excepted all things which are fairly included in the general language of any subsection of section 91 ?

Mr. MACLAREN—I did not mean to say that.

Lord DAVEY—The presumption is in favour of section 91.

Mr. MACLAREN—To a certain extent, no doubt.

Lord WATSON—It says that, notwithstanding what has gone before, it shall extend to all matters coming within the class of subjects next thereinafter enumerated. Now, if any matter comes within these classes of subjects, of which there are 29, do you say that any matter coming within these is a matter with which the Provincial Legislature could deal or could endow a municipal institution with power to deal ?

Mr. MACLAREN—My argument is that it could not, my Lord.

Lord HERSCHELL—Let me follow that up. Even although it is not one of the subjects which are given in terms to the Provincial Legislature, yet if it was a subject about which there had been legislation in relation to the municipalities, then it becomes a municipal institution. Do you say that ?

Mr. MACLAREN—If it had been comprised within the municipal institutions.

Lord HERSCHELL—I do not quite understand what you mean by "comprised within the municipal institutions." The thing itself obviously had not, because the question is whether particular legislation about it is good. It must mean that there had been legislation about a particular subject matter, endowing a municipal body with power in relation to it.

Mr. MACLAREN—Yes.

Lord HERSCHELL—Then wherever that had been the case, any legislation with relation to that in the direction of further or altered powers, you say is subject to the other ?

Lord WATSON—That would make the section an exception from the powers conferred by section 91. I do not doubt that under sub-section 8 the creation of municipal institutions is given them ; but on the other hand, with reference to matters as to which the Legislatures have powers to deal, does not it follow that they must look to the Dominion Parliament so far as the matter is committed to the Dominion Parliament on this subject ?

Lord DAVEY—I think there is a case on this very subject in which municipal legislation was held to include such matters.

Mr. MACLAREN—My argument is—and it is necessary for us to argue it in this case—that the words "municipal institutions " in sub-section 8 include not only the creation of corporate b dies and municipal corporations, but also the conferring upon them such powers as usually, at least, belong to such bodies.

Lord HERSCHELL.—But would it be " usually " ? They confer upon municipal institutions every power which they please. Why " usually " ?

Mr. MACLAREN—That they would probably put under one of the other enumerated classes. I was only arguing how much they might do under sub-section 8. They might, I think, confer upon the municipal institutions——

Lord HERSCHELL.—I do not understand myself under sub-section 8 how they have power to confer anything which they do not themselves possess. " Municipal institutions " means the creating of municipal bodies and giving them powers. What powers—all or any of those which they themselves have ? I cannot at present grasp the idea of their being able to give them more.

Lord WATSON—Nor I.

Mr. MACLAREN—My argument is that municipal institutions, as understood in Canadian legislation at the time of and before the passing of the British North America Act, included a large number of subjects which are not by name comprised within any of the other classes of subjects that are enumerated in section 92.

Lord HERSCHELL—As to what it comprised, surely it comprised municipal bodies, and it comprised every right and power which those municipal bodies had. It was not limited to particular subjects ; it included everything.

Mr. MACLAREN- -But there would be, as was mentioned a moment ago by your Lordship, taken out of those subjects which had formerly been included, powers which are not possessed by municipal institutions—at least, so far as local legislation would go. There would be taken out of that the power of the local Legislature to confer all the subjects that are enumerated in section 91.

Lord WATSON—For the first time it distributes the

power between the Dominion and the Provinces, and they must look to the Dominion for the authority to legislate on subjects which are within the Dominion, and they can only look to the locality to exercise authority on subjects which are within the locality.

Lord HERSCHELL—You say "Municipal Institutions" has a technical meaning but where do you derive the technical meaning from?

Mr. MACLAREN—I derive it from the course of Canadian legislation.

Lord WATSON—Prior to 1867?

Mr. MACLAREN—Prior to 1867.

Lord MORRIS—The word "Municipal Institutions" is a very vague phrase, and as I understand you suggest that it had at the time that Statute was passed a well-known meaning, that it comprised a well-known set of institutions and matters which the Legislature were in the habit of dealing with.

Mr. MACLAREN—Yes, my Lord.

Lord MORRIS—You say that it was a well-known phrase there, although not generally speaking known to me or to anybody else.

Mr. MACLAREN—Yes; my argument is that in Canada before confederation, the word "Municipal Institutions" had acquired a well-defined legislative meaning and that it was used in that sense in the Quebec Resolutions, and thereby became used in that sense in the British North America Act.

The LORD CHANCELLOR—I quite follow your argument, but kindly tell me what sense do you attribute to the words in their technical meaning?

Lord MORRIS—I do not know that it is technical; it is in the understood sense.

The LORD CHANCELLOR—But I am using the Attorney-General's own phrase, the sense which he insists upon; I want to know how you define it?

Mr. MACLAREN—I would define it by the powers which were under the Acts respecting Municipal Institutions conferred upon these bodies.

The LORD CHANCELLOR—But I want you to give a dogmatic exposition of what you say it does mean.

Lord WATSON—It includes the right not only to produce legislation and the right not only to create municipalities but to endow those municipalities with all the powers that had been usually given or entrusted to Municipal Institutions before the passing of the Act. Is that what you say?

The LORD CHANCELLOR—Is that what you mean? I want to hear from you what you say.

Mr. MACLAREN—No; I do not go so far as that. I take out of that all that is assigned to the Dominion by section 91.

Lord HERSCHELL—But you must in a sense go further than that, because it is not to endow them with the powers which they possess, it is to give them new powers in relation to subject matters with regard to which they possessed powers before, for you are on new legislation and not old.

Mr. MACLAREN—The legislation which is now in question in Question 7 was old and was before confederation, as I was going to show to your Lordships.

The LORD CHANCELLOR—You have not answered my question yet. Would you mind for the purpose of assisting me telling me what you mean by "Municipal Institutions?"

Mr. MACLAREN—By "Municipal Institutions" I think in subsection 8 is meant the creation of Municipal Corporations or bodies and the conferring upon them of such powers as under Canadian legislation had been understood to belong to such bodies.

Lord HERSCHELL—Canadian legislation of any Province or of all the Provinces do you mean?

Mr. MACLAREN—I was going to show your Lordship that so far as Municipal Institutions existed in the various Provinces, the powers are very much on the same lines.

Lord HERSCHELL—But are not there some that had not then a Legislature ?

Mr. MACLAREN—I was just going to call your Lordships' attention.'   .t in a moment and the class of legislation that was ac. .d.   Some of the Provinces went further than others.   There were at the time of Confederation Municipal Institutions in the sense in which they now exist and in the sense in which I think the phrase was used in the British North America Act.   In two of the Provinces there was a full system of Municipal institutions, that is in Upper and Lower Canada — the old Province of Canada.   In the Provinces of Nova Scotia and New Brunswick, Municipal Institutions as they are now understood, did not exist to the same extent.   I was going to point out to your Lordships the extent to which such legislation as is now in question existed.

Lord HERSCHELL—You say Municipal Institutions in this Act means the more limited powers which were possessed and which were possessed in common or at least such powers as were possessed by anyone—which do you mean ?

Mr. MACLAREN—Probably it would be between the two lines that are drawn by your Lordship.

The LORD CHANCELLOR—I should think that that was fatal to you because the inevitable result would be that you would have nothing.   Do you use the word " Municipal Institutions " in the sense in which you say it was understood in Canada before Confederation took place—is that your proposition ?

Mr. MACLAREN—That is.

The LORD CHANCELLOR—Then you can hardly answer the question in the way you have answered it—that it means neither in substance, because that is what no part of Canada adopted.   That seems fatal to your proposition.

Mr. MACLAREN—I do not know that I have made myself understood by your Lordship, but what I mean is this, that out of the larger powers are taken those subjects, so far as local Legislatures are concerned, that were assigned to the Dominion by section 91.

The LORD CHANCELLOR—Yes, but I do not know that, I wanted mere verbal exposition. The proposition put to you was that there were two senses in which the word was used. That was practically what you said and you were asked which you meant and you say neither, but something between the two. It seems to me that that is an impossible contention.

Mr. MACLAREN—My meaning was that out of the larger must be taken those subjects that are allotted to section 91 which reduced the larger and still left a residue.

Lord HERSCHELL—But if you take those out given in section 91, that is not the meaning of it. I am speaking of Municipal Institutions which you say were more fully developed in Canada than in Nova Scotia and New Brunswick. Now in what sense do you say " Municipal Institutions " here is used—as applicable to all the Provinces ? Do you suggest it meant that a different power was given in Canada from what was given in Nova Scotia and New Brunswick ?

Mr. MACLAREN—No my Lord.

Lord HERSCHELL—Then do you suggest that it meant, as regards Nova Scotia and New Brunswick, something broader than " Municipal Institutions " there meant ?

Mr. MACLAREN—Yes.

Lord HERSCHELL—It meant there something as broad as that which existed in Canada ?

Mr. MACLAREN—Less what was taken out by section 91.

Lord HERSCHELL—Never mind what was taken out by section 91. Does " Municipal Institutions " include the powers which municipal bodies had in Canada rather than those which they had in Nova Scotia and New Brunswick ?

Mr. MACLAREN—Part of my argument would be this, that the expression " Municipal Institutions " was borrowed and taken from the legislation of Canada, and that the expression itself, so far as I know was not used in the legislation of New Brunswick or Nova Scotia, so that it would be the powers as used with the exception which I have named, the powers, that is, which were enjoyed in Canada, and I say that these powers were given to the legislatures of Nova Scotia and New Brunswick if they saw fit to exercise them.

Lord HERSCHELL.—But could not they give a municipal body power to deal with anything that it had not power to deal with in Canada prior to the confederation ?

Mr. MACLAREN—I think so. Any of the powers that are given under any of the other subsections of section 92 could be conferred on a municipality.

Lord HERSCHELL.—Then " Municipal Institutions " does not mean only the power which municipalities had down to that time possessed ?

Mr. MACLAREN—My argument would be that the Province would have the power, not under subsection 8 relating to Municipal Institutions, but that it might have the power under some other section, and that having that power it could easily exercise it directly.

Lord WATSON—If that is part of that special meaning under subsection 8 which you desire to attribute to it, it must mean at all events a Municipal Institution which may be endowed with all the powers which the Provincial Legislature can give it by virtue of the legislative powers given by section 92. You might give them, as far as I can see, under subsection 8, entirely new powers and functions so long as these were powers and functions which the Legislature of the Province could exercise and legislate upon, and could therefore delegate to a municipal body. You cannot read it in the narrow meaning. You may say it implies the other also, but that cannot be the meaning of it. It is not to be construed in the light of municipal legislation, and if it were, according to your own argument there are a great many exceptions which would have to be made in respect of the legislation in Section 91. You do not dispute that so far as express power is given to the Dominion Parliament by section 91, that power cannot be delegated to or conferred upon the Provinces ?

Mr. MACLAREN—I quite admit that—I must admit that, my Lord.

Lord DAVEY—Is not it sufficient for your argument to say that " Municipal Institutions " is a phrase which requires definition and explanation, and you define it by the aid of what " Municipal Institutions " usually meant before ?

Mr. MACLAREN—I think that is so.

Lord DAVEY—I am not expressing any opinion.

Lord WATSON—A municipal institution means a great deal more than a mere municipal body or town council. It means the body created for the purpose of exercising and which does exercise certain powers of administration for the benefit of the public and the inhabitants of the municipality over which it presides.

Mr. MACLAREN—Yes; and I think in construing this and other sub-sections of section 92——

Lord WATSON—I do not quite follow you. You desire, you say, to obtain a meaning for the phrase from the examination of legislation in the Provinces prior to 1867, and you admit that after 1867 the Provinces cannot give the powers which are entrusted to the Supreme Legislature.

Mr. MACLAREN—Certainly.

LORD WATSON—Every power that is not entrusted, I take it, to the Parliament of Canada, which does not belong to it, is with the Province.

Lord HERSCHELL—No; it is the other way. Everything which is not expressly entrusted to the Province is with the Canadian Parliament.

Lord WATSON—But, taking it in that way, is there any meaning in it ? In construing section 92, I am using those things which are given by the larger section. It can be shown to belong to the Parliament of Canada in two ways : by showing either that it falls within one or other of the sub-sections from 1 to 29 inclusive—that is one method. Another way of proving or demonstrating that the legislation belongs to the Parliament of Canada is by showing that it is not given to the Provinces under any one of the sub-sections in section 92. In either case it equally belongs to the Parliament of Canada.

Mr. MACLAREN—No doubt, my Lord.

Lord WATSON—Now, if it can be shown to be within that, according to the assumption of your argument, it cannot be exercised by the Province, and it cannot be given as a power consequently to the municipal institutions. If it is without, it can. I take it that the whole legislative field which an Imperial Legislature in Canada could occupy is divided between these two bodies—the Provincial and the Dominion Parliament. There is no vacant ground. It belongs either to the Dominion by virtue of one of the sub-sections from 1 to 29, or by virtue of its not coming under section 92, in which case the last sentence of section 91 gives it.

Mr. MACLAREN—Yes, my Lord.

Lord HERSCHELL—I am not sure that I quite follow you as to "Municipal Institutions." You say that, supposing you cannot find the power anywhere else, you find it in "Municipal Institutions." Of course, if you can find it under any other section, well and good; but your point is, that although it cannot be found to be conferred in terms upon the Provincial Legislature, in which case presumably it is not in it, yet it is conferred by this sub-section on municipal institutions, because it is given to a municipality. You admit they could not legislate without it themselves for the whole Province.

Mr. MACLAREN—The Province—I do not know that that question is really necessary for the consideration of this question.

Lord HERSCHELL—It is rather a strange conclusion, that something which they cannot legislate about themselves for the Province because it is not within any of the others, they can confer upon the various parts of the Provinces power to legislate about.

Mr. MACLAREN—That is not my argument. My argument would be that, under the head of "Municipal Institutions," the Province could legislate upon such matters as are comprised within the term "Municipal Institutions," even other-

wise than by giving them to the bodies that were created—
incorporated bodies.

Lord HERSCHELL—It seems rather strange to me that
because the Provincial Legislature can legislate about Provincial institutions, it can legislate about something which
had no relation to municipalities.

Mr. MACLAREN—It would be comprised within what
could be understood by "Municipal Institutions" or matters.
I think the term "Municipal Institutions" has been decided
by your Lordships in the cases that have come before you
when this question has been under consideration to have a
wider meaning than the mere creation of these bodies.

Lord HERSCHELL—Certainly, the creation of bodies and
all powers given to the bodies—but I do not think this Board
has ever suggested that there was power to give to the bodies
something that it was not expressly competent to legislate
about itself.

Mr. MACLAREN—But I think your Lordships have
decided that they could give to a municipal body some power
that was not in any other of the enumerated subjects of
section 92.

Lord DAVEY—I do not think that the cases have gone
beyond this, that "Municipal Institutions" includes the
creation of Municipal Police, with all the police powers which
are necessary for the maintaining of the order and good
government of a municipality, and it may be (I do not know
whether it is or not), that this may come within this category.
I do not think the cases have gone beyond that.

Mr. MACLAREN—The case of *Hodge* v. *The Queen* [*] is
the case where your Lordships considered it, and powers
going very near the same length as the legislation that is
before your Lordships now, were considered.

Lord DAVEY—There is another case which I remember
I argued, but which I do not remember the name of, which
may come within that category, as to the regulation of billiard
rooms.

[*] L. R. 9. Ap. Cas. 117.—3 Cart. 144.

Mr. MACLAREN—That is *Hodge* v. *The Queen*. That is the billiard case.

Lord DAVEY—It is a case where a man was sentenced to hard labour because he kept his billiard room open during prohibited hours.

Mr. MACLAREN—That is *Hodge* v. *The Queen* my Lord.

Lord MORRIS—If this subsection 8 were limited to merely creating a Municipal Institution I could understand that, but if it goes beyond the mere creation and it is said that it may imply also a power to vest in the Municipalities matters incident to the Institution, then you open the door for seeing to what length it should go, and it would appear to be not unreasonable to say that at the time the Act was passed one could see what were exactly the matters that were entrusted to Municipalities, because you have opened the door beyond the mere fact of the creation of a Municipality, and you have opened the door to show that the question as to what length you may go must depend upon the circumstances of the case and not upon previous decisions. Previous decisions held the door was open to a particular length about police, but the door was opened beyond the mere creation of a Municipality.

Lord HERSCHELL—This Board has held that the prohibition of the local liquor traffic is a thing which is given to the Dominion Parliament under section 91.

Mr. MACLAREN—In *Russell* v. *The Queen* * which I was going to it is considered.

Lord HERSCHELL—And they say it cannot exist in the Provincial Parliament.

Lord MORRIS—My observation always assumes that it is not given under section 91. *Cadit questio* if it was.

Lord HERSCHELL—It is not open now to discuss that, is it ? *Russell* v. *The Queen* settled that.

Mr. MACLAREN — *Russell* v. *The Queen* settled the lawfulness of the Canadian Temperance Act.

Lord DAVEY—That was consistent with the making of

* L. R. 7. Ap. Cas. 829.—2 Cart. 12.

the Police Regulations of the Municipality for regulating the Police.

The LORD CHANCELLOR—*Russell* v. *The Queen* depended, I think, upon the subject matter being one which was intended to be regulated according to general orders throughout the whole Dominion ?

Mr. MACLAREN—Yes.

Lord WATSON—It will eventually come round to this question in my opinion—whether the Provincial Legislature have exceeded their powers of regulation in passing that Act —whether it is regulation at all or is in effect prohibition. That is another thing. It is one thing to regulate a thing within the Province and it is quite another thing to regulate it without the Province.

Mr. MACLAREN—In the case of *Hodge* v. *The Queen* where your Lordships were considering this question of Municipal Institutions and where the regulations sought to be upheld were based upon subsection 8, I think the ground laid down by your Lordships is really broader than the mere creation of these bodies.

Lord WATSON—We shall see presently what has been decided by this Board in *Hodge* v. *The Queen*, but I need not refer to it now. We can do that afterwards.

Mr. MACLAREN—I was about, with your Lordships' permission, to refer to the case of *Hodge* v. *The Queen* now.

Lord WATSON—Very well, do so.

Mr. MACLAREN—It is to show what was comprised within " Municipal Institutions " in that case. *Hodge* v. *The Queen* is reported in 9 Appeal cases, page 117. It is also reported in Mr. Cartwright's collection, the 3rd volume, at page 144. I read from page 160 in Cartwright :

> " Their Lordships proceed now to consider the subject-matter and legislative character of sections 4 and 5 of the ' Liquor License Act ' of 1877, chapter 181, Revised Statutes of Ontario. That Act is so far confined in its operation to Municipalities in the Province of Ontario, and is entirely local in its character and operation. It authorises the appointment of License Commissioners to act in each Municipality, and empowers them to pass under the name of resolutions what we

E

know as by-laws or rules to define the conditions and qualifications
requisite for obtaining tavern or shop licenses for sale by retail, of
spirituous liquors within the Municipality, for limiting the number of
licenses, for declaring that a limited number of persons qualified to
have tavern licenses may be exempted from having all the tavern
accommodation required by law, and for regulating licensed taverns
and shops, for defining the duties and powers of license inspectors, and
to impose penalties for infraction of their resolutions. These seem to
be all matters of a merely local nature in the Province, and to be
similar to, though not identical in all respects with, the powers then
belonging to Municipal Institutions under the previously existing laws,
passed by the Local Parliaments. Their Lordships consider that the
powers intended to be conferred by the Act in question, when properly
understood, are to make regulations in the nature of police or muni-
regulations of a merely local character for the good governme
taverns, &c., licensed for the sale of liquors by retail, and such ..
calculated to preserve in the municipality, peace and public decency,
and repress drunkenness and disorderly and riotous conduct. As such
they cannot be said to interfere with the general regulation of trade
and commerce which belongs to the Dominion Parliament, and do not
conflict with the provisions of the Canada Temperance Act, which does
not appear to have as yet been locally adopted. The subjects of
legislation in the Ontario Act of 1877, sections 4 and 5, seem to come
within the heads Nos. 8, 15 and 16 of section 92 of British North
America Statute, 1867."

Sub-section 8, as your Lordships are aware, is the sub-
section relating to Municipal Institutions, 15 is the clause
relating to fines and penalties for violation of Provincial
Laws, 16 relates to matters of a merely local and private
nature, so that I submit even in this case of *Hodge* v. *The Queen*,
that your Lordships are giving to sub-section 8 of section 92
a much wider meaning than the mere creation of Municipal
Corporations, and the conferring upon them of such powers
as are conferred upon the local legislatures by the other sub-
sections.

Lord HERSCHELL—I do not think it goes beyond that
at all. I do not think it even goes so far as that. They
found there that it was within one of the named clauses, 16,
(whether rightly or wrongly), and that it was also within 8;
because it was giving to a local body, namely, these Commissioners, powers to do something which was within one of
the enumerated classes. They never said there you could
give to a local body under 8, powers which you could not
find existing under any of the numbered classes.

Mr. MACLAREN—The subjects are enumerated.

Lord HERSCHELL—15 and 16 they say it was.

Mr. MACLAREN—Yes.

Lord HERSCHELL—Of course it was thought, wherever you have a municipal body empowered to do any of the things in sections numbered 1 to 16, no doubt it came within that number, but that is no authority for saying that it gives any extended meaning to "Municipal Institutions" beyond this, that within it is the power to enable municipalities to use any of the things which the legislature itself could use. I think so far it goes, but I do not think it goes farther.

Mr. MACLAREN—Yes. Now I desire to refer your Lordships to the course of legislation in Canada by which we claim that the words "Municipal Institutions" have been defined and have come to have a well defined meaning.

Lord HERSCHELL—A well defined meaning, where ?

Mr. MACLAREN—In Canada—especially in the Province of Old Canada. I will refer to the other as well but the expression "Municipal Institutions" so far as I am aware had been used in legislative enactments only in the Province of Old Canada.

Lord DAVEY—I suppose you would say that "Municipal Institutions" does not include merely the creation of Town Council and Aldermen and Mayor for instance, but would include for instance the creation of a market and municipal police.

Mr. MACLAREN—Quite so.

Lord WATSON—Or a separate body of commissioners for the purpose of supplying the locality with water ; I should say all those were Municipal Institutions.

Mr. MACLAREN—Yes.

Lord WATSON—Or institutions created for the benefit of the particular municipality.

Lord DAVEY—And I should suppose it might include the establishing a gas works.

Lord HERSCHELL—I should think it included every local

E 2

body and every power that you can confer upon that local body.

The LORD CHANCELLOR—You would add to that, that which was included in Canada.

Mr. MACLAREN—I think that would be part of my argument. Where the expression "Municipal Institutions" had in various Acts of Parliament been given a well known meaning. I would refer your Lordships to a joint Appendix of Statutes that has been put in by the parties—that is the Appellant in this case and the Distillers' and Brewers' Association to which they refer. It is a selection of statutes chiefly before federation which show the legislation. They are extracts from the statutes showing the regulations that had been in force in Canada upon the subject. The first Municipal Act in Canada was passed by the Province of Canada for Upper Canada alone.

The LORD CHANCELLOR—There is a difficulty in my mind as to whether I understand your argument, and the difficulty is this. I quite understand the Imperial Legislature using the word which had been usually used in Canada with reference to Canadian subjects; that would be true. I assent to that as reasonable, but I very much doubt unless you can make out a more limited meaning universally understood in Canada whether the Legislature were supposed to use it in a more limited sense than in the Imperial Parliament itself. Because in some parts of Canada particular powers are given to Municipal Institutions, therefore I understand you to say that the powers are universal.

Mr. MACLAREN—Not universal, and the expression "Municipal Institutions" I think was not universal, but I was going to show your Lordship a series of Acts in which the expression "Municipal Institutions" was used.

The LORD CHANCELLOR—You mean beyond those which you would say are generally incident to Municipal Institutions, do you?

Mr. MACLAREN—They are used as they are given there. They are not given in all countries. Of course different countries give different powers.

The LORD CHANCELLOR—We must consider what is usual in the place in question.

Mr. MACLAREN—I presume that "Municipal Institutions" in Canada means something different to what the words might mean here in England.

Lord WATSON—The meaning of institutions may be got at when the question is what powers had they, speaking with reference to the powers to be exercised by the institution, created or rather conferred upon the institution by the new Provincial Legislature.

The LORD CHANCELLOR—And merely by the use of that word.

Lord HERSCHELL—If you take the statutes themselves it is not used—it is not in the first Act.

Mr. MACLAREN—No, my Lord, I think the expression is not used in the Act of 1849.

Lord HERSCHELL—But in the Act of 1849 there are certain municipalities created and there are certain powers given.

Mr. MACLAREN—Yes, my Lord.

Lord HERSCHELL—Then comes the Act respecting Municipal Institutions of Upper Canada. That is the first.

Mr. MACLAREN—That is the first time in which it was used in the statutes.

Lord HERSCHELL—Then you have a number of provisions giving certain powers to certain municipal bodies, but the Municipal Institutions existed, did not they, before ever those powers were given?

Mr. MACLAREN—The general "Municipal Act of 1849," which is quoted here was the first general Municipal Act for the Province of Canada and applicable alone to Upper Canada, and it was not introduced in the Province of Quebec, that is, in Lower Canada, for some years afterwards.

Lord HERSCHELL—I should read the title of this as relating not to powers which they possess, but to bodies, because it is an Act relating to the Municipal Institutions of Upper Canada, that is municipalities that had been created, and they were going to give them further powers, but the Municipal Institutions of Upper Canada would not mean the powers which they were about to confer, but the bodies upon which they were about to confer those powers.

Lord WATSON—Do the parties mean to represent to us that before 1849 there was not a Municipal Institution there ?

Mr. MACLAREN—No, my Lord ; I think that is not so. The first general Act was passed in 1849.

Lord WATSON—There were municipalities before the first general Act ?

Lord HERSCHELL—But still even at the time of the first general Act in 1849 there are no such words used.

Mr. MACLAREN—The word was not used.

Lord HERSCHELL—Did you observe the title of that Act where the word is used : " An Act respecting the Municipal Institutions of Upper Canada "—does not that refer to the bodies rather than the powers that are about to be conferred upon those bodies ?

Mr MACLAREN—Well, my impression is that the word is used in the title very much as it is used in section 92 of " The British North America Act," that the local legislatures under section 92 might make laws upon the following classes of subjects, one of them being Municipal Institutions.

Lord HERSCHELL—No ; it is an Act respecting not Municipal Institutions in Upper Canada, but it is an Act respecting The Municipal Institutions of Upper Canada. It is the definite article that I am calling your attention to.

The LORD CHANCELLOR—It is recognising there the existence of constitutions, and giving them certain new powers.

Mr. MACLAREN—This was really a consolidation—it was embodied in the consolidated Statutes. The Act of 1859 is found on page 3 of the Appendix.

Lord MORRIS—The enacting part of section 92 should

be read in this way : " In each Province the Legislature may exclusively make laws in relation to matters coming within Municipal Institutions in the Province."

Mr. MACLAREN—Yes, my Lord ; I think that is the proper reading of section 92, and I submit that that is quite as broad as the title to 22 Victoria, chapter 99, found on page 3 of the Appendix. In this Act of 1859 there is found a section, 245, which your Lordships will see on page 4. On page 4 of the Appendix your Lordships will find a section, 245, which is substantially the same as that which is now considered in the question referred to. Section 245 of the Act of 1859 reads as follows :

> " The council of every township, city, town, and incorporated village may respectively pass by-laws."

Then follow a number of other sub-sections not in question here :

> " 6. For prohibiting the sale by r___ d of spirituous, fermented, or other manufactured liquors in any inn or __ __ __ house of public entertainment, and for prohibiting the sale there__ in shops and places other than houses of public entertainment, provided the b___ l___, before the final passing thereof, has been duly approved by the electors of the municipality in the manner provided by this Act."

That is, I think, the first enactment in the form of an Act almost identical with that which is now referred to.

Lord HERSCHELL—There is no provision in this Act about it being approved by the electors, is there ?

Mr. MACLAREN—Yes, my Lord.

Lord DAVEY—Was this Act in force at the time of the Confederation ?

Mr. MACLAREN—Yes ; at least, it was re-enacted immediately before Confederation. I was just coming to that.

Lord HERSCHELL—I see that it deals also with weights and measures.

Mr. MACLAREN—Yes, weights and measures. We are in this peculiar position, that there was legislation at the time of Confederation by the Parliament for the whole of Canada. There was other legislation for Lower Canada and Upper Canada separately, and there were certain powers given to

the municipalities to regulate some matters relating to
weights and measures in the Municipal Act.

Lord DAVEY—There is a section about existing legislation.

Mr. MACLAREN—Yes, section 129.

Lord WATSON—But all the powers given in the Act are
expressly taken away under section 91. I mean all the
powers given to the municipalities that the Act refers to are
taken away by the British North America Act, section 91.
What inference do you desire us to draw from that ?

Mr. MACLAREN—As to those that are taken away, there
can be no question that those are beyond the powers of the
local legislature.

Lord HERSCHELL—But the difficulty you have, as it
seems to me, is this—that everything is taken away which is
not expressly given. You cannot say that this enabled them
to confer upon municipal bodies or to legislate in relation to
all matters that municipal bodies had been empowered to
deal with before, because some of those are expressly mentioned in section 91. But then section 91 equally sweeps in
everything that is not expressly given in section 92.

Mr. MACLAREN—So far as this clause is concerned, I am
driven back to the same point that I previously mentioned to
your Lordship—that I think we must, so far as this argument
on this sub-section 8 goes, that sub-section 8——

Lord WATSON—It shows that in the matter the Imperial
Parliament cannot have given all the powers or the powers
belonging to municipalities before the passing of the Act.

Mr. MACLAREN—Certainly not ; we must admit that.

Lord WATSON—It must be sought elsewhere.

Lord HERSCHELL—You say " Municipal Institutions "
means the creation of the bodies and dealing with their
powers in all matters which are not given to the Dominion
Parliament by section 91 ?

Mr. MACLAREN—All powers which were conferred upon
them and not transferred to the Dominion—yes.

Lord HERSCHELL—But then there are given to the Dominion under section 91 not only the enumerated things, but everything which is not given in section 92 ?

Mr. MACLAREN—Yes.

Lord HERSCHELL—That seems to me very difficult to understand. Therefore can " Municipal Institutions " include the giving of powers in relation to any of the matters not to be found in 1 to 16 ?

Mr. MACLAREN—I think so far as the argument upon this sub-section goes we must claim that " Municipal Institutions " does mean more, that is, it means the powers, as I have said, which had been conferred upon municipalities and which are not taken and transferred to the Dominion.

Lord HERSCHELL—But everything is transferred to the Dominion which is not expressly given to the other.

Mr. MACLAREN—We may be arguing in a circle, but I come back to this with which I started.

Lord MORRIS—One of the things expressly given is all matters that had been previously considered common to Municipal Institutions you say ?

Mr. MACLAREN—Yes.

Lord MORRIS —They are given expressly ?

Mr. MACLAREN—They are given expressly.

Lord HERSCHELL—But you cannot say it is all matters expressly considered common to Municipal Institutions, because you have excepted out of them everything found in section 91.

Mr. MACLAREN - Yes.

Lord HERSCHELL—Then if so, amongst the things given to the Dominion Parliament is legislation in respect of all matters not expressly given to the Provincial Legislatures.

Mr. MACLAREN—But, my Lord, I think that is really overriding the whole of section 92 and taking away the whole power, for this reason : take, for instance, any of the subjects enumerated in section 92—take " property and civil rights," for instance, I think that the interpretation which your Lordships have put upon that section is this, that the Province may legislate respecting property and civil rights except as to the interference with property and civil rights by legislation by the Dominion upon any of the subjects that are enumerated in section 91, and I would ask you to apply the same rule here.

Lord HERSCHELL—No, because you see the difficulty is this, that you are seeking to extend the natural meaning, as it strikes me, of "Municipal Institutions." It is any municipal bodies you choose to create, or whose circumstances you choose to modify, and every power that you choose to give to those municipal bodies, all that is included in "Municipal Institutions" as I should understand it by the light of nature. But then you seek to put an artificial meaning upon it rather, and to say that it means the powers which had been in fact conferred, or rather powers of the nature of those which had been in fact conferred upon municipal bodies. But then you cannot maintain that to the full, because you are obliged to admit that it can only mean such of them as were not conferred upon the Dominion Parliament.

Mr. MACLAREN—Yes.

Lord HERSCHELL—Then I have pointed out to you that if you have to interpose that exception, then you except also everything that was not in terms given to the Provincial Parliament.

Mr. MACLAREN—As I tried to point out a moment ago, that would apply not only to 8 but to every other sub-section to section 92.

Lord HERSCHELL—I do not see that it applies to the others also, because if you can find it in any of these from 1 to 16, then no doubt there are exclusive powers given to the Provincial Legislature, and no general words in section 91 will enable the Dominion Parliament to take it out of the power of the Legislature.

Lord MORRIS—It still comes back to the question under sub-section 8, are these powers expressly given to the

Provincial Parliament ?   You say they are under the words
" Municipal Institutions," and you would be right if you
could show that " Municipal Institutions in the Province "
includes them as well as the others.

Mr. MACLAREN—Yes, and I was endeavouring to show to
your Lordships that " Municipal Institutions," as understood
in Canadian legislation, really comprises such powers as we
are now claiming under the Act that is impugned.

Lord HERSCHELL—Not such powers.   It applies to all
the powers that were given to municipalities.   For instance,
it did not comprise any particular one, but it comprised every
power that was given as I understand it.

Mr. MACLAREN—Every power that is not taken out by
section 91.

Lord MORRIS—As I understand it, you want to read
" Municipal Institutions " as though there were a glossary to
the Act, and your glossary is previous legislation.

The LORD CHANCELLOR—I can quite understand that, if
you were accurate in your statement as to what that was.

Mr. MACLAREN—I was just proceeding to show your
Lordships as well as I could what I meant by that.

The LORD CHANCELLOR—I thought you conceded that
there were different powers ?

Mr. MACLAREN—The legislation was not identical.

The LORD CHANCELLOR—Not uniform ?

Mr. MACLAREN—Not uniform in all the Provinces.

The LORD CHANCELLOR—But when you are treating that
as a mode of expounding a particular word it seems to me
impossible to follow your argument.

Lord WATSON—The fault of your argument appears to
be this : to suggest that there is some power or other which
might be given to a Municipality which it is not the province
of the Supreme Legislature to confer, and not within the
power of the Provincial Legislature to confer.   I am not
aware that there is any such legislative power to be found

within the four corners of the Act or outside the four corners
of the Act of 1867. It appears to me the whole legislative
power belongs to one body or the other.

Mr. MACLAREN—That I think is undoubted my Lord.

Lord WATSON—But if it is within your power under
section 92 what is the use of going to previous Statutes on
it? If it is outside your powers it is equally useless.

Lord HERSCHELL—You go to previous Statutes to show
what " Municipal Institutions " mean ?

Mr. MACLAREN—Yes.

Lord HERSCHELL—But my difficulty is, looking at these
Statutes, " Municipal Institutions " there means, if it refers
to powers at all and not to institutions, all powers that the
Municipalities possess, and it does not mean any new powers
that it is proposed to confer upon them.

Mr. MACLAREN—But this is an old power which had
been conferred by Canadian legislation upon Municipal
Institutions.

Lord MORRIS—If your definition of " Municipal Institutions " which obtained in Canada can be got out of the
previous legislation it is expressly given under sub-section 8.

Mr. MACLAREN—That is beyond argument.

Lord MORRIS—It is expressly given. It says so.

Lord WATSON—One object, or if not an object, certainly
a plain result of the Act of 1867, was to take away from the
Provincial Legislatures the power to do a great many things
which they had done and quite competently done before.

Mr. MACLAREN—No doubt.

Lord WATSON—And to hand over those powers. The
motive seems to have been to give over all those legislative
powers which were necessary for the general welfare of all
the Provinces, and in regard to those matters with respect to
which there ought to be uniform legislation throughout the
Provinces.

Lord HERSCHELL—Is there anything else here pointing to the " Municipal Institutions " ?

Mr. MACLAREN—There is, if your Lordship will turn to page 6, the " Consolidated Statutes of Upper Canada," you will find a title relating to Municipal Institutions of Upper Canada.

Lord WATSON—They mean existing institutions ?

Mr. MACLAREN—Yes, my Lord.

Lord HERSCHELL—" Municipal Institutions " there is used obviously in two senses because the title is " Municipal Institutions," and under that heading are such things as Building Societies and Municipal Institutions of that kind, so that apparently there was a broader and narrower meaning there.

Mr. MACLAREN—Apparently. Then there is chapter 54 which is referred to in the title on page 6 of the Joint Appendix. These Consolidated Statutes of Upper Canada of 1859 were a consolidation of the previous legislation and included the Act which was passed in the same year, to which we have just referred. Section 246 of that Act is identical with section 245 of the Act of the year 1859, which is found on page 4 of the Appendix.

Lord HERSCHELL—I do not understand what this is set out at page 5 " Consolidated Statutes of 1859." What does that come from ?

Mr. MACLAREN—That would be on another head of the grounds taken by the other side—" Trade and Commerce."

Lord WATSON—Is it distributed throughout the Act ?

Lord HERSCHELL—I cannot find it; I have the Consolidated Statutes of Upper Canada of 1859 and I want to see where this comes from. I cannot find it.

Mr. MACLAREN—It comes from the Index, my Lord.

Lord HERSCHELL—It is only a classified table of the Consolidated Statutes ?

Mr. MACLAREN—Yes, my Lord.

The LORD CHANCELLOR—I thought it would only turn out to be an index.

Lord WATSON—The destruction of wolves is a Municipal Institution.

Mr. MACLAREN—When the Municipalities looked after the destruction of them. In these Consolidated Statutes the Act of 1859 was consolidated, and section 246 is identical with section 245 of the Act of the year 1859.

Lord WATSON—The destruction of wolves goes beyond regulation.

Lord HERSCHELL—It commences " Existing Institutions continued," and then it goes on to New Municipalities.

Mr. MACLAREN—Yes.

Lord HERSCHELL—I should say that " Municipal Institutions " there was used in the sense of the body and not of its powers.

Mr. MACLAREN—The title of the whole Act. Of course the greater part of the Act is taken up with the powers and not with the Institution.

Lord HERSCHELL—It gives those Municipal Institutions powers, but the " Municipal Institutions " means the bodies, not the powers conferred.

Lord WATSON—Without reference to any power they may have had before. For the purposes of that enactment it is quite immaterial.

Mr. MACLAREN—The Act which was in force in Upper Canada (29 & 30 Vic. cap. 51) at the time of Confederation your Lordships will find on the same page 6, which Act was passed in 1866. That also, like the Act of 1859, is intituled, "An Act respecting the Municipal Institutions of Upper Canada," and section 249, which is cited on page 6, is almost identical with that which is found in the Act of 1859. Next, when we look at the Statutes of the whole Province of Canada that related to Lower Canada, we find an almost identical course of legislation upon this subject. The Act of 16 Victoria, cap. 214, provides for the consent of municipal

electors being necessary for the obtaining of a license. The
first General Municipal Act of Lower Canada (18 Vic. cap. 100)
is to be found on page 12, and was called "The Lower
Canada Municipal and Road Act, 1855." Section 23 of that
Act reads thus :

> "The powers and authority of each Local Council (in addition to
> the powers hereinbefore conferred upon all Municipal Councils) shall
> extend to the following objects :—6. To the regulating and governing
> of all shopkeepers, and storekeepers"—

and so on, and then on page 13, line 3, I read what is more
pertinent to what we have to deal with here, almost identical
with what we have in the present Act :

> "Or the preventing absolutely of the sale of wine or brandy, or
> other spirituous liquors, ale or beer, or any of them by retail, within
> the Municipality, and the making of such further enactments as may
> be deemed necessary for giving full effect to any such by-law, and for
> imposing penalties for the contravention thereof."

Your Lordships understand that I am reading from page 13
of the Joint Appendix of Statutes. Then, my Lords, comes
the exception :

> "Provided always that the selling of any wine, brandy or other
> spirituous liquors, ale or beer, in the original packages in which the
> same were received from the importer or manufacturer, and not con-
> taining respectively less than five gallons or one dozen bottles, shall
> not be held to be a selling by retail within the meaning of this Act."

Lord HERSCHELL.—There is no use of the term "Municipal
Institutions."

Mr. MACLAREN.—The term is not used with regard to
Lower Canada as far as I am aware.

The LORD CHANCELLOR—Does it not further strike you
that the section you are quoting is awkward for you ? This is
a peculiar and additional power given. What I mean is, so
far as your interpretation of the words is concerned, they are
not the same, and in the next place, if they were the same, it
is an addition in express terms.

Mr. MACLAREN—I submit the explanation of that is this :
certain powers were conferred on all Councils, and then
certain powers conferred upon County Councils.

Lord DAVEY—What is the meaning of Local Council is
it something different from a Municipal Council ?

Mr. MACLAREN—There were two Councils. There were Municipal Councils—County Councils and Local Councils. In addition to the powers conferred upon all Councils, that is County and Local Councils, powers were conferred upon Local Councils or the Councils of Townships and Villages.

Lord DAVEY—Then the Municipal Council is the genus and the Local Council is a particular species of the genus.

Mr. MACLAREN—It is one of the individual Municipalities. Then these Local Municipalities within the County were combined and there was a County Council composed of delegates from the various Local Councils. That is the explanation, I think, of this section.

The next Act to which I refer is 19 and 20 Vic., c. 101, in which the power is conferred upon County Councils:

"1. To prohibit and prevent the sale of all spirituous, vinous, alcoholic, and intoxicating liquors, or to permit such sale subject to such limitations as they shall consider expedient."

Then section 11 provides:

"* * * * * 5. Every Local Council shall have power to make by-laws, prevent or prohibit the sale of all spirituous, vinous, alcoholic and intoxicating liquors in any year when the County Council has failed in the month of March to regulate by by-law such sale."

Then on page 14 is found an illustration of a particular charter given to a city or town. The cities and towns were not under the General Act, and the Town of Three Rivers is taken as an example of the powers that were given to one of the towns. In the consolidated Statutes of Lower Canada we have the same thing.

The LORD CHANCELLOR—This seems rather a long way, does it not, from interpreting the phrase "Municipal Institutions?"

Mr. MACLAREN—I was endeavouring to show, my Lord, what was comprised within Municipal Institutions at the time of the passing of the British North America Act.

The LORD CHANCELLOR—But it strikes me that this is rather a long way from that.

Mr. MACLAREN—Then, my Lord, in the Province of Nova Scotia we have the legislation on page 21 of the Joint

Appendix of Statutes (Revised Statutes of Nova Scotia, cap. 75), where the powers as to the regulation of licenses were conferred upon a Special Sessions and the Council of the Municipality. In the Province of New Brunswick (page 22), " Public Statutes of New Brunswick (1854), cap. 15," the General Sessions of the Peace were empowered to grant wholesale and tavern licenses, and where there were incorporated Counties, by section 29 those powers were conferred upon the Counties.

Lord DAVEY—That was only the power to grant licenses.

Mr. MACLAREN—Yes, my Lord ; the power of prohibition is not included in that.

Lord DAVEY—Section 92 expressly confers the power to grant licenses.

Sir RICHARD COUCH—For revenue—only for revenue.

Mr. MACLAREN—For revenue. Up to page 22 of this Joint Appendix I think all the Acts show what the legislation was prior to federation in each of the Provinces which went to make up the Dominion of Canada ; and as I say the expression " Municipal Institutions " I think is found, so far as I am aware, only in the Acts applying to the Province of Canada. We find it in a series of Acts relating to Upper Canada. There have been a number of judicial decisions and interpretations with regard to this matter, and it has been considered by the Courts, although, as far as I am aware, your Lordships have never been called upon formally to consider it in connection with the question which is now before you. But the matter has been before the Courts in Canada—the Courts of the various Provinces and the Supreme Court ; and with your Lordships' leave, I will refer to some of the interpretations which have been placed upon the matter by the Courts with regard to Municipal Institutions and the meaning of that expression in sub-section 8 of section 92. The case I would first refer to is the case of *Slavin* v. *The Corporation of Orillia*, which was first reported in 36 U. C. Q. B. page 159, but is now to be found in the first volume of Mr. Cartwright's collection, at page 688.

Lord WATSON—What is the date of the Judgment ?

Mr. MACLAREN—1874. I will now read from page 702.

F

The LORD CHANCELLOR—I see the Chief Justice in the Judgment he gave repeats your observation, but he does not shrink from the generality of it.

Mr. MACLAREN—Yes, my Lord. As I remarked, I would take out of that all that is assigned to the Dominion in section 91.

Lord DAVEY—Of course you understand your own argument best, but it does not seem to me that that advances it much. I can understand the argument if you confine it to Municipal Institutions, which by section 129 have certain powers continued to them, and that this is an Act dealing with those powers and an Act relating to Municipal Institutions as they exist; but then you must go the whole length, you know.

Lord HERSCHELL—Then there is this difficulty. These powers may not have been primarily conferred. They exist, we will suppose; but can they be repealed, and then after a time be re-enacted? That is to say, a Province that had not had any provision of this sort before could not create, but the Province that once had had it, could—which would be rather an anomaly.

Mr. MACLAREN—I think we must admit that the powers of all the Provinces would be the same under section 92.

Lord DAVEY—Is that so, because section 129 continues to them their existing powers?

Lord WATSON—And on the other hand, although section 129 continued their existing powers, it gave a Province or a Provincial Legislature no power to meddle with these enactments. This is an action of the Province, and that is what is complained of. Section 129 is very express. The laws of each Province may be " repealed, abolished or " altered by the Parliament of Canada or by the Legislature of " the respective Province, according to the authority of the " Parliament or of that Legislature under this Act." The fact that it stood as an enactment in 1867 does not give any power whatever to any Provincial Legislature to deal with the matter.

Lord HERSCHELL—When did these provisions which you say are now re-enacted cease to exist ?

Mr. MACLAREN—They were repealed in 1869 by the Province of Ontario, and then re-enacted.

Lord HERSCHELL—But perhaps they are still in force ?

Mr. MACLAREN—That was the argument. When this was re-enacted, your Lordships will have observed the enacting is very peculiar, and it was done with this object: that under the repealing Act of 1869, if they had not the power to re-enact they had not the power to repeal.

Lord WATSON—I do not think they have. I do not know how you deal with section 129, but there was only one interpretation; statutes existing at the date of the passing of the Act, could be repealed or altered by the appropriate legislature. If it refers to a matter which in future the Dominion Parliament can alone deal with, the Provincial Parliament have no power whatever to touch it. On the other hand if it be a Provincial matter it is fully within their power to repeal, alter or vary.

Mr. MACLAREN—The Provincial Legislature having purported in 1869 to repeal, the Legislature in 1890 passed this peculiar Act to revive it.

Lord DAVEY—With a preamble.

Mr. MACLAREN—Yes, with a preamble explaining why the legislation was in that particular form.

Lord WATSON—If the re-enactment was invalid under section 129 I should say the repeal was equally invalid.

Mr. MACLAREN—If the Act was not repealed in 1869 then the Act of 1890 was declaratory. If it was repealed, the legislature meant to revive it.

Lord DAVEY—You were going to read to us the case of *Slavin* v. *Orillia*.

Mr. MACLAREN—Yes, my Lord. I was about to read the

F 2

remark of Chief Justice Richards, at page 702 of the
1st volume of Cartwright:

> " When then this Imperial Act uses the very words of the title of
> this Bill in giving as one of the class of subjects on which the
> Provincial Legislature may pass laws, viz., 'Municipal Institutions in
> the Province,' can there be any reasonable doubt that it was expected and
> intended that the 'Municipal Institutions' which were to be constituted
> under that authority would possess the same powers as those which
> were then in existence under the same name in the Province? I should
> think not."

Lord WATSON—I cannot read the words of section 129
without thinking, as it appears to me, that the Imperial
Legislation had in view that there were existing statutes
under which the legislative power required was that of the
Dominion Parliament as well as that of the Provincial
Legislature, and that it did not intend one way or the other
on that account to have the legislative power increased.

Lord DAVEY—There is no doubt that one or other has
power to do it.

Lord WATSON—According to the power given them by
the statute—they are not to lose their power of legislation;
it is not to be handed over to the Province from the Supreme
Legislature simply because it was dealt with in a former Act
along with other matters which fall within the jurisdiction of
the Provincial Legislature.

Lord HERSCHELL—How did the question arise in the
case you are reading?

Mr. MACLAREN—It arose on proceedings to quash a
prohibitory by-law.

Lord WATSON—A power given to a municipal body,
was it not?

Mr. MACLAREN—Yes.

Lord WATSON—By the Provincial Legislature?

Mr. MACLAREN—Under the Act of 1866, or a continuation
of that Act which I have just read.

Lord DAVEY—It must have been a new Act.

Lord HERSCHELL—It was a new by-law as I understand.

Mr. MACLAREN—A new by-law. The Act of 1866 had been re-enacted by the Provincial Legislature.

Lord WATSON—And that authorised the municipality to pass the by-law ?

Mr. MACLAREN—Yes, which was challenged by Slavin.

Lord WATSON—On the ground that the sanction of the Legislature was *ultra vires* ?

Mr. MACLAREN—Yes. In the case of *The Queen v. Taylor* which is reported in the same volume. (36 U. C. Q. B. 183.)

Lord WATSON—Can you tell me how you reconcile that with the case of Russell ?

Mr. MACLAREN—With your Lordships' permission I was proposing to take that up a little later. In the Province of Nova Scotia the question also arose in the case of *Keefe* v. *McLennan*, which is reported in the 2nd volume of Cartwright, commencing at page 400. I read from page 409, but I will point out first that on page 408, Judge Ritchie, in giving the Judgment of the Court, considers very much the questions which came before your Lordships in the case of *Hodge* v. *The Queen*, so that I need not refer to that, and will only quote a few sentences on page 409, where he says :—

> "In addition to what I have already said, I may remark that we are to assume that the framers of the British North America Act knew of the legislation which was in force in the several Provinces, and at the time of its passing, the law in this Province relating to the granting of licenses for the sale of intoxicating liquors recognised the right of the Court of Sessions to refuse licenses for the sale of them in small quantities within their respective counties, and that Act did not repeal the Provincial Law then in force, so that when the right of granting licenses was conferred on the Provincial Legislature it may very reasonably be presumed that the intention was that the right should continue to be exercised in the same manner as it was then exercised."

This matter also came before the Courts, and has been before the Courts of the Provinces and the Supreme Court on a reference to the Court of Appeal for Ontario under a Provincial Act very similar to that which is now under consideration, and in which the Court of Appeal for Ontario considered the question, and I have here the Judgments.

Those Judgments have been furnished to your Lordships. They are three Judgments which are not yet printed in Mr. Cartwright's book, and they are furnished in printed form. The first to which I will refer is the Decision of the Court of Appeal of Ontario (In *re* Local Option Act 18 O. A. R. 572), with regard to this very Act. Under a Provincial Act this very question was referred to the Court of Appeal for Ontario, with certain questions which your Lordships will find here. The first question is substantially the same question as we are now considering—the jurisdiction of the Ontario Legislature as to this very Act, and it was submitted by the Lieutenant-Governor in Council under the authority of a Provincial Act to the Court of Appeal for Ontario. We have the Judgment of the Chief Justice of Ontario, in which his Lordship reviews the legislation to which I have been calling attention, and which I need not read.

Lord WATSON—Can you tell me what the date of this Judgment was ?

Mr. MACLAREN—September 23rd, 1891. This question was referred to, and after a review of the legislation, the Court of Appeal for Ontario answered the question, and gave as their opinion that this legislation was not *ultra vires* of the Province. I need not trouble your Lordships with reading that part which is a summary of what I have been endeavouring to give. His Lordship goes on to say :—

> " Under the Confederation Act ' Municipal Institutions in the Province' are in the class of subjects within exclusive Provincial regulation. It may be safely said that there is no apparent intention in the Confederation Act to curtail or interfere with the existing general powers of Municipal Councils, unless the Act plainly transfers any of such existing powers to the Dominion jurisdiction."

Lord HERSCHELL.—If there was no intention to curtail any existing powers they were all preserved, because they were under Acts which were preserved.

Lord WATSON—It rather misses this point, that the intention of the Act clearly was to distribute these powers between two Legislatures.

Lord HERSCHELL—No ; to distribute the power to deal between the two Legislatures. Then it says there is no apparent intention to curtail or interfere with the existing powers—the existing powers were all preserved.

Mr. MACLAREN—Under Section 129 all existing legislation was preserved.

Lord HERSCHELL—Of course it might be altered, if it was within one of the Dominion subjects, by the Dominion.

Mr. MACLAREN—Yes.

Lord HERSCHELL—The question is not curtailing the existing powers, the question is dealing with the subjects which have been committed to the Municipalities.

Lord WATSON—The argument is very much the same as you are addressing to us. The argument in the first part of the learned Judge's opinion is really to this effect: that prior to the passing of the Act of 1867, certain powers of dealing with these Municipal Institutions and granting certain powers to them had been vested in the Provincial Legislature, and it was then practically within the province of the Imperial Parliament, and therefore he finds in the Act, or certain passages of the Act, that it was not the intention of the Imperial Parliament, after the passing of the Act, to deprive the Provincial Legislature of any power to continue to deal with these matters. In fact, the learned Judge holds that the power to deal with them was in these circumstances to be implied as included in the words "Municipal Institutions."

Mr. MACLAREN—Yes, my Lord. There is an observation in the same judgment to which I will call your Lordships' attention which may come up as to the scope and effect——

Lord WATSON—Yes; he sums up the argument there, and says the effect is to leave the power in the Municipality as it was for so many years before. That is his conclusion.

Mr. MACLAREN—His Lordship then considers the question of its being an interference with trade and commerce. As to the interpretation of this I would also refer to the judgment of his Lordship Mr. Justice Burton in the same case. He says:—

"It is proper to enquire therefore what was the extent of the grant given under that designation. Does it mean only the creation and erection of municipalities with such powers as are of the essence of municipal institutions, and necessarily incident to and essential to their existence, or does it include the powers and functions which at the time of confederation were ordinarily exercised to a greater or less extent by the municipalities of all the Provinces? It may not without some reason be contended that there is no inherent connection between the liquor traffic and municipal institutions, which is perfectly true; but there was, if I may so express myself "——

Lord DAVEY—The 2nd paragraph (on page 7) is rather an important paragraph having regard to your argument :—

" Having that power, it was clearly competent to the Legislature to confide to a municipal council or any other body of its own creation, or to individuals of its selection, authority to make by-laws or resolutions as to subjects specified in the enactment, with the object of carrying it into effect ; and the provision in question being found therefore within a Municipal Act in one of the Provinces furnishes no conclusive evidence that by the words ' Municipal Institutions ' it was intended to confer every power which might be contained in such an Act upon the Legislatures of the Provinces."

That has rather an important bearing upon your argument.

Mr. MACLAREN—Yes ; that all the powers were not conferred. He goes on to consider this in the following paragraph——

Lord WATSON—But the learned Judge proceeds really to grapple with the question in the words following. He argues it.

Mr. MACLAREN—Yes, my Lord.

" It may not without some reason be contended that there is no inherent connection between the liquor traffic and municipal institutions, which is perfectly true, but there was, if I may so express myself, a constitutional connection. In, I believe, all the Provinces the power to regulate, by the granting licenses to sell intoxicating liquors, existed ——"

They are expressly given and they are expressly taken away.

Lord WATSON—It does not matter whether they are expressly taken away or otherwise, if they are taken away.

Mr. MACLAREN—

" —— whilst in many the power to regulate even to the extent of prohibiting it altogether existed as a matter of police or municipal regulation, so that we have to regard it in the view that at that time the regulation and prohibition had come to be regarded as municipal

regulations which were guaranteed to the Provinces under Confederation, and made part of their rights by section 92."
I do not know that there is anything else important.

The Lord CHANCELLOR—I should have thought there was
an essential difference between regulation and prohibition.

Mr. MACLAREN—Prohibition may be partial or total and
regulation may be restrictive; I suppose it is difficult to say
when regulation is not complete.

The Lord CHANCELLOR—I should have thought it was
not at all difficult to say where there was prohibition that
that was not regulation.

Lord WATSON—To prescribe the conditions under which
a thing is to exist is a very different thing to prescribing that
it shall not exist at all.

Mr. MACLAREN—That of course refers to the abstract.

Lord HERSCHELL.—I suppose it would amount to prohibition if you said no man should sell less than 10,000
bottles of wine at a time. That is very near prohibition
although it purports to be regulation.

The Lord CHANCELLOR—It would purport to be regulation
but it would be prohibition and I should think any Court
would so hold and that that would be a colourable evasion.

Mr. MACLAREN—I would also refer your Lordships to
page 13 of the same book to the remarks of his Lordship
Mr. Justice MacLennan in the same case, where he is
discussing this question of the prohibition. He says:

" The enactment in question then, in 1866 and 1869, and until it
was repealed by 37 Vic. c. 32, sec. 61, was merely a power granted to
municipalities to prohibit the *retail* traffic in liquors. It was not a
power of *total* prohibition, but a comparatively small power confined
to retail business, and was the same which was conferred first in the
year 1853, and which was possessed by the municipalities unimpaired
at the time of the Confederation."

I would next refer your Lordships to the Judgment of the
Court of Appeal of the Province of Quebec in the case of *The
Corporation of the Village of Huntingdon* v. *Moir.* That is to be
found at 7 Montreal Law Reports, p. 281. Q. B. That was

a case in the Province of Quebec. The Province of Quebec had legislation similar to that of the Province of Ontario.

Lord DAVEY—Your section that you are defending prohibits the sale of liquor altogether ?

Mr. MACLAREN—No, my Lord.

Lord DAVEY—Only in retail ?

Mr. MACLAREN—I was coming to that ; that was a later part of my argument, and I was going to take that up presently. The effect of it is this——

Lord HERSCHELL—Does section 18 of 53 Vict. c. 56 (Ontario), define retail ?

Mr. MACLAREN—Yes ; retail, your Lordship will find defined in the Appendix of Statutes.

Lord HERSCHELL—But did this Statute itself define retail ? ·

Mr. MACLAREN—It defined it in this way, that it said what was not involved in that—no license was necessary—your Lordship will find that provision on page 4 of the Joint Appendix of Statutes.

Lord HERSCHELL—But those are the earlier Statutes. I am speaking of the Law now in force. We are supposing those earlier Statutes to be swept away except so far as they are dealt with in the Act of 37 Victoria, chap. 32.

Mr. MACLAREN—It referred to taverns and shop licenses, and your Lordship will find a definition on page 23 of the Joint Appendix of Statutes ; and perhaps I might just deal with that as explanatory of the Act. The License Act of Ontario, which is chapter 194 of the Revised Statutes of Ontario, intituled " An Act respecting the sale of fermented or spirituous liquors," contains the definition.   That is :

" 2. Where the following words occur in this Act or in the Schedules thereto, they shall be construed in the manner hereinafter mentioned, unless a contrary intention appears : ' 2. Tavern license ' shall mean a license for selling, bartering or trafficking by retail in fermented, spirituous or other liquors, in quantities of less than one quart, which may be drunk in the inn, ale or beer-house, or other house of public entertainment in which the same liquor is sold : ' 3. Shop license ' shall mean a license for selling, bartering or trafficking by retail in such liquors in shops, stores or places, other than inns, ale or beer-houses, or other houses of public entertainment, in quantities not less than three half-pints at any one time to any one person, and at the time of sale to be wholly removed and taken away, in quantities not less than three half-pints at a time."

Then : " 4. License by wholesale ? "——

Lord HERSCHELL—That does not apply to retail; " tavern license " means selling by retail in quantities of less than a quart, and " shop license " means selling quantities by retail of not less than half-a-pint. Those are definitions of "tavern license " and " shop license," not a definition of " retail."

Mr. MACLAREN—Your Lordship will see the effect of it, which is contained in the Act of 1890, is to abolish either tavern licenses or shop licenses.

Lord HERSCHELL—But it does not show what retail means.

Mr. MACLAREN—It shows what tavern and shop licenses are.

Lord HERSCHELL—It means selling by retail in different quantities.

Mr. MACLAREN—They were, I think, both considered retail.

Lord WATSON—I suppose retail means sales of every description which are not covered by the wholesale license.

Mr. MACLAREN—I think so—anything under the quantity authorised to be sold by the wholesale license is retail, because your Lordship will see that the word retail is used both in the definition of a tavern license and of a shop license.

Lord WATSON—Yes : retail is used both with regard to a tavern and a shop.

Mr. MACLAREN—In answer to the question put as to whether this Act is a total prohibition, my answer is that it is not. The Act provides :

" The Council of every township, city, town and incorporated village may pass by-laws for prohibiting the sale by retail of spirituous, fermented or other manufactured liquors in any tavern, inn or other house or place of public entertainment, and for prohibiting altogether the sale thereof in shops and places other than houses of public entertainment. Provided that the by-law, before the final passing thereof, has been duly approved of by the electors of the municipality in the manner provided by the sections in that behalf of the Municipal Act. Provided, however, that nothing in this section contained shall be construed into an exercise of jurisdiction by the Legislature of the Province of Ontario beyond the revival of provisions of law which were in force at the date of the passing of the British North American Act, and which the subsequent legislation of this Province purported to repeal."

Lord HERSCHELL.—I can see the reason of that. That is to save them if it turns out that they have not power to enact, by falling back on the fact that the old statute did not repeal.

Mr. MACLAREN—Yes, I think that was the intention.

The Lord CHANCELLOR—I am afraid it does not affect it much because if they were right they were right, and if they were wrong it would not help them.

Lord WATSON—That question is not before us at all.

The Lord CHANCELLOR—If it was not repealed it would be in force.

Lord WATSON—That is not the question before us. There is nothing to raise the point for our consideration just now as to what the effect of those Statutes may be.

Mr. MACLAREN—I submit that this Act which is now before your Lordships is not an Act of total prohibition by repeal.

Lord HERSCHELL—They can sell if they sell in less than a dozen bottles or five gallons.

Mr. MACLAREN—Yes, municipalities have two powers under this Act of 1890.

Lord DAVEY—I suppose it being part of the object of the municipal institutions to preserve order and to prevent disorder in a municipality, they would have power to make regulations for conducting traffic in such a way as to prevent drunkenness.

Mr. MACLAREN—Yes.

Lord HERSCHELL.—Are you going to argue the question that this is within 16 ?

Mr. MACLAREN—I am afraid my Lord that *Russell* v. *The Queen* may interfere with my having the full benefit of that argument.

Lord HERSCHELL.—Of course *Russell* v. *The Queen* interferes with your argument a good deal. I am quite aware of that.

Mr. MACLAREN—I would say this my Lord, my answer would perhaps be a qualified one to that, considering *Russell* v. *The Queen*, in showing why I think this question can be answered in our favour without interfering with *Russell* v. *The Queen*, and I prefer to give the qualified answer which I had intended to give. On this point my argument is this : On page 23 we have the Ontario License Act——

Lord HERSCHELL.—If it is within the specific subjects mentioned in section 91, then clearly all matters although merely local if they are within any of those specific subjects are under section 91.

Mr. MACLAREN—Yes.

Lord HERSCHELL.—And, therefore, out of the power of the Provincial Legislature. But if it is not to be found in any of the specific subjects in section 91 and is merely local, then the question arises whether there is anything in section 91 to take it out of the full operation of the Act.

Lord WATSON—If you can show that the enactments in the Statute in question do not go beyond regulation, it strikes me that *Russell* v. *The Queen* is a judgment in your favour, because it does decide that laying down the lines of trading is within the competency and belongs to the Dominion Parliament, yet there resides in the Local Legislature the power of regulating local sale, and the question is whether you can show that this is regulation.

Lord DAVEY—Regulation of the Liquor Traffic for municipal purposes.

Lord WATSON—It is a question of regulation and the powers of regulation and if the Dominion Parliament were to give power to a municipality to pass a by-law by which no drink could be sold between 8 a.m. and 10 p.m. I am inclined to think that that would raise the question of mere regulation.

The Lord Chancellor—We will deal with that when it arises. The only thing I should say as to that would be that it was in form regulation but was really intended to be prohibition. I suppose if that proposition were true you might make it from 6 a.m. to 7 a.m.

Lord Watson—With an hour for meals.

Mr. Maclaren—This Act of 1890 as your Lordships will see is an Act amending the License Act of Ontario, and I submit that the proper test of this Act as to whether it is valid or not is to look at it not so much as an isolated piece of legislation, but to look at the effect of the Act as amended by this amending Act. It is part of an Act amending the Liquor License Act and is now embodied in it.

Lord Herschell—But it does not follow that you can amend that Act, does it? That is the whole question. There were many Acts which you could not amend after the Confederation Act was passed. I do not see how you advance your case by saying that it is merely the amending of the previous Act.

Mr. Maclaren—It is an amending of the Act which was before your Lordships in *Hodge* v. *The Queen.*

Lord Herschell—Still something in that Act may be perfectly valid, but you may amend it for example in this way. Taking the case of *Hodge* v. *The Queen* as good law, you might alter the hours but that would not have been good, because there was an amendment of the Act; it would be good if there were no such Act existing at all.

Mr. Maclaren—Yes. In the License Act of Ontario, of which this is an amendment, the legislature has made three classes of licenses: tavern, shop and wholesale. Tavern may sell one quart or less which may be consumed on the premises; the shop may sell in quantities not less than three half-pints, which shall not be consumed on the premises; the wholesale may sell not less than five gallons. Now the

effect of this Act of 1890 is this. It says in effect to the
municipalities—" you may pass a bill that there shall be no
tavern licenses granted " : that would leave shop and wholesale ; " or, you may pass a bill saying that there shall be no
more shop licenses granted " : that would leave tavern and
wholesale ; or, you may pass a bill or bills saying that " there
shall be neither tavern nor shop licenses granted "; in any case
there might be wholesale licenses in the municipality, that is
for the sale of five gallons, or not less than one dozen bottles.
So I submit that it was quite competent as a license law and
as a regulation—a regulation of the drink for the Province of
Ontario to enact, or to authorise municipalities to enact, that
there should not be a total prohibition of the sale of liquor,
but that there should be not less sold in a particular municipality than five gallons at one time or less than a dozen
bottles, and that that legislation can be sustained under a
police regulation for the amendment of the trade in intoxicating liquors. And that is the Act which your Lordships have
to consider, so that under this question which we are now
considering, it is not a question of entire prohibition at all :
it is a matter merely of the withholding of tavern licenses and
of shop licenses ; so that I submit, that even though in
answer to some of the previous questions, your Lordships
should hold that the Province has not the power——

The Lord CHANCELLOR—Putting it in different language
to make it more intelligible, that liquor should never be sold
except wholesale.

Mr. MACLAREN—That is with the definition of wholesale.

Lord WATSON—It is a prohibition of the retail trade.

Lord HERSCHELL.—The sale of twelve bottles at a time
might even be called retail. The distinction, as I understand
it between wholesale and retail generally, has no application
to quantity, but it means that the wholesale dealer is a person
who sells to other dealers to retail, and the retail dealer is the
person who sells to the public.

The LORD CHANCELLOR—I rather think our law in this
country makes a distinction. I think it is 2 dozen bottles
which constitutes a wholesale dealer—a wholesale dealer
cannot sell less than 2 dozen bottles.

Lord WATSON—I think there is an arbitrary distinction made by statute, but the real distinction is that the wholesale dealer does not sell to private customers or is supposed not to do so.

Lord HERSCHELL—Wholesale I take it means selling it to other people to retail.

Lord WATSON—Yes; and the retail dealer I understand sells to the public who consume. The wholesale dealer does not sell to the consumer but he sells to those who supply the consumer.

The LORD CHANCELLOR—It comes to this you know, that any one who cannot afford to buy a dozen bottles can get no liquor at all.

Mr. MACLAREN—That would be the effect.

The LORD CHANCELLOR—That is the intended effect.

Mr. MACLAREN—That is if the Municipality should pass a Bill abolishing not only taverns but shops. Of course it would be to prevent the sale and the purchase.

If your Lordships will allow me there is one other case to which I wish to refer upon this point but I will not detain your Lordships by reading it. It will be found in the book of special printed cases, and it is the last of the three contained in it—*Lepine* v. *Laurent*. I cite it, especially because it embodies the judgment of the Court of Appeal of the Province of Quebec which is not elsewhere reported. It will be found on page 17 of these printed cases, I refer especially to the part of the case commencing at page 18, in which his Lordship Mr. Justice Lynch refers to a case which had been decided—the case of *Sulte*, and also the judgment of the Court of Appeal which is not elsewhere reported, as was stated by his Lordship Mr. Justice Lynch, who acted as one of the Counsel in the matter. He quotes, no doubt, from the printed case which went to the Supreme Court, and he refers specially to the remarks of the Court of Appeal of the Province of Quebec. I first refer to the remarks of the late Sir Antoine Dorion, and then on page 19 to the remarks of Mr. Justice Ramsay. Then at the foot of page 19 your Lordships will find the remarks of Mr. Justice Cross, which put in a very strong way some of the points and arguments to which I was endeavouring to call your Lordships' attention upon the matter.

Adjourned for a short time.

Mr. MACLAREN—My Lords, I think the only other case to which it is necessary to refer your Lordships at the present time on the subject I was addressing you upon before the adjournment, is the Judgment of Mr. Justice Taschereau in the case of *Huson* v. *South Norwich*, which raised this same question.

Lord HERSCHELL—Where do you find that?

Mr. MACLAREN—It is in the Joint Appendix of Statutes, beginning at page 31. The Judgment is one of considerable length and part of it covers the same ground as that which I have been going over, and is referred to in the other Judgments. I will refer your Lordships only to some short extracts.

Lord WATSON—I see this was in January, 1895.

Mr. MACLAREN—Yes, the same day as the Judgment was given from which the present Appeal comes.

Lord WATSON—He was the other Judge?

Mr. MACLAREN—The 6th Judge.

Lord WATSON—The Judge who brought the balance to an equipoise?

Mr. MACLAREN—He was one of the first five—one of the majority in the first case—but he did not sit in the second case. He was one of the three who dismissed the Appeal of *Huson* v. *South Norwich,* upholding the validity of the Provincial Act, but he did not sit in the second case.

Lord WATSON—*Huson's* case was the first case?

Mr. MACLAREN—Yes.

Lord WATSON—The result of the two cases, because they seem to have involved the same question very much, and the same considerations, was that the Supreme Court was equally divided.

Mr. MACLAREN—Yes.

Lord WATSON —Though there was a majority in the case now before us.

Mr. MACLAREN—Yes; there was a majority the other way in the case of *Huson* v. *South Norwich* which involved the same point.

Lord WATSON -Arising from the fact that the opinion of the whole Court was taken, the Judges were equally divided.

Mr. MACLAREN -That was the result, and I refer your Lordships to this partly because his Lordship discusses the question that was put to me by one of your Lordships a short time ago, and that is about the case of *Russell* v. *The Queen*. His Lordship, on page 34 of the Joint Appendix, is discussing the " Canada Temperance Act," which was in question before this Board in the case of *Russell* v. *The Queen*, which he calls the " Federal Act of 1878," and he is pointing out the distinction on page 34 between that Act and the present one.   He refers to your Lordships' Judgment in the case of *Hodge* v. *The Queen*, on which he says :

> " The Privy Council in *Hodge* v. *The Queen* (9th Appeal Cases 117), considered that the 'Ontario License Act' does not conflict with the 'Federal Temperance Act of 1878.'   *A fortiori* would I say, two prohibitory Acts need not necessarily conflict with one another."

Lord WATSON I do not follow what *a fortiori* there means.   They were held to conflict because one was a prohibitory Act or a prohibitory Act was contemplated.   It was supported on the ground that it was a regulating Act and not prohibitory.   Why should it be *a fortiori*.   It is a strong proposition, and not easy to digest at first sight.   Can you throw any light upon it ?

Mr. MACLAREN I think his Lordship meant to refer to the application of the two Acts.

Lord WATSON Let me put the proposition before you. If a power of A. to grant a prohibitory Act is not inconsistent

with B. granting a regulating Act, how does it follow *a fortiori*
that the power of A. to grant a prohibitory Act is not inconsistent with B.'s granting one?

Mr. MACLAREN—I think that is to be taken into account
with the remarks that follow, in which his Lordship goes on
to point out the difference between the Act of 1878 and the
Act of 1890, which was in question in the case under consideration.

Lord WATSON—He means that the prohibitory Acts may
be of such a different character.

Mr. MACLAREN—Yes; and he goes on to consider it in
the second paragraph following that I have just read, and he
says:—

" The Federal Act cannot at all be considered as legislation over
the powers of the Municipalities. It does not purport to be anything
of the kind. It has no connection whatever, and could have none,
with the municipal system of the different Provinces. It is controlled
altogether by a majority of federal electors, but that, it is obvious, may
not be at all the majority of the municipal electors in a municipality,
when that is required, as in the Province of Quebec, and in fact under the
Statutes at present in force in some of the Provinces, whereby women,
for instance, are entitled to vote at municipal but not at federal elections.
Likewise, for the provincial electors, where, as in Ontario, these by-laws
under the Provincial Act depend on their votes, the majority of them
may not be at all a majority of federal electors, or *vice versa*; and the
Respondents, I assume, would not have any objection to submit to the
Temperance Act of 1878, if it was put into force in the county of
which they form part. All what they claim is Home Rule—the right
to put a stop to drinking and to taverns within their own territorial limits,
even if the rest of the province or all the other municipalities of their
county choose to do otherwise for their own people. They should be as
free to do so now as they were before Confederation, though the Provinces
of British Columbia, Prince Edward Island, Quebec, or all of them, and
all the other municipalities of Ontario, may favour within their territorial
limits a different policy. Whenever the Federal Parliament prohibits
entirely the liquor traffic in the Dominion—assuming always, for the
purposes of this case, that they have the power to do so—the Respondents
will not complain: the very object they are now contending for will be
attained. What they ask is to be at liberty to do so for themselves till
Parliament does so for the whole Dominion. And again, by an express
provision of the Temperance Act of 1878, if the Act is rejected by the
federal electors, it cannot be submitted to them again for a period of
three years. Now, if within these three years a local municipality and
a majority within it of the provincial or municipal electors, where that

G 2

is required, desire to prohibit the liquor traffic within its limits, is there anything in allowing them to do so inconsistent with the Temperance Act of 1878, or repugnant to it?"

Lord WATSON—All that is hardly argument. It merely goes this length, that it is a benevolent sort of legislation that advances the line of legislation that has been followed by the Canadian Parliament, but if the Canadian Parliament have the power to initiate that prohibitory legislation, where resides the power of the Provincial Parliament to carry it further by supplemental legislation? Those are the points I should like you to address your argument to, or at least those are the points that raise difficulty in my mind. It is possible that it is not insuperable by any means.

Mr. MACLAREN—The argument on that point would be that this power which the Provinces exercise and profess to give to the municipalities under the present Act falls short of the power of the Dominion.

Lord WATSON—In other words, though the Dominion Parliament has power to initiate the legislation and carry it so far as to stop there, it is within the power of the Provincial Parliament to step in and carry it further. On what do you found that? I know what you found your arguments on on the first point, namely, that they derived it from the legislation before 1867. These observations you are reading us now do not proceed on that argument.

Mr. MACLAREN—No.

Lord WATSON—Because, if that argument were well founded to the core, it would follow that the Provincial Legislature have the exclusive power of beginning the legislation and carrying it on. This assumes that the Dominion Parliament has the power of initiating. I want to know where you find it in the Statutes. That throws overboard altogether the view that the Provincial Legislature had it because it was implied in the very words "Municipal Institutions." This assumes that that did not oust the Dominion Parliament, and as far as I can see he is going to say that the Dominion Parliament must have carried it on. If they had carried it on, by the same rule it would apply to all the different Provinces of the Dominion.

Mr. MACLAREN—I think this is to be interpreted by the second following paragraph in which his Lordship asks the question :—

> " And can it not be said of the enactment now under consideration what their Lordships said of the Statute in *Hodge* v. *The Queen*, that it is ' confined to Municipalities in the Province of Ontario and is entirely local in its character and operation.' "

That, I think, is to be read in connection with the preceding paragraph.

Lord WATSON—Then on the other hand if that power of prohibition is given to the Dominion Parliament, why should not they have the power to carry it further ? Where is the limit on that power of prohibition, to put my difficulty more shortly before you ? Where is the limit to this power which at a certain time deprives them of power to go further and hands over the power to go further to the Provincial Legislature ?

Mr. MACLAREN—This would appear to my mind rather to be an exercise of a power which falls short of that law which might be exercised by the Province when the Dominion has not legislated.

Lord WATSON—What is there that gives it to the Province after the Dominion have gone so far ? Because if this argument has any foundation that is legislation belonging to the Province. It follows on that reasoning if it were well founded according to my view that it was the Province and not the Dominion which had the power to carry it this distance.

Mr. MACLAREN—That this might be a power the Province would have and might legislate upon so long as it was not overridden by any Legislation of the Dominion on one of the subjects committed to the Dominion. That is part of his Lordship's view, that this was a local matter—a Police regulation.

Lord WATSON—That the field was unoccupied.

Mr. MACLAREN—Yes, that the field was unoccupied, and I think that has force in this respect, that although the Canada Temperance Act which we shall consider further in *Russell* v. *The Queen* presently——

Lord Watson—That is a doctrine which was applied in a recent case on the question of bankruptcy, but what I wish to ask is this—Has this Board ever affirmed that you could have a field of that sort partly occupied where there was not an express clause authorising it?

Lord Herschell—I suppose you point to the express clause as to matters of a local nature and you say, dealing with the condition of drinking and the amount of drinking, and the limitations upon drinking in a particular Province is of a local nature; that it may be that the Dominion Parliament with reference to the Dominion generally and its legislation if it touched all Provinces would override anything the Province did, but in so far as the Dominion Parliament has not dealt with it the Provincial Legislature may deal with it as a matter of local character which touches nobody outside the Province. Of course you could not contend that, if it is within any of the specific clauses of section 91. If it is excluded by reason of its being trade and commerce, then you would be out of Court.

Mr. Maclaren—Yes.

Lord Herschell—On that point this Board has not yet pronounced, but they left it open in the case of *Russell* v. *The Queen*. In *Russell* v. *The Queen* it said that the Dominion Parliament was not excluded from dealing with it as being merely a local matter, because it was of interest to the Dominion Parliament that there should be a uniform regulation of the liquor traffic throughout the whole Dominion. But that would still leave open the question whether it was competent to the Provincial Legislature to deal with it as regards its own Province in a manner not inconsistent with any Dominion legislation.

Mr. Maclaren—Yes.

Lord Herschell—I have been refreshing my memory by referring to the case of *Russell* v. *The Queen*. I do not think there is anything in *Russell* v. *The Queen* which precludes that point.

Lord Watson—I think in *Russell* v. *The Queen* they distinctly held that the legislation in question there was not legislation under subsection 16 of a merely local and private nature. They expressly ruled that.

Mr. MACLAREN—Because it was general for the whole Dominion.

Lord DAVEY—The legislation in *Russell* v. *The Queen* was defended on the ground of the general words as to good order.

Mr. MACLAREN—Yes.

Lord HERSCHELL—They did not say that within each particular Province it would not be a matter of a local nature which the Provincial Parliament could deal with. What they said was, that dealing with it as they were doing as a general matter for the whole of Canada was not trenching upon the province of the Provincial Legislature to deal itself with matters of a local character. That was all they said in *Russell* v. *The Queen.*

Mr. MACLAREN—That, I think, is the point.

Lord HERSCHELL.—That certainly leaves open the question whether the liquor traffic could be prohibited or put under fetter in a Province by a Provincial Legislature in a manner not inconsistent with Dominion legislation.

Mr. MACLAREN—We have then to consider—and I think we cannot claim more than that—that this Act which we are now considering might, perhaps, be overridden by Dominion legislation, if the Dominion should legislate under some of its powers. Our claim is that until the Dominion so legislate, this legislation is good. Of course we shall be told in the first place that this is really conflicting with the Canada Temperance Act of 1878.

Lord HERSCHELL.—That is another question.

Mr. MACLAREN—That is the other question. My answer to that is that this legislation which is now in force here would in the nature of things only apply to places where the Canada Temperance Act is not in force. The Canada Temperance Act, as your Lordships are aware, is an Act which is to be brought into force by proclamation of the Governor-General after an affirmative vote of the Federal

electors, that is, the electors who elect the Members to the
House of Commons.   Until that vote is taken, and until that
proclamation of the Governor-General issues putting the
Canada Temperance Act in force, so far as regards any portion
of any Province the Canada Temperance Act does not exist.
It does not practically exist, it is not a law in any part of the
Dominion until it is put in force by a proclamation.

Lord WATSON—That Act gives local option to certain
districts as to whether they will or will not adopt its provisions
as part of the measure ?

Mr. MACLAREN—Yes.

Lord WATSON—But then it is quite possible that a district
which has that local option, the option between two things
under the Act of Canada, may be deprived of an option by
some vote or regulation of a municipal body.

Mr. MACLAREN—I hardly think that could arise in this
case.   The present Act applies only to local municipalities,
that is, to small areas, not to parishes in the Province of
Ontario, but townships, villages, towns, or cities.   Those
are what are called local municipalities.

Lord WATSON—The legislation of Canada if not adopted
gives them one rule ; your legislation if adopted by these
authorities may apply a different rule.

Mr. MACLAREN—In small localities, that is as a rule, with
the exception of cities.

Lord WATSON—A man who has succeeded in preventing
the Canada Temperance Act applying may find himself under
this Statute.

Mr. MACLAREN—If the Canada Temperance Act is not
applied in the larger area, that is the county ; as to cities
they might be co-terminous, but if the Canada Temperance
Act is not applied in the larger area of the county because it
is not a matter of general interest——

Lord WATSON—Any Statute of that sort which would
carry prohibition so far is by plain implication an empowering
Statute ; it enables them to do what is not forbidden under

that Act. So far as the Legislature of Canada can do it, it authorises, subject to these restrictions, the sale of liquor and the consumption of liquor. On the other hand the Legislature may seriously interfere with that Act.

Mr. MACLAREN—I think I may say that with reference to the Dominion legislation, if the Dominion should have power to legislate under section 91 on this subject, that would probably override any permissive action.

Lord WATSON—It is an Act which is providing certain restrictions, but it is an Act plainly, which in substance, authorises the trade in liquor, wholesale and retail, to be carried on in the Provinces. Subject to those restrictions, and as long as they are observed they are within the law. The introduction of the local areas and the power given to local areas to prohibit on some other ground and for some other causes, surely is an interference with the system established by the General Act.

Lord DAVEY—Then the Temperance Act is only what it is the fashion now to call an adoptive Act?

Mr. MACLAREN—Certainly.

Lord DAVEY—And if not adopted by the Province it is not the law of the Province?

Mr. MACLAREN—Not by Provinces—by counties—small areas.

Lord WATSON—That alters the question. The law does not apply until that happens, but it is the only law restraining them until it is adopted. They may be free to sell and buy without it.

Lord HERSCHELL—Take this case. Supposing your Act had been repealed, or purported to be repealed, would the passing of the Canada Temperance Act have prevented its operation in the Province of Ontario, or such parts of the Province of Ontario as have not adopted the Canada Temperance Act? I do not know.

Mr. MACLAREN—I do not know why it should.

Lord HERSCHELL—If so and if it is not impliedly

repealed by it, is not that one test as to whether it is inconsistent ?

Mr. Maclaren.—I should think that would be the proper test. Then I would refer your Lordships also to what Mr. Justice Taschereau says on page 38, referring to the Province of Quebec, which throws some light on this question :—

" I need hardly say that it results clearly from it whatever its consequences may be on the question now under consideration, that the whole system of legislative supervision over the liquor traffic was so closely identified with the municipal system of the Province," (that is the Province of Quebec, and we have been hitherto speaking chiefly of the Province of Ontario) " and so blended with it that they formed only one. The ' Constitutional connection ' between the two to use Mr. Justice Burton's expression—was complete. And up to the present day the two are so worked and put in operation as one, that every year, in a large number of municipalities, the only, or at least the principal question at the election for councillors is prohibition or no prohibition ? This is a matter of public notoriety in the Province. Now, not long after the coming into force of the " British North America Act " the Quebec Legislature, in 1870, enacted a *Municipal* Code, and in continuance of the policy that had theretofore prevailed in the Province, of treating the control over the liquor traffic as a part of the Municipal Institutions, and leaving it to be as theretofore a marked feature of the power vested in the municipal authorities, it conferred upon each local council, by section 561 thereof, the power to prohibit, and this by extension of the power ' *at any time* ' during the municipal year, the retail sale of intoxicating liquors. And that enactment with slight amendments (Art. 6118 Rev. Stat. of 1888) has remained in force up to the present day unchallenged by the federal authority, and has been acted upon through the Province in a number of municipalities.

" And at this very moment there are no less than 158 localities " (he means municipalities) " in the Province, as I gather from official sources, where the retail sale of liquor is entirely prohibited under that Statute. That has been in the Province the average yearly number of such by-laws since 1867."

Lord Watson—That seems to involve this result which may or may not be good, namely, that so long as the Dominion Parliament do not proceed to enact a total prohibition it will always be within the power of any Province to supplement that by making the prohibition total within the Province; that may have been what was contemplated by the Act of 1867.

Mr. Maclaren—Of course I have called your Lordships'

attention to the fact that this Act we are now considering is not an Act of total prohibition.

Lord HERSCHELL.—If there was no power to make this enactment there seems strong argument in favour of there having been no power to repeal it, and if so a strong argument in favour of this previous legislation being still in force, and the question is whether that is overridden in that case by the "Canada Temperance Act" until any place within the Province adopts it. If they do not adopt it it is difficult to see what can have got rid of the old law. It is a little strange why the question was not asked whether the previous statute had been validly repealed, because there seems to be rather a dilemma. If it cannot be validly enacted it is difficult to see that the former Act has been validly repealed, because it is dealing with precisely the same subject-matter. If it could not be validly repealed then it is in force. One of those questions is asked. Do you know why the other is not?

Mr. MACLAREN—I was speaking of the Ontario legislation, and confining myself to that.

Lord HERSCHELL.—The question is not put whether such an enactment is in force. The question is put whether it had jurisdiction to enact the 18th section. It may not have had jurisdiction to enact it, but the Act may be in force because there was no power to repeal the Act which previously existed. We are not asked that question.

Mr. MACLAREN—I believe that it is doubtful whether the Act may not have been repealed by the Dominion in the general repealing clause in connection with the Revised Statutes.

Mr. BLAKE—It has been.

Lord WATSON—Then that accounts for it.

Mr. BLAKE—I can show your Lordship the repealing clause in the Revised Statutes of Canada.

Lord WATSON—Read the clause, Mr. Blake.

Mr. BLAKE—There is a general provision which is that

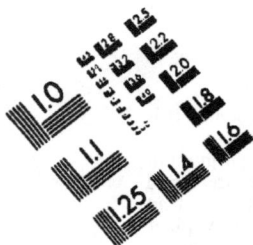

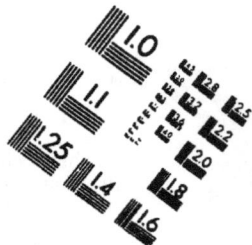

IMAGE EVALUATION
TEST TARGET (MT-3)

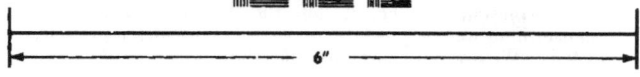

6"

Photographic
Sciences
Corporation

23 WEST MAIN STREET
WEBSTER, N.Y. 14580
(716) 872-4503

parts of Acts are repealed by a Schedule.   Schedule A, page 9, includes 59 : " An Act respecting municipal institutions of Upper Canada ; the whole except section 409." This is not section 409.

Lord HERSCHELL—Then the Dominion Parliament has purported to deal with this very thing.

Lord WATSON—They repealed the Act which the Province have now re-enacted.

Lord HERSCHELL—If they could repeal it, it seems to me clear that the Province could not re-enact it.

Mr. MACLAREN—If it is in Dominion jurisdiction.   It cannot be in both.

Lord HERSCHELL—If the Dominion Parliament had enacted provisions inconsistent with it, dealing with the whole Dominion, it may be that they could repeal it.   I am not quite sure that it follows they could repeal simply a local enactment applied to a particular Province without substituting anything for it.

Mr. BLAKE—We contend that the Canada Temperance Act does supply the deficiency.

Mr. MACLAREN—That we shall consider when we come to *Russell* v. *The Queen*.   The question is whether our contention is correct, that this is a municipal matter.

Lord WATSON—I think if they had power to repeal anything coming within trade or commerce, they would have a right to repeal a particular enactment of a particular Province passed before 1867 with a view to the requirements of that Province under the clause enabling them to deal with trade and commerce.

Lord HERSCHELL—If it came within any of the specific subjects mentioned.

Sir RICHARD COUCH—Section 129 is " repeal, abolish or alter."

Mr. MACLAREN—They had power to repeal or alter if within their jurisdiction.

The LORD CHANCELLOR—That comes back to the old question, does not it?

Mr. MACLAREN—That would come back to the same question, whether this is within the jurisdiction of the Dominion or the Province.

Lord HERSCHELL—It is conceivable that the matter of dealing with the liquor traffic may be in the Dominion or in the Province or both. It may be that in the Province, quite apart from the question of Municipal Institutions, you could deal with the liquor traffic for the Province alone as being a matter of a local nature. It may be said that the Dominion Parliament has power, as a matter of good government of the Dominion at large, to deal with the liquor traffic throughout the Dominion. I apprehend that in so far the Dominion legislation must override the Provincial legislation if the two are inconsistent. I am supposing it is not excluded from the Province by being within trade and commerce. That is another question. If it is within trade and commerce that includes it, but supposing it not to be within any subject in section 91, it may be that the Provincial Legislature may deal with it and the Dominion Parliament also.

Mr. MACLAREN—Quite so, for different purposes, and that it would come within the subjects which are specified in the Judgment of this Board in *Hodge* v. *The Queen* where they are distinguishing *Russell* v. *The Queen*.

Lord HERSCHELL—It is quite clear that matters of a private and local nature, or of a local nature at all events, must have a large scope. I do not see that Police comes within anything mentioned there. It does not come within the administration of justice, and you cannot say it comes within that; I do not see that it comes within anything, yet they have power to create a system of police.

Lord DAVEY—It is supposed to come within Municipal Institutions.

Mr. MACLAREN—A constable is a municipal officer as a rule.

Lord HERSCHELL—The difficulty is this, that if it comes

within Municipal Institutions that is because of the very difficulty raised in your argument on the first point. You say it comes within Municipal Institutions because it had been one of the things dealt with by municipalities.

The LORD CHANCELLOR—I do not think so because a policeman is a municipal officer himself.

Lord WATSON—I must confess for my own part I have considerable difficulty in reading "Municipal Institutions" in sub-section 8 as meaning anything more than the creation of such institutions, and that the power to be communicated to them must depend on the meaning you give to the other sub-sections of the clause. I do not think it is necessary to say you must find within sub-section 8 all the powers. Any matter coming within the class, that is what you communicate to them. There are, I venture to say, five-sixths of the powers given to municipal institutions that are much better described in sub-section 16 than sub-section 8.

Lord HERSCHELL—I certainly do not see any reason for putting a narrow construction on "matters of a local nature." It must be something the effect of which is confined to the Province, but if the effect of it is confined to the Province, and if it is not one of the things specifically mentioned in section 91, I do not see why the Provincial Legislature should not deal with it.

Lord WATSON—Then you come round to the last clause 16 "all matters of a merely local or private nature." I do not think they are necessarily implied in the words "Municipal Institutions," but having created a Municipal Institution, whatever its character, it is entirely within the power of the Provincial Legislature to clothe it with such powers and authorities as are within themselves. They can delegate their powers.

Lord HERSCHELL—I do not quite see why you "shy" at that clause 16. It seems to me it is better for you than 8. If the thing is one of the things specifically mentioned in section 91 then you are thrown.

Mr. MACLAREN—We are out in any event.

Lord HERSCHELL — If it is not one of the things specifically mentioned in section 91 and it is local in its character and nature and does not go beyond the locality, why should it not be within 16 ?

Mr. MACLAREN—When your Lordship suggested 16 I confess I thought your Lordship was leading me on to the consideration of that clause as in *Russell* v. *The Queen*, and I was in fear of being landed in a dilemma there.

Lord HERSCHELL.—The question arose in *Russell* v. *The Queen* from exactly the opposite point of view. In *Russell* v. *The Queen* it was sought to exclude it from the purview of the Dominion by saying it is a thing of a local nature. The answer to that was, if you give that construction to a thing of a local nature by way of excluding the Dominion action you would exclude them from everything which dealt with the Dominion as a whole, because it must deal also with the parts. That was the argument rejected in *Russell* v. *The Queen*, but *Russell* v. *The Queen* certainly did not say that you might not legislate in the Province for a thing which affected only the Province provided it was not one of the things specifically mentioned in section 91.

Mr. MACLAREN—I was about to consider that.

Lord DAVEY—Subject to any legislation in the Dominion ?

Lord HERSCHELL.—Subject to any legislation for the whole of the Dominion that is not made one of the specific clauses. The specific clauses exclude it, but when you are dealing with anything of a local nature everything in the Province and all legislation within the Province might b. said to be of a local nature, but when you are dealing with a general term like that it is obvious that that must be overridden by any specific legislation by the Dominion Parliament for the Dominion as a whole.

Mr. MACLAREN—No doubt.

Lord HERSCHELL—If you cannot bring it within any of the sub-sections 1 to 15 of section 92 and have to rely on sub-section 16 it must always be subject to being overridden by the action of the Dominion Parliament for Canada as a whole, but subject to that I do not quite see why there should not be Provincial Legislation.

Mr. MACLAREN—I wish to claim the benefit of 16, but I thought it better to consider it in conjunction with *Russell* v. *The Queen*, and in considering the Canada Temperance Act which was under consideration in *Russell* v. *The Queen* and the present Act, the distinction is one that has been drawn by this Board in a number of cases. Though the word "exclusive" is used it has been laid down that that word "exclusive" does not really exclude one or the other body from something which may have been unoccupied, that if there were legislation on the part of the body whose legislation would override that, that would preclude the legislation on behalf of the other body.

The Lord CHANCELLOR—I think you are quite justified in saying that more than one judgment points to that distinction. I have great difficulty in following it. Because its powers were distributed some to one and some to the other, it does not appear to me that the fact of one not having exercised it is any argument to shew that the distribution has not taken place.

Lord WATSON—I think you must admit that is due to two considerations. I do not think that this Board have ever held that to be the law except where these two things occur; in the first place that the thing the power of doing which is in question could be done effectively by the Dominion Parliament as incidental to power expressly given them by section 91, and in the second place that it falls expressly within powers given as exclusive powers to the Provincial Legislature.

Mr. MACLAREN—Yes.

Lord WATSON—It may be that it ought to be carried further. I do not think it has yet been carried further.

Mr. MACLAREN—I was about to argue that the length to which it has been carried is all the length to which I require to go.

Lord WATSON—The last case we had was one where clearly the matter at issue was a matter of civil rights and it was held that the legislation was good, though it would be quite competent to the Dominion Parliament to set it aside and repeal it, or render it of no effect whatever by introducing certain provisions to the contrary in dealing with the question of bankruptcy, because there are a number of powers given with which it is perfectly clear you cannot interfere without interfering more or less with civil rights. How can you interfere, for instance, with copyright without affecting the right of the rest of the public and their civil interests ? How can you interfere with bills of exchange or promissory notes without interfering with the interests of others, and the civil rights and interests of persons outside the Province, and many others in the same way ?

Mr. MACLAREN—I think there are two cases in which that has been specially considered and which I think I need not press upon your Lordships as being any extension of the principle. The first case is *L'Union St. Jacques de Montreal* v. *Belisle*, to which your Lordship has referred, which is in Law Reports 6 (Privy Council) page 31, and in the first volume of Cartwright, page 63. That was a question respecting a benevolent society which was altering its basis in proportion to its members, and it was a question whether that was an interference with the Dominion right relating to bankruptcy and insolvency, and your Lordships held it was not such an interference and that it belonged to property and civil rights and to prevent bankruptcy taking place. That was further considered in the case of the Attorney-General of Ontario and the Attorney-General of the Dominion in the matter relating to the Assignment Act of the Province of Ontario in the Law Reports of last year (1894) Appeal Cases, page 189, in which your Lordships upheld the validity of certain enactments of the Province of Ontario which it was claimed were *ultra vires* on the ground of relating to bankruptcy and insolvency a matter which is assigned exclusively to the Dominion.

Lord WATSON—We held that these enactments were warranted by sub-section 13 of section 92.

Mr. MACLAREN—Yes.

Lord WATSON—They were enactments with reference to civil rights which the Province were entru ed with, but it was pointed out that the Dominion Parliament had legislative power with reference to bankruptcy which might occasion the nullifying of the legislation.

Mr. MACLAREN—But the Dominion not having legislated the Province had the right to legislate under the authority of "Property and Civil Rights." That, I think, is the effect of the Judgment.

The Lord CHANCELLOR—That is to say so long as it does not conflict with the bankruptcy legislation of the Dominion.

Mr. MACLAREN—That I think is the expression used. With regard to the case of *Russell* v. *The Queen*, I think the effect of that has been so fully stated by one of your Lordships that I need not go into it in detail. The difference between the Canada Temperance Act and the present Act is very marked, and although they relate to a certain extent to the same subject yet I think the rule should be adopted which your Lordships have a number of times laid down that it is necessary to look at the nature and character of the legislation in order to determine the authority which has the jurisdiction in the premises. Now the Canada Temperance Act is an Act very different from the present and it has nothing whatever to do with municipal bodies. Municipalities are not mentioned at all except as to the limits of counties and cities. Beyond the geographical extent I think the municipalities have nothing to do with it. There are no municipal by-laws.

Lord MORRIS—Where is it in the Canada Temperance Act ?

Mr. MACLAREN—The enacting Clause is in the Canada Temperance Act, Revised Statutes of Canada (1886) cap. 106 section 99. There are other Clauses bringing it into force.

Lord HERSCHELL—Can you rely much on that, that it has no reference to municipalities ? Supposing it were adopted in Ontario, would you say that the Ontario Act we are considering remained in force ? You say it has no reference to municipalities, but should you contend that if the Canada Temperance Act were adopted in Ontario in a given district that the Act we are now considering would remain in force none the less?

Mr. MACLAREN—I think it would not. It would be a matter of a local or private nature that would be superseded by general legislation of the Dominion.

Lord HERSCHELL—You would admit it was superseded in any part of Ontario where the Canada Temperance Act came into operation?

Mr. MACLAREN—I think we should have to admit that. I think, considering section 91 and *Russell* v. *The Queen*, that if the Canada Temperance Act were in force—I mean put in force by act and Proclamation—that in such case the present legislation would be inoperative; that this is a mere local matter simply regulating a matter of a local and private nature in the Province, or indeed any particular municipality in the Province which, by virtue of the power conferred by section 92, the Province itself may legislate upon or delegate to the municipalities, until that is overridden by Dominion legislation which comes actively into force. I think that is the position which I should require to take in connection with this legislation, that it is very much like the legislation to which I have referred, that was considered in the case of *L'Union St. Jacques* v. *Belisle*, and in the insolvency case—that it was good legislation on its own ground and in its own locality so long as there was no Dominion legislation on the general subject or of a general nature overriding it. That, I think, is the extent to which it would be enforced, and that is all which I should claim for this Law in the present case. Then, with your Lordship's permission, I would refer to two or three cases in which this matter has been specially considered, and the first of those cases is the case of *Russell* v. *The Queen*. As I was saying, that was, I think, an Act of an entirely different nature. That was not a matter of a local or private nature. Your Lordships have so decided and based it on the ground that it was not a matter of a local or private nature in the Province so as to oust the jurisdiction of the Dominion. The nature of the Act was entirely different; it was brought into force entirely by Federal authority. It is the Federal Parliament which prescribes the limits in which it is to be put into operation, namely, counties and cities. The Federal electors—those who vote upon it—are those that are created only by Federal legislation, though at one time, by virtue of Federal legislation, they adopted the Provincial franchise. But that is not the case now. It is almost entirely brought into operation by enactments within the purview of the Dominion Parliament.

Lord WATSON—The prohibition in *Russell* v. *The Queen* was that no person, by himself, his clerk, servant or agent, should "expose or keep for sale, or directly or indirectly, on any pretence, or upon any device, sell or barter, or in consideration of the purchase of any other property, give to any other person, any spirituous or other intoxicating liquors, or any mixed liquor capable of being used as a beverage, and part of which is spirituous or otherwise intoxicating." (Canada Temperance Act, 1878, sec. 99.) Why is that prohibition not of a local nature as much as the prohibition of the Act we are dealing with? It was held not to be so in that case.

Lord HERSCHELL—It was held not to be a local matter, that is to say, not excluded from the Dominion jurisdiction as a local matter, because the Dominion Parliament might deal throughout the whole of Canada with any subject that was not specifically described in the other heads of section 92 wherever they thought it was for the good of the country there should be such legislation, and then each Province could not say: "Oh, but you cannot do that because it applies to us and is therefore a local matter." That is all that *Russell* v. *The Queen*, as I understand it, decided.

Mr. MACLAREN—I think that is the effect of the decision.

Lord HERSCHELL—It was an attempt to prevent the Dominion Legislature dealing with a matter not within any of the headings in this section 92 because it was a local matter. That was the argument. Their Lordships said that it is not a local matter. They say :

"Their Lordships cannot concur in this view "—

that is that it is local.

"The declared object of Parliament in passing the Act is that there should be uniform legislation in all the Provinces respecting the traffic in intoxicating liquors with a view to promote temperance in the Dominion. Parliament does not treat the promotion of temperance as desirable in one Pro 'nce more than in another, but as desirable everywhere throughout the Dominion. The Act, as soon as it was passed, became a law for the whole Dominion, and the enactments of the first part relating to the machinery for bringing the second part into force took effect and might be put in motion at once and everywhere within it. It is true that the prohibitory and penal parts of the Act are only to come into force in any county or city upon the adoption of a petition to that effect by a majority of electors, but this conditional application of these parts of the Act does not convert the Act itself into legislation in relation to a merely local matter. The objects and scope of the legislation are still general, viz. : to promote temperance by means of a uniform law throughout the Dominion."

Therefore they say you, the Provincial Legislature, cannot say, "We have exclusive dominion, for this is a local matter." That, I think, was all.

Mr. MACLAREN—That, I think, is the extent of the Judgment in *Russell* v. *The Queen*. So that there is another point that I think might in a doubtful matter weigh, and that is this—the disposition there might be to uphold the legislation, but if the legislation were even doubtful——

Lord WATSON—I can quite understand the argument that there may be some matter involving local considerations which makes it fit to be dealt with under sub-section 16— considerations which do not arise in legislation of another kind.

Lord DAVEY—Their Lordships said the case might have a double aspect.

Mr. MACLAREN—They said that in speaking of *Russell* v. *The Queen*. I think it is unnecessary to refer further to the case of *Russell* v. *The Queen*. That case is explained in the case of *Hodge* v. *The Queen*, which is reported in the 9th Appeal Cases, at page 117, which your Lordships will also find in the 3rd volume of Cartwright, at page 144. Your Lordships will see there the comment that their Lordships made upon *Russell* v. *The Queen*, which goes to explain it, and, as I think, very strongly in our favour. Your Lordships will find it at page 160.

"It appears to their Lordships that *Russell* v. *The Queen*, when properly understood, is not an authority in support of the Appellants' contention, and their Lordships do not intend to vary or depart from the reasons expressed for their Judgment in that case. The principle which that case and the case of the Citizens' Insurance Company illustrate is that subjects which in one aspect and for one purpose fall within section 92 may in another aspect and for another purpose fall within section 91."

Now I claim the benefit of that: that they are discussing *Russell* v. *The Queen*, and that they say in words that the subject-matter of *Russell* v. *The Queen* is one which in one aspect might fall under Dominion authority and in the other aspect may fall under Provincial authority.

Lord WATSON—Surely under such a different aspect as to make it substantially different. The words are not happily selected, and I do not quite understand what was meant.

Mr. MACLAREN—So that *Russell* v. *The Queen*, as explained by *Hodge* v. *The Queen*, would, I think, go to sustain our contention here. In fact, they say that the subject-matter of *Russell* v. *The Queen* was just such a one as that of the Citizens' Insurance Company, in which there are different aspects, and that there might be on the same subject valid Dominion legislation and valid Provincial legislation.

Lord MORRIS—Which is to prevail ?

Lord WATSON—If to the same effect it does not matter.

The LORD CHANCELLOR—As a broad proposition that would not be adopted. You might have, for instance, what was put in *Hodge's* case. You might have the regulation of hours within which shops in a particular place might be open for the sale of liquor, but if it was effected to enact that no liquor should be sold, in that case other considerations would apply. What I mean is, the mere proposition that you might have regulations in a Province, where it is not two subject-matters but one subject-matter which may be within the province of one legislation and within the province of the other——

Lord HERSCHELL—Supposing that the Dominion Parliament had not passed any legislation on the subject at all, would there have been anything to prevent the Legislature of any one of those Provinces (supposing it not to come within " trade and commerce ") from regulating as it pleased the sale of drink within those borders ?

Lord DAVEY—Let us take the sale of poisons or dynamite, or the sale of firearms.

Mr. MACLAREN—As a matter of fact the Provinces have legislated on these very subjects; poison is dealt with by all the Provinces in the Pharmacy Acts, the sale of poisons and the licensing of Pharmacists and the like. I submit that we are in this position here, as our claim is that this legislation need only be enforced where the Canada Temperance Act is not in force—we are in the same position as if the Canada Temperance Act had never been passed. If these local regulations are only to be operative where the Canada Temperance Act or any other overriding legislation is not in force, then we are in the position of there being no Dominion legislation on the subject.

Lord HERSCHELL—If it is one not specifically mentioned in section 91, then you cannot bring it in under any general provision of 92.

Mr. MACLAREN—Then of course the ground is entirely taken from us if it is taken from the enumerated subjects. If to the Dominion is given the exclusive regulation of trade and commerce, anything that comes within that meaning would be taken out of the power of the Provinces.

The LORD CHANCELLOR—I agree.

Lord DAVEY—Trade and commerce has been construed by this Board as meaning the trade regulations for regulating the traffic between the Provinces.

Lord HERSCHELL—It put rather a narrow construction on trade and commerce. I argued the case. I was always in doubt whether that regulated the trade and commerce throughout the whole of the Dominion. Where people are dealing with one another in different states and passing from one state to another they should be all living under the same commercial law.

Lord WATSON—I doubt whether there is any definition of the word "commerce," which has ever been laid down by this Board since I remember sitting here. Definitions have been laid down for the purpose of particular occasions but they are not for universal application.

Lord HERSCHELL—You may give a very broad construction to " trade and commerce," and yet it may be that it would still leave open a very large power of dealing in such a way as to incidentally affect trade without its being a part of the regulations made within such meaning.

Mr. MACLAREN—My Lords, the other case to which I wish to refer is an Order or Judgment on the " Liquor Licensing Act of 1883." That is not reported in the regular reports, but your Lordships will find the Order in Council in the 4th volume of Cartwright, at page 342. As your Lordships are aware that arose upon the " Dominion Act ; " the " Liquor Licensing Act of 1883," and the " Amending Act of 1884," being referred first to the Supreme Court and afterwards brought before your Lordships here. Questions were asked whether the Dominion Act of 1883 and the Act of 1884 were valid in whole or in part. The Supreme Court of Canada to which the questions were first referred by the Governor-General answered the questions that they considered the Acts were *ultra vires* as far as the licenses were concerned except as regards wholesale and vessel licenses, and there were some amendments to the Canada Temperance Act. That was brought before your Lordships, and the Order in Council is found in the foot-note at page 342 of Cartwright's Reports, Vol. 4. The effect of that answer was this. I may just read as it is very short. It says :—

" The Lords of the Committee have taken the said Humble Petition into consideration and having heard Counsel thereupon for the Dominion of Canada, and likewise for the Lieutenant-Governors of the respective Provinces of Ontario, Quebec, Nova Scotia and New Brunswick, and having been attended by the Agents for the Province of British Columbia, their Lordships do this day agree humbly to report to your Majesty as their opinion in reply to the two questions which have been referred to them by your Majesty, that the ' Liquor License Act, 1883, and the Act of 1884 ' amending the same, are not within the legislative authority of the Parliament of Canada. The provisions relating to adulteration if separated in their operation from the rest of the Acts would be within the authority of the Parliament, but as in their Lordships opinion they cannot be so separated, their Lordships are not prepared to report to your Majesty that any part of these Acts is within such authority."

Now those, of course, were licensing Acts, but I would wish to call your Lordships' attention to the fact that the provisions in those Acts are similar.

Lord HERSCHELL—It seems to be clearly involved in this that this Board held that they did not come within "the regulation of trade and commerce," because if they had come within "the regulation of trade and commerce" they must have been *intra vires* the Dominion Parliament. That seems to me to be the effect.

Lord DAVEY—We have not got the reasons before us, but I think it turned upon the particular provisions of the Canadian Act of 1883. The machinery of the Act was to create a licensing system through the municipal authorities and in fact to create new municipal authorities.

Mr. MACLAREN—It was not municipal, there were federal officers.

Lord DAVEY—Yes, they were appointed, but in fact it was argued that they were municipal officers.

Mr. MACLAREN—They were municipal officers. There were three commissioners in each district, who were composed of the county court judge, the chairman of the police commission, and the warden of the county.

Lord DAVEY—We do not know the reasons which influenced their lordships' mind, but I remember a great point was made in the case that although they were federal officers and called federal officers they were in fact municipal bodies.

Mr. MACLAREN—For performing municipal functions.

The LORD CHANCELLOR—The idea broadly was this— I do not know whether it was right—but the idea was that the Parliament of Canada had thought proper to interfere with the interior regulation of their municipalities. It was not really the question of licensing at all. I mean the argument was not directed to that at all. It was because they wanted the question of licensing to be properly administered that the Parliament had thought proper to appoint certain persons. I do not know the exact names of the officers.

Lord WATSON—They appointed a Board of Licensing Commissioners.

The LORD CHANCELLOR—In each case; and I think it was supposed that that was interference with the internal government of each Province.

Lord WATSON—They constituted a court by their authority within the Province, who were to be provincial officers, and take part in the administration.

Lord HERSCHELL—If what they were to take part in was the regulation of trade and commerce you were appointing only officers to take part in that which was exclusively limited to the Dominion Legislature, and I have a difficulty in seeing how it would be *ultra vires* although they may have appointed local authorities to carry out that which was *ultra vires*.

Lord DAVEY—That was the argument of the learned counsel.

The LORD CHANCELLOR—I sat in that case I think.

Mr. MACLAREN—Yes. I think as far as one can understand that was put broadly upon the ground that the Dominion could not pass a licensing Act of the nature that is there.

Lord WATSON—In section 3 of chap. 181 of the Revised Statutes of Ontario (1877), I see it says:

> "There shall be a Board of License Commissioners to be composed of three persons to be appointed from time to time by the Lieutenant-Governor for each city, county, union of counties or electoral district, as the Lieutenant-Governor may think fit; and any two of the said Commissioners shall be a quorum, and each of them shall cease to hold office on the 31st day of December in each year, but he may be re-appointed; and the said office shall be honorary and without any remuneration."

Then section 7 of the Canada Act defines licenses, hotel licenses, saloon licenses, shop licenses, vessel licenses, wholesale licenses.

Lord HERSCHELL—It had already been held that you might legislate for the whole of Canada for its peace or for its government in the way of permitting or enabling prohibition of liquor traffic. Then arose the question whether if that was so you might equally legislate not for a particular

Province but for the whole of Canada as a matter for its peace or good government. If controlling it by license is regulating trade and commerce, then that would be dealing with that as for the whole of Canada and within the exclusive jurisdiction of the Dominion, and therefore it would hardly be held to be *ultra vires*. I do not see how it was possible to hold this Act *ultra vires* except by holding that it was not regulating the trade and commerce.

Mr. MACLAREN—It must have involved that it was not the regulation of trade and commerce.

Sir RICHARD COUCH—Here is section 4 as to the establishment of provincial officers and the employment and appointment of provincial officers.

Lord WATSON—They appointed license officers and they exacted license fees, and they raised money by those fees, which was to be paid to the Dominion officers, who were certainly doing work to maintain order in the Province.

Lord HERSCHELL—That was not for provincial purposes, because they were Dominion officers appointed throughout the whole of the Dominion.

Mr. MACLAREN—They were appointed for the whole of the Dominion in different localities. I think I am correct in saying that there was merely a nominal fee of five dollars to cover the expenses of administration. It was claimed that the expenses of the administration was little more than the amount the fee would cover. Of course that decision settles the fact that licensing such as that Act of 1883 was not within the competency of the Dominion Parliament.

Lord WATSON—It is not a decision.

Mr. MACLAREN—I will call your Lordship's attention to two parts of this Act of 1883 which are almost identical with the provisions which we are now seeking to maintain.

Lord WATSON—All that comes within the arguments on sections 91 and 92.

Mr. MACLAREN—At page 29 of the Joint Appendix of Statutes your Lordships will see the sections of the Act of 1883

which were before your Lordships in the Liquor Licensing
Act Case.   Section 45 contains a provision that

> "No provision in this Act contained shall affect the powers con-
> ferred on the Municipal Councils in the Province of Quebec, of each
> county, city, town, village, parish, and township by the laws in force
> in the said Province on the 1st day of July, 1867, to restrict or
> prohibit the sale of intoxicating liquors in the limits of their respective
> territorial jurisdiction and the said powers and the by-laws now in
> force passed under the authority of the said laws are hereby preserved
> and confirmed."

The LORD CHANCELLOR—Sir Montague Smith, in one of his
observations, points out that in his view the meaning of the
legislation is to give them full power to grant those licenses
and to give them exclusive jurisdiction over licenses : that is
what Sir Montague Smith thought.

Mr. MACLAREN—I would call your Lordship's attention
to the amending Act of 1884 which was also before your
Lordships on that reference.   The shorthand notes say that
these sections were dwelt upon and that the attention of your
Lordships was called to them.   Your Lordships will find
section 45 at page 29 of the Joint Appendix.

Lord WATSON—They were fully argued no doubt, but I
have not been able to discover from any of the interruptions
by the learned Judges in what direction their minds were
running.

Lord DAVEY—I think the gist of the argument for the
Respondents was contained in one sentence, page 105 of the
report :—

> "If the legislation is in its character local, that is to say, if the
> scope and character of the legislation is such as to be of a local
> character, to take the present instance erecting a number of local
> licensing boards exercising jurisdiction within a restricted locality and
> making by-laws for that particular locality, then you do not bring it
> within section 91 by enacting a general Act for the whole of Canada,
> if the character of the legislation is such that it falls within any of the
> enumerated articles in section 92."

Lord HERSCHELL—That is a little inconsistent with
Russell v. *The Queen* because that case said it is not of a
local character within the Province, the intention is to deal
with the matter for the general purposes of temperance.

Lord DAVEY—I think what was intended was this—that the machinery of the Act was local in its character, that is to say, it created local boards with the power to make local by-laws ; I think that was what was intended.

Lord WATSON—I can only derive one conclusion from it and it is not to my mind so full and satisfactory as I could desire, and that is that for some reason or other they arrive at the conclusion that the legislation in question did not deal with trade and commerce in any aspect presented by section 91. I think they must have come to that conclusion.

The LORD CHANCELLOR—I quite agree as to that. Subject to what the other Counsel may say as to what was meant by that.

Mr. MACLAREN—I would call attention to the Amending Act of 1884 as found at page 30 of the Joint Appendix, which the argument shows was considered by their Lordships. That section is almost identical for the Province of Quebec with the Act for the Province of Ontario which is now before your Lordships. Your Lordships will see that it is as follows :—

"12. Section 45 of the said Act " (that is the Liquor Licensing Act of 1883) "is amended by adding the following thereto as sub-section two : ' 2, In every town, village, parish, or township in the Province of Quebec the Municipal Council thereof may, by by-law, restrict or prohibit, within the limits of such town, village, parish, or township, the sale of intoxicating liquors.' "

This Act, which your Lordships held to be *ultra vires* the Dominion, was almost verbatim the provision which we are now considering. This provision went with the Act, and your Lordships were asked to say whether the whole Act was *ultra vires* and if there were any parts of it which were within the jurisdiction of the Parliament of Canada and your Lordships did not save those prohibitory clauses which were in the Act of 1883 and in the Act of 1884 and which the shorthand notes show were specially brought before your Lordships.

The LORD CHANCELLOR—That I can answer for. I think the Board at that time did determine that there were parts of it that might have been, but that the two things were so intertwined by the Act itself that they could not separate them.

Mr. MACLAREN—Your Lordships selected the question of adulteration.

Lord WATSON—It would almost have taken all the bones out of the Act.

The Lord CHANCELLOR—It would have taken the machinery out and it was so bound up that you could not separate them.

Mr. MACLAREN—But your Lordships did select the subject of adulteration and said that would have been good if it had stood alone, and then this provision almost identical with the one now under consideration was in that Act and did not depend to any extent upon the machinery, because this section 45 which I have just read and which is found at page 30 of the joint Appendix says—

> "In every town, village, parish or township in the Province of Quebec the Municipal Council thereof may by by-law restrict or prohibit within the limits of such town, village, parish or township, the sale of intoxicating liquors."

Mr. BLAKE—It was agreed by the counsel on both sides that if the Act of 1883 failed the Act of 1884 must go too. That is not in the Act of 1883.

Mr. MACLAREN—There is a provision on that point in the Act of 1883. It is an amending Act but it amends section 45 which I read a moment ago and which shows that this subject was dealt with by section 45 of the amending Act.

Lord WATSON—We should be driven to speculate what the reasons were for that judgment.

Mr. MACLAREN—I was only referring to a part of the Act which was in the two Acts, which was referred to specifically by counsel and which their Lordships did not bring within the reserving clause as to adulteration and the like.

The Lord CHANCELLOR—I have the words before me, but if I remember rightly I do not think their Lordships said that was the only matter, for instance the adulteration clauses might do. I am speaking with an unrefreshed memory, but the whole thing was so wrapped up together that they could not possibly give effect to one without the other.

Mr. MACLAREN—I would read it to your Lordships :

"Their Lordships do this day agree humbly to report to your Majesty as their opinion in reply to the two questions which have been referred to them by your Majesty, that the Liquor License Act 1883 and the Act of 1884 amending the same are not within the legislative authority of the Parliament of Canada."

The first question is "is the Act good " then " if it is not good entirely is there any part that is good." In answering the second question your Lordships said :

"The provisions relating to adulteration, if separated in their operations from the rest of the Acts would be within the authority of the Parliament, but as in their Lordships opinion they cannot be so separated, their Lordships are not prepared to report to your Majesty that any part of these Acts is within such authority."

That is the text of the decision, so that I claim in the first place as to this decision that although we have not the grounds upon which it went it must have decided these three things, first that that Act was not a regulation of trade and commerce, secondly that the Dominion could not pass a licensing Act, and thirdly in a subsidiary way that these prohibitory clauses regarding the municipalities were invalid.

The Lord CHANCELLOR—I do not quite follow you there. Take this position, supposing that it was " trade and commerce," but supposing it involved something else, an undue and improper interference with the provincial privileges as to appointments and the regulation of their own internal affairs. It would not necessarily be within the competence of the Canadian Parliament because it related to trade and commerce. I think it is a misuse of that argument to assume that because it related to trade and commerce that therefore the things that were included within it would necessarily belong to the Dominion Parliament.

Lord WATSON—It might not justify a construction of the Act so as to justify their engrafting upon it as to the municipal management of the licensing system something of the Dominion licensing system, that is to say an interference with the existing administration of the municipalities. I can quite understand that. At the present moment there is

nothing in any of the observations to suggest any other ground
for the judgment.

Lord Herschell.—If it shews that licensing, in the sense
of saying that certain persons shall sell or shall not sell
under certain conditions, is not exclusively committed to the
Dominion Parliament as a regulation of trade and commerce
that is one thing.   Of course if it were exclusively, they
would have as part of the regulation of trade and commerce
power to appoint persons to license in the Provinces and it is
a licensing law for the whole of the Provinces.

Lord Watson—My reason for taking the view that I
have already expressed is the answer given by the noble
and learned Lords in giving their opinion, and in singling
out the Board of Commissioners and the licensing system
carried on under their supervision as the vicious part of the
Statute for which there was no authority in fact.   They
singled that out.

Lord Herschell—My difficulty at present is this : If
the regulation of trade and commerce includes any regulations as to licensing or controlling their selling, and that is
committed to the Dominion Parliament, it is difficult to see
why any machinery which is exclusively designed for carrying
out a legislation, which in its nature is committed to them,
would make the whole Act bad.   Of course if it is something
that is not committed to them, that is another thing.

Mr. Maclaren—But if it were a proper subject of
legislation——

Lord Herschell—The United States appoint their
judges who sit in the different States, although the States
have their own judicature.   The United States judge is the
creation, I should say, of the United States and not of the
particular State, that is to say, he is appointed for a particular
district, and he there sits and administers justice.   That is
not at all interfering with the judicature of the State—it is
carrying out a system of judicature that is left to the
Confederate Government.

The Lord Chancellor—The Act of 1867 is the one we

are construing.   I am not aware under what Statute the United States appoint their judges.

LORD HERSCHELL.—What I mean is this : If the regulation of trade and commerce has so wide a scope as to cover all provisions for licensing or controlling the way in which people shall carry on their trade, then I do not see how it can be *ultra vires* to create the machinery for carrying out that which is left to the Dominion Legislature.   It all depends upon the construction to be put upon " trade and commerce."   I do not know what was in the mind of the learned judges who took part in that case, but to my mind there is essentially involved in it, as at present advised, a decision as to that regulation—as to the meaning of trade and commerce in the Canada Act.

The LORD CHANCELLOR—Supposing some Provincial Legislature said—anyone who sell poisons shall have them in blue bottles on a particular shelf.

Mr. MACLAREN—I think the Provinces have so enacted.

The LORD CHANCELLOR—In one sense that would be trade and commerce.

Mr. MACLAREN—It would be in a sense.

Lord WATSON—In another sense it would be for the protection of the lives of the inhabitants.

Lord HERSCHELL.—Then there comes in exactly the question—if there is a trade which many people think analogous to the sale of poisons and the object is the public health, whether that cannot be dealt with locally as a local matter without it coming within the trade and commerce clause, subject, of course, to the power which the Dominion Parliament has to deal with the thing as a whole.

Lord DAVEY—Section 91 is—" It shall be lawful for the Queen by and with the advice of the Senate and House of Commons, to make laws."   You must read " the regulation of trade and commerce," and all these subjects as being subject to an exclusive jurisdiction in certain matters of the trade of the Provinces.   It is trade and commerce so far as it does

I

not trench upon the exclusive jurisdiction of the Provincial Legislature.

Lord HERSCHELL—I think it is very important, because it seems to me to intimate that unless it is brought within the subjects enumerated, if its operation is local it may be dealt with as a local matter, but if it is not, you must bring it within the earlier part of 91 in order to exclude it.

Mr. MACLAREN—You must bring it within the enumerated clauses.

Lord DAVEY—You cannot pass a bankruptcy law for that Province and say that was within the jurisdiction of the Provincial Legislature.

Mr. MACLAREN—Because that is over-ridden by bankruptcy and insolvency being assigned to the Dominion as one of the enumerated subjects.

The LORD CHANCELLOR—Just in the same way as trade and commerce are assigned.

Lord HERSCHELL—Your earlier point as regards the extension of the meaning of municipal institutions I think is a difficult one. To my mind I am not sure that it has not a bearing on this part of the case. The fact that at the time of this Act of 1867, legislation was in force in these Provinces regulating, for the good order and sobriety of the community, the liquor traffic and the local traffic—I think there is a good deal to be said for that being regarded as one of the subjects of a local nature.

Lord WATSON—I am rather wearying for the time when the learned Counsel will address himself to section 91, because there are the words "trade and commerce." I do not know whether it can be suggested that they are not local matters in each Province. We shall be probably enlightened in the course of the argument, but I do not know of any trade or commerce that is not in some sense local.

Mr. MACLAREN—These words have been considered—the regulation of trade and commerce—in the case of the *Citizens' Insurance Company* v. *Parsons*, which is reported in the 7th Appeal Cases at page 96, and also found in the 1st volume of Cartwright, page 265. I take the liberty of reading two short paragraphs in the *Citizens' Insurance Company* v. *Parsons*, at page 112 of the former. Your Lordships were considering the meaning of the words, " regulation of trade and commerce."

> " The words ' regulation of trade and commerce' in their unlimited sense are sufficiently wide, if uncontrolled by the context and other parts of the Act, to include every regulation of trade— ranging from political arrangements in regard to trade with foreign Governments, requiring the sanction of Parliament, down to minute rules for regulating particular trades. But a consideration of the Act shows that the words were not used in this unlimited sense. In the first place, the collocation of No. 2 with classes of subjects of national and general concern affords an indication that regulations relating to general trade and commerce were in the mind of the Legislature when conferring this power on the Dominion Parliament. If the words had been intended to have the full scope of which in their literal meaning they are susceptible, the specific mention of several of the other classes of subjects enumerated in section 91 would have been unnecessary : as, 15, banking : 17, weights and measures ; 18, bills of exchange and promissory notes : 19, interest ; and even 21, bankruptcy and insolvency."

Lord WATSON—Do you lay any stress upon these words, " general trade and commerce," as being an observation in your favour ? It seems to me to be an observation the other way.

Mr. MACLAREN—Your Lordships were then construing a local act. I submit with deference this is the chief case.

Lord HERSCHELL—They allowed to the Provincial Legislature a very considerable power of dealing with trade within its own limits—within its own borders.

The LORD CHANCELLOR—That is a case in which you have got the Judgments—the reasons there are given.

Mr. MACLAREN—Yes ; I am reading from the reasons given by their Lordships.

Lord HERSCHELL—We contended that the legislation of the Provinces was *ultra vires*. They were regulations with regard to an insurance company. We contended that they were regulations of trade and commerce. Undoubtedly it is a very strong decision that everything that regulates trade is not excluded from the Province.

Mr. MACLAREN—With your Lordships' permission, I will read a few words further.

Lord WATSON—That case was a decision upon two sections, upon trade and commerce, and it is a decision upon section 92. It was held that really and truly in that case the Province had dealt with what it was competent to deal with—namely, something made by the Company within the Province, and that that was a matter of civil right.

Mr. MACLAREN—It says, L. R. 7th Ap   . Cases at p. 112 :

" ' Regulation of trade and commerce '   y have been used in some such sense as the words ' regulations of trade ' in the Act of Union between England and Scotland (6 Anne chap. 11.)"

Lord WATSON—They held that it was clearly and properly within sub-section 13, I think.

Mr. MACLAREN—Yes ; property and civil rights.

Lord HERSCHELL—It is very like regulating.

Lord WATSON—I venture to make this further observation with regard to that case—that it was said to be an Act which came into collision with the Dominion Act. It was held that that was not so. It does not necessarily follow that the Dominion Government might not have power to legislate. Until they came into the field it was open to the Parliament of Ontario to regulate that matter. It was purely a matter of civil contract. Contracts between the Insurance Company no doubt and Insurers.

Lord HERSCHELL—The Act said certain conditions shall be deemed to be part of every contract. That is rather like regulating the business of a Fire Insurance Company.

Mr. MACLAREN—Then there is this at page 113 :

" It is enough for the decision of the present case to say that, in their view, its authority to legislate for the regulation of trade and commerce does not comprehend the power to regulate by legislation the contracts of a particular business or trade such as the business of fire insurance, in a single Province, and therefore that its legislative authority does not in the present case conflict or compete with the power over property and civil rights assigned to the Legislature of Ontario by No. 18 of section 92."

We put forward the same claim in this case, that the

regulation of trade and commerce must be taken in that broader and more general sense, and cannot refer to matter of a merely local and private nature.

Lord HERSCHELL.—It is very difficult to draw the line.

The LORD CHANCELLOR—It is a series of conundrums.

Lord HERSCHELL.—The provision that poisons shall not be sold except under certain restrictions is a regulation with regard to that particular trade, yet it is hardly conceivable that that should be intended to be taken away from the Province and that there should be nothing at all done except by an Act dealing with the whole Dominion. I could put many other instances. Where you are to draw the line between these matters of local regulation and general regulation I do not for the moment see.

Mr. MACLAREN—Our claim is that this is a valid regulation—a regulation so well known that there is no conflict with the Dominion legislation.

Lord MORRIS—If it is exclusively within the Province under section 92, what arises?

Mr. MACLAREN—It would be claimed, I think, that the opening part of section 91 which provides that the Dominion may legislate on the subjects therein enumerated——

Lord WATSON—I think these three classes are explained by Sir Montague Smith in *The Queen* v. *Parsons*. There may be three positions; they may be exclusive; they may be that the Dominion merely excludes the other from exercising some statutory power; and it also may be that the Dominion have the power to set aside the Provincial legislature and to upset it.

Lord MORRIS—If you come under sub-section 16 of section 92 that your legislation is of a merely local or private nature as regards that prohibition, it is exclusively given to you on the assumption that it comes within sub-section 16.

Lord HERSCHELL—What they said in *Russell* v. *The Queen* was this, that although it may be a local matter exclusively within your jurisdiction when you are legislating for your own Province and your legislation is confined to that, it becomes a different matter and not merely a local matter, and therefore not excluded from the Dominion Parliament when it is dealt with as a matter essentially with regard to the peace, order and good government of the Dominion, and therefore is to be treated throughout the Dominion alike. That is what I understand was said in *Russell* v. *The Queen*.

Lord WATSON—I think that is so, and I think there is one other case, the name of which I forget at present, where the language is susceptible of this interpretation, that it is a sufficient change of aspect that the one is passed for merely local and provincial matters and the other is passed for Dominion purposes. I have done my best to understand it.

Lord HERSCHELL—You might put various illustrations. A local Act with reference to carrying firearms might be purely local, and that would be exclusively for the local Legislature. On the other hand, you could not exclude or intend to exclude the right of the Dominion Parliament, if it thought fit and necessary to take steps for the safety of the whole community, to make more stringent regulations and to say you shall not carry firearms at all while war is going on. That would be a matter for the peace, order and good government of the whole Dominion, and would not be inoperative because a mere police regulation within the Province would be good Provincial legislation.

The LORD CHANCELLOR—I do not quite follow that.

Lord HERSCHELL—You might have a matter perfectly within the functions of the Provincial Legislature as a matter of a local nature within sub-section 16, and yet that same matter might be overridden by the superior legislation of the Dominion Parliament under its general powers.

Lord WATSON—There is both a head and a tail to the 91st section; you require to read them both.

Lord HERSCHELL—I understand the view to be this: if it is a matter in which the whole Dominion is interested, and which the Dominion Parliament so determines, then it ceases to be a merely local matter in the Province whilst it is so, and the Dominion Legislature will legislate about it.

Lord Morris—It does not cease to be local. It is only made local. It only purports to deal with it from a local point of view. How can that ever be altered ?

Lord Herschell—As I understand the Dominion Act comes into operation and says, " we do not consider this as a matter of a local nature."

Mr. Maclaren—The expression used by several of the Judges is, that it is the nature and character of the legislation that must be looked at.

Lord Davey—Every legislation of the Dominion does more or less affect either the property or the civil rights of the subjects.

Adjourned to the next day.

SECOND DAY.

Mr. Maclaren—My Lords, in support of the proposition that the words " The regulation of trade and commerce " in section 91 of the British North America Act meant general regulation, and not such specific matters as might be involved in the Act which is now before your Lordships, in addition to the cases of *The Citizens Insurance Company* v. *Parsons*, and the Liquor License Act Case to which I referred yesterday, I should desire to refer your Lordships to a few sentences that are found in the case of *The Bank of Toronto* v. *Lambe*, which is reported in 12th Appeal Cases at page 575, and in the 4th volume of Cartwright at page 7. This was a case involving the question of the right of the Province to tax Banks. It was resisted by the Banks on the ground that it was a regulation of trade and commerce : and in that case their Lordships considered this sub-section 2 of Section 91, which I am now discussing. I would read that part of the judgment commencing near the foot of page 585 of the 12th Appeal cases :

> " It has been earnestly contended that the taxation of Banks would unduly cut down the powers of the Parliament in relation to matters falling within Class 2, viz. : The regulation of trade and commerce; and within Class 15, viz. : Banking and the incorporation of Banks. Their Lordships think this contention gives far too wide an extent to the classes in question. They cannot see how the power of making Banks contribute to the public objects of the Provinces where they carry on business can interfere at all with the power of making laws on the subject of banking, or with the power of incorporating Banks. The words 'regulation of trade and commerce' are indeed very wide ; and in Severn's case it was the view of the Supreme Court that they operated to invalidate the license duty which was there in question, but since that case was decided the question has been more completely sifted before the Committee in *Parsons'* case, and it was found absolutely necessary that the literal meaning of the words should be restricted in order to afford scope for powers which are given exclusively to the Provincial Legislatures It was there thrown out that the power of regulation given to the Parliament meant some general or inter-provincial regulations."

Lord WATSON—Do you regulate a man when you tax him ? Is it regulating a man to tax him ?

Mr. MACLAREN—Taxation was held not to be regulation of trade and commerce.

Lord HERSCHELL—May it not be necessary to regard it from this point of view to find what is within regulation of trade and commerce, what is the object and scope of the legislation ? Is it some public object which incidentally involves some fetter on trade or commerce, or is it the dealing with trade and commerce for the purpose of regulating it ? May it not be that in the former case, it is not a regulation of trade and commerce, while in the latter it is, though in each case trade and commerce in a sense may be affected.

The LORD CHANCELLOR—And I should think the lines may sometimes approach so near each other that it must be a question of degree. Take this very case you are now referring to ; I can quite understand that a tax upon banks might be very proper, but supposing the tax was imposed to that degree that practically it extinguished the banks in the

Province.   That would be rather beyond the line would it
not ?

Mr. MACLAREN—The tax was a heavy one in this case.

The LORD CHANCELLOR—I am not talking about that case,
but about the principle.   You might have what was in form
a mere regulation, so extreme as really to interfere with trade
and commerce generally.   Then I suppose it would be
beyond the line.

Lord WATSON—It would be difficult to imply from these
words " The Regulation of Trade and Commerce " whilst the
power of direct taxation is given to the Province—the clauses
must be read reasonably together—it would be difficult to
suppose that regulating commerce meant the passing of an
Act by the Dominion Legislature exempting banks from
Provincial taxation, for practically that is what the argument
in that case had to come to; that under the words " Regulating Commerce " was implied a power of exempting a bank
from Provincial taxation or the liability to be taxed by the
Provincial Parliament.

The LORD CHANCELLOR—Curiously enough I see this
passage at page 586 of the same case :

> " Then it is suggested that the Legislature may lay on taxes so
> heavy as to crush a bank out of existence and so to nullify the power
> of Parliament to erect banks.   But their Lordships cannot conceive
> that when the Imperial Parliament conferred wide powers of local self
> Government on great countries such as Quebec it intended to limit
> them on the speculation that they would be used in an injurious
> manner."

I suppose that implies that if they did, it would be beyond
their powers ?

Mr. MACLAREN—The latter part of the paragraph seems
to imply that once they have the power, they can use it to
the full extent.

The LORD CHANCELLOR—I do not know.   I should think
that the meaning of it was this, that the Court will not
presume they will do anything so outrageous.

Mr. MACLAREN—If your Lordship will allow me, I will
read the latter part of the paragraph which throws, I think,

some light on the view of their Lordships. It says at p. 586 :

> " People who are trusted with the great power of making laws for property and Civil rights may well be trusted to levy taxes. There are obvious reasons for confining their power to direct taxes and licenses because the power of indirect taxation would be felt all over the Dominion, but whatever power falls within the legitimate meaning of classes 2 and 9 is, in their Lordships' judgment, what the Imperial Parliament intended to give."

Lord WATSON—That is saying in other words that you must not assume that a power that is conferred is not meant to be given because it is capable of being abused.

Mr. MACLAREN—Or being used unwisely. And to place a limit on it because the power may be used unwisely as all powers may, would be an error and would lead to difficulties in the construction of the Federation Act. The only other words I think it necessary to read are those following the concluding part of the preceding paragraph on page 586 in which they say :

> " No further attempt to define the subject need now be made, because their Lordships are clear that if they were to hold that this power of regulation prohibited any Provincial Taxation on the persons or things regulated so far from restricting the expressions, as was found necessary in Parson's case, that would be straining them to their widest conceivable extent."

Lord WATSON—If any construction of that sort had been adopted it would go a long way. You could not tax a patent. You could not raise a tax upon a copyright or on a patent. That would be a difficult question perhaps ; it is " Banks and the Incorporation of Banks."

The LORD CHANCELLOR—With reference to what I was saying it appears to me what their Lordships meant in that judgment was that however extravagant it was it would be valid, and then that would be a reason for the Imperial Parliament to repeal it, but they go on to say that they are not to assume they would do such a thing.

Mr. MACLAREN—They say, as they say in some other cases, that large powers of self-government are given and that the remedy is with the people. If the Parliament abuses its power they have responsible government, and it is left to the people; some such expressions are used in some of the cases on that particular point. The cases, I think, show that so far as this Board has dealt with the subject, those three decisions especially would go to show that by the words "the regulation of trade and commerce" are meant general regulation.

Lord WATSON—It goes this length at all events, that they do not trench on the power broadly given to the Province of raising money by Provincial taxation.

Mr. MACLAREN—That is the last case.

Lord HERSCHELL—And they go further in *Hodge's* case, although of course the trade or commerce of dealing in liquor was affected by the Act; no one would have doubted it affected it; it limited the mode in which it was to be carried on, and yet they say that it was within the power of the Local Legislature and was not a matter taken out of their power by section 91, sub-section 2.

The Lord CHANCELLOR—That was the question as to the billiard table.

Mr. MACLAREN—It involved the question of the power of making regulations by the License Commissioners to regulate taverns and limit their numbers.

The Lord CHANCELLOR—The actual thing decided was that it was within their power to make a regulation for the period during which a billiard room might be open and inflict a penalty if it was disobeyed.

Mr. MACLAREN—Attached to a tavern.

The Lord CHANCELLOR—It may be; but still the particular regulation was as to a billiard room.

Mr. MACLAREN—Yes, and the regulation was directing that the billiard room should be closed when the statute required the tavern to be closed.

Lord HERSCHELL—Here you cannot play billiards in a licensed house if I remember rightly within the prohibited hours.

Mr. MACLAREN—That was the precise regulation.

Lord HERSCHELL—That is the law here.

The Lord CHANCELLOR—I have got the conviction here, 9 Appeal Cases 117 :—

> " Did unlawfully permit a billiard table to be used and a game of billiards to be played thereon in his tavern in the conviction named and described as the St. James Hotel, situate within the city of Toronto during the time prohibited by the ' Liquor License Act.' (Revised Statutes of Ontario cap. 181.) "

Lord HERSCHELL—Have you got the statute in question in *Hodge's* case, cap. 181 ?

Mr. MACLAREN—It is cap. 194 in the present Revised Statutes. That was the Revised Statutes of 1887.

Lord HERSCHELL—The reason I mentioned that was that one does not quite see what relation that has to the sale of liquor. It is true the offence can only be committed by a person who has a tavern. That is the only point of connection, that the hours were the same.

Mr. MACLAREN—There was this that your Lordship will see from the report of the case a little further on, that though there was the conviction yet the Courts of Canada and this Board considered the whole scope of sections 4 and 5 of the Act which gave very large powers to the Commissioners amongst which was the power to limit the number of tavern licenses which might be issued in a city or municipality. It was sections 4 and 5 of cap. 194 that were in question in *Hodge's* case.

The Lord CHANCELLOR—I daresay you are quite right, but it is obvious to remark if it was so it was entirely *obiter*.

Lord HERSCHELL—There is nothing about billiards in terms.

The Lord CHANCELLOR—

> " For that he the Appellant did on the 7th day of May 1881, unlawfully permit and suffer a billiard table to be used and a game of billiards to be played thereon in his tavern in the conviction named and described as the St. James Hotel."

Sir RICHARD COUCH—Contrary to the regulation.

Mr. MACLAREN—It came about in this way: The statute said that all taverns should be closed at 7 on Saturday and not opened till 5 o'clock on Monday morning. The License Commissioners made a regulation saying that billiard tables should not be used in connection with a tavern during the hours in which liquors were prohibited from being sold. Then came the question under sections 4 and 5 of the Act as to the validity of these regulations. The conviction was with reference to a billiard table but it involved the question of the sale of liquor, because the billiard tables were required not to be used during the prohibited hours.

Lord HERSCHELL—It was an Act respecting the sale of spirituous liquors. The idea was that if you opened the house for billiards it would open the house for the sale of liquors.

Mr. MACLAREN—Yes.

Lord WATSON—It simply appeared in the form of a condition attached to the license.

The Lord CHANCELLOR—It is what we should call an act done against the tenor of the license.

Lord HERSCHELL—It was a fetter imposed on the manner in which a man carried on his business as a licensed victualler.

Mr. MACLAREN—Quite so.

Lord MORRIS—Do you draw any limit at all as to the power of the Provincial Legislature to legislate on the liquor question, and do you say they could pass an Act in Ontario like the Maine Liquor Act to prevent the sale of spirituous liquors?

Mr. MACLAREN—That is the next question that is raised and comes under question 1 and is one of the following questions, and I was, with your Lordships permission, about to address myself to that point. That is all that I wish to say to your Lordships regarding the question which I was discussing, and the discussion of that question has really involved the points that are in the other questions so that

I think I shall find it necessary to say but little on the preceding six questions as it is largely one subject.

Lord WATSON—It goes to the root of them all.

Lord HERSCHELL—Except that there may be different considerations with reference to question 4, whether the Provincial Legislature has power to prohibit the importation of liquor. In some of the maritime provinces that would affect Customs duties that go to the Dominion.

Mr. MACLAREN—In all of them it would. It would affect the Dominion Revenue ; both as to Customs and Excise— as to Customs if they imported liquor, and as to the Excise with reference to liquor manufactured in the Dominion——

Lord DAVEY—That looks much more like the regulation of trade and commerce.

Lord HERSCHELL—That cannot be treated as a merely local matter, because inasmuch as it directly affects the revenue of the Dominion it cannot be a local matter to the Province.

Mr. MACLAREN—I was going to rely on the case of *Russell* v. *The Queen* as an authority on this, in answer to the question just put, that if the local Legislature has the power, it has the power, no matter what effect it may have on the revenue of the Dominion.

Lord HERSCHELL—From a certain point of view that might be so, but the difficulty is this : Can you treat the importation and the conditions of importation in a Province as merely a local matter ?

Mr. MACLAREN—That is another matter. I am addressing myself to the Revenue.

Lord HERSCHELL—I am supposing now that you bring it within your "Municipal Institutions" clause ; but still more, if you bring it within sub-section 16 as a merely local matter, there is a difficulty about importation.

Mr. MACLAREN—Quite so.

Lord DAVEY—All the Judges were agreed about Questions 3 and 4.

Mr. MACLAREN—Yes; the Judges were unanimous in answering those in the negative.

Lord HERSCHELL—I am not sure there may not be a possible distinction between manufacture and importation. It is difficult to say that importation is a local matter, but manufacture in the Province may be said to be a local matter. Take the case of a dangerous manufacture : supposing the Province said, " We will not have dynamite made in our Province because it is dangerous to the neighbourhood."

The LORD CHANCELLOR—Supposing that was the only source of supply in the Dominion, which was necessary for mining purposes elsewhere ? I should think that was a serious question.

Mr. MACLAREN—That might broaden it and take it out of the local nature. " Has a Provincial Legislature juris- " diction to prohibit the sale within the Province of spirituous, " fermented or other intoxicating liquors ?" That is really the question which we have been discussing under Question 7, with this exception, that that would seem to imply the putting down of wholesale licenses in the Province of Ontario, as well as shop and tavern licenses.

Lord MORRIS—Why not ? If they have the power under the regulation of matters local, to prohibit in part, why should not they have power to prohibit altogether ?

Mr. MACLAREN—I was about to observe that I think the decision of this Board in the Liquor License Act case of 1883 is an authority for the proposition that there is substantially no distinction between what are known as retail licenses— that is, shop and tavern licenses—and wholesale licenses.

Lord DAVEY—That is an artificial distinction.

Mr. MACLAREN—It is an artificial distinction, and what is called wholesale there, is in reality retail.

Lord WATSON—Those cases involved quite a different sort of question. It is not now disputed, and I do not think any of the Judges in the minority in this case would have disputed, that a license in this matter is local.

Lord HERSCHELL.—All the argument you have addressed to us applies to Question 1.

Mr. MACLAREN—Yes ; and the second question : " Or " has the Legislature such jurisdiction regarding such por- " tions of the Province as to which the Canada Temperance " Act is not in operation ? "

Lord HERSCHELL—That is *a fortiori*. It is one subject, because the points that have been discussed have reference to the question whether there is any conflict between the Canada Temperance Act and any particular Act.

Mr. MACLAREN—That is a general question.

Lord HERSCHELL—Supposing that there was an Act validly passed by the Dominion of Canada within its powers for the whole of Canada, which affected the Province of Ontario, you would not then contend, would you, that the Province of Ontario could, as a merely local matter, defy that ?

Mr. MACLAREN—No. If there was valid general Dominion legislation, I admit that would supersede anything the Province had done under matters of a private and local nature.

Lord HERSCHELL—Is the Canada Temperance Act in operation in Ontario ?

Mr. MACLAREN—No. It was in operation, but it has been repealed so that it is not in operation in any part of Ontario at the present time.

Mr. BLAKE—The Act has not been repealed.

Mr. MACLAREN—The adoption has been repealed.

Mr. BLAKE—The by-law was repealed.

Mr. MACLAREN—It was not a by-law but a proclamation of the Governor-General, and the Governor-General issued his proclamation that the Act was in force ; but after the adverse vote, he issued a proclamation declaring that the Act was not in force.

Lord DAVEY—It is one of the Acts which it is the fashion now-a-days to call an adoptive Act.

Lord HERSCHELL—Then you come to question 3.

Mr. MACLAREN—Yes; question 3. " Has a Provincial " legislature jurisdiction to prohibit the manufacture of such " liquors within the Province." I claim that the manufacture is a local matter and of a private nature, and one on which the Province has power to regulate.

Lord WATSON—That may or may not be.

Mr. MACLAREN—To the question as framed here, I say we are entitled to an affirmative answer on the ground that the Provincial legislature has jurisdiction to prohibit the manufacture of liquors within the Province on the ground of its being a matter of a private and local nature. This is manufacture, and the Province has the right over manufactures, especially those that might be considered injurious.

The LORD CHANCELLOR—You must go to the extent of saying, to prohibit the manufacture altogether.

Mr. MACLAREN—It involves it if they have the power to prohibit their being manufactured in a city or within a certain limit of a city.

Lord WATSON—Supposing the manufacture was for the Canadian service, would that be a local matter ?

Mr. MACLAREN—I do not know that I am prepared to answer that question.

Lord WATSON—Supposing a manufacturer supplied all his produce to the Canadian Government for the Navy or for other purposes ?

Mr. MACLAREN—I do not know that the fact of the personality of the customer would really affect the power if they have the power to prohibit.

Lord HERSCHELL—Supposing there was a Government manufactory of Cordite in a particular Province, could the Provincial legislature prohibit it as a merely local matter ?

Mr. MACLAREN—I think this question does not contemplate Government manufactories.

K

Lord HERSCHELL—I know it does not.

Lord WATSON—The answer would embrace it.

Mr. MACLAREN—If it was answered absolutely.

Lord DAVEY—The Cordite manufacture might be carried on, as it is partially in this country, by means of private firms manufacturing for the Government. The Government has its own manufactories in this country, but also buys Cordite from private manufacturers.

Mr. MACLAREN—I assume the Province would have a control over these manufactories as being a matter of a private and local nature.

The LORD CHANCELLOR—The word control is ambiguous. By control you mean absolute prohibition.

Lord MORRIS—The question is " prohibit."

Sir RICHARD COUCH—Then it is liquor not Cordite.

Mr. MACLAREN—I do not know that the material makes much difference.

Lord WATSON—It rather occurs to me that if any question as is now suggested arose, the legislature of Canada would have full power to legislate under the general words with which section 91 commences and which are not limited by the words which follow. Any subject may be dealt with which is necessary, which in the opinion of the Government is required for the peace, order or good government of Canada. If they could not govern Canada properly without a supply of Cordite from these works I see no reason why they should not pass a law saying these factories shall be there notwithstanding.

Lord DAVEY—This is a speculative question.

Lord HERSCHELL—There has never been any proposal to prohibit the manufacture. I should question whether it is right that a number of conundrums should be submitted for solution to this Board under the Act. They were intended to be questions having a practical bearing on immediately intended or actual legislation.

Lord Morris—Except that they may have surmised that if the Province has begun by prohibiting the sale of liquor, it may follow it up by prohibiting the manufacture of liquor.

Lord Watson—Every one of these questions seem to be purely academical.

Lord Herschell.—The question of dealing with liquor has been in operation in the Province for 40 years I should think.

Mr. Maclaren—Prohibition has been in force since 1853 in the Province of Ontario.

Lord Herschell—Over 40 years. That is a practical question, but there has never been any proposal to prohibit the manufacture.

Mr. Maclaren—Not by actual legislation, but it is a matter of discussion as to one of the ways of dealing with the liquor traffic.

Lord Herschell.—It seems rather premature to submit a question of that sort.

Mr. Maclaren—The questions have been submitted by the Governor-General and we are brought here to answer them.

Lord Davey—Have you got the 54th and 55th Victoria, chap. 25, section 4 ?

Lord Herschell.—I should like to see the power because it seems a questionable matter to put a number of speculative questions and insist that this Board should answer them.

Mr. Maclaren—I think the Act is very sweeping.

Lord Watson—I do not think this Board is bound to answer them. It is the duty of the Board to comply with the Statute as far as reasonable. The Legislature of Canada by passing an Act cannot lay a duty on this Board of that kind to answer questions. One is willing to dispose of all questions that are necessary.

Lord Morris—Is not question 1 also to a certain extent speculative in that way ? You have not altogether prohibited the sale.

K 2

Lord HERSCHELL—The sale by retail ?

Lord MORRIS—They have not passed any Act of Parliament within question 1. If question 3 is speculative it appears to me question 1 is speculative also.

The LORD CHANCELLOR—That is so.

Lord HERSCHELL—Question 1 is not quite so speculative. It is on the lines of existing legislation.

Lord MORRIS—I suspect they are not put speculatively.

Lord WATSON—I have not the least doubt that they are not put speculatively in this sense that they are with a view to the future guidance of the action of the Governor-General.

Lord MORRIS—And with a view to something that they see coming.

Mr. MACLAREN—There is, no doubt, an agitation in Canada for such legislation.

Lord DAVEY—Prohibiting the manufacture ?

Mr. MACLAREN—That is one of the propositions. If I may speak of Resolutions introduced into the House of Commons, such Resolutions have been introduced into the House of Commons of Canada, year after year, for prohibiting the manufacture, importation and sale of intoxicating liquors, and that is the reason no doubt for this question if I may know what reasons moved this.

Lord WATSON—The difference is that we can give no judicial opinion upon some of these questions which are academic. We cannot give anything like a judicial decision except upon a substantial case.

Lord HERSCHELL—I see the 4th section of the Act (54 and 55 Victoria, chap. 25, Dominion Statute) says:

"Important questions of law or fact touching Provincial legislation, or the appellate jurisdiction as to educational matters vested in the Governor in Council by 'The British North America Act, 1867,' or by any other Act or law, or touching the constitutionality of any legislation of the Parliament of Canada or touching any other matter with reference to which he sees fit to exercise this power may be referred by the Governor-in-Council to the Supreme Court for hearing or consideration."

The LORD CHANCELLOR—The words are rather wide. I do not see how you can get out of it.

Lord WATSON—Except that it is beyond the power of the Canadian Legislature to lay that duty upon this Board.

Lord DAVEY—They have laid it on the Supreme Court.

Lord WATSON—They may lay it on the Supreme Court as much as they like, but they cannot lay it on this Board.

Mr. MACLAREN—The Supreme Court answered these questions and Her Majesty has given special leave to appeal to this Board.

Sir RICHARD COUCH—Special leave to appeal has been given ?

Mr. MACLAREN—Yes.

Lord WATSON—We need not enter into a discussion on that point. It would come to this that they have the right to remit to us.

Lord HERSCHELL—No doubt it may be that the Supreme Court of Canada would be bound by this Statute to express its opinion on any matters submitted to it; but it may be that this Board would say it is a matter of so thoroughly speculative a character, and with no immediate reference to any legislation either passed or introduced into Parliament, that we decline to express any opinion upon it.

The LORD CHANCELLOR—I doubt that very much—It says (sub-section 6) :

> "The opinion of the Court upon any such reference, although advisory only, shall, for all purposes of appeal to Her Majesty in Council be treated as a final judgment of the said Court between Parties."

Lord HERSCHELL.—That is a Canadian Statute.

Mr. MACLAREN—Special leave has been given in this case.

Lord WATSON—It reminds me of what occurred in my practice at the Scotch Bar. On two or three occasions I and two other gentlemen, members of the Scotch Bar, were consulted as to the meaning of a Statute, and we gave a very long number of replies in return for a handsome fee, and we eventually discovered that the object of consulting us was not to defend any Action, but that somebody might write a book on the subject and state in the introduction to it that it had the influence of our authority. They came afterwards on an amending Statute that was passed, but we declined to give any opinion. If somebody is going to write a Treatise on the Liquor Laws, a few more questions might be in[.] to assist their labours.

Mr. MACLAREN—With regard to question 4, notwithstanding what is said, I shall ask your Lordships to answer that in the affirmative, as ancillary to the right to prohibit the sale. If the Province has the right to prohibit the sale, and in order effectually to carry that out it becomes necessary to prohibit the manufacture and importation of the liquor, I submit that the right to prohibit the importation would follow the right to prohibit the sale.

Lord DAVEY—I think you would have to deal in connection with questions 3 and 4 rather more closely with the regulation of trade and commerce. It seems to me, without expressing any opinion, to be more near a regulation of trade and commerce than the others.

Mr. MACLAREN—Yes, there is no doubt that No. 1 and even No. 7 interfere with trade and commerce, but whether it is a regulation of trade and commerce I think that we should need to look at such legislation, if it were passed, to ascertain its true nature and character.

Lord DAVEY—Even under the definition of Sir Montague Smith it regulates trade and commerce between the Colonies. It is a regulation of trade and commerce between the Provinces, or between Canada as a whole and some Foreign Countries, including England.

Lord HERSCHELL—That is importation.

Lord DAVEY—And manufacture.

Lord HERSCHELL—You are on No 4.

Mr. MACLAREN—I ask for an affirmative answer to No. 4 as an accessory to No. 1.

Lord Morris—Does not No. 4 deal with more than a colony by preventing importation? Does not it deal with persons outside the Province? •

Mr. Maclaren—Only persons in the Province. It would only affect persons in the Province importing into the Province.

Lord Morris—Does not it affect the question of exporting? If there is an import there must be an export.

Lord Davey—Importation must mean into a Province if it is into Canada, because Canada consists of the Provinces. It must be in the Province therefore, and if you could prohibit it on the ground that it is a local matter because it is imported at Halifax, if the ship arrives and unloads at Halifax, then you do away with the right of Canada to regulate trade and commerce.

Lord Herschell—It might be liquor consigned viâ Halifax to some other Province. How can you prohibit the importation if you would prevent the people of other Provinces getting it? How could that be said to be a merely local matter?

Mr. Maclaren—It might be qualified in the way your Lordship suggests. Then question 5, " If a Provincial Legis- " lature has not jurisdiction to prohibit sales of such liquors " irrespective of quantity, has such Legislature jurisdiction to " prohibit the sale by retail according to the definition of a " sale by retail either in statutes in force in the Province at " the time of confederation or any other definition thereof."

Lord Herschell—That is covered by what has been said.

Mr. Maclaren—Yes. Then question 6, " If a Provincial " Legislature has a limited jurisdiction only as regards the " prohibition of sales, has the Legislature jurisdiction to pro- " hibit sales, subject to the limits provided by the several " sub-sections of the 99th section of The Canada Temperance " Act, or any of them (Revised Statutes of Canada, cap. 106, " section 99.) " That would mean subject to the Canada Temperance Act and to the ground covered by that, and I should ask your Lordships to answer that in the affirmative.

Lord WATSON—That is one of the matters we can answer. What are asked are questions submitted for our adjudication. According to my view a court of law cannot adjudicate upon a section of a statute. The thing is nonsense. It is not adjud... ... They cannot adjudicate except upon a substantial ...

Lord DAVEY—Look at section 99, and see what it says.

Mr. MACLAREN—Your Lordships will find section 99 in the Joint Appendix of Statutes. It is a prohibition of the sale of liquor. It was the section under consideration in *Russell* v. *The Queen*, and your Lordships will find it at pages 26 and following of the Joint Appendix of Statutes.

The LORD CHANCELLOR—

" * * * * .* No person shall * * * * expose or keep for sale or directly or indirectly on any pretence or upon any device sell or barter or in consideration of the purchase of any other property, give to any other person any intoxicating liquor."

Mr. MACLAREN—That is section 99. Then there are the exceptions.

Lord HERSCHELL—I do not quite understand why this 6th question is put as distinct from the others. If it has the power, why should its power be regulated by the provisions of the Canada Temperance Act?

Mr. MACLAREN—That question I think is meant to involve this—Assuming the Canada Temperance Act to be a Superior Act, question 2 puts the question : Has the Province the right to legislate where the Canada Temperance Act is not in force?

Lord HERSCHELL—If they had a right to legislate because it is not in force, why must this legislation follow the lines of the Canada Temperance Act, or why can it be better because it does follow those lines?

Mr. MACLAREN—It would be on the assumption that the Canada Temperance Act having been declared to be within the competency of the Parliament of Canada, the question is put here to ascertain whether they can legislate subject to it.

Sir Richard Couch—Whether that does not put a limit to their power ?

Mr. Maclaren—Yes.

Lord Herschell—That can only be brought into operation in a particular way, which is by the Act of the Legislature, and I do not see how the Canada Temperance Act whose provisions can be brought into operation in a certain way can guide us as to what the Provincial Legislature can do.

Lord Watson—It is putting in another form this question to us—If a Provincial Legislature has a limited jurisdiction only as regards the prohibition or sale, their Lordships of the Privy Council are asked to determine what is the limit of its limited jurisdiction ; do the limits of their jurisdiction extend to an enactment which does not go beyond the lines of the Canada Temperance Act ?

Lord Herschell—What I fail to see for the moment is how that can be a test within the limit you put. Supposing they have power to limit in the direction of prohibition—if they have none there is an end of it, and *cadit quæstio*—but if they have power to limit in the direction of prohibition how can the extent of their powers be determined by what the Dominion Parliament has done ?

Mr. Maclaren—It might mean this I think : that the Dominion having, even where they have enacted prohibition to the full extent to which they have in the Canada Temperance Act, rendered legal certain sales named in these several provisos for sacramental purposes, for medicinal and mechanical purposes, having given certain rights to distillers, to vine growing companies and to manufacturers of native wines, whether that is the limit ?

Lord Herschell.—If it is within the function of a Provincial Legislature, how can they in their legislation be fettered by a view expressed by the legislation of the Dominion Parliament ; because that is what it comes to. It is not that that Act is in operation—it is not in operation.

Mr. Maclaren—No.

Lord Herschell--But an Act passed for the whole of

Canada, which may be adopted by the different parts of Canada, embodies the views of the Dominion Parliament we will suppose as to desirable legislation, but how can that be the test of the powers of the Provincial Legislature, assuming that it has power to legislate in that direction, which you must assume. If you are right in your first point then of course you do not need that, but if you are wrong in your first point I feel a difficulty as to how you can be right to the limited extent suggested in question 6.

Lord DAVEY—Is the meaning this—that if any county or city in the Province of Ontario should adopt the Temperance Act, will the Temperance Act enable the excepted person to carry on the trade notwithstanding the total prohibition ?

Lord HERSCHELL—I think the question is whether it is within the jurisdiction of the Provincial Legislature.

Lord WATSON—It is a question whether they can enact prohibition to the same extent to which prohibition is enacted by the Temperance Act and no further—that seems to be the question. But then that is of course on the assumption that you have not the power contended for.

Mr. MACLAREN—That there is only the limited power—not more.

Lord WATSON—In fact the question is put entirely on the assumption that the Provincial Legislature has not power to deal——

Mr. MACLAREN—With the whole question.

Lord WATSON—With the question of sale or interfering with the sale of liquor as a local matter.

Mr. MACLAREN—I submit these questions to your Lordships. My learned friend, Mr. Haldane, who is with me will read the judgments.

The LORD CHANCELLOR—Before you finish will you kindly answer one question. I see that in the judgment of Mr. Justice Taschereau a reference is made to the Declaratory Act, 1891, 54 Victoria, chapter 46, and he says that disposes of the question of the complete prohibition of the liquor traffic.

Mr. MACLAREN—Yes. Your Lordship will find that at the foot of page 2 of the Appellants' Case.

The LORD CHANCELLOR—Have we got the Act?

Mr. MACLAREN—It is printed in its entirety in the Appendix to the Case of the Respondents, the Distillers' and Brewers' Association. The 1st section is on page 2 of the Appellants' Case, and it is referred to in question 7. Your Lordship will find it copied in full in paragraph 4 at the foot of page 2. The Act of the Legislature of Ontario, 54 Vict., chapter 46 also referred to in the 7th question, is as follows: and that is declaratory that the restriction was not to go further than the limitation prescribed in the Act of 1866.

The LORD CHANCELLOR—That is a Declaratory Act?

Mr. MACLAREN—Yes my Lord, that is declaratory.

Lord HERSCHELL—It does not touch the Canada Act?

Mr. MACLAREN—It touches the Act which was in force at the time of Confederation; and the Act of 1891, was passed to declare——

Lord HERSCHELL.—It meant this, not to go further than the former Act which was kept alive by section 129.

Mr. MACLAREN—Yes, that is the effect of the Act of 1891.

The LORD CHANCELLOR—I see Mr. Justice Taschereau says that that clears the ground, and the only question is whether—

Lord WATSON—Whether it is or is not the law. Of course if the first question were answered against you, it appears to me that that Act would be standing by virtue of section 129.

The LORD CHANCELLOR—I think you have sufficiently answered my question Mr. Maclaren.

Mr. MACLAREN—If your Lordship pleases, my learned friend, Mr. Haldane, will read the Judgment of the Court below, and further discuss the questions.

Mr. HALDANE—My Lords, there are two observations I should like to add to my friend's argument before I go to the Judgment. Your Lordships are always loth in construing the Confederation Act to draw an abstract line, and indeed it is almost impossible to do it, but there are some land-marks which the authorities have established, and if we find a concrete question lying near these land-marks it affords indication at all events, that it is on one side of the boundary line or the other. Now there are two things which seem to be settled by the decisions of this Board on previous occasions and on which one may lay hold in arguing this case. The first is that the words conferring the regulation of trade and commerce upon the Dominion Parliament do not include the whole or nearly the whole of the regulation of the liquor traffic. That is quite plain. There are two decisions—the decision in the Liquor License case of 1883, and in *Hodge* v. *The Queen*, which have made it plain that certain things at all events in connection with the liquor traffic are reserved for the Provincial Legislature.

Lord WATSON—I should like to know what your view is upon this question, how far does the power of the Dominion Parliament to make a rule—we will say, partially prohibiting or entirely prohibiting the sale of liquor—assuming they pass such an Act, how far would their legislative power be attributable as a regulation of the liquor trade, or would it be attributable in reality and substance to their general power to make laws for the good order and government of Canada ? That is a question which may not be without importance to consider in the present case.

Mr. HALDANE—Quite so, my Lord.

Lord HERSCHELL—I think *Russell* v. *The Queen* distinctly says it is within the second proposition—the peaceable government, but in that case they avoided expressing any opinion whether it was within the other point.

Mr. HALDANE—Yes, they did.

Lord WATSON—It may be a question whether in any case the words " mere regulation " would include prohibition necessarily, but entire prohibition might be justified on the ground that it was for the well being of the community.

Lord HERSCHELL—That seems to be distinctly the judgment—that it is within the power to legislate for the peaceable government, but they avoid expressing any opinion as to whether it was within the first proposition.

Mr. HALDANE—Yes, I think that is so. It is a little difficult to see why prohibition should not come within the regulation of trade and commerce.

Lord WATSON—It might, and legislation might take such a form as to be entirely within it.

Lord HERSCHELL—But may the test not be whether the object of the legislation is directed to the question of peace and order such as various police purposes, sanitary purposes, or whether it is directed to a trade purpose ? May it not be often the test whether it is within the one category or the other ?

Mr. HALDANE—You must look at the entire Statute, my Lord.

Lord WATSON—Incidentally you may affect trade and commerce, but as to whether it is within the regulation of trade and commerce may be doubtful. These sections are not limiting words, they are words expressly declared by the section.

Mr. HALDANE—I should have thought, my Lord, the right test would be to do what Lord Herschell suggests, and look at the entirety of the Statute and see what its scope and purposes were. If its scope and purpose were simply prohibition as a matter of peace, order and good government, then you would naturally refer it to the initial words of section 91. If it is really a matter of regulation of trade and commerce, as it might be although involving prohibition to some extent, then it may be within regulation of trade and commerce ; but you must see what the prohibition is.

Lord WATSON—The effect of the original first words—they have not been a great deal considered, and may some day require considerable attention—appears to me to be to override to a certain extent nearly all the clauses giving jurisdiction. If that is thought good for one, each Province may enact for itself, because it thinks it for the benefit of the Province. The Dominion Parliament apparently have power if they are really justified, and I assume they are acting fairly and honestly in the matter, to enact that as a general regulation.

Mr. HALDANE—These words " peace, order and good government " are the common form words in which the power of making laws has been given to every Colony of Great Britain. I think they have been used always, at any rate in every recent Act.

Lord HERSCHELL—It is the general law-making power.

Mr. HALDANE—It is the general law-making power; therefore my Lords you must take the Provincial power as an exceptional power. I think that must be so and that the enumeration in section 91 is only for greater certainty, as is stated.

Lord DAVEY—The enumeration has some value besides that, because if it comes within the enumerated matters, then it is not of a local or private nature, because it is confined to the locality, so that it has something more than that value.

Mr. HALDANE—After all my Lords we are brought face to face with the question what does come within what is enumerated.

Lord WATSON—There are many things enumerated which might be in a sense local.

Lord DAVEY—You might pass a local bankruptcy law for instance.

Mr. HALDANE—That could not be, that would be something which would clearly come within the Dominion Law.

Lord HERSCHELL — You could hardly pass a local bankruptcy law unless all the man's creditors were within a particular state, that is to say, you could not pass a law if it were to apply to all a man's creditors, people in other provinces, in addition to which it would be hampering provincial trades.

Mr. HALDANE—Your Lordships remember in the In-

solvency Case last year there were a number of provisions
which were passed by the Province which were appropriate
to a general Bankruptcy Statute, and it was said on behalf of
the Dominion that those provisions were appropriate provisions
to be contained in a Dominion Bankruptcy Act, and that it
ought not to be passed by a Province, but your Lordships
said : It is true these are appropriate provisions in a Bankruptcy Statute, but there are also appropriate provisions with
regard to property and civil rights, and in the absence of
special legislation they are proper things to be brought in in
dealing with property and civil rights.   So it may be here that
there are things which are quite appropriate in a general
prohibition law.

Lord WATSON—There was another case which we
decided last year in which the Dominion had legislated. The
question was raised there as to whether that legislation was
valid or not.

Lord DAVEY—I think it was where some particular usage
had grown up in the lumber trade, but I forget the name of
the case.

Lord WATSON—There was an enactment passed with
regard to receipts ; it authorised a bailee who was also owner
to grant a receipt to pass goods in the market ; that was the
effect of it ; and the question was whether that man was to be
called an Assistant.   We sustained in that case the validity
of the Dominion Act.   I think the case was from Montreal.

Mr. HALDANE—Yes it was.

Lord DAVEY—That case was an appeal, I believe, from
the Court of Appeal of Montreal.

Mr. HALDANE—In that state of the law my Lords it
becomes important to see exactly what has been decided with
regard to the liquor trade, and as I have said not only has
the regulation of it been decided to be in some aspects and
for some purposes within the provincial competence but even
qualified prohibition is decided to be *intra vires* of the Province.

The LORD CHANCELLOR—The consideration of the matter
it seems to me is very difficult in view of the way in which
the question comes before us. .

Mr. HALDANE—I have learnt on very high authority how the question came to be put in this form. In Ontario the Temperance party in Parliament there, is pressing very strongly for legislation and the difficulty with the Government is that they do not know what is *ultra vires*. If it had got to the stage of a bill of course your Lordships would have known exactly what the question was.

The LORD CHANCELLOR—But the moment you are urging what you are urging now, those considerations must come into the matter. The question of degree and the question of aspect in which it may be looked at is a very difficult question.

Mr. HALDANE—It certainly makes the ti   very difficult one for your Lordships. It is important, I think, to look a little carefully at the case of *Hodge* v. *The Queen* in order to see exactly what it was that that case decided, and I take that, as coming earlier than the Liquor License Act. *Hodge* v. *The Queen* decided it to be within the competence of the provincial Parliament— I am not going over that case again, but there are one or two sections of the Act which I wish to call your Lordships' attention to—*Hodge* v. *The Queen* dealt with an Act which certainly had some provisions for prohibition in it. Section 43 prohibited the sale of intoxicating liquors from and after the hours of 7 of the clock on Saturday, and before 6 of the clock on Monday morning, and the conviction was for an infringement of that rule. It was a conviction of a licensed holder who had bound himself to obey the provisions of the Statute, but who had kept his billiard table going an hour afterwards.

Lord HERSCHELL—It was for the purpose of fettering the mode in which the licensed victualler carried on his business.

Mr. HALDANE—Yes, that was so. There you have a general prohibition ; you have, in fact, Sunday closing enacted, and Sunday closing in Municipalities appears therefore to be a thing within the competence of the Provinces. I can quite conceive that there are other forms of qualified prohibition which would stand on the same footing, for instance, the Municipality might prohibit, as a Municipality sometimes does, the sale of liquor in any shop the front of which was not open to the public, so that the police could inspect it. That would be another form of qualified prohibition. Or, they might put it under further restrictions, they might shorten the hours very much, and they might prohibit the sale of liquors altogether on election days. One can conceive, looking at these things, that the purpose of them would be in the nat·re of police regulations.

Lord WATSON—To a great extent these powers are really exercised in the administration of the law.

Mr. HALDANE—Yes, the due administration of the law, my Lord.

Lord WATSON—Consistently with police powers.

Mr. HALDANE—Yes, they may be perfectly necessary.

Lord WATSON—They may have it within their power, and it may be within their power. Even assuming the whole regulation of the liquor traffic rested with the Dominion Parliament, it would not follow that in administering the Act within their own Municipalities the Local Legislature might not have given them a great deal of police power.

Mr. HALDANE—And not only so, but it might vary in localities.

Lord WATSON—Quite so, for local considerations.

Mr. HALDANE—Yes, my Lord, for local considerations. For instance, in a country borough. We know it is the law in Scotland that the country towns close sometimes at half-past nine and ten o'clock, whereas in large towns eleven o'clock is the rule, and it may well be that it is necessary that that should be so.

Lord WATSON—It may go further than that. Before the Dominion Act this liquor question had been dealt with by the different Provinces. I think it was shown to us that all the Provinces had dealt with it, but it was quite clear that they had all dealt with it differently, and one can quite well see that the local circumstances in one Province might be such ·as to render a very strict liquor law necessary, while in another it

L

might not be so. If that were so, that would be on account of the local conditions, and that raises the question whether dealing with those local conditions is not dealing with a small local matter.

Mr. HALDANE—And your Lordship notices the questions raise that in two forms, because question 7 relates to the validity of the 18th section of the Act of 1890, which proposes to put the power of prohibition into the hands of the Council of every township, city, town and incorporated village. That is, of course, Municipal only. In the other case your Lordship put, in the case of a Province, there you have a locality proposed to be entrusted with the power of prohibition, but a locality of a wider nature.

Lord WATSON—Of course, it might be too that the evil only existed in one part of a Province, and that there alone a very stringent law was necessary. The natural way of meeting that would be by legislation of the Province, giving power to that particular locality to deal with the matter.

Mr. HALDANE—Yes, it may be purely local. The first observation I make upon question 7, and indeed the main observation I wish to make upon it, is that that deals with a particular kind of locality—with the Municipality, whereas question 1 is directed to the wider question of whether the Province, taken as a locality, or part of a Province, as your Lordship suggests, taken as a locality, can be entrusted by the Province with the same kind of power. I need not say more upon *Hodge* v. *The Queen*, because it is plain that it did involve prohibition of some kind, and prohibition for what you may call a local purpose, and the power in section 18 of the Act of 1890, which is under discussion, is also of a qualified kind. It is a power to the local Council to " prohibit the sale " by retail of liquor in any tavern, inn, or other house or place " of public entertainment." That is the first branch of it, and, secondly, for prohibiting altogether the sale of it in shops and places other than houses of public entertainment. Then that must be read together with the amending Act which enables you to buy in the shop,—for example you may buy it anywhere, because it says :—

" No tavern or shop license shall be necessary for selling any liquors in the original packages in which the same have been received from the importer or manufacturer, provided such packages contain respectively not less than five gallons or one dozen bottles."

It comes to this—that in some localities it is desirable that the public house, or inn, or place where the liquor is sold, is a place where you are not to buy less than a dozen bottles. The scheme of the Act is local, and its purpose is to deal with something in the nature of a local regulation or restriction. Now in the Liquor License Case you get the same thing upon the other side. I will not go over it again, but on pages 4, 6 and 7 of the report, you have the kind of provision which was put into that Act. One cannot tell of course what was the ground of their Lordships' decision, but one cannot help seeing that the contest largely turned upon whether the whole Act was not in substance an attempt to get hold of what was a local or municipal matter under cover of a Dominion Statute.

Lord DAVEY—I have read the argument again and I think it turned very largely on the machinery which was used in that enactment.

Mr. HALDANE—Yes, your Lordship remembers that the Act had been drawn with considerable care, and the electors, who had been chosen, were the electors of the Dominion constituency, and they took localities which corresponded very nearly to the Municipal localities under the Ontario legislation, but this Board decided that the mere variation of the machinery did not prevent the machinery from being a machinery of a municipal and local character—indeed the Act was of that nature.

Lord HERSCHELL—I do not think that carries the matter really further than the decision in *Hodge's* case, because whether it is right or wrong, *Hodge's* case having decided that any licensing functions were within the power of the Provincial Legislature, I do not know that it is very material for the present purpose—if it is so—to consider whether those functions were also within the powers of the Dominion Parliament. The Liquor License case held they were not, but whether they were or not, having been so held, that is the class of case we are now considering.

Mr. HALDANE—It is the converse of the case your Lordship had before you in the Insolvency Case—the field was already occupied.

Lord WATSON—The power is given to the Dominion Parliament, exclusive power, or power which, if used, might deprive the Municipalities of their own power of self regulation ?

Mr. HALDANE—That is really what it comes to.

Lord WATSON—If it were within the powers, the Dominion Parliament might interfere and regulate the hours, and the Police might have no jurisdiction.

Mr. HALDANE—And do it through a set of Authorities which would be doing the same work exactly which the Police ought to be doing, for instance, the looking after the conduct of the public-houses, the limit of prohibition and so on. It is not a case of sweeping away the whole of the public-houses.

Lord WATSON—The point in that case was not so much the regulation as the administration of the law for Municipal purposes, which is a very different thing. It is one thing to say the Dominion Parliament might have power to legislate, and another thing to say they could take away the administration of the law and the Police powers in reference to that law from the Municipal bodies in the Province.

Mr. HALDANE—Yes. I do not think I need read the judgments as fully as they are sometimes read in these cases, because we have really covered so much of the ground. I will refer to the substance of them. If your Lordships will turn to page 76 of the Record, the Chief Justice, who is favourable to the Appellants' contention, after stating his opinion that all the questions except those relating to manufacture, should be answered in the affirmative, says very much what I have just been arguing that the Court is precluded by the decision of the Privy Council in *Russell* v. *The Queen*, from holding that the exclusive power prohibiting the sale of liquor by retail was given to the Provinces as an incident to the Police power conferred by the words

" Municipal Institutions." Then he refers to *Hodge* v. *The Queen*, and says :

> " The question then is narrowed to this :—Have the Provinces under this sub-section 8, a power concurrent with that of the Dominion to enact prohibitory legislation to be carried into effect through the instrumentality of the Municipalities or otherwise, either generally or to the extent of the power of prohibiting which had been conferred on Municipal bodies by legislation enacted prior to Confederation and in force at that date."

Then he quotes *Russell* v. *The Queen* and says—

The Lord CHANCELLOR—I think what he says there about that is material because he gives his exposition of how he understands that decision.

Mr. HALDANE—Yes, at the top of page 77 :

> " But, as I understand that decision, such Dominion laws must be general laws, not limited to any particular Province."

It may be that that is stating it more widely than it is necessary to state it ; it may be enough to say for the purposes of general legislation as distinguished from general administration or local and police legislation. Then a little lower down he says :—

> " Therefore it appears to me that there are in the Dominion and the Provinces, respectively, several and distinct powers authorising each, within its own sphere, to enact the same legislation on this subject of prohibitory liquor laws restraining sale by retail."

Lord WATSON—I am not sure ; it is always dangerous to lay down a proposition of that kind. I do not know that they must be general laws not limited to any particular Province, that they must be for the benefit of the whole of the Provinces.

Mr. HALDANE—Yes.

Lord WATSON—It is much too narrow to say that.

Mr. HALDANE—Yes, you must look at the whole scope of the Statute.

Lord WATSON—The legislation runs very much on the lines and to the same extent as the interests given by the Act to the Provinces.

Lord HERSCHELL—But to legislate in a matter which is

a local matter for one Province only and merely say that we
thought it would be for the benefit of all Canada that Ontario
should be made a very sober place would be to my mind
legislation about which there would be a good deal of
question. I think it is too narrow to say that the law must
extend to every Province, but on the other hand the general
idea that it must not be local legislation in a particular
Province though it is by the Dominion Parliament——

Lord Morris—I think the Chief Justice is only dealing
with the local option laws. He says, at foot of page 76, the
Dominion of Canada " may' pass what are denominated local
" option laws. But as I understand that decision "—that is
the decision on the very question—" such Dominion laws
" must be general laws." It is the local option laws, and I
think he is strictly right.

Mr. HALDANE—About the middle of the page his reason
is given :—

> " To neither of the legislatures is the subject of prohibitory liquor
> laws in terms assigned. Then what reason is there why a local legis-
> lature in execution of the police power conferred by sub-section 8 of
> section 92 may not, so long as it does not come in conflict with the
> legislation of the Dominion, adopt any appropriate means of executing
> that power, merely because the same means may be adopted by the
> Dominion Parliament under the authority of section 91 in executing a
> power specifically given to it ? It has been decided by the highest
> authority that there are no reasons against such a construction. This
> is indeed even a stronger case for recognising such a concurrent power
> than the case of *The Attorney-General of Ontario* v. *The Attorney-
> General of Canada.*"

That is the insolvency case—

> " because bankruptcy and insolvency laws are by section 91
> expressly attributed to the exclusive jurisdiction of the Dominion. In
> the event of legislation providing for prohibition enacted by the
> Dominion and by a Province coming into conflict, the legislation of
> the Province would no doubt have to give way. This was pointed out
> by the Privy Council in *The Attorney-General of Ontario* v. *The Attorney-
> General of Canada*, and although the British North America Act con-
> tains no provision declaring that the legislation of the Dominion shall
> be supreme, as is the case in the constitution of the United States, the
> same principle is necessarily implied in our Constitutional Act, and is
> to be applied whenever in the many cases which may arise, the
> Federal and Provincial Legislatures adopt the same means to carry
> into effect distinct powers."

Lord WATSON—It is not quite correct in my opinion to call that concurrent power when the concurring provincial legislation must give way.

Lord DAVEY—There is a passage you left out which may be of importance on questions 3 and 4, between lines 10 and 20 :

> "Such provincial legislation cannot, however, be extended so as to prohibit importation or manufacture, for the reason that these subjects belong exclusively to the Dominion under the head of trade and commerce, and also for the additional reason that the revenue of the Dominion derived from Customs and Excise Duties would be thereby affected."

Lord WATSON—And not only so, the Provincial Legislature can only deal with that which is really a matter of civil right. They cannot propose, for instance, to deal with bankruptcy.

Lord HERSCHELL—I should like to know what you have to say about the question of importation, because the question of importation seems to me to be very different. Do you say it is a question of a local nature ? The question of manufacture in any Province would *prima facie* seem to be of a local nature unless it comes within trade and commerce, but then supposing it to be otherwise than of a local nature, would it be excluded because the Dominion Parliament raised part of their revenue by excise.

Mr. HALDANE—I think the question would be whether it was necessarily a thing that came within matters of a local nature. If it was something which came within matters of a local nature and could be properly dealt with in that capacity then I take it that notwithstanding there would be some interference with the Dominion revenue that would not be sufficient reason for saying the Province had not the power.

Lord HERSCHELL—Supposing the Dominion Parliament has used it for the purpose of taxation, can it be said that it would be simply of a local nature, when it directly affects the raising of revenue under a law passed by the Dominion Parliament ? That seems to me to be a very serious question, because otherwise you see, supposing they had raised a great deal of their revenue in that way, the Provincial Legislature might for the very purpose of checkmating, in some controversy between the Province and the Dominion, prohibit particular manufactures.

Mr. HALDANE—That would be clearly bad ; if it were a statute passed for that purpose it would be clearly bad.

Lord HERSCHELL—Supposing it has immediately that effect, can it be said to be merely of a local nature when it affects the revenue of the Dominion directly ?

Mr. HALDANE—Again I think you must look at the purpose and scope of the whole statute.

Lord HERSCHELL—Whatever its scope and purpose, it must be merely of a local nature, that is : not touching by its immediate and direct operations those outside the province. If you do this you at once stop a source of revenue of the whole of the Dominion.

Lord MORRIS—Do you not do very much the same thing if you stop the drinking of whisky altogether ? You stop the manufacture of it practically for nobody will be fools enough to manufacture that which nobody can drink.

Lord DAVEY—You reduce the excise undoubtedly if you restrict drinking liquor (without prohibition) by a licensing system.

Mr. HALDANE—Your Lordships had this very point before you in the *Russell* Case, only the other way. It was argued in the *Russell* Case that if the Dominion had the power of prohibition, that was destroying the right of the Province to the revenue from liquor licenses which undoubtedly it had, and this was said in the judgment :—

"But supposing the effect of the Act to be prejudicial to the Revenue derived by the Municipality from licenses, it does not follow that the Dominion Parliament might not pass it by virtue of its general authority to make laws for the peace, order, and good government of Canada. Assuming that the matter of the Act does not fall within the class of subject described in No. 9, that sub-section can in no way interfere with the general authority of the parliament to deal with that matter. If the argument of the Appellant that the power given to the Provincial Legislatures to raise a Revenue by licenses, prevents the Dominion Parliament from legislating with regard to any article or commodity which was or might be covered by such licenses were to prevail, the consequence would be that laws which might be necessary for the public good or the public safety could not be enacted at all. Suppose it were deemed to be necessary or expedient for the national safety or for political reasons to prohibit the sale of arms or the carrying of arms it could not be contended that a Provincial Legislature would have authority by virtue of sub-section 9, (which alone is now under discussion) to pass any such law, nor, if the Appellants' argument were to prevail, would the Dominion Parliament be competent to pass it, since such a law would interfere prejudicially with the revenue derived from licenses granted under the authority of the Provincial Legislature for the sale or the carrying of arms." L. R. 7. App. Cas. 837.

Lord HERSCHELL—That does not seem to me to help us on this question, because that is dealing with supreme legislative power. You cannot be deprived of that because it may affect the taxing power of a particular Province, but it does not help us on this question, which is, is legislation of a "merely local nature," which are the words we have to deal with, "in the Province" which does in this way directly affect the Dominion? I mean that is a different question and does not help us. I am expressing no opinion upon it of course.

The LORD CHANCELLOR—It is impossible to solve these conundrums without having a specific thing before us. You have just now quoted if it should be necessary for the purpose of good government to prohibit the carrying of arms, they might have to import a new state of facts in order to show what would or what would not be within the power. That seems to me to prove the impossibility of answering these things in the abstract. The infinite variety of human circumstances may or may not render it desirable.

Mr. HALDANE—Your Lordships are asked to deal with all the contentions of the temperance party in advance.

The LORD CHANCELLOR—Not only that, but all the things which may happen in the course of this world's history which may or may not render the temperance legislation or any other legislation proper.

Lord WATSON—How can I deal with and adjudicate upon a question of that kind? I can hazard an opinion, but that is another matter. We do not give opinions, not judicially.

Mr. HALDANE—I will pass from this point with this observation, that the power of raising revenue, a power which the Provinces and the Dominion have in different forms, is a power which must be necessarily subject to the alteration of the subject matter from which the revenue is to be raised under the powers which are conferred upon these two Parliaments respectively. It cannot be merely because the Dominion Parliament has a right to put an indirect tax, for instance, to put a tax upon bread——

Lord HERSCHELL—I do not think because it has a right : I should not be pressed with that difficulty at all. You cannot interfere with the scope of Provincial legislation in a matter otherwise local by saying " it is a matter with which the Dominion might find it convenient to deal." I should have no difficulty upon that, but where the Dominion Parliament has dealt with it by way of raising revenue, then the question arises whether you do not directly affect the Dominion legislation when you prohibit manufacture.

Mr. HALDANE—It is only dealt with for the purpose of raising revenue in a general fashion.

Lord HERSCHELL—As I understand, it raises revenue distinctly by the manufacture. It has nothing to do with the sale. Of course it is true if you prohibit sale that may indirectly affect the manufacture. That is only an indirect and incidental effect, but if the taxation is distinctly upon the manufacture, if you prohibit the manufacture, you directly attack the revenue.

Lord WATSON—A distillery is a mere local matter, but the moment you tax all its productions for the purpose of filling the Exchequer, it may be a question whether it does not then cease to be a matter of local interest merely.

Mr. HALDANE—Yes.

Lord WATSON—The ratepayers throughout the Dominion are interested in it, the Government of the Dominion is interested in it.

Mr. HALDANE—Yes, my Lord, there are a number of subjects which are handed over.

Lord WATSON—You affect it by dealing with it in the way it is proposed other than in regard to the local interests.

Mr. HALDANE—Yes, of course one may, by a particular Act of legislation of the Province, be simply striking at the source of revenue. It might well be, one can conceive, that from the point of view of police the existence of the manufacture of drink——

Lord WATSON—Whether you can legislate on the ground that it is a purely local matter to an extent which would immediately destroy that interest of the general ratepayers of Canada and of the Canadian Government, it may be questioned whether that within the meaning of the Statutes is purely local.

Mr. HALDANE—Supposing the Dominion Government to raise a revenue partly from licenses for the manufacture of dynamite or cordite and the Provincial Legislature were to say " in none of our towns shall there be a manufactory of this kind," that, I take it, would be within the power of the Provincial Legislature on the ground of local safety, and yet it would affect the revenue in the same way as this. That is a case which comes very close to something which is necessary in the interests of the locality.

Lord HERSCHELL.—That is the difficulty you see. Apart from the point of Municipal Institutions, if you bring yourself within 16 you must bring yourself within the terms that it is merely of a local nature. Then if your Act operates outside the province it ceases to be so and the question is whether it is or is not of a local nature.

Mr. HALDANE—I think you must look at the effect of the whole thing.

Lord HERSCHELL—I quite understand your argument. You say that because incidentally it affects the revenue of the Dominion that that does not prevent it being dealt with locally.

Mr. HALDANE—Yes, my Lord.

Lord WATSON—It goes to raise a question of fact.

Mr. HALDANE—I think it comes to this, that there is hardly a question on the construction of these two sections that can be decided except in a concrete form.

Lord HERSCHELL—That is the difficulty. Taking the very case of its being merely of a local nature, one would want to know what the exact thing was, what the exact facts were about the Dominion Act, and how it would affect the revenue or anything else under that Act before you could answer the question.

Lord WATSON—Probably the most satisfactory answer would be to say, though not perhaps to those who asked the question, in certain circumstances it will and in certain circumstances it will not. It is quite capable of that answer.

Mr. HALDANE—I turn now to the top of page 78 of the Judgment. There is nothing more in the preceding page that I need trouble your Lordships with—

> "That a general police power sufficient to include the right of legislating to the extent of the prohibition of retail traffic or local option laws, not exclusive of but concurrent with a similar power in the Dominion, is vested in the Provinces by the words 'Municipal Institutions in the Province' in sub-section 8 of chapter 92 is, I think, a proposition which derives support from the case of *Hodge* v. *The Queen.* It is true that the subject of prohibition was not in question in that case, but there would seem to be no reason why prohibitory laws as well as those regulating and limiting the traffic in liquors should not be included in the police power which under the words 'Municipal Institutions' it was held in *Hodge* v. *The Queen* to the extent of licensing, the Provinces possessed."

Lord HERSCHELL—I think it is not quite accurate to say that they possessed it under sub-section 8. It was held they possessed it under 8 and 16. I am by no means sure that the decision of this Board in *Hodge* v. *The Queen* would have been the same if they had thought it had come under 16. If it could not be brought within any of the other specific ones I doubt whether they would have held it could be done under 8 alone. At all events, whether they would or would not, it is not accurate to say they held it to come under 8, they held it to come under 8 and 16.

Mr. HALDANE—Yes. Under one or the other.

> "The difference between regulating and licensing and prohibiting is one of degree only.
>
> "As regards the objection that to recognise any such right of legislation in a Province not extending to the prohibition of importation and manufacture would be an infringement of the

power of the Dominion to regulate trade and commerce. I am not impressed by it. The retail liquor traffic can scarcely be regarded as coming directly under the head of trade and commerce as used in the British North America Act, but as the subjects enumerated in section 92 are exceptions out of those mentioned in section 91 it follows that if a police power is included in sub-section 8 of the former section the power itself and all appropriate means of carrying it out are to be treated as uncontrolled by anything in section 91. Moreover *Hodge* v. *The Queen* also applies here, for although in a lesser degree, yet to some extent the restriction of the liquor trade by a licensing system would affect trade and commerce. On the whole, I am of opinion that the provincial Legislatures have power to enact prohibitory legislation to the extent I have mentioned though this power is in no way exclusive of that of the Dominion but concurrent with it."

Lord HERSCHELL—I think that is going a little too far to say that the Dominion has concurrent power because that might imply that they could legislate for the particular Province. I should say rather than concurrent power an overruling power, if they considered such legislation necessary for the purpose of good Government and order of the whole Dominion.

Mr. HALDANE—Yes. The last part of the Judgment I do not read because it simply states the argument.

Lord WATSON—It is not quite co-extensive and it is not concurrent. In the case of concurrent power the general rule is that the authority which first exercises it prevails.

Lord HERSCHELL—One sees what the learned Chief Justice means. It is a verbal criticism rather than otherwise.

The LORD CHANCELLOR—I think the next four or five lines are important, as emphasising what the Chief Justice means.

Mr. HALDANE—Yes. I will read them :—

"If I am wrong in this conclusion, it is sufficient for th.. decision of this Appeal to hold, as I do, that the Legislature of Ontario had power to repeal and re-enact the legislation in force at the date of the Confederation Act, which gave Municipal Councils the right to pass by-laws absolutely prohibiting the sale of liquor by retail within certain local limits. Having regard to the history and objects of Confederation, I can scarcely think it possible that it could have been intended by the framers of the British North America Act to detract in any way from the jurisdiction of the Provinces over their own several systems of Municipal Government,"

Lord HERSCHELL—But they did detract from the jurisdiction of the Provinces over their own several systems of Municipal Government, because it is admitted that they did interfere with the power of the Municipality. Is that one of those things in which they have interfered ? It is too broad, surely, to say that it was not " to detract in any way from the jurisdiction of the Provinces over their own several systems of Municipal Government " ?

Lord DAVEY—I think this observation of the learned Chief Justice is only important if he is right in his previous conclusion.

Mr. HALDANE—Yes.

Lord WATSON—If he is wrong he does not seem to have adverted to the concluding language of section 129, which gives to each of them the power. The old law is to stand, but the Dominion Parliament are to have power to deal with the whole of the legislation.

Mr. HALDANE—Section 129 makes the federal power have the power of repeal—it follows up sections 91 and 92.

Lord WATSON—On the same lines as the right of legislation ?

Lord HERSCHELL—It would seem almost to follow. I should have thought that if there was no power to enact this there could be no power to repeal it. If there is no power to enact, and the Chief Justice is wrong in his point, it is because that is taking away from the Provincial and giving to the Dominion Parliament. If so, it must follow that the power to repeal the existing legislation is taken from the Provincial and given to the Dominion Parliament in that section 129, and it rather strikes me that is the same question. If he is right in his first point, then it is for the Provincial Parliament alone to deal with the repeal. If he is wrong, it was for the Dominion Parliament to deal with the repeal.

Mr. HALDANE—The fact that municipal bodies, prior to Confederation, possessed this power shows that to some extent it was regarded as a matter of local power.

The LORD CHANCELLOR—I should have thought it was

the other way—that they had plainly the power at that time in everything.

Mr. HALDANE—They all had it, more or less.

Lord HERSCHELL—They all had the full power; they had delegated that power, some of them more and some less, to particular local bodies, but differently in each State.

Lord WATSON—They had the same plenary power in those days within the Province as the Dominion Legislature and all the other legislatures put together.

Mr. HALDANE—Yes; and they were in the habit of giving to municipal bodies these powers.

Lord HERSCHELL—They were in the habit of giving them some powers in relation to dealing with drink differing in different Provinces. How does it follow from that that it was intended that each of the Provinces should have the power of giving any powers they pleased in relation to drink to any municipal bodies?

Lord DAVEY—It might be put in this way: it occurs to me that if it gives them power to legislate on any matter relating to Municipal Institutions, and *de facto* at the passing of the Act certain municipal bodies had certain powers, the repeal of those powers would be a matter relating to an existing Municipal Institution.

Lord WATSON—I have arrived at the conclusion that the right to enact and the right to repeal old enactments did not stand upon exactly the same footing, but whichever legislature the one belonged to must necessarily have been possessed of the other.

Mr. HALDANE—That seems to have been the intention of section 129. However, that is the only way that the argument can be put.

Then Mr. Justice Fournier concurs, and Mr. Justice Gwynne gives a very long Judgment the other way. I think I need not read the whole of it, as it would take a long time, but I will read such portions as seem to be necessary, and if my friends think I am missing anything they can rectify it.

Lord HERSCHELL—We have probably all read the Judgments. Although you pass over certain passages, it must not be taken that we have not informed ourselves of them.

Mr. HALDANE—That is so, and I think it would be only wasting your Lordships' time for me to read them further.

Lor.' HERSCHELL—If there is any part to which you wish to call special attention do so, but it is not necessary to read the whole of them as we have read them ourselves.

Mr. HALDANE—There is no comment on these Judgments which your Lordship will not hear from the other side.

Lord MORRIS—This passage on page 85 seems to be material—

"Now the several questions in the case submitted to us are resolvable into this one. * * * * "

That is very satisfactory.

Mr. HALDANE—Yes, Mr. Justice Gwynne takes rather a strong view. There are a great many very edifying things like speeches from people who introduced these things into Parliament, and a number of things which are of great historical value but not otherwise pertinent. In this Judgment of Mr. Justice Sedgewick's your Lordship will get the arguments more satisfactorily put.

Sir RICHARD COUCH—Mr. Justice Sedgewick's Judgment gives them better than any other I think.

Mr. HALDANE—Yes, it is a very good Judgment.

Lord HERSCHELL—There is some very forcible reasoning which certainly impressed me very much in all these Judgments with regard to this coming under "Municipal Institutions" and coming under nothing else. I think it is very clearly put in Mr. Justice Sedgewick's Judgment on page 101.

Sir RICHARD COUCH—It is better put there than in any other.

Lord HERSCHELL—

"What meaning then is to be given to Municipal Institutions in the Province ? Three answers may be advanced. First, it may mean that a Legislature has power to divide its territory into defined areas, constitute the inhabitants a Municipal Corporation or Community, give to the governing bodies of officers of such Corporations or Communities all such powers as are inherently incident to or essentially necessary for their existence, growth and development, and confer upon them as well all such authority and jurisdiction as it may lawfully do under any of the enumerated articles of section 92. That is the narrowest view. Or, secondly, it may mean that a Legislature may also confer upon Municipalities, in addition to these powers, all those powers that were possessed or enjoyed in common by the Municipalities or Municipal Communities of all the confederating Provinces at the time of the Union, the *jus gentium* of Canadian Municipal law ; or, finally, it may mean that a Legislature may confer upon Municipalities all those powers which in any Province or in any place in a Province, any Municipality at the time of the Union, as a matter of fact, possessed by virtue of legislative or other authority."

Those are three possible cases.

Mr. HALDANE—Yes. Then he says that he dissents from putting the case in the widest view.

"The first view in my Judgment is the proper one, a view which gives scope for liberal interpretation as to what may constitute the essence of the Municipal system and give due effect in that direction to the Municipal *jus gentium* of the three old Provinces, and I entertain the strongest doubt if it ever was contemplated by the use of the words 'Municipal Institutions' to make any particular reference to the liquor traffic at all."

Then he states certain reasons for thinking that, and he refers to class 9 of section 92 and to the Quebec Resolutions. My Lords, it does seem a little odd to refer to those things which took place and which were no doubt the basis of the Act which afterwards became the Confederation Act, for that is certainly not what your Lordships have got to interpret. They are very interesting, but they are the words of the promoters in Canada of this Act, promoting objects which, for aught we know, may have been modified by Lord Carnarvon and his advisers when they came to frame the statute which was afterwards passed into law.

Lord HERSCHELL—Were they passed into law in the terms settled on ?

Lord WATSON—What is the date of this case ?

Mr. HALDANE—It is last year.

Lord HERSCHELL—The same date ?

Mr. HALDANE—The same date, and the Judgments were given the same day, the same afternoon.

Lord HERSCHELL.—They gave their Judgments the same day, but the case had been heard before Courts differently constituted.

Mr. HALDANE—Yes, a long time had elapsed in both cases between the arguments and the Judgment. My Lords, I think I should be only taking up your Lordships' time if I went into this, because my friends will call your attention to any points in the Judgment which they think of importance.

Mr. NEWCOMBE—If your Lordships please, I appear for the Attorney-General of the Dominion of Canada. The subject of the Reference I take it may be regarded as prohibition. I think that is the subject to which the various questions are directed, and that was the question which was dealt with by your Lordships' Board in the case of *Russell* v. *The Queen* which has been referred to, but which I think it will be necessary for me to refer to at some greater length than has already been done. That case excluded the subject of prohibition, as dealt with by the Canada Temperance Act, from provincial authority.

Lord HERSCHELL.—How do you put that?

Mr. NEWCOMBE—I submit it must be held to have gone to that length.

Lord HERSCHELL.—It did not exclude legislation on such a subject within the Dominion, but I think it excluded it in the direction of prohibition from the Provinces.

Mr. NEWCOMBE—My proposition is this, my lord, that it necessarily did exclude the subject from provincial authority having regard to the power of the Province to enact prohibition as to the whole Province generally. The question of the effect of the assignment to the Province of private and local matters may be another question, but it seems to me that the case was approached by your Lordships in *Russell* v. *The Queen* and decided in such a way as to exclude the subject generally from provincial competency. That is the effect of the decision.

Lord HERSCHELL.—I will tell you at once my difficulty, and you will deal with it no doubt. This Board expressed no opinion as to its coming within the two, it founded its judgment entirely upon the earlier part of the section, its coming within the general power to legislate for all Canada. Now the provision at the end of section 91 is to the effect that the power of the provincial legislature to legislate on matters of a merely local character shall be excluded and shall not be taken to extend, where the limits of the legislation be local only, to matters coming within the enumerated provisions of section 91. This Board did not decide that the prohibition of liquor came within any of those enumerated sections; it decided it upon the ground that it came within the first provision. Now if you read the words at the end of section 91 they imply that so far as their limit is merely local and the effects are merely local, the Provincial legislature may legislate on matters with which nevertheless the Dominion Parliament may have power to legislate generally as being a matter for the peace or good government of Canada. The very express words at the end of section 91 appear to me to imply that there may be cases in which you may legislate locally by Provincial legislative authority and nevertheless the Parliament of Canada may legislate generally.

Mr. NEWCOMBE.—For peace or good government.

Lord HERSCHELL—Yes.

Mr. NEWCOMBE—That is so long as it does not come within the enumerated clauses.

Lord HERSCHELL—Yes. Of course if they have decided it on the ground that it came within the regulation of trade and commerce, one of the enumerated things, then no doubt that would have been a strong point, but I am only speaking of the scope of *Russell* v. *The Queen*. I am not speaking of this case only. So far as *Russell* v. *The Queen* is concerned it does not seem to me to go further than that. That is why I say it does not strike me that the ground upon which the decision in *Russell* v. *The Queen* is based excludes the provincial power from dealing with the matter locally.

Lord WATSON—I do not think there is any decision of

this Board which settled the power, if any, in this matter of the Dominion Parliament as being limited to such subjects.

Mr. NEWCOMBE—No, my lord.

Lord WATSON—If it did that it may be so, but it has not been so held, and I feel a certain amount of difficulty upon that subject.

Mr. NEWCOMBE—For the purpose of considering really what has been decided by the case of *Russell* v. *The Queen* I should like to refer for a moment to the part of the Act which was then under consideration—the Canada Temperance Act section 99 which is the prohibiting clause. It is set out in the Joint Appendix section 99 on page 27. The main section is generally prohibitive, and then follows a sub-section which is stated to have been merely declaratory that licenses shall not have effect where this Act is in operation. Then we have certain exemptions established, namely, sales for sacramental purposes, sales for medicinal and mechanical purposes, sales by producers of cider, or licensed distillers or brewers, sales by vine growing companies and sales by manufacturers of pure native wines, also sales by merchants and traders in wholesale quantities; but these exceptions, except with regard to sales for sacramental purposes and medicinal purposes and mechanical purposes, are limited to sales in quantities of 10 gallons or more. Therefore what is really prohibited by the Canada Temperance Act is sale in quantities of less than 10 gallons.

Lord HERSCHELL—But it does not do so everywhere. There is only power to the Government generally to bring the Act into force.

Mr. NEWCOMBE—Yes; and I mean in those localities where it is brought into force, that is the effect of it. The prohibition is as to quantities for sale of less than 10 gallons. That is prohibition of the retail sale. That I submit to your Lordships is the effect of the Statute which was under consideration in *Russell* v. *The Queen*, a Statute passed by the Parliament of the Dominion of Canada providing for prohibition of sales throughout the Dominion in retail quantities, in so far as prohibition, limiting the sales to quantities of 10 gallons or more, constitutes retail.

The LORD CHANCELLOR—There is nothing in the essential nature of the thing in that respect. That is an arbitrary line, very properly drawn perhaps.

Mr. NEWCOMBE—It is an arbitrary line ; that is so, but it has regard to small quantities.

The LORD CHANCELLOR—I suppose if one had the facts before one, which one has not, one would conjecture that that would mean that the greater number of people in the Provinces would not get it at all.

Mr. NEWCOMBE—Yes, my Lord.

Lord HERSCHELL—But supposing that I put another case which will equally illustrate it. Supposing that the Dominion Parliament thought that certain regulations were necessary for the peace, order, and good government of Canada, and supposing that in a particular Province a state of things existed which rendered it unsafe for the public that regulations so little stringent should exist, that is to say that it would be necessary that some further and more stringent regulations should be in force if peace was to be maintained there, then it does not follow that because the Parliament of Canada considered that for the Dominion generally you must at least do this, that the Provincial Legislature could not, as a merely local matter where the locality needed something much more drastic, so legislate—I do not see why not. It is a merely local matter. They do it for their locality and it affects it only. It may be the Legislature in question think it proper not for the whole Dominion, but for their locality, and what is the inconsistency between those two acts of legislation ?

The LORD CHANCELLOR—There might be, I suppose, such a condition of things as this. Take the question of travelling from one part of the country to another. If the Provincial Legislature has thought it proper to put in force such regulations as to make travelling perfectly impossible, such legislation, although competent as regards the extent of its own jurisdiction would affect seriously the whole country.

Lord HERSCHELL—Of course one might take many cases that would be of a merely local nature, and I wanted to take a case that was of merely local nature and affecting only the inhabitants of the locality. Take sanitation for example; supposing that the Dominion Parliament had, with a view to the health of the whole Dominion, passed certain regulations and supposing in a particular Province a particular disease was raging which rendered it necessary for the safety of all those within the Province, that much more stringent regulations as to the inhabitants of the houses should come into force. Why should not that be considered a merely local matter? If it is so, it is intended to be dealt with, and you limit your regulation to the locality and why is that inconsistent with legislation which is on the same lines as that which is in force in the Dominion at large?

Mr. NEWCOMBE—It may come to this, that if the Dominion has legislated in pursuance of an express power conferred upon it under section 91, then that power is exercised exclusive of any power conferred upon the Province.

Lord HERSCHELL—You mean one of the enumerated powers?

Mr. NEWCOMBE—Yes.

Lord HERSCHELL—Take one which is not so; may not one imagine many cases where you might have legislation properly under the first part of the section by the Dominion Parliament for the whole of Canada, there being very different legislation necessary at an existing time and for existing circumstances for a particular Province?

Mr. NEWCOMBE—That must depend upon the jurisdiction of the legislation. If the Legislature has intended to occupy that field and cover the ground, with respect to that subject, I submit it would be improper to allow the Province to interfere also in the matter.

Lord HERSCHELL—One cannot help having certain doubts as to whether the Parliament of Canada could legislate as regards the sanitary arrangements of houses in a particular town in a Province under this general power for the peace, good order and government of Canada, which must mean Canada at large, in general. It must mean something in a particular place, and it is difficult to suppose then that the Parliament of Canada could legislate for what may be a temporary measure required to meet a local exigency at a particular time in a particular town in a Province, and if the Parliament of Canada cannot legislate, it is very difficult to suppose that the Provincial Legislature cannot, and that there is no power of legislation about it at all because all legislative power was intended to be in one or other of the Provinces.

Mr. NEWCOMBE—Yes.

Lord WATSON—Supposing the Parliament of Canada passed an Act compelling the vaccination of every child within six months, and that within one of the Provinces, owing to an outbreak of small-pox the Provincial Legislature thought it necessary to enact that the vaccination should be repeated every seven years, would that be beyond the power of the Provincial Legislature, or would it be in conflict with the Dominion legislation? I do not see that the Dominion Parliament could provide that a child was never afterwards to be vaccinated during its life.

Lord HERSCHELL—There might then be a question whether that would be within the powers of the Dominion Parliament, whether it would not be that kind of legislation which is negative merely.

Mr. NEWCOMBE—There would be the question whether the Dominion had that power.

Lord HERSCHELL—Supposing this to be within the power of the Dominion Parliament: that they could enact that every child must be vaccinated before it reaches the age of three months, the Province could not say that it would be enough if it is vaccinated before the age of eight months because that would be in direct conflict, and the Provincial Parliament would be dealing with a matter which *ex hypothesis* was within the jurisdiction of the Dominion Parliament. That they could not do.

Mr. NEWCOMBE—They could not do that. In *Russell* v. *The Queen*, your Lordships' Board approached the case from the standpoint of the Provincial powers, and the question was, was this legislation within the power of the

Province ? It was urged that it was within the power of the
Province under the several heads which are always invoked
for the purpose of conferring that jurisdiction. " Shop,
" saloon, tavern, auctioneer and other licenses for the purpose
" of raising revenue for Provincial purposes " was the first
head dealt with by the Judgment, and it was held that the
Province could not enact prohibition under that clause. Then
under " property and civil rights " the same conclusion was
come to. Then we come to the question with regard to
No. 16 : " generally all matters of merely local or private
" nature in the Province." What was said on that subject is
at pages 24 to 26 of the Report as found in 2 Cartwright's
cases, and L. R. 7 App. Cas. at page 840. It begins in
this way :—

> " It was not of course contended for the Appellant that the
> Legislature of New Brunswick could have passed the Act in question
> which embraces in its enactments all the Provinces, nor was it denied
> with respect to this last contention that the Parliament of Canada
> might have passed an Act of the nature of that under discussion, to
> take effect at the same time throughout the whole Dominion. Their
> Lordships understand the contention to be—— "

Lord HERSCHELL—We had a large admission made there
by those who represented the Provincial Legislature, on the
question of whether the Parliament of Canada could or could
not pass such an Act for the whole Dominion, that is to say,
an Act coming into force at once for the whole Dominion.

Mr. NEWCOMBE—Yes.

Lord HERSCHELL—The only point there made was that
they could not pass an Act for the whole Dominion which
was to affect localities separately.

Mr. NEWCOMBE—Yes.

> " Their Lordships understand the contention to be that, at least
> in the absence of a General Law of the Parliament of Canada the
> Provinces might have passed a local law of a like kind, each for its
> own Province, and that as the prohibitory and penal parts of the Act
> in question were to come into force in those counties and cities only in
> which it was adopted in the manner prescribed, or, as it was said ' by
> local option,' the legislation was in effect and on its face upon a matter
> of a merely local nature."

That is the argument that was urged, because it came into
effect in localities, in counties.

Lord WATSON—A great deal of the argument was founded upon this, that if the Dominion Parliament chose to exercise that power they must do so by means of an imperative Act; that to make the Act permissive was to enable some Provinces to escape from its incidence altogether, and that was not what was inte .ded at all.

Mr. NEWCOMBE—Yes.   Then follows a quotation from the Judgment of Chief Justice Allen, in which he says :—

"'Had this Act prohibited the sale of liquor, instead of merely restricting and regulating it, I should have had no doubt about the power of the Parliament to pass such an Act, but I think an Act which in effect authorises the inhabitants of each town or parish to regulate the sale of liquor, and to direct for whom for what purposes and under what conditions spirituous liquors may be sold therein, deals with matters of a merely local nature, which by the terms of the 16th sub-section of section 92 of the British North America Act are within the exclusive control of the Local Legislature.'   Their Lordships cannot concur in this view.   The declared object of Parliament in passing the Act is that there should be uniform legislation in all the Provinces respecting the traffic in intoxicating liquors, with a view to promote temperance in the Dominion.   Parliament does not treat the promotion of temperance as desirable in one Province more than in another, but as desirable everywhere throughout the Dominion.   The Act as soon as it was passed, became a law for the whole Dominion and the enactments of the first part, relating to the machinery for bringing the second part into force took effect and might be put in motion at once and everywhere within it."

Now with regard to the consideration urged that as the prohibitory and penal parts of the Act in question were to come into force in those counties and cities only in which it was adopted in the manner prescribed, or as it was said by "local option" the legislation was in effect, and on its face upon a matter of a merely local nature, I submit as to matters of a merely local and private nature that that expression must be construed to mean something less—a matter of a public and provincial nature.   Notwithstanding the word "local," of course it is not urged and could not be urged that this is a private measure.   But the word "private" probably throws some light upon the word "local," and may assist in the interpretation of that word.

Lord HERSCHELL—It is "local or private."

Mr. NEWCOMBE—Local or private; it is alternative; but the two are grouped together disjunctively.   But where the

Province is authorised to pass a measure with regard to a local matter, that is a matter which does not affect the Province generally—it does not affect the entire Province. If so, it would be taken out of the category of "local." Perhaps it would be fair to construe those words as having regard to local or private bills. They could pass local and private measures under that sub-head of the British North America Act, section 92. They could pass a measure which would ordinarily be given effect to by a private or local Bill, but not a matter of general and equal application to the entire Province. I submit that that is a construction which may be placed upon the words "private and local matters" for the purpose of saying that it is involved in the decision of *Russell* v. *The Queen*, and I say that the Province cannot pass a Prohibition Act, an Act prohibiting the sale of liquor, coming into force in the Province at large, coming into force generally throughout the Province. It cannot give effect to prohibition within its borders by its own legislation.

Lord DAVEY—The words are "generally all matters" which looks as if things not previously enumerated were considered as being within it.

Mr. NEWCOMBE—I submit the construction is that there are a large number of things enumerated in section 92 as to which authority is given to the Province, and it may be that the 16th sub-clause does not carry the Provincial legislative authority very much beyond what has been already conferred upon it, but whatever is conferred by those words is a general grant, in the last sub-section of section 92, which would enable the Province to deal with matters which are merely local and private. You have the word "merely" there, thus accentuating as I submit the limited character of the legislation which may be enacted under that Clause. In the case of *L'Union St. Jacques de Montreal* v. *Belisle* (L. R. 6 P. C. 31), there was a question raised as to legislation with regard to what were merely local or private matters, and their Lordships said, at Cartwright, page 68 of that case :—

> "The subject matter of this Act, the 38 Vict. chap. 58, is a matter of a merely local or private nature in the Province because it relates to a Benevolent or Benefit Society, incorporated in the City of Montreal within the Province which appears to consist exclusively of members

who would be subject *prima facie* to the control of the Provincial Legislature." And again " clearly the matter is private. Clearly it is local so far as locality is to be considered, because it is in the Province and in the City of Montreal."

I submit that is an illustration of what would be a private or local matter, and I am not aware of any decision of your Lordships' Board in which a matter has been considered local.

Lord WATSON—Would a matter be a matter of private nature if it affected every person in the Province ?

Mr. NEWCOMBE — I submit it would not be a local matter.

Lord WATSON—Do you say not : it is alternative, local or private? A private Bill here would simply relate perhaps to the affairs of some individual or company, but if it affects everybody in Britain it would not be a private Bill, and I do not see why we should include in local measures a measure which would affect every person in the Province. The word " local " so far as I have seen here may mean local as regards particular Provinces as distinguished from the whole Dominion, or local as regards part of a Province in contradistinction to the whole Province. It may be local as regards a particular locality, or it may mean practically the whole Province which would be local in respect to the whole Dominion.

Lord MORRIS—What you want is, local in the Province.

Lord WATSON—Look at the object of the enactment here. The object of the enactment here is to give legislative power to a Provincial Legislature with respect to matters that are provincial—shortly speaking ; I do not say that is a full definition—and to give to the Dominion Parliament matters which, as far as Canada is concerned, relate to the whole Dominion.

Mr. NEWCOMBE—I submit that the words " local matter in the Province " must be construed as meaning something less than the whole.

Lord WATSON—In any case the word must either apply to the Province, or concern some subject which belongs to the Province as distinguished from the Dominion, or must refer to some matter in which the Provinces have a common interest. Supposing the Parliament of Canada were under the impression that it would not be for the benefit of some of the Provinces to have certain legislation, but that it would be for the benefit of other Provinces to have it, is there power given under this Act to enable them to effect that legislation, or is it your contention that the power is taken away?

Lord Morris—What you are contending is that it is not given by these words.

Mr. Newcombe—It is not conferred ; general powers are not conferred.

Lord Morris—It is of a local or private nature in the Province, because it implies that that is not legislation affecting the whole Province in contradistinction to the Dominion.

Mr. Newcombe—It implies a grant to legist te with regard to a limited area within the Province—a limited locality in the Province as we speak of localities. Now the Canada Temperance Act, while it is an Act of general application to Canada does not in effect bring about uniformity of legislation in the various districts in which it may be brought into force. It does not contemplate equality of condition with regard to the right to sell spirituous liquors. It contemplates the opposite ; it brings about diversity of condition as to the several localities, as to the several counties, that is. There is the option of the electors which is to be exercised and which of course may work differently in different communities ; and then there is a provision in the Act which says, that if the Act be brought into force it is not to be repealed by the exercise of the popular will for a period of three years ; or if an election be held for the purpose of bringing the Act into force and the electors declare against it, then there shall be no election for the purpose of bringing it into force again for the period of three years. Therefore it brings about by force of Dominion Legislation this condition of things : that there may be a county in which it is illegal to sell spirituous liquors in quantities exceedi ₁ 10 gallons, and another adjoining county in which it is lawfu. to sell those liquors and in which it will remain lawful to sell them for a period of three years. In that

way while the legislation is general in its application it brings
about inequality and diversity with regard to the prohibition,
with regard to the right to sell intoxicating liquors.   In that
way, my Lords, I submit it involves a power to prohibit in a
locality and a power to declare freedom from prohibition
in a locality.   It is legislation relating to localities.   The
effect of the Judgment would seem to be that the Dominion
Parliament has authority to prohibit locally and as an illustration of that principle or as an illustration of what, I submit,
the Dominion has a right to do with regard to the prohibition
of the sale of liquors, take the Act which is found in the
Dominion Revised Statutes with regard to the preservation of
order near public works ;   that is an Act which provides that
where any public work is in course of construction under the
authority of the Canadian Government, a district may be
proclaimed in which the act shall come into operation, and
then in that district the sale of liquor is prohibited.   Now
that is legislation which is purely local, which can never come
into effect under the scope of the Act except as to localities,
and yet I submit that within the decision in *Russell* v.
The Queen it is an Act which is within the authority of
Parliament.

Then if legislation of that character is within the authority
of Parliament, it is legislation with regard to a particular
subject, the subject of prohibition that is, and I submit
that that is one subject which can only be regarded in one
aspect, which is only brought about for one purpose, and the
decisions of your Lordships' Board in which certain subjects
have been held to come within the Provincial jurisdiction and
also within the Dominion jurisdiction, having regard to the
standpoints from which they are regarded or the purpose for
which the legislation is enacted, are not applicable to this
case where we have a single subject, single as to aspect,
single as to the purpose in which it is to be dealt with.

Then there is a provision in section 94 of the British
North America Act with which your Lordships are familiar,
which provides for legislation as to uniformity of laws which
makes special provisions with regard to the Dominion authority
to legislate for uniformity of laws which section does not
include the subjects under consideration.

Now upon the question of Municipal Institutions, I

submit the exclusive power of the Legislatures with regard to
those Institutions is not intended to go further than to enable
the Legislatures to establish them, and any authority which
they may validly confer on Municipal Institutions must
be derived through or have regard to the other subjects
enumerated in section 92, which do not, I submit, include the
power to prohibit, and there appears to be no connection
between the Municipal Institutions and the subject of prohibition regarded in the abstract.   I would like to refer your
Lordships to the Judgment of Mr. Justice King, upon
page 108, at the top of the page, in which he says—

> "In treating of the exclusive powers of the provincial legislatures
> clause 8 of section 92 respecting Municipal Institutions was not in
> terms referred to in *Russell* v. *The Queen*, and this fact has sometimes
> been made use of in the way of criticism of that case.   Indeed in the
> argument of the Dominion License Act one of their Lordships expressed
> the opinion that clause 8 of section 92 had not been argued in *Russell*
> v. *The Queen*, but the Counsel then arguing (the present Lord
> Chancellor) stated that it appeared from a shorthand note of the
> argument that the point had been distinctly urged.   When *City of
> Fredericton* v. *The Queen* (which is known to be substantially the same
> case) was before this Court, the point was argued.   Mr. Lash, Q.C.,
> one of the Counsel for the Act thus alludes to the argument as adduced
> by the other side :   ' It is also contended that this law having for its
> ' object the suppression of drunkenness is a police regulation, and so
> ' within the powers of Municipalities,' &c.   In *Regina* v. *Justices of
> Kings*, Chief Justice Ritchie had previously dealt with the like conten-
> tion, and in *City of Fredericton* v. *The Queen*, adhered to that decision.
> To that case I beg to refer.
>
> "But what is more pertinent is the fact that after clause 8 of
> section 92 had been fully considered and given effect to in *Hodge* v.
> *The Queen*, their Lordships as though it might be thought to make a
> difference with *Russell* v. *The Queen* took occasion to re-affirm that
> decision :   'We do not intend to vary or depart from the reasons ex-
> pressed for our Judgment in that case.'"

Then on page 109 he says at the foot of the page :

> " Then is the power to prohibit reasonably or practically necessary
> to the efficient exercise   by the Province of an enumerated power ?
> It is urged that this is so with regard to clause 8 respecting Municipal
> Institutions   The licensing system is ordinarily associated with that
> subject and licensing is also pointed at in clause 9, but there is no
> inherent or ordinary association of prohibition with Municipal Institu-
> tions.   Neither in England nor the United States is this so.   The
> state of things in the Confederating Provinces at the time of Union will
> be referred to hereafter.   What is reasonably incidental to the exercise
> of general powers is often a practical question, more or less dependent
> upon considerations of expediency.   In several Judgments of the

Privy Council have placed the respective powers of the Dominion and
Provinces upon the subject on a wise and practical working basis,
affirming on the one hand the exclusive right of the Provinces to deal
with license and kindred subjects, and affirming on the other the right
of the Dominion to prohibit, either directly or through the method of
endowing the several provincial municipalities with a faculty of
accepting prohibition or retaining license. Wherein is it reasonably
necessary for purposes of Municipal Institutions that the Provinces
should have like power of suppression, to be exercised either directly
upon the entire Province or through the bestowment of a like faculty
upon the municipalities ? Why (in any proper constitution) should a
considerable trade be subjected to prohibition emanating from different
legislative authorities in the one country ? The suppression of a lawful
trade impairs the value of the power to raise revenue by indirect
taxation. *Prima facie* the power that levies indirect taxation has
the power to protect trade from suppression and the sole power of
suppression. And in a system of government where the Provinces
receive annual subsidies out of the Dominion treasury it seems
repugnant that the Provinces should through mere implications respecting Municipal Institutions possess the power to destroy a large
revenue-bearing trade. It is for the Dominion to determine for itself
whether or not such a trade shall be suppressed, and, if so, how and to
what extent. The Dominion has so expressed itself. It has entered
every municipality and offered to it the suppression within it of the
liquor trade under sanctions of Dominion law.

"It is further contended, however, that prohibition is local and
municipal, because that at the time of the Union two out of the
three original members of the Union (having then, of course, full
power of legislation) had conferred upon the municipalities a local
option of prohibition (within wider or narrower limits) and had
incorporated this provision in the Municipal Acts. Even had this
been general with all the Provinces I do not think that the conclusion
drawn from it is warranted in view of the whole of the British North
America Act, nor perhaps would it support the claim to deal with
the matter otherwise than through the like method of municipal local
option. But, assuming that a common understanding of words in an
unusual sense might be inferred from such a state of things, if it had
been general, the fact that in one of the confederating Provinces (New
Brunswick) there was no such provision, deprives the argument of the
weight that only an entire concensus could give to it. In New Brunswick
there were at the Union two groups of Municipal Institutions, the
representative kind (as in Upper and Lower Canada) throughout part
of the Province and the system of local government of counties through
the justices in session (as in Nova Scotia) throughout the remaining
part. But in neither kind was there vested the power of suppressing
the liquor trade. The Act in force in New Brunswick was 17 Victoria,
cap. 42 as from time to time revived and continued. This is important
for temperance legislation had gone further in New Brunswick than in
any other Province. In 1855 an Act was passed prohibiting throughout
the Province the importation, manufacture, and traffic in intoxicating

liquors. This was repealed in 1856 amid great political excitement, and the absence of local option at the time of the Union was not a casual omission. Notwithstanding the great weight of judicial authority the other way, I cannot, in view of this, give to the words Municipal Institutions as used in the British North America Act a meaning not inherent in them simply because of this extension of power to the municipalities in several, but not all, of the confederating Provinces. It seems to me that the contention in question comes to this, that the words Municipal Institutions are to be read not only as meaning everything inherent in or ordinarily associated with them, but also all other powers exercised by the municipalities of any of the confederating Provinces. I must add that, even if the practice had been general, such an excrescence on the municipal system would be removed by "... other provisions of the British North America Act."

Those were the observations of Mr. Justice King, and I submit that while " municipal institutions " might cover what would ordinarily be incidental to the exercise of municipal power they would not refer to what would be regarded as special or extraordinary such as the power to prohibit a trade, the power to prohibit the sale of intoxicating liquor. It might be possible that under Municipal Institutions the Provinces would have the power to prohibit a nuisance, to prohibit that which was obnoxious, but the prohibition of a trade brings one into contact with a different class of ideas, with a class of ideas that is not ordinarily associated with Municipal Institutions. The contention of the other side too, I submit, comes to this, that because under Municipal Institutions previous to confederation the Provinces had conferred upon the Municipalities the power to prohibit, therefore the Provinces may still confer the like power upon the Municipalities. That involves the idea, I submit, that the Provinces may now confer upon the Municipalities power which, so far as this particular subject of Municipal Institutions is concerned, they could not directly exercise. That is, they may do through the medium of Municipal Institutions what they could not do directly, and a construction of that kind, I submit, could not be reasonably adopted. Such a departure from the ordinary legislative procedure, if contemplated by the Act, one would have expected would have been expressly enacted.

Now, if your Lordships please, I submit that the subject of prohibition comes within Dominion authority under the general words of section 91 as legislation for the purpose of

the order and good government of Canada, having regard to
the subject of Criminal Law as stated in the case of *Russell* v.
The Queen. The two things are associated together in that
case.

[*Adjourned for a short time.*]

Mr. NEWCOMBE—If your Lordships please, I was, when
your Lordships adjourned, taking the point that the subject of
prohibition was within the scope of Dominion authority as to
legislation for the peace, order and good government of Canada,
having regard to Criminal Law, and upon that point I refer
your Lordships to the case of *Russell* v. *The Queen* (L. R.
7. App. Cases at page 838) at pages 21 to 23 in the 2nd volume
of Cartwright's Cases, from which I formerly cited. Their
Lordships said this :—

"Next their Lordships cannot think that the Temperance Act in
question properly belongs to the class of subjects 'property and civil
rights.' It has in its legal aspect an obvious and close similarity to laws
which place restrictions on the sale or custody of poisonous drugs or of
dangerously explosive substances. These things, as well as intoxicating
liquors, can of course be held as property, but a law placing restrictions
on their sale, custody or removal, on the ground that the free sale or use
of them is dangerous to public safety, and making it a criminal offence
punishable by fine or imprisonment to violate these restrictions, cannot
properly be deemed a law in relation to property in the sense in which
those words are used in the 92nd section. What Parliament is dealing
with in legislation of this kind is not a matter in relation to property
and its rights, but one relating to public order and safety. That is the
primary matter dealt with, and though incidentally the free use of
things in which men may have property is interfered with, that incidental interference does not alter the character of the law. Upon the
same considerations the Act in question cannot be regarded as legislation in relation to civil rights. In however large a sense these words
are used it could not have been intended to prevent the Parliament of
Canada from declaring and enacting certain uses of property and certain
acts in relation to property to be criminal and wrongful. Laws which
make it a criminal offence for a man wilfully to set fire to his own
house on the ground that such an act endangers the public safety, or
to overwork his horse on the ground of cruelty to the animal, though
affecting in some sense property and the right of a man to do as he
pleases with his own, cannot properly be regarded as legislation in
relation to property or to civil rights. Nor could a law which prohibited or restricted the sale or exposure of cattle having a contagious
disease be so regarded. Laws of this nature, designed for the promotion of public order, safety or morals, and which subject those who

contravene them to criminal procedure and punishment, belong to the subject of public wrongs rather than to that of civil rights. They are of a nature which fall within the general authority of Parliament to make laws for the order and good government of Canada, and have direct relation to criminal law, which is one of the enumerated classes of subjects assigned exclusively to the Parliament of Canada."

Then if your Lordships please that is the passage from the decision of *Russell* v. *The Queen* which refers the subject of prohibition to the general words "peace, order and good Government of Canada," and their Lordships state that it belongs to legislation of that character but having direct relation to Criminal Law, which is one of the enumerated subjects; and if by force of the connection of those two subjects it is to be referred to the two jointly or to the subject of Criminal Law singly, then we have a condition of affairs where the words "local and private matters" under section 92 would not admit of a construction which would entitle the Province to legislate. In the case of *Tennant* v. *The Union Bank* which has been referred to and which is in the Appeal cases, 1894, page 45, their Lordships stated what is probably merely a re-statement of the words of the Act :—

> " But section 91 expressly declares that 'notwithstanding anything in this Act' the exclusive legislative authority of the Parliament of Canada shall extend to all matters coming within the enumerated classes which plainly indicates that the legislation of that Parliament, so long as it strictly relates to these matters is to be of paramount authority."

so long as it strictly relates to what is enumerated in section 91 ; and as I understand the Judgment in *Russell* v. *The Queen* it was held there that the subject with which your Lordships were then dealing directly related to the subject of Criminal Law. Hence the authority of these two cases would be to refer the subject to one of the enumerated classes under section 91. That would override any authority which the Province otherwise might have under "private and local matters." It would also appear to follow I submit from these decisions that whatever authority a Province may have as to prohibition of Trade it could not pass a law as to the Province, as to its own legislative jurisdiction territorially speaking, in the words of the Canada Temperance Act.

Lord WATSON.—Do you maintain that the terms of sub-section 2 of section 91 gives to the Dominion Legislature power to prohibit or abolish a particular trade?

Mr. NEWCOMBE—Yes, my Lord, I submit that, because sub-section 2 is " all subjects dealing with Trade and Commerce."

Lord WATSON—Do you think that in any proper sense " Regulation " involves abolition ?

Mr. NEWCOMBE—In dealing with a general subject I submit so. The Regulation of Trade and Commerce is a large subject.

Lord WATSON—If it had been " Trade and Commerce " I could quite well have understood that these words might have implied abolition as well as regulation, but when the power given expressly is confined to the regulation of the liquor trade could they abolish it. I could quite understand their doing it in virtue of the general power given them at the commencement of the section

Mr. NEWCOMBE—If instead of the words " Regulation of Trade and Commerce " we had the words " the Regulation of the Liquor Trade," I should conceive that under that the Dominion Legislature could not destroy the subject by legislation which had been assigned to it. It could not say there shall be no liquor trade.

Lord WATSON—Are they to do away with that which is to be regulated ?

Mr. NEWCOMBE—They could not do away with that which is to be regulated, but it seems to me that the construction of the words which we have admit of the other view. While you could not in legislating with regard to Trade and Commerce or in regulating Trade and Commerce destroy Trade and Commerce entirely, you can regulate the subject generally. You can say that Trade and Commerce shall exist in certain commodities. You can in the exercise of that general power of regulation prohibit a particular trade. You do not destroy as you do in the other case the subject matter of legislation. You do not do away with the trade which is to be regulated because that section is not confined to any

s 2

particular trade. Now upon that question of the regulation
of trade, we contend, if your Lordships please, that legislation
of this character does come within sub-section 2 of section 91,
and in that connection I should like to refer to sections 122
and 132 of the British North America Act, section 122
says :—

> "The Customs and Excise Laws of each Province shall, subject
> to the provisions of this Act, continue in force until altered by the
> Parliament of Canada."

Section 132 says :—

> "The Parliament and Government of Canada shall have all powers
> necessary or proper for performing the obligations of Canada or of any
> Province thereof, as part of the British Empire towards Foreign
> Countries arising under Treaties between the Empire and such Foreign
> Countries."

Of course I do not refer to section 122 for the purpose of
showing that the Dominion has authority to levy Customs
and Excise. That of course we get under other provisions
of section 91, but *prima facie* it seems to me, absolutely the
power which may levy Customs and Excise, may also prohibit
importation or manufacture, and if importation and manufacture, therefore sale. We have under section 122 a
declaration of the Imperial Parliament that the Customs
and Excise laws which were in force in the several
Provinces at the time of confederation shall remain
until altered by the Parliament of Canada. Now I
will assume for the purpose of the argument that the
prohibitory power is what the Province asserts, not exclusively necessarily, but that they have power to prohibit ; and
supposing such a law had been enacted by the Province before
any change was made by the Parliament of Canada in the
customs and excise laws prevailing at the time of the Union,
then you would have prohibition and also legality so far as
customs and excise were concerned. You would have illegality
in the importation and in the sale so far as importation
and sale were concerned, but so far as levying Excise and
Customs' Duties upon the commodity were concerned you
would have a law authorising it. You would have a trade
legal for one purpose and illegal for the other purpose, which
is, I submit, a construction that cannot be reasonably adopted.

Lord WATSON—The exercise of that power by the Province

would not alter the Customs' Law. It would simply result in diminished revenue.

Mr. NEWCOMBE—No, my Lord, it would not alter the Customs' Law, but that is an argument to show that the Province does not have it.

Lord WATSON—It might affect more than the import trade of the Province. It might affect the import trade of the country.

Mr. NEWCOMBE—Yes.

Lord WATSON—The second ground makes it doubtful whether that power belongs to the Province. It is not at all likely that a power of that kind would be a power with reference to a local object within the meaning of sub-section 16. A municipal prohibition to take effect within the limits of a municipality may be a local subject within the meaning of sub-section 16, when a general prohibition of all imports would not be local.

Mr. NEWCOMBE—I was endeavouring to urge that this morning.

Lord WATSON—There are considerations affecting the one that do not affect the other. Supposing a man in Quebec or Lower Canada sends a quantity of spirits en route to Manitoba, and in Manitoba it is not allowed. Would that be a provincial matter, the stoppage of spirits not intended to stop in the Province and not intended to be consumed there? At present it does not appear to me it would be a provincial matter. It may be a provincial matter to the man affected in Quebec.

Mr. NEWCOMBE—And the position I was endeavouring to explain is this : if the Dominion may levy a Customs' Duty and the Dominion establishes a customs' law, it cannot be contended that the Province, by prohibiting the importation of the article on which the Dominion has declared there shall be collected a Customs' Duty, can thereby repeal the Dominion Statute. Then we have an article imported into Canada which is illegally brought in, but upon which a tax is legally levied. I submit, my Lords, that is an incongruous construction of the constitution. Upon this point I would refer your Lordships to the case of *Regina* v. *The Justices of Kings*, in the Supreme Court of New Brunswick, reported in 2 Cartwright at page 499, and particularly to the remarks of Chief Justice Ritchie on page 505. This is a decision of the Supreme Court of New Brunswick at the time when Chief Justice Ritchie was Chief Justice there. He afterwards became Chief Justice of the Supreme Court of Canada, and if your Lordships will permit me, I will read a few words—his Lordship said :—

> "To the Dominion Parliament of Canada is given the power to legislate exclusively on 'the regulation of trade and commerce' and the power of 'raising money by any mode or system of taxation.' The regulation of trade and commerce must involve full power over the matter to be regulated, and must necessarily exclude the interference of all other bodies that would attempt to intermeddle with the same thing. The power thus given to the Dominion Parliament is general without limitation or restriction, and therefore must include traffic in articles of merchandise, not only in connection with foreign countries, but also that which is internal between different provinces of the Dominion, as well as that which is carried on within the limits of an individual Province. As a matter of trade and commerce the right to sell is inseparably connected with the law permitting importation. If, then, the Dominion Parliament authorise the importation of any article of merchandise into the Dominion, and places no restriction on its being dealt with in the due course of trade and commerce, or on its consumption, but exacts and receives duties thereon on such importation, it would be in direct conflict with such legislation and with the right to raise money by any mode or system of taxation if the local Legislature of the Province into which the article was so legally imported, and on which a revenue was sought to be raised, could so legislate as to prohibit its being bought or sold and to prevent trade or traffic therein, and thus destroy its commercial value, and with it all trade and commerce in the article so prohibited, and thus render it practically valueless as an article of commerce on which a revenue could be levied. Again, how can the local Legislature prohibit or authorise the Sessions to prohibit (by arbitrarily refusing to grant any licenses) the sale of spirituous liquors of all kinds without coming in direct conflict with the Dominion Legislature on the subject of inland revenue, involving the right of manufacturing and distilling or making of spirits, &c., as regulated by the Act 31 Vict., c. 8, and the subsequent Acts in amendment thereof, and the excise duties leviable thereby, and the licenses authorised to be granted thereunder."

This is the case in which the Supreme Court of New Brunswick decided that a Province had not the right to prohibit as arising under a Statute which provided that no liquor should be sold without license, and that the Justices should have power to refuse a license.

Lord HERSCHELL.—That seems to conflict with *The Queen* v. *Hodge*.

Mr. NEWCOMBE—I was referring to the case on account of the remarks of the Chief Justice with reference to trade and commerce.

Lord HERSCHELL.—How do you reconcile the remarks of that learned judge with what was laid down by this Board in *The Queen* v. *Hodge* ? Do you say they are reconcilable or how do you propose to reconcile them ?

Mr. NEWCOMBE—We are dealing with the case of an absolute prohibition, and I understand the case of *The Queen* v. *Hodge* merely to decide that the Provinces may regulate.

Lord HERSCHELL.—That is what the Judgment of the Chief Justice really had reference to, regulation not prohibition.

Mr. NEWCOMBE—He says in so many words in this Judgment that the Provinces may prohibit.

Lord HERSCHELL.—He goes beyond prohibiting. His Judgment deals with regulating as well as prohibition and finds that that is illegal and *ultra vires* because it may interfere with the Revenue.

Mr. NEWCOMBE—Yes, my Lord. But when you take that case in connection with a case to which I was intending to refer of *Fredericton* v. *The Queen*, from which case *Russell* v. *The Queen* was in effect an Appeal, it seems to me that your Lordships have not intimated any dissent from the remarks of the learned Chief Justice as to the subject falling within trade and commerce, because in *Russell* v. *The Queen*, while your Lordships came to a conclusion favourable to Dominion jurisdiction by a process of excluding the legislative authority from section 92, yet it is stated in that case that no dissent is intimated from the Judgment of the Chief Justice of Canada in which he, having regarded the subject from the standpoint of Dominion authority, had come to the conclusion that the subject is within the regulation of trade and commerce.

Lord Herschell.—I dare say that they do not dissent, but that is not saying they assent.

Mr. Newcombe.—I was merely saying that that point is open, and that therefore I am entitled consistently with the decisions of this Board to rely upon what was stated in those two cases.

Lord Watson.—We are always inclined to stand on what is the main substance of the Act in determining under which of these provisions it really falls. That must be determined *secundum subjectam materiam* according to the purpose of the Statute as that can be collected from its leading enactments. When a legislature proceeds to enact that not less than a certain quantity of liquor shall ever be sold retail, what is the object of it? Is it for the physical benefit of the population that they are legislating? Is it because small quantities should not in their opinion be sold to any one that wants a drink? Or is it because they want to regulate the trade?

Mr. Newcombe.—If in fact it is a regulation of trade; but if in effect it is a prohibition of trade having regard to all the circumstances, and if it practically prevents the trade from being carried on, then it seems to me, assuming your Lordships are going to put a construction on the words " trade and commerce," which would throw the subject of regulation——

Lord Watson.—This legislation derives its vigour as much from the initial part of section 91 as from sub-section 2.

Mr. Newcombe.—If it derives anything from sub-section 2 it must be excluded from section 92.

Lord Watson.—They are simply introduced for the purpose of further specification but they are all contained in the first part of the section.

Mr. Newcombe.—They are all contained in the first part.

Lord Watson.—They are legislative charters to pass laws to the following effect.

Lord HERSCHELL—You are right in this, that if you could bring it within sub-section 2 then it is excluded from local matters under sub-section 16.

Mr. NEWCOMBE—I submit if I have to go to sub-section 2 at all to draw it within the Dominion authority, if it is necessary to invoke No. 2, then it cannot be within 16 or any Provincial power.

Lord WATSON—I quite admit it is a material part of your argument to bring it within sub-section 2.

Mr. NEWCOMBE—I quite admit the difficulty of that undertaking, but I submit that the legislation does come within No. 2, and I submit that if in effect we have legislation which regulates a trade generally or which affects a trade generally to the extent of destroying a trade by such legislation as might be passed——

Lord WATSON—We are not dealing here with any legislation, and we have no fact before us to start from as to legislation.

Mr. NEWCOMBE—I admit that.

Lord WATSON—All these suggestions as to what the Dominion Legislature might do are mere speculations. We are indulging in speculation in possible facts with the view of trying to illustrate the meaning of these two clauses in this Act. The Dominion Legislature have not passed any legislation.

Lord HERSCHELL—You say you are entitled to show it is legislation within trade and commerce, and that they alone could legislate?

Mr. NEWCOMBE—Yes; because the aspect of all these questions is prohibition. That is the question referred—the prohibition of trade. While the Dominion Parliament is given the right to regulate trade and commerce, it is inconsistent, I submit, with that, that the Province should prohibit a trade. If they prohibit a trade they take away that which the Dominion is to regulate.

Lord HERSCHELL—There is nothing left to regulate.

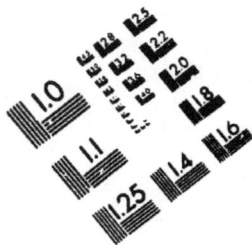

**IMAGE EVALUATION
TEST TARGET (MT-3)**

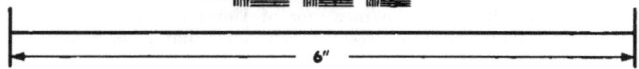

Photographic
Sciences
Corporation

23 WEST MAIN STREET
WEBSTER, N.Y. 14580
(716) 872-4503

Mr. NEWCOMBE—No ; there is nothing left to regulate.

Lord HERSCHELL—That would be true if they prohibited all trades, but it does not follow that they cannot prohibit one.

Mr. NEWCOMBE—It is only by a process of exclusion ; you would have to draw the line somewhere.

Lord WATSON—It would be regulating a trade if they regulated an import trade which conflicted with home production. If, in the interest of the home producer and his trade in Canada, they were to prohibit the importation of an article which he manufactures, into Canada, would not that be regulating trade ?

Mr. NEWCOMBE—I should think so ; but my point is this—tnat the effect of legislation which the Province could pass (if your Lordships were to give an affirmative answer to these questions as to prohibition), under the general affirmation of power in the Province to do these things, would be to interfere with the Dominion authority to regulate trade and commerce. I submit, my Lords, that this is the way in which these questions should be regarded. They are put categorically for the purpose of getting an affirmative answer.

Lord WATSON—Assuming this would be a regulation of trade, the next question is whether the extent of power given by sub-section 2 is such as to exclude anything in the nature of regulation of trade which is enacted for merely local purposes by the Provincial Legislature, or whether a mere general regulation of trade is not contemplated by sub-section 2.

Mr. NEWCOMBE—That enquiry would only affect the seventh question.

Lord WATSON—That is the next question to consider in the line of argument you have pursued.

Mr. NEWCOMBE—Supposing I have succeeded hitherto, it would involve a negative answer to each of the first six questions. It is the seventh question that contemplates that state of things.

Lord WATSON—I do not think the language you have got—assuming you are right as far as you have gone—warrants a favourable answer to the question when you consider the next point.

Mr. NEWCOMBE—I have tried—I fear unsuccessfully—to deal with that.

Lord WATSON—If you are content to intimate that it is immaterial to your argument, I will not discuss it with you any further.

Mr. NEWCOMBE—I admit we have to deal with that question of prohibition in the locality.

Lord MORRIS—Are you dealing with Clause 1 now?

Mr. NEWCOMBE—I am dealing generally with all.

Lord HERSCHELL—You are dealing with them altogether. If you bring it within trade and commerce you get rid of them all.

Mr. NEWCOMBE—Yes.

Lord HERSCHELL—If you bring it within trade and commerce in the sense which excludes any Provincial legislation, then that answers all the questions.

Mr. NEWCOMBE—Yes, my Lord. Now, I submit on that point that the exercise of Provincial authority as to regulation or whatever authority it may have with reference to trade must necessarily stop at the point of conflict between Dominion legislation and Provincial legislation. The power to prohibit sale, I submit, would necessarily imply the power to prohibit importation. The two go together. They cannot be separated as a trade problem—as a matter of trade and commerce.

Lord HERSCHELL—I do not think you need labour that. Whoever cannot prohibit sale *à fortiori* cannot prohibit importation. If you prove that the Province cannot prohibit sale, it cannot prohibit importation. You need not labour that.

Mr. NEWCOMBE—No, my Lord. Then look at section 132 of the British North America Act which I have referred to,

which gives the Dominion Government power to give effect
to trade obligations between the Empire and Foreign
Countries. The subject of trade and commerce and the
matter of the interchange of goods and commodities is a
subject which frequently is regulated by treaty.

Lord WATSON—It simply enacts that the Dominion
Government shall be the representative of the State in all
questions as to relations with Foreign Countries.

Mr. NEWCOMBE—Then, my Lord, a treaty is made
between Great Britain and France providing for the importation of wine into Canada.

Lord HERSCHELL—That it shall be admitted at certain
duties ; you have a strong case as to importation ; I should
think you might leave that.

Mr. NEWCOMBE—Does not it follow, if importation, then
sale ?

Lord HERSCHELL—Not at all, because all those grounds
you are speaking of are wholly inapplicable to sale. The
importation affects the whole Dominion of Canada. To allow
a Municipality to put fetters on the sale of something in a
particular district is one thing. You might as well say
because we have wine treaties here with France we could not
pass a Local Option Bill, or a Local Veto Bill. That is exactly
the same point. A good many people have been opposed to
the Local Veto Bill, but that is not a point which has ever yet
been taken, and I should not think it is a very hopeful one.

Lord WATSON—You might as well say that importation
into the Thames is a local question for London only.

Mr. NEWCOMBE—It would seem to go this far—that if
The Queen v. *Russell* has not already gone that far, the result
of that consideration would seem to be that a Province could
not prohibit generally for itself, I submit.

Lord WATSON—If it was shewn it was not a matter per-
taining to the Province, *prima facie* on the face of section 92
the Provincial Legislature would have no power to deal with it.

Lord MORRIS—The way it strikes me is that the first

question implies that the Province would have the power of prohibiting the trade of a publican because it could prohibit the only way he could exercise the sale of his intoxicating drink. Is that consistent with sub-section 2 of section 91 which gives the legislation as to trade to the Dominion ? It abolishes the trade of a publican.

Mr. NEWCOMBE—Then it in effect abolishes the whole trade.

Lord MORRIS—It abolishes the trade of a publican if he cannot sell or carry on.

Mr. NEWCOMBE—It abolishes the trade of the importer and the manufacturer also, because they are deprived of the means of getting their commodity to the consumer which is necessary for the effective carrying on of all trade.

Lord MORRIS—The license is only applicable to the individual that is refused ; but if they refused all licenses it would amount to the same thing.

Lord HERSCHELL—My difficulty of course is that you may affect trade just as much by limiting it to licensed people and making your qualifications for a license as tight as you may do, as by prohibiting sale. In the one case you hit a few people and in the other many. Each of them regulates trade, and this Board has held in *Hodge* v. *The Queen* that in that sense you may regulate. That is the difficulty.

Lord WATSON—On other grounds that it must be a local matter within the meaning of sub-section 16.

Mr. NEWCOMBE—In the *Hodge* case it was referred to three separate things, to Nos. 8, 15 and 16, but the legislation in the *Hodge* case was merely regulation.

Lord HERSCHELL—If it was merely regulation it is more fatal to you. You use the very word. Regulation of what ? Of the trade of a publican. You say that cannot be done by regulation of trade and commerce under sub-section 2 of section 91. It is just as fatal. In what sense is compelling a person to take out a license, and saying nobody shall sell who is not licensed, regulation, in which it is not equally regulation to say nobody shall sell at all ?

Lord WATSON—You must accept the start. Regulation such as you had in *Hodge* v. *The Queen* is not regulation of trade within the meaning of sub-section 2. It necessarily follows.

Mr. NEWCOMBE—I admit that.

Lord WATSON—Why does the extension of a regulation of that sort, which instead of being partial is total prohibition become a regulation of trade? Why does the partial prohibition of a right to sell fail to constitute regulation of trade, and, if so, why does prohibition entirely constitute regulation of trade?

Lord MORRIS—Does not regulation of trade imply that the trade is to exist under certain circumstances?

Mr. NEWCOMBE—Yes.

Lord MORRIS—The trade is to exist, but to exist under certain circumstances; but abolishing such trade is not regulating it.

Lord HERSCHELL—The Act does not say the regulation of this trade. It is the regulation of trade generally. One may be said to regulate trade by prohibiting or putting a fetter on a particular trade. If you prohibit all trades, you certainly do not regulate trade; but you may be said to regulate trade by saying certain trades shall be unlawful. But then it has been already held that the Provincial Legislature may regulate trade in the sense of putting very large fetters upon a particular trade. Why may not they more completely fetter it, without regulating trade in the sense of sub-section 2, if they do not regulate it by putting the milder fetter on it? Each of them interferes with the trade and the way it is carried on. That is the difficulty I feel.

Mr. NEWCOMBE—The whole Act is to be read and construed together. Dealing with the regulation of trade in *Hodge* v. *The Queen*, the decision was that in the exercise of police authority the Legislature had the right to impose restrictions to limit the number, to prescribe the hours as to taverns and so on. It was under these powers which are conveyed either by "Municipal Institutions," by "the imposition of fines and penalties for the violation of Provincial Statutes," or "private and local matters," their Lordships held that there was a power vested in the Provincial

Legislature to regulate the particular trade as a trade more
or less noxious and more or less harmful, which might have
a bad effect on the community. Now what that case decides
is that such a power is vested in the Provincial Legislature
for the good of the community, but it does not go to the
length at all of deciding that they have a right to destroy it.
I submit that their Lordships did read into section 92 for
the purpose of deciding *Hodge* v. *The Queen* " Regulation of
the Liquor Trade," that is, the decision proceeds, as if
those powers had been given to the local Legislature. The
decision cannot be put any higher or stronger than that
against me. But when we come to the " prohibition " of
the trade, that is an entirely different thing. That is a
thing which I submit the Provinces have no power to do
under any one of the enumerated classes in section 92 and I
submit that the decision in *Hodge* v. *The Queen* does not
controvert that proposition. If I want any authority upon
the point I am arguing with regard to trade and commerce,
I refer to the case of *Frederickton* v. *The Queen*, which is
reported in 2 Cartwright's cases, page 27.

Lord DAVEY—Before you leave the subject of " trade and
commerce," I should be very glad to know what you say is
the meaning of those words, and how far, if at all, you accept
the definition given by Sir Montague Smith in the *Citizens
Insurance Company's* case?

Mr. NEWCOMBE—I am going to refer to that.

Lord HERSCHELL—*Frederickton* was the case in which
Russell was the Appeal?

Mr. NEWCOMBE—Yes, my Lord. I will not detain your
Lordships by reading it at length, but I would refer your
Lordships to the remarks of the learned Chief Justice on
pages 39 and 40 of the Report in the 2nd volume of
Cartwright. In that case his Lordship expressly re-affirms
the decision which I referred to, given while he was Chief
Justice of New Brunswick, in the case of *Regina* v. *The
Justices of Kings County*, and he uses these words which I
would like to read :—

" I think it equally clear that the local legislatures have not "·e
power to prohibit, the Dominion Parliament having not only   ıe

general powers of legislation, but also the sole power of regulating as well internal as external trade and commerce, and of imposing duties of Customs and Excise; and having by law authorised the importation and manufacture of alcoholic liquors——"

Lord WATSON—The only question that is raised there is the power of the Dominion Parliament. There was nothing done against it or proposed to be done. He is construing the section.

Mr. NEWCOMBE—He is construing the section and referring to the subject of trade and commerce, he says :—

"——and having by law authorised the importation and manufacture of alcoholic liquors, and exacted such duties thereon, and so far legalised the trade and traffic therein, to allow the Local Legislatures, under pretence of police regulation, on general grounds of public policy and utility, by prohibitory laws, to annihilate such trade and traffic, and practically deprive the Dominion Parliament of a branch of trade and commerce from which so large a part of the public revenue was at the time of Confederation raised in all the Provinces, and has since been in the Dominion, never could have been contemplated by the framers of the British North America Act, but is, in my opinion, in direct conflict with the powers of Parliament, as well over trade and commerce as with their right to raise a revenue by duties of import and excise."

Those are the observations which were before their Lordships in *Russell* v. *The Queen*.

Now my Lords, in the case of *The Citizens Insurance Company* v. *Parsons* (1 Cartwright, page 277), there are some observations upon this subject. That was a case in which the power of the Province to annex statutory provisions to insurance contracts was questioned. Counsel for the Respondent in arguing that case stated that :—

"With regard to the validity of the Act the real question is whether insurance is trade and commerce within the meaning of section 91, number 2, of the Act of 1867. If the other side can establish their definition of trade as that of carrying on business for a profit there is nothing more to be said, but they gave no authority for that definition which rests only on imagination."

Reference was made to show that insurance was not a trade. The point that appears to have been urged there was whether the business of insurance was a trade or not within the meaning of the section. In the Judgment of their Lordships the meaning of the words " the regulation of trade and commerce " is referred to not apparently as necessary for the purpose of the decision, but some observations were made upon that subject. This was one of the earlier cases under the British North America Act, and it was stated—at L. R. 7 App. Cas. p. 112 :—

"The words regulation of trade and commerce, in their unlimited sense, are sufficiently wide, if uncontrolled by the context and other parts of the Act, to include every regulation of trade ranging from political arrangements in regard to trade with foreign Governments, requiring the sanction of Parliament, down to minute rules for regulating particular trades. But a consideration of the Act shews that the words were not used in this unlimited sense. In the first place, the collocation of No. 2 with classes of subjects of national and general concern affords an indication that regulations relating to general trade and commerce were in the mind of the Legislature when conferring this power on the Dominion Parliament. If the words had been intended to have the full scope of which in their literal meaning they are susceptible, the specific mention of several of the other classes of subjects enumerated in sect. 91 would have been unnecessary; as—15 Banking; 17 Weights and Measures; 18 Bills of Exchange and Promissory Notes; 19 Interest, and even 21, Bankruptcy and Insolvency. 'Regulation of trade and commerce' may have been used in some such sense as the words 'regulations of trade' in the Act of Union between England and Scotland (6 Anne, c. 11), and as these words have been used in Acts of State relating to trade and commerce; Article 5 of the Act of Union enacted that all the subjects of the United Kingdom should have 'full freedom and intercourse of trade and navigation' to and from all places in the United Kingdom and the Colonies; and Article 6 enacted that all parts of the United Kingdom, from and after the Union, should be under the same 'prohibitions, restrictions and regulations of trade.' Parliament has at various times since the Union passed laws affecting and regulating specific trades in one part of the United Kingdom only, without its being supposed that it thereby infringed the Articles of Union. Thus the Acts for regulating the sale of intoxicating liquors notoriously vary in the two Kingdoms. So with regard to Acts relating to bankruptcy and various other matters. Construing, therefore, the words 'regulation of trade and commerce' by the various aids to their interpretation above suggested, they would include political arrangements in regard to trade requiring the sanction of Parliament; regulation of trade in matters of inter-provincial concern, and it may be that they would include general regulation of trade affecting the whole Dominion. Their Lordships abstain on the present occasion from any attempt to define the limits of the authority of the Dominion Parliament in this direction. It is enough for the decision of the present case to say that, in their view, its authority to legislate for the regulation of trade and commerce does not comprehend the power to regulate by legislation the contracts of a particular business or trade, such as the business of Fire Insurance, in a single Province, and therefore that its legislative authority does not in the present case

o

conflict or compete with the power over property and civil rights assigned
to the Legislature of Ontario by No. 13 of Section 92."

Those were the remarks of the Judicial Committee in the
case of *The Citizens Insurance Company* v. *Parsons*, and I observe
that in a much later case of *The Bank of Toronto* v. *Lambe*
(which is reported in 12 App. Cas. 575 and the 4th Cartwright page 21) there is this statement——

Lord Herschell—That case you have already referred
us to.

Mr. Newcombe—I think my learned friend called your
Lordships attention to that, but I am going to refer to the
same passage that he did for the purpose of showing what
my point is upon it.   It was said there :—

> " The words ' regulation of Trade and Commerce' are indeed very
> wide, and in *Severn's* case, it was the view of the Supreme Court that
> they operated to invalidate the license duty which was there in question.
> But since that case was decided, the question has been more completely
> sifted before the Committee in *Parsons'* case, and it was found
> absolutely necessary that the literal meaning of the words should be
> restricted in order to afford scope for powers which are given exclusively
> to the provincial legislatures."

Now as *The Citizens Insurance Company* v. *Parsons* is interpreted
and explained by the case of *The Bank of Toronto* v. *Lambe*,
it only affects the point with which I am dealing to this
extent that it is necessary to limit and restrict (to what degree
is not decided) the interpretation of the words " regulation
of trade and commerce" in order to afford scope for the
powers which are given exclusively to Provincial Legislatures.
Here the power is not given exclusively to the Provincial
Legislature.

Lord Watson—The Judgment which was delivered by
Lord Hobhouse contains some points which are of very great
importance, and in *Parsons'* case a similar question arose.
One question that ought to be raised and considered in this
case is how far sub-section 2 of 91, and sub-section 16 of 92
ought to be read together.   There is a very marked illustration
of that in *Parsons'* case, as to whether one sub-section of 91
gives a general power of raising taxation by any means.
There is a sub-section in 92 which gives to the Province
direct taxation.   It was held that although the sub-section
of 91 read by itself was wide enough to include the power of

both sub-sections, yet construing the one in the light of the other it is said it is evident that it is not intended to include direct taxation within the Province in the previous sub-section.

Lord DAVEY—Both parties may have the power of direct taxation.

Lord WATSON—His Lordship said :—

"Then is there anything in section 91 which operates to restrict the meaning above ascribed to section 92 ? Class 3 certainly is in literal conflict with it. It is impossible to give exclusively to the Dominion the whole subject of raising money by any mode of taxation, and at the same time to give to the Provincial Legislatures, exclusively, or at all the power of direct taxation for provincial or any other purposes. This very conflict between the two sections was noticed by way of illustration in the case of *Parsons.*"

Then he quotes what their Lordships said.

Lord HERSCHELL—In that case if you found anything enumerated in 92 the Provincial Legislature had it even although there may be something in 91 which in wide terms would include it, but at the end of 91 there is a provision which only applies to item 16 in 92, and that provision is that you cannot get in under those words "local and private nature" anything which is in one of the enumerated classes of 91. That is your stronghold on this point. If you can bring it within 92.

Mr. NEWCOMBE—That is my point, my Lord, that it is enumerated there.

Lord HERSCHELL—It may throw light upon the construction which you put upon 91.

Lord WATSON—I do not think their Lordships went further than to say you may fairly read one with the other, and compare one clause with the language of the other in order to ascertain how far it was meant to give a more comprehensive or a less comprehensive power to the Dominion than 91.

Lord DAVEY—Do you accept the definition given, or have you any criticism to give on the definition given by Sir Montague Smith in *Parsons'* case, namely, that the regulations of trade and commerce related to regulations of inter-provincial trade, or trade of the Dominion with outside nations ?

Mr. NEWCOMBE—I submit that it must have a larger scope than that.

Lord DAVEY—What do you say it means ?

Lord MORRIS—I do not know how you can define it more than what it says.

Lord DAVEY—Are you prepared to carry it so far as to say that whenever any enactment touches trade and commerce, and in any way interferes with or affects trade and commerce, that that would be *ultra vires* of the Provincial Legislature ?

Mr. NEWCOMBE—That is a very broad proposition.

Lord HERSCHELL—You can hardly go so far without saying that *Hodge* v. *The Queen* was wrong, because no one can say that that particular trade was not most materially affected by the fetters imposed.

The LORD CHANCELLOR—You do not use such a word as "affected." The truth is you cannot give any effect to such a word without saying that the whole region of thought is excluded from legislation if you use that word. It affects it if it touches it at all.

Lord HERSCHELL—Could you deny that that Act which was in question in *Hodge* v. *The Queen* did regulate the trade of licensed vitualling or selling spirits within the Province of Ontario ? It prescribed conditions under which alone it could be carried on. Is not that regulating ?

Mr. NEWCOMBE—It regulated it by means of the exercise of police powers.

Lord HERSCHELL—You may call it a police power, but it determined it. That was the purpose and object of doing it —not what was done. What was done was to regulate and prescribe the conditions under which alone it could be carried on.

Mr. NEWCOMBE—Perhaps I could make myself clear by this illustration. Suppose instead of intoxicating liquors it had been groceries or dry goods, or something that was not harmful to the community. I submit that the decision does not involve that the Province should pass a similar license law as to dealing in sugar for instance.

Lord Morris—Or flour?

Mr. Newcombe—Or flour.

Lord Davey—If you say that the Dominion has an exclusive regulation of the trade and commerce, if it did regulate trade and commerce it may have been within it.

Mr. Newcombe—That is an illustration of what your Lordships have laid down about a matter having two aspects and two purposes.

Lord Herschell—You may admit it has two aspects, whether it is flour or anything else.

The Lord Chancellor—I do not quite understand what you mean by a distinction between spirituous liquors and flour. What is the difference?

Mr. Newcombe—I was dealing with the case of *Hodge* v. *The Queen*, in which it was held that Statute which dealt with the sale of intoxicating liquor in the way of putting restrictions on it——

The Lord Chancellor—"Intoxicating liquor" is a phrase which has been often quarrelled with. What is the difference between liquor in the category of trade and commerce and innocent flour?

Lord Davey—Or tobacco?

Lord Watson—Or milk, or soda water?

The Lord Chancellor—I thought you said there was a difference.

Lord Morris—There is a police regulation everywhere as regards the sale of intoxicating liquors.

The Lord Chancellor—I am not aware that there is.

Lord Morris—I think so.

Mr. NEWCOMBE—Their Lordships decided in *Hodge* v. *The Queen* that under 8, or under 15, or under 16—

Lord HERSCHELL—Not under each of those separate or alone. To my mind, unless it came under 16 it could not have come under 8 or under 15; 15 cannot stand by itself, because 15 is only imposing penalties for the purpose of any of the things remitted to the Province. Therefore it could not have come under 15.

The LORD CHANCELLOR—Before you go to *Hodge* v. *The Queen* would you kindly tell me what is the difference in your view between flour and liquor ?

Mr. NEWCOMBE—This is the point I was endeavouring to make about it under these sub-sections of section 92 in *Hodge* v. *The Queen*.

The LORD CHANCELLOR—Please try to forget *Hodge* v. *The Queen*.

Mr. NEWCOMBE—It is with reference to *Hodge* v. *The Queen* that I make the distinction. If your Lordship excludes that I cannot distinguish it.

The LORD CHANCELLOR—Do you say *Hodge* v. *The Queen* has raised a distinction between those two subjects ?

Mr. NEWCOMBE—I base the distinction upon *Hodge* v. *The Queen*—that is, that *Hodge* v. *The Queen* upheld the power of the Provincial Legislature to regulate the trade in the way of restricting and imposing conditions in the exercise of police powers which were conferred for the good of the community generally, under the several sub-heads to which his Lordship has referred.

Lord MORRIS—They expressly held, which is the important part of it, that a regulation of that kind was not a regulation within the meaning of sub-section 2.

Mr. NEWCOMBE—That it was the regulation of a trade which was, or in the view of many people is, held to be harmful, noxious and dangerous to the community.

Lord HERSCHELL—Inasmuch as we have here to deal with this very trade if this Board differentiated it from all

others why cannot we now put all others aside and deal
with it.

Mr. NEWCOMBE—Very likely. I was endeavouring to
answer his Lordship the Lord Chancellor when he asked me
to distinguish between flour and liquor.

Lord HERSCHELL—You introduced it. If it is not
regulating trade within the meaning of sub-section 2 of 91
to put twenty fetters on it, does it become so if you put
twenty more ?

Mr. NEWCOMBE—If you go to the extent of prohibition
I submit, yes.

Lord HERSCHELL—Why is one regulating more than the
other ?

Mr. NEWCOMBE—Because it is destroying that which is
to be legislated about.

Lord HERSCHELL—I could have understood an argument
that prohibition was not regulating while that of fetters was ;
but I do not understand an argument which says that you
may fetter it by one fetter after another and prescribe one
condition after another of its being carried on, that that is
not regulating the trade, but if you say it is not to be carried
on at all that is regulating the trade. The converse I could
understand but not that.

Lord WATSON—That is to say it begins to come within
the clause when it ceases to be a regulation.

Lord DAVEY—One must give some meaning to the words
" trade and commerce " which is consistent with the fact of
the provincial legislature's having certainly the right to fetter
and I should say to make regulations prescribing the conditions under which trade must be carried on, not only
because the Board so decided in *Hodge* v. *The Queen*, but
because I find, among other things, power to require them to
take out licenses, true only for revenue purposes, but still
that is a fetter on a person carrying on a trade, that he
cannot do so without paying a certain sum for a license.
That is a fetter and a regulation.

Lord WATSON—The difficulty I find raised is a difficulty that arises in other cases. That case determines what in a general sense constitutes regulations of a trade ; that you cannot say that imposing fetters and conditions on the way in which it was to be carried on which affected the trade and the mode of carrying it on are not regulations of a trade within the meaning of sub-section 2 ; and that at once raises a question where does the distinction begin between that kind of regulation and that which is to be taken to be regulation within the meaning of sub-section 2. You put it (I cannot follow the argument) that whenever it becomes prohibition you are within sub-section 2. To my mind you are out of sub-section 2 when you get a prohibition. You have no longer a regulation when you have got the length of prohibition. It is for these reasons that I cannot follow the line of argument.

Mr. NEWCOMBE—Sub-section 2 is general, and in the regulation of trade and commerce as a general subject it would be competent to prohibit a particular trade while under a provision authorising the regulation of a particular trade they could not prohibit it.

Lord WATSON—That expression was used in *Parsons'* case. I am not sure it was a very happy one, but it is apt to be misused, and it is apt to mislead. It is not general as including all particulars, but it is general as distinguished from certain particulars. The decision is that certain particulars would be general if you were to read the word in all its general senses, but you may make certain conditions general in a sense if they apply to all trades. At the present moment I am not prepared to say what the proper definition of that is, or what was precisely meant, but it certainly was intended to suggest this, that while special regulations might be made by the Dominion Parliament the function of the Supreme Parliament was to enact regulations of a more general description. It is very difficult to define it.

Mr. NEWCOMBE—I submit that the case of *The Bank of Ontario* v. *Lambe* is an authority for confining the decision in the *Citizens Insurance Company* v. *Parsons* to something which would not interfere with my argument in this case,

because it is established that this is not a case in which the
Province has exclusive authority.   Now, leaving the subject
of trade and commerce, I submit that, however this question
might be regarded if the Dominion had not legislated upon
the subject, by the enactment of the Canada Temperance
Act we have occupied the field of legislation, and that there
is no room for Provincial enactment upon the subject.   In
other words, the Provincial Legislature are precluded from
interfering with prohibitory legislation inasmuch as such
interference would affect the Dominion Statute.

Lord WATSON—I suppose you read the provisions of that
Act as being directly restrictive and as giving a license to sell
freely in those localities where it has not been adopted ?

Mr. NEWCOMBE—Yes, my Lord.

Lord WATSON—Do you read that as expressing both these
things ?

Mr. NEWCOMBE—I think so.

Lord HERSCHELL—I think you must.

The LORD CHANCELLOR—I think so.

Lord WATSON—The field is not occupied unless that is so.

Mr. NEWCOMBE—The field must be occupied consistently
with the Judgment in *Russell* v. *The Queen.*

Lord WATSON—It has no effect except in those regions
where it has been adopted.   Outside these localities it is not
operative and not intended to be operative, in fact there is no
law applicable to them, but there is a law applicable to them if
you read that as a law dispensing with all restrictions.   I
should think it was almost necessary to your argument to
read it in that way.   If you say the field is occupied, it must
be in that sense.

Lord DAVEY—What you mean, I presume, is this, that
assuming for a moment that there is in one sense a concurrent
line of legislation, if the Dominion has legislated on the
subject, then the Dominion Legislation is paramount over any
Provincial Legislation.

Mr. NEWCOMBE—Yes, we have dealt with the subject and it must prevail.

Lord WATSON—If anybody was to go to a part of Canada where the Temperance Law has not been adopted, would it be true to say that there was any Statute law applicable to that place until it had been adopted ? Would it not be more correct to say that there was no law as yet applicable ?

Mr. NEWCOMBE—There is legislation which it is open to the community to bring into force.

Lord HERSCHELL—Supposing that this is not within 91 and 92 at present, but it is legislation which the Parliament of Canada had power to enact by virtue of the provisions for peace, order and good government of Canada, and if they thought with a view to the benefit of the whole community of the Dominion that this legislation was sufficient, what would there be in that inconsistent with a particular Province coming to the conclusion that in its particular case some other legislation in respect of liquor, further legislation owing to its local circumstances was necessary and desirable ? Supposing that apart from the Dominion Legislation, which is again the hypothesis, it would be competent for it so to enact under 16, and supposing it was therefore within its legislative power ? I do not quite follow you.

Mr. NEWCOMBE—The idea of uniformity——

Lord HERSCHELL—The hypothesis on which you are going is this : that it was within the legislative power of the Provincial Legislature notwithstanding that it was within the power of the Dominion Parliament to legislate for the whole community as it thought necessary with reference to liquor. Of course that would prevent the Provincial Legislature from interfering in any way with the legislation of the Dominion, but why should it prevent it exercising its existing legislative competence in a manner not so inconsistent, which would not in any way interfere, but which might remain side by side and be operative as well as the Dominion Legislation ?

Lord WATSON—Does not that depend to some extent on

whether the power of the Dominion Parliament is derived from sub-section 2 ?

Lord HERSCHELL—I am asking the learned Counsel to assume it is not within the sub-section 2. If it is within sub-section 2, the Provincial Legislature could not do it at all ; therefore, for your present purpose—saying that the field has been occupied—you assume that the Provincial Legislature could do it, and you assume therefore that the law is against you as regards its being within sub-section 2. You are then driven to assume it to be within 91—1. Then I put it to you, in such a case, what is there to prevent the Legislature of the Province legislating for the Province on the same subject as the Dominion Parliament has legislated upon it, but in a manner not inconsistent with it, and in a manner confined to that Province ?

Mr. NEWCOMBE—Because that would produce that state of inequality which it was the object of the Canada Temperance Act to overcome ?

Lord HERSCHELL—This Board, in *Russell* v. *The Queen*, did not decide it on the ground that it was intended to overcome that at all, but that it was intended to deal with the question of temperance to that extent, at all events, as a matter in which the whole Dominion was interested, and not merely any particular Province. That is what *Russell* v. *The Queen* said.

Lord WATSON—I do not quite understand how far you carry that idea of equality and inequality. Do you say where there is an Act passed for the benefit of the Province under the first rule of the section, the Dominion Parliament must enact equally the same rule over all Provinces. If so, it raises rather an argument against you, because it would come to this, that the Dominion Parliament — the paramount Parliament—although they were satisfied that a particular locality and a particular Province required special treatment and special provisions to be made for its welfare, yet they would be absolutely helpless to do so ; and this curious result would follow if that is the right result—that they being unable to do it, and it not being given according to your argument to the Provincial Legislature, that power to enact

this piece of legislation has been kept out of the British
North America Act by the Imperial Parliament here.

Mr. NEWCOMBE—My argument involves, I think, the
opposite to that.

Lord WATSON—It may be that I am pressing that a
little too far, because it may be possible that in passing an
Act having a similar view and intended to produce the same
state of things throughout all the Dominion of Canada, that
there may be power (I am not prepared to negative the proposition) to adapt this means to the circumstance of any
particular Province. I have heard the other point put as if
it was an iron rule. I am not altogether satisfied that that
must be so.

Mr. NEWCOMBE—I am arguing from *Russell* v. *The Queen*.
So far as the point your Lordship makes is concerned, I
would concede this as a matter of illustration: Supposing it
was admittedly desirable that there should be a bankruptcy
and insolvency law for the Province of Ontario, and none for
the rest of Canada—supposing that was desirable for the
peace, order and good government of Canada, I should have
thought that the Dominion Parliament could give effect to
such a law. Either it must be so, or else that is a question
which does not admit of solution in Canada. I think all the
authority which was previously vested in the Provinces must
have been distributed.

Lord HERSCHELL—That is a case in which clearly the
Province could not legislate for itself. It may very well be
that the Province who desired legislation could only get it
through the Dominion Parliament, and it does not follow that
it can only get it at the expense of all the other colonists
who do not want it.

Lord WATSON—They have no power to effect bankruptcy
except in their power to deal with civil rights, and we have
very recently held that they may exercise that power so
long as there is no bankruptcy system with which the enactment comes into collision.

Mr. NEWCOMBE—So far as it is property and civil rights
as distinguished from bankruptcy.

Lord WATSON—They are absolutely excluded from legislating in bankruptcy, and they are not absolutely excluded from legislating in local matters.

Mr. NEWCOMBE—I thought my proposition involved this, that as to any subject as to which legislative authority is exclusively conferred upon Canada, Canada might limit the operation of its legislation upon that subject to the particular part of its territory. But the decision in *Russell* v. *The Queen* L. R. 7 App. Cas. at page 841, proceeds on the point of uniformity :—

> " The declared object of Parliament in passing the Act is that there should be uniform legislation in all the Provinces respecting the traffic in intoxicating liquors with a view to promote temperance in the Dominion."

That assumes this, that the Dominion Parliament has considered this matter and come to the conclusion, that for the peace, order and good government of Canada it is necessary that there should be uniform legislation in order to promote temperance. They have effected a uniform system.

Lord HERSCHELL—Anything less like a uniform system than a system to be adopted or not at the will of a particular part of the Dominion I cannot conceive. If that was necessary for the Judgment in *Russell* v. *The Queen*, I should be in doubt whether the Judgment in *Russell* v. *The Queen* is right.

Mr. NEWCOMBE—" Parliament does not treat the promotion of temperance as desirable in one Province more than in another."

Lord HERSCHELL—Quite so—the promotion of temperance, but what they meant by a uniform system was that they should have a system capable of application to every part of the Dominion as distinguished from treating temperance as a matter solely to be confined to each Province.

Lord DAVEY—This is how Mr. Justice Sedgewick (at p. 105) states it :—

> " The Federal Parliament has already seized itself of jurisdiction. It has passed the Scott Act. It has prescribed the method by which in Canada prohibition may be secured ; and is not any local enactment

purporting to change that method or otherwise secure the desired end for the time being inoperative, overridden by the expression of the controlling legislative will?"

That is the argument you adopt.

Mr. NEWCOMBE—Yes, my Lord, I adopt that.

"The objects and scope of the legislation are still general, namely, to promote temperance by means of a uniform law throughout the Dominion."

That is another extract from the Judgment in *Russell* v. *The Queen* at p. 841. My understanding of this Judgment was that it did depend upon uniformity of the law, because it is so referred to a good many times in the Judgment.

Lord HERSCHELL—Uniformity of the law would not necessarily promote temperance better, if side by side with the existence of that law, there was in a particular Province a law still more stringent, always supposing that stringent legislation promotes temperance. Their object which is said to be temperance would not be advanced by that. They may have gone as far as they thought public opinion would render it possible for them to go, but if in the Dominion public opinion would promote something even further, what is there to conflict with the Dominion Act or its operation? It is all working to the same end.

Mr. NEWCOMBE—If the Legislatures can supplement this system or can enact prohibition, then you have them defeating that which was the declared object of Parliament.

Lord HERSCHELL—This seems to me sometimes a little apart from the assumption. The assumption is that this is a matter within the power of the Provincial Legislature; it was down to the date of the Canada Temperance Act. You have to show that that power is gone. Can it be gone by anything but a law of the Dominion which would make their enactment inconsistent with it. If the two could operate side by side without any conflict of the one with the other how can their legislative power have been taken away by Canada passing that Act?

Lord WATSON—If the intention of the legislature was to keep a man sober, in this sense never to let him get more than half drunk, would their intention be defeated by someone keeping him sober ?   Is not that the question we are asked to consider ?

Lord DAVEY—I suppose you would say that the Canada Temperance Act is in a sense permissive because it permits the sale of sacramental wines (I take that because it comes first) or medicine.   A man may be convicted in a county which has adopted the Canada Temperance Act which allows the sale for medicinal purposes, but here there is an Act prohibiting the sale altogether.

Lord HERSCHELL—Where it is once adopted in a place it is law there and your Act would absolutely conflict ; the one would allow something which the other prohibited.

The LORD CHANCELLOR—The Canadian Act would be paramount.

Lord HERSCHELL—The Canadian Act would be paramount. I take it you could not legislate in a Province so as to conflict with an *intra vires* Dominion Act.

Mr. NEWCOMBE—No.

Lord MORRIS—It deals with the subject, and it deals with the subject of prohibition in a particular way, and is it not to be fairly argued that that is the only way in which prohibition is to be carried out ?

Lord HERSCHELL—What should you say as to my illustration which was put in one of the cases.   The Provincial Legislature has full power, we will suppose, to legislate with reference to the carrying of firearms, I suppose it is difficult to imagine it has not.   For the order and good government of the Dominion there is an Act passed putting certain restrictions on firearms which would apply to the whole.   Clearly they would have a right to do it for the order and good government.   They have occupied the field in that sense.   But in a particular Province the state of affairs in that Province renders it necessary for them to go further, and the Dominion Parliament has made a law saying that no one in the Dominion shall carry firearms at night.   But the state of the Province is such that the Provincial Legislature considers it necessary to provide that nobody shall carry firearms in the day time or possess them. Under those circumstances would there be anything to take away their power to pass that Act which they had before, because the Dominion Parliament had dealt with the subject in that more limited way? Your proposition goes a long way.

Mr. NEWCOMBE—Perhaps so my Lord.

The LORD CHANCELLOR—If you could reverse the hypothesis put to you and say that the Dominion Parliament prohibited the use of firearms generally, but the circumstances of the particular Province rendered it essential to the protection of everybody that they should carry firearms, I am afraid the Dominion Parliament, notwithstanding the necessity which is by the hypothesis put to you, would have had power to prohibit the use of arms altogether, and the Provincial Legislature would have no power to say what was necessary for the purpose of defence.

Lord HERSCHELL—I suppose that it is clear that, even in a matter within their province, if it is also within the province of the Dominion the Provincial Law would have to give way.

Mr. NEWCOMBE—Yes.

Lord HERSCHELL—But the question is whether it may not supplement; which is a different question.

Lord MORRIS—If it deals with the subject at all, is it not conflicting?

The LORD CHANCELLOR—If it is supposed to be exhaustive, of course, then it would be conflicting. If it enacts that this shall be the only law for the Province.

Lord WATSON—If it stated in positive terms that in those districts where the law had not been adopted every man who had got a license should be at liberty to sell without restriction or in any quantities.

The LORD CHANCELLOR—I should go a little further than that, I think. If the law made by the Dominion was supposed to occupy the field in the sense of occupying it exclusively the Province can have no power.

Lord WATSON—That legislation being within their power.

Lord HERSCHELL.—If they have left the matter alone where it has not been adopted, they have said everybody shall be free to sell liquor anyhow. If that is the total meaning of it I do not see how *Hodge* v. *The Queen* could be arrived at, if they have occupied it in that sense by the Canada Temperance Act.

Mr. NEWCOMBE—My present point involves, of course, the proposition that the subject is within section 92, and would remain there but for the exercise of the Dominion Authority under section 91. The case of *Russell* v. *The Queen* has upheld this statute of 1878, the Canada Temperance Act.

Lord HERSCHELL—It is not only *Hodge* v. *The Queen* but it is that subsequent Act before this Board, the Dominion Act of 1883, because it has held that the Canada Temperance Act had not so completely dealt with it but that the Province and they alone could deal with all licensing regulations.

Mr. NEWCOMBE—With the question of licensing.

Lord HERSCHELL.—That is dealing with it; licensing is dealing with it.

Lord WATSON—It restricts the trade to licensed people which is unquestionably in one sense of the word a regulation of the trade.

The LORD CHANCELLOR—I think one must bear in mind that you are not at liberty to construe these words in their ordinary natural meaning ; you must take the words as used by the Legislature, and I am not at all certain that where you are dealing with such words as are in No. 2, " the regulation of trade and commerce " that you are at liberty to go outside and consider what would be a regulation of " trade and commerce " ; I cannot help thinking that you must give what I will call the statutory meaning to those words.

Lord HERSCHELL.—You are on the point supposing it to come within the earlier part of order and good government. Your present point is whether the fact of this Temperance Act excludes a pre-existing power of the Provincial Legislature ; I should say it does, and any legislation inconsistent

P

with it, but my difficulty is in seeing how consistently with
the decisions of this Board it excludes any other power.

Mr. NEWCOMBE—I was endeavouring to make a point as
to which your Lordship made an unfavourable observation,
but I would like to complete that point with regard to
uniformity. The statute begins with the recital : —

> "Whereas it is very desirable to promote temperance in the
> Dominion, and that there should be uniform legislation in all the
> Provinces respecting the traffic in intoxicating liquors."

Lord HERSCHELL—You cannot by citing the Dominion
Act, limit the power of the Provincial Legislature.

Mr. NEWCOMBE—I admit that, but it would seem to me
that the decision may involve the view that for the purpose
of uniformity and for general law applicable throughout
Canada, the Dominion Parliament may legislate upon the
subject of prohibition where otherwise it might not be able to
legislate. It appears to me that the case for the purpose of
this point may involve that view. The present legislation is
clearly meant to apply a remedy to an evil which is assumed
to exist throughout the Dominion, and the local option, as it
is called, no more localises the subject and scope of the Act
than a provision in an Act for the prevention of contagious
diseases in cattle, that a public officer should proclaim in
what districts it should come into effect would make the
statute itself a mere local law for each of these districts.

Lord WATSON—I do not think any of the cases afford a
definition or anything like a precise definition of what
precisely is meant by the expression "regulation of trade" in
sub-section 2. There are explanations of it but the explanations as far as I can find, require as much explanation as the
section itself.

Mr. NEWCOMBE—My Lord, so far as this branch of the
case is concerned, what I submit is this ; that the Dominion
Legislation which was enacted for the declared purpose of
uniformity has been upheld, and the legislation was enacted
with a view to produce uniformity, to have a general law
applicable to all Canada and uniformity. If on account of
the uniform character of the legislation which was then
considered desirable, the legislation which then followed in

the form of the Canada Temperance Act has been upheld, then it would certainly be inconsistent with that for the Provinces to come in and produce diversity of legislation to provide anything different. Therefore so far as uniformity is concerned if that is an element, as I submit with all deference it is under that decision, the ground would be fully occupied. The subject would be exhaustively dealt with by the Dominion Parliament and the Provinces could not legislate while the Canada Temperance Act was in force. I refer to the case of the *Union of St. Jacques* v. *Belisle* (L. R. 6. P. C. 31 and 1 Cartwright p. 63) on that point which I have previously referred to. That case foreshadowed, I think, the decision which their Lordships of this Board arrived at in *The Attorney-General of Ontario* v. *The Attorney-General of Canada*, reported in the Appeal Cases of 1894. In the former case their Lordships said at page 36 :—

> "The hypothesis was suggested in argument by Mr. Benjamin, who certainly argued this case with his usual ingenuity and force, of a law having been previously passed by the Dominion Legislature to the effect that any association of this particular kind throughout the Dominion on certain specified conditions assumed to be exactly those which appear on the face of this Statute, should thereupon, *ipso facto* fall under the legal administration in bankruptcy or insolvency. Their Lordships are by no means prepared to say that if any such law as that had been passed by the Dominion Legislature it would have been beyond their competency, nor that if it had been so passed it would have been within the competency of the Provincial Legislature afterwards to take a particular association out of the scope of a general law of that kind so competently passed by the authority which had power to deal with bankruptcy and insolvency. But no such law ever has been passed, and to suggest the possibility of such a law as a reason why the power of the Provincial Legislature over this local and private association should be in abeyance or altogether taken away is to make a suggestion which, if followed up to its consequences, would go very far to destroy that power in all cases."

Then, my Lords, I refer to the case of *The Attorney-General of Ontario* v. *The Attorney-General for the Dominion of Canada*, reported in Appeal cases (1894) at pages 200 and 201, in which it is said :—

> "In their Lordships' opinion these considerations must be borne in mind when interpreting the words 'bankruptcy' and 'insolvency' in the British North America Act. It appears to their Lordships that such provisions as are found in the enactment in question, relating as they do to assignments purely voluntary, do not infringe on the exclusive legislative power conferred upon the Dominion Parliament."

The LORD CHANCELLOR—It may be material that I should mention now that their Lordships will only hear two Counsel.

Mr. BLAKE—We understood that, my Lord.

The LORD CHANCELLOR—Therefore when we begin again on Tuesday you will arrange which of you will address us.

Mr. BLAKE—Very well, my Lord.

Mr. NEWCOMBE—

"They would observe that a system of bankruptcy legislation may frequently require various ancillary provisions for the purpose of preventing the Scheme of the Act from being defeated. It may be necessary for this purpose to deal with the effect of executions and other matters which would otherwise be within the legislative competence of the Provincial Legislature. Their Lordships do not doubt that it would be open to the Dominion Parliament to deal with such matters as part of a bankruptcy law, and the Provincial Legislature would doubtless be then precluded from interfering with this legislation inasmuch as such interference would affect the bankruptcy law of the Dominion Parliament. But it does not follow that any such subjects as might properly be treated as ancillary to such a law and therefore within the powers of the Dominion Parliament, are excluded from the legislative authority of the Provincial Legislature when there is no bankruptcy or insolvency legislation of the Dominion Parliament in existence."

Lord WATSON—That case is distinguishable in all the points that create the leading difficulties in this. There, that the right under the sub-section of legislating for bankruptcy pertained to the Dominion and to the Dominion only, was made perfectly clear. It is not a subject that is included in any of the sub-sections of section 92, and no pretext could be made by the Provincial Legislature that it could legislate on the subject of bankruptcy. It could legislate on the subject of civil rights, and what we held in that case was that although in dealing with bankruptcy it might be necessary to touch civil rights, that the Provincial Legislature is free to deal with civil rights and legislate upon them until the Dominion has legislated in bankruptcy. After that, so far as civil rights are competently involved in their bankruptcy legislation, the Provincial Legislature has no power.

Mr. NEWCOMBE—I merely cited the case as an authority upon the point that the Dominion legislation would prevail. Now suppose, as an example of the inconsistency which would

result if the Province could meddle with the subject of
prohibition in view of the Canada Temperance Act, an attempt
made under the Statute to bring the Canada Temperance Act
into force in a County, and the Act was rejected by the electors,
then I submit that section 95 of the Act is in effect a declaration
on behalf of the Dominion Parliament within its competence
that there shall be freedom as to the sale of intoxicating
liquors within that County for three years. If the Province
could legislate the liquor seller is subject to another contest
perhaps the next week under a Provincial statute, or prohibition may be forced upon him by the Province notwithstanding
he has succeeded in getting it rejected in the manner provided
by Parliament.

Lord WATSON—Your argument is that not only in those
cases where it is adopted there is an immense restriction, but
so far as there is no restriction it provides that there shall be
free liberty to sell.

Mr. NEWCOMBE—Yes, my Lord. Then upon the question
of wholesale and retail I point out that the Canada Temperance Act was a retail Act so far as the question depends
upon quantity. It has been held to be in force, and no
unfavourable distinction can be drawn so far as the Dominion
is concerned in respect of wholesale dealings. In so far as
the case of *Russell* v. *The Queen* is an authority in our favour
it seems to show that it supports our case upon the
wholesale aspect of it.

The seventh question, I submit, takes the Provincial
view no further than the previous questions. The question
is one of prohibition under whichever question you like, and
I submit that the case for the Province of Ontario under
the seventh question is no stronger than the case of Nova
Scotia or New Brunswick would be if they were to enact
a similar Statute, although neither of those Provinces had
enacted previous to confederation any such Statute. My
Lords, I submit on these considerations that the answers of
the majority of the Supreme Court should be upheld.

The LORD CHANCELLOR— We will resume the consideration
of this Appeal on Tuesday next.

[Adjourned to Tuesday next (August 6th) at **10.30.***]*

THIRD DAY.

Mr. BLAKE—I appear, my Lords, for the Respondents, the Distillers' and Brewers' Association of Ontario.

Perhaps I may be permitted, before entering upon what I have to address to your Lordships on the case, to say a word or two with reference to the meaning of the questions, and to some suggestions which were made as to difficulties in dealing with them, owing to the form in which the matter comes before your Lordships.   Of course my clients have Judgment in the case ; but your Lordships have already been informed of the actual condition of judicial opinion in the Court of final resort in the Dominion, and it need hardly be said that a Judgment under such circumstances is eminently unsatisfactory, and cannot be considered to settle the question, even locally.   Your Lordships have had before you, in the case of the Dominion License Act, an attempt, expedited by the authority, and at the special instance of the Parliament of the Dominion, to procure a solution of somewhat analogous questions ; and it is public, and I presume fit to be alluded to here, what the reasons were for that course being taken.   It was because of the enormous public inconvenience, harassment and expense occasioned by an Act of that description, the Dominion License Act, which ran so wide and so intimately affected the relations of the community, being put into operation while its constitutionality was in doubt, and in the end it was found that those doubts were well founded.

Lord DAVEY—The Dominion License Act is the Act of 1883 ?

Mr. BLAKE—Yes.   An enormous public expense, a tremendous amount of private inconvenience and loss were occasioned by the putting of that Act into actual operation, it being found in the end that it was an Act which had no legal operation.   Obviously, like difficulties would be created, and similar inconveniences would arise from the putting into operation of an Act of either Legislature of such a nature as is suggested as possible by these questions ; and it was there-

fore, I submit, not unreasonable to make some effort to decide
in advance upon the validity of such suggested legislation,
Nor are the questions purely academic and speculative,
in the sense in which, as I apprehend, those terms were
applied the other day. Because matters have gone so far in
this connection that an Act was passed in 1893 by the
Legislature of the Province of Ontario, being Chapter 41 of
the Statutes of that year, to enable the electors of that
Province to pronounce upon the desirability of prohibiting
the importation, manufacture and sale as a beverage of
intoxicating liquors. The preamble of that Act is this :—

> " Whereas it is desirable that opportunity should be afforded to the
> Electors of this Province to express a formal opinion as to whether or
> not the importation, manufacture and sale into or within this Province
> of intoxicating liquors as a beverage should be immediately prohibited.
> And whereas such opinion can most conveniently be ascertained by
> ballot in the manner hereinafter mentioned."

The Act may be cited as the " Prohibition Plebiscite Act."
It is provided by the 2nd section that :—

> " Upon the day fixed by law for holding polls for the annual
> election of members of municipal councils, in the month of January,
> 1894, the clerk of every municipality other than a county, shall submit
> to the vote of the electors hereinafter declared qualified to vote on the
> same, the question whether or not the said electors are in favour of the
> prohibition by the competent authority of the importation, manufacture
> and sale as a beverage of intoxicating liquors into or within the
> Province of Ontario."

Then there are detailed provisions for carrying out that poll,
and the directions for the guidance of voters in voting contain
the following expression (*see* Schedule C) :—

> " Voters in voting ' yes ' on this question will be considered as
> expressing an opinion in favor of prohibition to the extent to which the
> Legislature of this Province or the Parliament of Canada has jurisdic-
> tion, as may be determined by the Court of Final Resort."

That plebiscite was taken and resulted in a large majority in
favour of immediate prohibition. Similar legislation has taken
place in the Province of Manitoba, with I believe a similar
plebiscite and a similar result, so that your Lordships will see
there is a degree of public interest, and if I may use the
phrase, the question has reached a degree of maturity as to
public opinion—at any rate in the Provinces, where these two
Acts have been passed—which puts not in the area of remote
speculation but within the scope of the immediate future the

prospect of legislation by one body or the other, so soon as it is found that the legislation is within the competency of the Legislature.

Next, my Lords, it seems to me, with reference to the suggestions that there is a difficulty in dealing with these questions greater than there would be in dealing with an Act, that what one has to do is to turn them into Acts. I think for example that the point your Lordships have to solve—taking the first question—would be precisely the same one as if a short Act was passed by the Legislature of Ontario, to the effect " that the sale within this Province of spirituous, fermented or other intoxicating liquor is hereby prohibited," with an appropriate penalty. There you have got the bald, naked proposition of the question turned into a short Act. If more is wanted in order to give a full answer, that more would not exist upon such an Act, and cannot be imported into this case ; but still on a prosecution for a penalty under an Act which turned that question into a clause of an Act of Parliament, your Lordships would have precisely the same question with the same difficulties as they exist of absence of further information as to circumstances, purpose, motive and extent.

Lord WATSON—The first question is really a concrete question. You must assume an Act passed to that effect.

The LORD CHANCELLOR—I do not feel that difficulty. When dealing with an absolute prohibition, I should agree with you—the matter is clear enough ; but supposing some question should arise in our minds as to whether or not the particular form of prohibition in terms might be only regulation and not with reference to hours, we will say, or limitation of the mode of sale or the quantity of sale, it is there the difficulty comes in, because you have to exhaust every possible hypothesis to pronounce an opinion. If you had an actual Act before you, you could say that was within or without a reasonable application of those terms.

Mr. BLAKE—I quite agree ; but what I venture to say is that what we at the Bar, and what, if I may respectfully suggest so to your Lordships, you have to do, is to assume that question turned into a clause of an Act of Parliament.

The LORD CHANCELLOR—That particular one I should agree. Prohibition or non-prohibition is clear enough.

Mr. BLAKE—Quite so.

Lord WATSON—Take the questions one by one. The first question you can see involves a substantial concrete question.

Mr. BLAKE—And so the second——

Lord WATSON—Would an Act of the Legislature absolutely prohibiting the sale within the Province of spirituous liquors be within its province? The next raises the question does the legislation of the Canadian Parliament oust the jurisdiction of the Provincial Legislature in those portions of the Dominion where the Temperance Act has been adopted by the inhabitants and is in force, and is it or is it not ousted as regards those portions of the Dominion where it has not been adopted and is not in force? The next two questions are quite clear. The 5th question I understand to be this. That if they have not power to enact a total prohibition, has the Provincial Legislature jurisdiction to regulate retail sales so as to prohibit liquor being sold by retail in quantities, less than those specified in the Statutes in force at the time of confederation. Then come these last words "or any other definition thereof." I do not understand that they intend to modify the quantities to be sold or to allow a little larger quantity or a lesser quantity to be sold than that Act allows. The next question, I understand (you will put me right if I misapprehend it) to involve this question or conundrum. If they are possessed of a limited jurisdiction such as is indicated in question 5, have they the power, within those parts of this Province, where the Canada Temperance Act is not in force to enact a law which will practically impose the provisions of the Canada Temperance Act upon that part of the Province, observing the limits of the Canada Temperance Act, but merely applying that Act without its being adopted in the manner specified in the Act itself in the Dominion. Then comes the 7th question which is on the section that gives rise to this controversy. It is a concrete question no doubt.

Mr. BLAKE—I was about to adopt the method your Lordship has been kind enough to take of dealing one by one with the different questions; and I had dealt with the first one. The second, I understand your Lordship to agree, is open to the same observation. It is quite clear that one may suggest an Act in those terms.

Lord DAVEY—That opens larger considerations. It opens the very large consideration of the relation of the Dominion Parliament and of the Provincial Legislatures to each other on those matters where this Board has said th'ir legislation overlaps.

Mr. BLAKE—Doubtless.

Lord DAVEY—That is a very large question.

Mr. BLAKE—I agree; large, complicated, more difficult, more doubtful perhaps of solution, but then that does not affect my present object.

Lord DAVEY—It is soluble ?

Mr. BLAKE—My present object is to find whether it is a question which you can turn into a clause of an Act of Parliament.

Lord WATSON—I think one question that may arise for our consideration, and which we shall have to consider, and which if determined one way or the other would appear to me to influence to some extent my opinion in this case at all events, is this; whether the legislation on these matters—the Drink Traffic Prohibitions enacted by the Dominion of Canada—are in reality and substance enactments for the purpose of regulating Trade and Commerce, or are in substance and reality enactments passed for the welfare of the inhabitants and with a view to suppressing drunken habits, that being under the first general part of section 91 which precedes the special sub-sections.

Mr. BLAKE—Yes my Lord.

Lord DAVEY—The second question appears to me to affect not so much the power of the Provincial Legislature to legislate as the effect of such legislation when made. It may well be that they have power to pass an Act for total prohibition throughout the Province, but then comes a Dominion Act which is to a certain extent in conflict with it, and the question is which Act the inhabitants are to obey, because the mere fact of the Parliament of the Dominion having passed a particular Act, which I will assume is within its jurisdiction, cannot affect the abstract question of the power of the Provincial Legislature to legislate.

Lord WATSON—You see the importance of the distinction between these two—whether it is legislation under the general part of section 91, or an enactment under sub-section 2. The distinction may be important when you come to consider the enactments of the last clause of section 92.

The LORD CHANCELLOR—Mr. Blake is only pointing out that these particular propositions are propositions capable of being answered as if they were concrete, in an Act of Parliament. He is not arguing the question at present at all.

Mr. BLAKE—I was not arguing the question at present, but I was desirous of saying that I think we can turn the second question, although it is in itself more complicated, into a clause of an Act as easily as the first.

Lord DAVEY—You put it as an Act for the total prohibition in those parts of the Province in which the Canada Temperance Act is not at the time in operation.

Mr. BLAKE—That is all I wanted to say just now.

Lord DAVEY—If you answer the first question in the affirmative then the second question must be answered in the affirmative?

Mr. BLAKE—Doubtless; the second question assumes a negative answer to the first. Then questions 3 and 4 are open to the same observations clearly. As to the 5th question I think I cannot ask your Lordships to make the same assumption with regard to the last limb of it.

The LORD CHANCELLOR—Because there comes the very question.

Mr. BLAKE—You are put in search of a definition. The tribunal is called upon to look all the world over.

The LORD CHANCELLOR—Itself an arbitrary definition.

Mr. BLAKE—I cannot tell whether you can find one, but you are called upon to find whether you can make any definition and what definition; and I admit, as to the second limb of that question, I am unable to take the clear and simple ground I take with reference to the others. As to the first limb it is more complicated, but the first limb is capable of being made concrete.

The LORD CHANCELLOR—I am not certain I follow you there because the words " has a limited jurisdiction " may raise the same question to my mind.

Mr. BLAKE—I suppose it may be put thus : Supposing an Act was passed prohibiting the sale by retail of liquors according to the definition which had obtained by reference to the local Acts or Statutes in force in the Province at the time of confederation : Supposing it is an Ontario Statute for example, " The sale by retail of liquor within the Province of Ontario according to," and then turn to the Statute of Ontario in force at confederation, "such a definition," whatever definition existed, " is prohibited." There is an Act.

The LORD CHANCELLOR—I should require some facts to solve that question myself. That is by no means so clear. I can quite imagine that the circumstances of a particular Province require a limitation on the general sale and that the circumstances were provincial, partial and territorially exceptional ; that might be one thing. If it was only done for the general enforcement of temperance ; that would be a totally different thing.

Mr. BLAKE—That may arise with reference to any of these questions. I am at present only considering whether I can put them in the same position.

The LORD CHANCELLOR—That is exactly what I mean ; any kind of limitation.

Lord DAVEY—Could you say that they could pass an Act prohibiting the sale of liquor by retail, leaving the Courts to find out what retail is ?

The LORD CHANCELLOR—That is exactly what I mean.

Mr. BLAKE—That would be an answer included in " or any other definition thereof " being no definition at all.

The LORD CHANCELLOR—That is exactly it.

Mr. BLAKE—I am limiting myself to the first.

The LORD CHANCELLOR—I do not think you escape the difficulty by the first, because the moment you speak of a limited jurisdiction you are immediately encountered by the difficulty, what is your limited jurisdiction, and in what respect may it be limited and to what extent and with what view.

' Mr. BLAKE—I must find out what the definition of a sale by retail is. Take Ontario as an example, I must find what the definition of a sale by retail in the Province of Ontario was at the time of confederation, and say " the sale in the Province of intoxicating liquors by retail," according to that definition which I insert in the Act " is hereby prohibited."

The LORD CHANCELLOR—I quite follow you. I do not wish to interrupt you further, only you were passing it over as if it was as plain as the others. I confess it is not to me.

Mr. BLAKE—I do not at all now say as to any of these that if they were in the position of an Act of Parliament, which is all I am trying to get them into, your Lordships might not say : " Well, we cannot tell, we want more facts."

The LORD CHANCELLOR—That is exactly what I meant.

Mr. BLAKE—But these would not be facts appearing on the Act of Parliament; they would be extrinsic facts based on either evidence or admission, so I get over the difficulty of the case being in the form of a question instead of an Act of Parliament.

Lord WATSON—One difficulty appears, which is only a difficulty in the event of our coming to certain conclusion : if they had not power to enact, they could not repeal tnat Act.

Mr. BLAKE—That is No. 7. I am sorry I had only got as far as No. 5.

Lord WATSON—Still, it is involved in No. 5, according to the definition of " retail " by the Statutes in force. If that Statute was a Statute which only the Canadian Parliament could pass, it is unrepealed at this date, and in force in the Province.

Mr. BLAKE—Unless the Canadian Parliament has repealed the definition.

Lord WATSON—It is not expressly repealed ?

Mr. BLAKE—I am really not able to answer that question. I will enquire.

Lord WATSON—There might be a question as to their power to repeal ?

Mr. BLAKE—Yes, my Lord. I think we might go on from now to Christmas if we entered into all the questions which ingenuity might suggest in this case.

The LORD CHANCELLOR—As we are anxious to conclude to-day, we had better let you go on.

Mr. BLAKE—Then as to No. 6. I frankly confess I do not understand the question myself. I do not understand it as Lord Watson understands it. I incline to believe that a different interpretation is to be given to that question.

Lord WATSON—You have to assume first that the Provincial Legislature has a limited jurisdiction—if we come to that conclusion under Question 5, it assumes that Question 5 is answered in the affirmative. If the Provincial Legislature is found under Question 5 not to have any jurisdiction—even a limited jurisdiction—as regards prohibition of sale, this Question No. 6 would fail, would not it ?

Lord DAVEY—I understand Question 6 as meaning this : Having regard to the fact that the Canada Temperance Act is not an Act for total prohibition, but for prohibition with certain exceptions, does the fact of the Dominion Parliament having legislated in that way cut down the legislation of the Province—if the power to legislate exists ?

Lord WATSON—It looks like, in other terms, but in substance, as being a question to this effect : Can the Pro-

vincial Legislature enforce the provisions of the Canada
Temperance Act in those parts of the Province where that
Act is not adopted ?

Mr. BLAKE—The difficulty about that view is that that
is really No. 2.

Lord DAVEY—It seems to be a repetition of No. 2.

Lord WATSON—No, no ; I think they are quite different.
In Question No. 2 you are dealing with total prohibition.
Has the Provincial Legislature a free hand in those parts of
the Province where the Canada Temperance Act is not in
force ?   Question 6 does not put the question whether they
have a free hand to legislate if they choose and prohibit to
any extent, but it puts this : Can they prohibit to the extent
to which it is prohibited within those parts of Canada where
the Canada Temperance Act applies ?

Mr. BLAKE—I did not understand your Lordship's
earlier exposition as your Lordship now puts it.   That is
more like what I understand the question to be as far as I
can reach its meaning.

Lord DAVEY—Has it power to make the Canada Temperance Act compulsory in the case of counties and townships
where it has not been in force ?

Mr. BLAKE—I think it is not that.

Lord WATSON—I think it is alternative to Question
No. 2.   Question No. 2 says : " Can the Legislature wholly
prohibit the sale of liquor within those parts of the Province
where the Canada Temperance Act is not in force ? "   If they
cannot wholly prohibit or to such extent as they think
expedient can they 'prohibit to the extent that would be
provided by the Canada Temperance Act if it were in
operation ? "   Can they do exactly what the Dominion has
done ?

Mr. BLAKE—I own I find it more difficult to understand
what the question is than to answer it.   Because I believe
the arguments I shall submit to your Lordships are of a
character that excludes anything but a negative answer to
this question, whatever it means.   Question 7 is admitted to

be a concrete question. So much with reference to the difficulty of these matters coming in the form of questions instead of in the form of Acts.

Lord WATSON—These questions are something like the provisions of section 91 and section 92—they overlap.

Mr. BLAKE—And possibly conflict, my Lord. It follows then—taking the main questions, the large questions—that a solution is demanded of the question whether a Province has the power to make an absolute and all-embracing prohibitory law as to each of these matters, a law less local in its practical application, less dependent on local option, and wider in its extent than the Canada Temperance Act itself ? It seems to me that that is really the main and most important class of questions with which your Lordships have to deal. Now, before I proceed to deal with those two questions which Lord Watson has suggested are the questions—the question of the authority of the Parliament of Canada under the general powers with all which that involves, and the question of its authority under the enumerated power "trade and commerce," may I briefly say, not by way of elaboration at all, but by way of general statement, what I conceive may fairly be laid down as the propositions in the line of which I purpose to argue the case. It seems to me that a competent Legislature may treat any trade by prohibition and thus make it unlawful, which of course prohibition would; firstly, because either on social or moral grounds it is bad for public morals, order or safety, the grounds which are all mentioned in the Judgment of this Board in the *Russell* case,—or, secondly, because of some fiscal, economic or political reasons including treaty reasons. There are these two classes, of which the second has different branches, and I am going to contend that both under the general and under the enumerated powers of the Dominion the jurisdiction to prohibit on any of these grounds rests in, and rests solely in, the Dominion. The second mode of treating a trade may be by ordering it, (I use that word for the moment instead of "regulating,") as a trade intended to exist and recognised as lawful, but requiring to be ordered on any of those grounds which I have mentioned. And here I am going to contend that there is a distribution of power. There may be, to quote

the language that was used in *Parsons'* case, "minute matters
of regulation affecting the particular trade," or to refer to,
without at this moment quoting the language used in the
Hodge case, a police power to meet the varying views and
conditions of different minor localities ; and within those
elastic limits which are indicated in principle,—although it
may be very difficult in each case to draw the exact line (when
it comes to be drawn) in *Parsons'* case and in *Hodge's* case
and in the *Dominion License* case,—I submit that the power
has been decided to be exclusively Provincial. In the case in
which your Lordships shall adjudicate that it is minute
regulation affecting a particular trade, there *Parsons'* case says
that is local. In the case in which your Lordships shall
adjudicate according to the language which, as I say, I refer
to without at this moment quoting because I shall have to
quote it presently, that it is within " the police power," there
your Lordships have held that it is exclusively local. Then
drawing that line which is to be drawn in principle, in general
statement in every case and in exact application,—a much
more difficult task when the particular case arises—drawing
that line and cutting off as exclusively Provincial what falls
within these two descriptions, there are yet regulations which
march wider, which cut deeper, which are of more general
application, which go beyond minute regulations affecting a
particular trade, which go beyond simple " police matters "
dealing with the varying circumstances and conditions of
small or differently-circumstanced localities. As to those
I am going to contend that they are in the Dominion, and
wholly in the Dominion, under both its powers, the general
and the special. Of course, the line of demarcation is difficult,
and fortunately it is not amongst the things that have to be
decided to-day. In point of fact that line cannot be drawn
except with reference to the particlar case which arises, and
the particular legislation with which your Lordships are
dealing at the time. But dealing with that in the particular
case and then drawing the line, you find where the Dominion
and where Provincial powers reside.

The LORD CHANCELLOR—I made an observation the other
day which, I think, I ought to retract upon consideration.
What occurred to me was, and it is relevant to our present

discussion, that those words " Regulation of Trade " could not be satisfied by its prohibition. I think I was too hasty. Trade generally may be regulated by prohibiting a particular trade. Take the case of the prohibition of the exportation of wool with which this country was familiar at one time. That was a regulation of trade, and it was the prohibition of a particular trade.

Mr. BLAKE—Quite so.

The LORD CHANCELLOR—And it may well be that whenever you are dealing with the entire prohibition of a particular trade that may be regulation of trade in the strictest sense.

Mr. BLAKE—Quite so.

Lord WATSON—We regulate the trade of these Islands in tobacco by prohibiting its production except to a very limited extent.

Mr. BLAKE—You prohibit the production and you prohibit the sale of the manufactured article. That is one of the instances I was about to cite to your Lordships.

The LORD CHANCELLOR—My mind was directed to the Provincial area. There it might be true enough to say that it is not regulating it. There it is prohibiting it altogether. That is a question of dealing with a particular trade.

Mr. BLAKE—A separate question. I was about to say, and I am very happy to hear your Lordships observations, that my argument will be that when you draw the line of demarcation and find where the local power stops and where the Dominion power begins, you must find that the latter goes on to the end, even to the extent of prohibition, and this under the title of regulation as well as under the general power. That is the observation I was about to make, that all the varying shades and phases of dealing with trade which go beyond these two, which I have admitted to be upon the authorities local, are exclusively Dominion right down to prohibition, and that within "regulations" as well as under the general powers. Those are the general positions I shall take.

Now it is obviously convenient to take them in their order when one comes to deal with the question of powers, and to

take first of all the general power. That is convenient, because
it is the firs power given ; and it is convenient also because
it is the power acted on in the concrete case, which so
intimately bears upon the decision of this question, in the
Russell case. It is the power upon which this Board acted
in determining that that Act was within the powers of the
Dominion Parliament. I am sorry, my Lords, to have to
refer again to sections 91 and 92.

The LORD CHANCELLOR—I do not wonder at it : the whole
thing turns on it really.

Mr. BLAKE—Quite so ; but yet I am sorry to have to ask
your Lordships to give a consideration, which I will try and
make as brief as possible, to the effect of this genera.
provision :—

> " It shall be lawful for the (Dominion) to make laws for the peace,
> order and good government of Canada in relation to all matters not
> coming within the classes of subjects by this Act assigned exclusively
> to the Legislatures of the Provinces."

Now these general words, leaving out the exception for
the moment, are extensive enough to grant all powers
whatever, whether local or private, in any part of Canada.
Nothing so minute, nothing so local, nothing so large,
nothing cutting so wide or deep, but it is included in
those words, because they are, as has already been stated,
the common form words under which the general legislative
power given to the domestically self-governing Colonies has
been granted for a long time, first of all in instructions and
commissions, and afterwards in Acts of Parliament. These
words are deliberately chosen as expressing in their generality
the character of the powers that are given to the Dominion,
and they are cut down only by the expression " in relation to
" all matters not coming within the classes of subjects assigned
" exclusively to the Legislatures of the Provinces." I observe
first, then, that there is here, even with reference to the
general powers, no idea of concurrence. It was not to be
expected in looking at the whole Act that you would find it
there, for section 95 gives you two express particular subjects
of concurrent powers of legislation, with reference to agriculture and with reference to immigration.

Q 2

Lord HENSCHELL—This Board has held it may in a sense be concurrent. We can hardly go back from that; that is to say that there are .matters which the Provincial Legislatures may deal with as to which they might be overridden by the action of the Dominion legislation.

Mr. BLAKE—I am going to discuss the rulings of the Board on the subject. I quite recognise the fact that I a.. not entitled to combat anything that has been decided, but hope to show your Lordships that nothing that has been decided is inconsistent with or disables me from presenting this view of the case. You find, as I say, an express provision for each power making laws in relation to agriculture and immigration, and you find an express provision as to the degree of validity which the provincial law shall have in that case. It shall have effect in and for the Province as long and as far only as it is not repugnant to an Act of Parliament of the Dominion. So that there is power in each to legislate, and the power of the Province is subordinated to the executed power of the Dominion. That being so we would not expect to find in other provisions of the Act a scheme of concurrent powers, either express or implied, and we do not, as I submit, find it here; because, while there is a general power given in these first words to the Parliament of Canada for everything, that power is limited by cutting out from it all those specified powers which are assigned exclusively to the Legislatures of the Provinces. Therefore, there is a sharp line of division; all the things which are assigned to the Provinces belong to the Provinces; all the rest belong to the Dominion. Then it is to be observed as bearing only upon the interpretation of the prior part of section 91 for the moment, and not entering otherwise on the argument in reference to the enumerated powers which comes under a separate head—it is to be observed that the meaning of that part which preceeds the enumeration is consistent with what I have said :—

" For greater certainty but not so as to restrict the generality of the foregoing terms of this section it is hereby declared that (notwithstanding anything in this Act) the exclusive legislative authority of the Parliament of Canada extends to all matters "   "   "   ".

It is indicated that there were matters which were intended by Parliament to be embraced within the general exclusive authority, within that same legislative authority which is given under the prior part of section 1, and which was itself clearly exclusive. But as to these particular subjects, for various reasons some of which are stated very clearly in some of the judgments now under appeal, it was obvious that there might be doubt, conflict, and difficulty of ascertainment as to whether, having regard to the enumerated powers in section 92, some of these things were within or without the area of Provincial legislation, and therefore " for greater certainty but not so as to restrict the generality of the foregoing terms." And thus by words indicative of the view that they were, in fact, and in intention embraced within those general terms, the enumeration took place.

Now let me state another difference. You have the powers limited, when you come to the Province by the area and the objects; provincial area and provincial objects are the scope. I think each one of the provincial powers is indicated in itself to be for provincial purposes. Instead of setting that out generally at the commencement, in each one of the Articles it is specifically stated. But you find on the contrary, unlimited, save by the express exception, general powers both as to scope, area, and objects in the Dominion. There is therefore, as I submit, nothing whatever to indicate in the least degree that the power of the Parliament of Canada was so limited as to those subjects on which it might enact that it could not, if the welfare of the whole community, in its opinion, demanded, enact with reference to particular parts of that community, the legislation which the condition of that part might, in the interest of all, specially demand. It is quite true that it was hoped and expected, and it was a reasonable hope and expectation, that, as a rule, the legislation would be general, extending over the whole area, the subjects being common. But there is nothing in these powers which prescribes any such limitation, and it is perfectly clear that the peace, welfare, and good government of the whole community may demand within the undisputed bounds of the legislative powers of the Dominion, an Act of Parliament affecting directly, not the whole area, not the whole community, but some part of that community as to these matters on which the Dominion has power to legislate for all.

Lord Herschell.—I should have found a difficulty in drawing the line if you put it so broadly as that, because nothing could be said in that sense to be of a local character. Everything : ʼ: is for the benefit of a part is in its degree and sense fo.   benefit of the whole, and therefore you could say noth.,   was local.   You might legislate for a particular Province because you might say the prosperity of that Province is the prosperity of the Dominion, and though it is a mere local matter though it is legislation confined within this limit, yet nevertheless it is within the authority of the Dominion.   Your proposition seems to me to be so broad as to embrace that and it would make it difficult to draw a line that would exclude it.

Mr. Blake—It hangs on the phrase " merely."

Lord Herschell.—Then in that sense nothing is *merely* local.   You may say it is for the peace of Canada to legislate in a particular way—in a particular part of the Province. That is because the advantage or the prosperity of that Province may affect the prosperity of the Dominion.   Should you say that that is a case in which they might legislate ?

Sir Richard Couch—You take away a good deal of the meaning of the word " exclusive."

Mr. Blake—I do not put it in that way.

Lord Watson—I quite agree with your suggestion that there is no such thing conferred by these two clauses as concurrent legislation—as I understand the words concurrent legislation.   The legislation to be effective must be by one or the other. I do not think they are joined together, but I think the result—and that does not render the present question less difficult to deal with—of recent judgments of this Board have been to establish that there are some powers of legislation which may be exercised by the Provincial Legislature, and so long as they are not interfered with by the Dominion Parliament they will stand and be effectual.   I understand that this Board has gone this length further, that these enactments may be overridden by an Act of the Dominion Parliament, competently legislating within its own field, but my impression as to the meaning of the

opinions which this Board has expressed is this, that whilst
the Dominion Parliament could override it by an enactment
that came into collision with the Provincial enactment, the
matter would not be so exclusively within the jurisdiction of
the Dominion Parliament as to enable that Parliament to
repeal.   That is another question ; it might overpower it but
not repeal it.

Lord DAVEY—The proviso to section 91 seems to
contemplate that the Dominion Parliament may legislate on
matters which are local if they come within the enumerated
subjects of section 91.

Lord HERSCHELL.—Nothing can be said to be merely
local which comes within those sub-sections, that is clear.

Mr. BLAKE—I agree.

Lord HERSCHELL.—But you are speaking of the general
power in the earlier part.

Mr. BLAKE—Quite so.

Lord HERSCHELL.—And I should not differ as at present
advised from your saying that it would not necessarily require
that the legislation should be legislation applicable to every
part of the Dominion ; but when you say they can legislate
as to a place in a particular Province, then it seems difficult
to draw the line between that and the local legislation referred
to in section 92.

Mr. BLAKE—As your Lordship put it a moment ago, I
can understand that very difficult questions of power would
be raised.   Difficult questions of power may be raised on
many clauses of this Act, and it may be very hard to draw
the line in numerous cases which may be suggested.

Lord HERSCHELL—That is why I begin to doubt whether
one can determine any such questions in the abstract by
general propositions as to the mode in which the two sections
are to be interpreted.   I think it is difficult to deal with anything but a concrete case.

Mr. BLAKE—Yes, my Lord ; I opened by trying to find
how nearly we were concerned in concrete cases to-day, and

I quite agree, but it is only because I want to examine a little later the phrases—- -

Lord WATSON—The two sub-sections which raise most difficulty in questions of this kind are those which give power to the Provinces under sub-sections 13 and 16, the one referring to all civil rights which are Provincial, and the other referring to all matters Provincial which are merely local.

Mr. BLAKE—Yes; what I was going to say about that is, that you get perhaps in a larger sphere, but in principle you get the same degree of difficulty that you get if you are called upon to determine where the limit of a police regulation is, which as I venture to suggest is, speaking broadly, the limit of the Provincial power on the reference which is in question.

Lord HERSCHELL—" Police regulation " is a very vague phrase. I am quite aware that that was used in *Hodge's* case; but it only means something conducive to the good order of the Dominion. It has nothing to do with the police.

Mr. BLAKE—It is rather borrowed from what is called the police power which we know has a larger interpretation.

Lord HERSCHELL—Saying that licensed premises shall not be open between prohibited hours is not a police regulation. The police have nothing to do with it except to see the law is not broken as in every other case

Mr. BLAKE—I assumed rather the phrase had been used in *Hodge's* case in the sense I suggest.

The LORD CHANCELLOR—We have substituted the word " Police " for " Constable," and if you get the old Common Law word there is a thread of theory that ran through it which was the preservation of the peace.

Mr. BLAKE—Yes.

Lord DAVEY—If you look at the derivation " Police," I expect it means the maintenance of Municipal order.

Mr. BLAKE—Yes.

Lord WATSON—We are apt to use these expressions which really are not definitive of the thing enacted but are descriptive of the executive body entrusted with the execution of the Statute.

Mr. BLAKE—Yes.

Lord WATSON—It becomes a police matter, and we use the words " Police regulation " whenever it is entrusted to the police for enforcement.

Mr. BLAKE—Yes.

Lord WATSON—But that word does not define the nature of the enactment or the object of the legislature in passing it.

Mr. BLAKE—No, my Lord.

Lord WATSON—Sanitary arrangements and that kind of thing are entirely for the benefit of the community.

Lord HERSCHELL—There is nothing about " Police " in section 92 at all.

Mr. BLAKE—No, my Lord. I am sorry I used the word. I thought I borrowed it from one of the cases.

Lord HERSCHELL—It was used in *Hodge's* case. It was thought it pointed to a distinction which helped one. I confess you may call them Police Regulations; but it does not help one with reference to other cases to call them Police Regulations.

Mr. BLAKE—No, my Lord. I quite agree, and what I was saying was that you would find it very difficult when you came to draw the line to find what is " Police " and what is not " Police," within the sense in which that term is used in *Hodge's* case, and so you find it difficult to determine what is merely local or private and what is beyond it. One can suggest extreme cases in which it would be perfectly clear. For instance with reference to a small ordinary travelled road in one portion of a great Province you might say in one sense—that in which your Lordships put it—that the prosperity of the whole Dominion depends on the prosperity of each of the inhabitants : there are 20 people that live on this road ; the whole Dominion will be infinitesimally better off, but still better off, if these 20 are better accommodated ; and therefore it is a Canadian matter to see to the repair of that road or legislate with regard to it. I should say that that proposition would be obviously absurd, and that that matter would be obviously a merely local or private matter. There must be some reasonable suggestion to sustain the proposition that there is a common interest in the condition of the question and of the treatment of it by the Parliament concerned.

Lord DAVEY—If there were larger elements of disorder and rebellion against government in one particular Province it would be a matter of the peace, order and good government to prohibit the sale of firearms in that Province ?

Mr. BLAKE—Yes, and it would be, as I submit, within the power of the Parliament of Canada. We have had cases in the earlier times, and also in the later history of the country, where disturbances took place of a grave description, but absolutely local, not affecting, except incidentally, the other parts of the Dominion, and no one ever doubted, or could doubt, I think, that the dealing with those matters by force or by law—and special laws have been passed—was appropriately and necessarily and exclusively a Canadian transaction ; and yet they did not touch, excepting in the sense in which I put it, the peace, order, and good government of the whole country, but that peace, order and good government was doubtless incidentally affected by the disturbance in the particular place.

Lord DAVEY—In Webster's Dictionary "Police" is said to be a French word, and to mean " regulation and government of a City or County or Union as regards the inhabitants." That does not carry one very far.

The LORD CHANCELLOR—That is very wide.

Lord HERSCHELL—Supposing it was not necessary as to the peace, order, and good government of Canada, but it was necessary for local purposes that you should prohibit the sale or carrying of firearms, or anything you please with regard to them. It is difficult to see why the Provincial Legislature should not deal with it, if it was a merely local matter ; but it is difficult, on the other hand to see why because the, have dealt with it as a merely local matter when it was a local matter, the Dominion Parliament when some provision with reference to fire-arms became necessary for the peace, order and good government of the whole Dominion, should be thereby precluded from dealing with it or should be unable to deal with it in that way. I can conceive both dealing with it in that way. A matter may be a merely local question at one time, but the state of the Dominion may make it something much more than a local matter at another time. I do not see any difficulty in saying that then the Dominion power would come into force, and it would not be inconsistent with that that there had been an exercise of power by the Provincial Legislature.

Mr. BLAKE—I own I find it difficult to define in my mind the condition of things which your Lordship suggests as local, with reference to prohibiting or restraining the carrying of fire-arms, which would not make it a Dominion matter. It may be suggested that there are turbulent spirits in particular portions of the Dominion, that there is a reckless habit of carrying fire-arms, that there have been criminal offences committed by the wanton use of them, and that people have been killed or wounded in those particular places. All those things seem to me to point to one conclusion and that is that it is a matter for Canadian action.

Lord HERSCHELL—I do not see if that is the case why the provisions discussed in *Hodge* v. *The Queen* were not Canadian. The object of them was that you should not have disorder, that you should not have drunken people committing crimes or troubling the community, and you might just as much say as to the carrying of fire-arms that it was not merely local but that it was a matter concerning the peace, order and good government of Canada. It seems to me you cut very deep into what is merely local though you admit the evil is one confined to the provincial area to be determined by the circumstances of the provincial area. If you come to that, what is " merely local " ?

The LORD CHANCELLOR—The difficulty about it is that you have two words to construe. You have the word "merely" and the word " exclusively " to be construed and those words have to be satisfied by something.

Mr. BLAKE—Yes, and where I find a difficulty is this:

I find a difficulty in adopting the proposition that if your transaction is merely local in its nature, and if there is the exclusive power—if the fact that it is local in Province A gives that Province the exclusive power of dealing with it, and it turns out that it exists also locally in Province B, which therefore has the exclusive power of dealing with it—that by this occurrence it ceases to be local anywhere and becomes general.

Lord HERSCHELL—This Board said something very like that in *Russell* v. *The Queen*. They indicated there that though a thing might be merely local viewed in relation to the particular Province yet nevertheless it might be necessary to have some general legislation for the whole of Canada for its peace, order and good government.

Lord DAVEY—Then it would not be "merely."

Lord HERSCHELL—It is not "merely local" when it becomes necessary to deal with the matter generally. That I understand to be the view taken in *Russell* v. *The Queen*.

Mr. BLAKE—May it not be said to be general where there is a sort of danger of contagion or disturbance spreading over the whole of the Dominion, because it is sporadic in different Provinces. If the matter be merely local or private and the condition which requires legislation exists in one Province only, it is suggested that the Dominion should not have power to legislate——

Lord HERSCHELL—Sanitary regulations certainly *prima facie* within a Province would be a matter merely local for which the Provincial Legislature would have power to legislate, and yet there may be a condition of things which renders some general sanitary legislation necessary for the safety of the whole Dominion.

Lord WATSON—In one Province there may be a local evil peculiar to one Province, it may be wholly a local matter and apparently section 92 in that case gives the local legislature the right to deal with it. Then it may attain such dimensions as to become a threatened danger to the whole Dominion and in that case I should be sorry to doubt that there is power given to the Dominion Parliament to intervene.

There may be an evil of the same nature which is local in each and every one of the Provinces and apparently the Dominion of Canada would be justified in that case in applying a uniform remedy to the whole.

Mr. BLAKE—Although it is merely local in nature.

Lord WATSON—I can quite understand that there is one thing, the disease is sporadic.

Lord DAVEY—Is not that the answer—that it is not merely local.

Mr. BLAKE—I am not certain that that is exactly the answer—that it is a full answer. It would depend on that which prevented it from being merely local. Is the special circumstance that it happens to exist in some little corner in a second Province to remove it from the area of mere locality?

The LORD CHANCELLOR—Take for example the prohibition of firearms. Do you shrink from saying that that can only be dealt with by a General Law or not?

Mr. BLAKE—I do not. I happen unfortunately to have been the author of a General Law dealing with that very topic.

Lord HERSCHELL—I do not think it is suggested that it could not be dealt with by a General Law if thought necessary for the safety of the Dominion, but do you do so if not so thought that the Province might deal with it by a Local Law on account of the local conditions that did not exist elsewhere?

Mr. BLAKE—It was not with reference to any insurrection or outbreak that the law that I referred to was passed, but with reference to a habit which for certain reasons was getting more general of carrying pistols.

The LORD CHANCELLOR—Whether that is so or not, I think the answer Lord Davey made to you just now that the words "not merely local" would apply there. If there is an outbreak in each particular Province that is not merely local I should take it. Do you affirm or deny that the Local

Legislature would have a right to deal with the question of prohibition—putting it in the broadest form—altogether ?

Mr. BLAKE—I should have said they would not have power, that would be my view.

The LORD CHANCELLOR—I thought that was your argument.

Mr. BLAKE—Certainly.

Lord HERSCHELL—Both on the hypotheses that it was a matter required by the particular Province, and the Dominion Parliament did not think it necessary to deal with it ?

Mr. BLAKE—I submit we must not affirm that determination of the Dominion Parliament as to whether legislation is beneficial or otherwise on a particular topic, is to be otherwise than conclusive within their scope of action.

Lord HERSCHELL—No.

Mr. BLAKE—If the thing is within their power, and they decide as a matter of policy that they ought not to legislate, that does not differentiate the case, as I submit. They decide on the whole that it is not well to legislate, they may prefer that Canada should be free rather than sober, to quote a phrase used in another country.

Lord HERSCHELL—Does not section 91 point to this, that if it can be brought within any of the enumerated clauses, and it is legislation confined to the locality it is *prima facie* within the Provincial power ? At the end of the clause they draw a distinction between those enumerated clauses and the general words at the beginning.

Lord DAVEY—I do not understand why you shrink from saying, Mr. Blake, that if the circumstances of a particular Province—say where there was a large mining population, rather rough in their habits—rendered it necessary in that particular Province to restrict the carrying of firearms, the Provincial Legislature should not treat it as a merely local matter, though it might be within the jurisdiction of the Dominion Parliament to legislate for the peace, good order and good government of Canada generally.

Lord HERSCHELL—I think I understand why Mr. Blake hesitates at that.

Mr. BLAKE—I do not shrink from it in the least degree. If your Lordships ask me the question whether, when there is a distinct local aspect in which the local legislature deals with the subject, I should say the local legislature has the jurisdiction—I should agree. The difficulty I feel is in agreeing to the view that where the aspect is the same there is a double jurisdiction ; that I have not been able to see.

The LORD CHANCELLOR—I am not quite certain that I follow your phrase, " the aspect."

Mr. BLAKE—Borrowed again, my Lord, only borrowed.

Lord DAVEY—Do you suggest the words bind the Board in their ultimate decision ?

The LORD CHANCELLOR—Whatever may be said about the ultimate decision of this Board, I protest against particular phrases being used so as to bind it.

Mr. BLAKE—I ventured to assume that your Lordships would understand the language that your Lordships had used.

Lord HERSCHELL—The language that this Board used it used *secundum subjectam materiam ;* and to detach a phrase that in a concrete case it used with reference to a particular matter, and which it may be perfectly proper to treat in that way, as a sort of phrase that determines something with reference to another matter, I rather protest against.

Mr. BLAKE—I agree, and I should be very sorry to do so. It will be found, I think, that it is used in a second case and after some years of consideration, as a general exposition of the principle laid down in *Parsons'* case ; that it is the measured and reasoned and considered language in which the Board sought to state and stated its definition. I think it says, " one purpose and one aspect, and another purpose and another aspect." I think it uses the two phrases. However, I think the meaning of what I have aimed at is plain——

Lord HERSCHELL—It may be very material to see whether, when you are enquiring with reference to trade and commerce, the object of legislation is to regulate and deal with the trade, or whether it has some other purpose than that, although it may incidentally produce some effect on that. I think that is a distinction.

Lord WATSON—That word "aspect" which you used just now in those passages is not to be taken alone from those passages, for, if I mistake not, there are other passages in the same case which are corroborative of the meaning which you repudiate.

Mr. BLAKE—One has to apply the same principles of construction as to these Judgments as are applied to sections 91 and 92.

Lord HERSCHELL—I do not think in this case we can lay down any proposition in such terms as to cover all cases and settle the confines of sections 91 and 92.

Mr. BLAKE—I agree, my Lord; I should be very sorry to make the attempt.

Lord HERSCHELL—You may tell in a particular case whether or not it comes within it.

Mr. BLAKE—I was really rather anxious to present the view that there may be a local aspect of some particular matter or subject which is different from some general aspect of that same matter or subject.

Lord WATSON—In other words, that there may be local circumstances warranting local legislation which are different from the circumstances that prompt the legislation of the Dominion Parliament.

Mr. BLAKE—But the local cause which prompts legislation and which indicates the necessity for legislation may be a cause of a nature which would justify the Dominion in legislating, though it had not gone further. That is what I mean.

Lord WATSON—In other words, the aspects would in some cases be the same ?

Mr. BLAKE—Yes, my Lord, if I may be allowed to continue using the phrase. In that case, I say wherever I can find a different local aspect from the general aspect, and the effect of the Provincial legislation remains merely local and directed to that different local aspect, not merely is that legislation good but that legislation cannot be touched by the Dominion's dealing, unless it deals with it in the way in which, in an insolvency case for example, the Dominion would deal with it.   •

Lord WATSON—What do you say to this ? It has been said that in determining the nature of legislation you must look to what it does and to the effect it produces or is calculated to produce rather than to the motive of the legislation being passed.

Mr. BLAKE—I suspect that where an Act of Parliament is passed, perhaps even if there be, but certainly if there be not, an absolute exposition in the statute of the object of the legislation, it would be very difficult for a Court to determine against the legislation if the Parliament had any power whatever of any nature under which it could have passed the legislation. That is stated very clearly in reference to the Canada Temperance Act, on the point that its professed object was the merely social aspect of the case : and yet the Judges in the Court below held it good under the regulation of trade and commerce, and the fact of the Preamble indicating a particular reason whi h might be a difficult reason to apply——

Lord WATSON—I can quite understand that an Act like that might be passed in reality regulating trade, and with that view, but producing in the result temperance.

Mr. BLAKE—Yes ; quite so.

Sir RICHARD COUCH —But must not you look at the Act and see what it does directly and not indirectly ?

Mr. BLAKE—I think you must look to what it does directly, and see if that which is directly done is within its power.

Sir RICHARD COUCH—It may have some indirect operation, but you would not look to that, would you ?

R

Lord WATSON—An Act might be passed for the regulation of trade, and the result of that Act might be to produce temperance.

Mr. BLAKE—Surely, when you come to the enumerated powers, which I hope to reach some time——

Lord HERSCHELL.—The difficulty about that regulation of trade is this. In a sense, no doubt to say you shall only carry on trade within particular hours, within particular buildings, by particular persons particularly qualified, is a regulation of trade, and nobody can dispute that, and yet this Board has held that it is not a regulation of trade within the exclusive power of the Dominion Parliament.

Mr. BLAKE—Certainly, I agree.

Lord HERSCHELL.—And yet it is not everything that regulates trade in that sense.

Mr. BLAKE—Yes, as I ventured to contend in the opening of my argument, there is a distribution of power as to that which in the broader sense of the term might be termed regulation of trade, and I said there were decisions of this Board that there are regulations within the power of the Local Legislature, and that there are others which fall beyond that and fall within the exclusive jurisdiction of the Dominion Parliament. I was about to make an observation on what your Lordships said as to the effect of the final phrase in sec. 91. I would ask the Court to consider that the express purpose and object of that last paragraph is to deal with the effect of enumeration, and not to deal impliedly or indirectly with the effect of that which is outside of enumeration and within the general powers—

" And any matter coming within any of the classes of subjects enumerated in this section shall not be deemed to come within the class of matters of a local or private nature comprised in the enumeration of the classes of subjects by this Act assigned exclusively to the Legislatures of the Provinces."

The very purpose for which the enumeration at any rate in part took place was to avoid doubt or conflict on certain subjects as to whether they fell within the one or the other, and that purpose would not be fully accomplished without an express provision taking the one set of specific provisions out of the operation of the other.

Lord HERSCHELL.—Take the case of a postal service. A postal service strictly confined within the limits of the Province, that is to say, a postal service from house to house in Toronto for example would be a merely local matter if anything is, but being a postal service it is not to be deemed to be merely confined to that. That is a good illustration. That seems to be the object of it.

Lord WATSON—From the earliest cases down to the most recent I think it has always been recognised by this Board that within these sections there is a power given to the Dominion Parliament which, when exercised, operates as an exception. Take the case of making a particular rule a rule of bankruptcy legislation, say affecting civil rights and illustrating the civil law of the Province, in that particular the law of the Dominion Parliament would be exercised and the previous legislation in the Province with regard to the same matter must give way.

Mr. BLAKE—Yes, I am about to trouble your Lordship with a few remarks upon the last instance of that ruling.

Lord WATSON—I think that was first pointed out by Sir Montague Smith.

Mr. BLAKE—But at present I was just endeavouring to answer the suggestion made by Lord Herschell.

Lord WATSON—In those cases really no exception exists in regard to that particular matter until the Parliament of Canada has legislated.

Mr. BLAKE—Yes, my Lord, I am going to trouble your Lordships with something upon that subject, but I would desire to say a word at present with reference to this paragraph at the close of section 91 to get rid of it, and at any rate, to say all I have to say about it, that it was indicated that conflicts would arise——

Lord WATSON—I remember in a recent case where the Dominion Parliament had passed a law which we considered fairly incidental to their powers to regulate Bankruptcy, we held accordingly that that Statute was effective in the Province and abrogated the Common law of the Province upon the subject.

Lord DAVEY—And what constituted the evidence of a debt on which a person might be sued was affected.

Lord WATSON—Yes.

Mr. BLAKE—The purport of the phrase at the close of section 91 is stated at pages 271 and 272 of 1st Cartwright in *Parsons'* case to be practically the same, to complete the object of enumeration altogether. Cases of probable conflict and of doubt were apprehended and enumeration was resorted to in those cases.

Lord HERSCHELL—But more than that, surely. The effect of that provision at the end of section 91 was to exclude from sub-section 16 of section 92 certain things that otherwise would distinctly have been within it.

Mr. BLAKE—I do not know, my Lord, that it was necessary at all.

Lord DAVEY—Surely they could not trench on the enumerated subjects by passing an Insolvency Act, and by saying that it was merely local and only applied to the Province.

Mr. BLAKE—Yes, but even apart from the phrase at the foot of section 91, I doubt whether they could have done that, because your Lordship will find in that portion of the section which precedes the enumeration this—

" For greater certainty, but not so as to restrict the generality of the foregoing terms of this section it is hereby declared that (notwithstanding anything in this Act) "

that is notwithstanding what is said in section 92.

Lord DAVEY—And for greater certainty still.

Lord WATSON—They put it for greater certainty twice over.

Mr. BLAKE—Yes.

Lord HERSCHELL—Then this might be contended—this

argument might be addressed to this Board with a good deal of force—that that was one of those subjects affecting the Dominion, more or less, generally—that where it was merely local, for example a Postal Service within the Province, which did not go outside it, and only dealt with places in the Province, that was merely a local matter, and was not within the Postal Service as intended in sub-section 5 of the main section.

Lord WATSON—I think one of the oldest principles to be found is this, that notwithstanding the terms of that last clause in section 91 there are matters with which the Province can deal, which are not excepted from their legislative jurisdiction until the Dominion Government has proceeded to act upon the powers given to it by certain sub-sections of section 91.

Mr. BLAKE—Yes, my Lord, and I propose to deal with that topic independently. I submit with reference to Postal Services that there is another consideration altogether which applies. It is well known that it is absolutely essential to the existence of the Postal Service that it should be a monopoly. The public are prohibited from carrying letters here.

Lord DAVEY—It might be said that it was detrimental to the Postal Service between the Dominion and Foreign Governments, as somebody said about another section as to trade and commerce.

Mr. BLAKE—Yes, but would somebody have been listened to ?

Lord WATSON—It would apply to the different streets in a Provincial Town.

Mr. BLAKE—Yes, and it would prevent its being possible to carry on a postal service at all such as is recognised here. Then my submission is that that is the purpose, and that no more is accomplished in effect by the end of section 91 than to make surer the provision which was in the beginning of it with reference to the effect of the enumeration, and I say that it leaves the general language of section 91 just where it was.

Lord WATSON—In the case of a Postal Service in construing the meaning of the words, we are not entirely left to the terms of section 91 and section 92, because there are provisions in the Act, if I mistake not, which vest the Dominion of Canada with the whole property, and everything that belonged to the Provincial Governments for the purpose of carrying on the past postal service.

Mr. BLAKE—Yes, the works and Post Offices and Custom Houses and so on, and it shows, of course, what is meant by it. My suggestion, of course, does not go so far (and that idea has been repudiated by this Board) as to say that Canada could, by legislating for all or more than one Province, deal with strictly Provincial topics; because that would be absolutely destructive of the Provincial powers, and the general result of it is that the federal system has, if I may adopt the phrase, the defects of its qualities. There is a lack of universal legislative power in any one body, for all aspects and all places, and one has got to recognise that there may be a desirable uniformity which yet you cannot have, which you must sacrifice in order to obtain the compensating advantages of the federal system. Then I come down to this that the principle is that of two aspects and two purposes of legislation. For example, take the case of licenses for revenue. The express power of No. 9 is for the purpose of raising revenue, and it has been adjudged, I understand, that that limits the power granted in respect of licenses in that aspect; that under No. 9, it must be for the purpose of raising a revenue. But that leaves the same matter subject to be dealt with in other aspects. Indeed it has been adjudged a subject to be dealt with in another aspect by the Province under—I do not know very well what to call it—but under what I have called the police power; and it leaves it to be dealt with under a still different aspect by the Dominion either under the general or under the enumerated powers, as we contend. How widely to be dealt with by the Dominion is one of the things to be disposed of, as also is the capability of its being dealt with by the Dominion under other powers and under other aspects. But what I submit is that the same subject cannot be treated by both under the same aspect, the only real difference being that in the one case it is treated as within the Province, and in the other case as both within and without the Province. I fail to find the over-riding power of the Federal Parliament which is sometimes suggested——

Lord HERSCHELL.—I will tell you where it strikes me it is found. At present the Dominion Parliament has power to make laws for the purpose of the order and good government of Canada in relation to all matters not within the classes of subjects. Now if a matter can only be found in section 92 under sub-section 16, if you can shew that there is a Dominion purpose to be served by dealing with something existing throughout the Dominion, then I should say that it comes within the general Dominion power and would not be within the class of subjects prescribed, because it would not be merely of a local nature, but yet it might deal with the same subject matter which the Province could deal with itself as being merely local. When you say you see no over-riding power, that is where I see it, and where I think according to *Russell* v. *The Queen* it exists.

Mr. BLAKE—I think your Lordship will find that it is not decided ; but indicated certainly.

Lord HERSCHELL.—No, I do not mean decided.

Mr. BLAKE—That is the only reason why I venture to submit this argument to your Lordship—that I do not think it has been decided. I agree that if you find some purpose or aspect, to use the phrases which have been used, in which from a Dominion point of view legislation should take place different from the purpose or aspect for which it is suggested the Province should legislate under merely " local or private " there is a right to legislate and there is no difficulty about it. What I contend is that when the purpose or aspect in which you are dealing with the subject is the same there is no right in both to legislate, and if there is such a right, I fail there to find any ground upon which to say that the Dominion power shall predominate. There is a provision that if it is within the enumerated powers it shall predominate, but there is no provision that if it is within the general powers it shall predominate ; and therefore you find and must, I submit, grapple with the proposition that there is then a conflict——

Lord WATSON—Your argument suggests that there cannot be a matter which is merely local in its nature and at the same time may be of interest to the Dominion.

Mr. BLAKE—Yes, my Lord, that is a part of the argument unquestionably, and my argument is——

Lord WATSON—And that if it be determined to be of interest to the whole Dominion so that the Parliament of Canada can legislate, it can no longer be regarded in the aspect of being merely local and private.

Mr. BLAKE—No, and if not " merely " local and private, it does not come within section 16.

Lord WATSON—It is not " local and private." I do not think " private " has any application.

Mr. BLAKE—No; I should have said "local or private."

Lord HERSCHELL—Supposing this matter had been dealt with by the Provincial Legislature as merely a local matter, and that then the Dominion Parliament had considered that it was a matter to legislate on for the whole Dominion, supposing that is so, and it passed a law with reference to it, of course the Provincial Legislature then could not contravene that Dominion legislation; but does the fact that the Dominion can so legislate prove that the Provincial Legislature never had the power to pass the legislation which it had passed ?

Mr. BLAKE—I think if the Dominion always had the power the Province never had it.

Lord HERSCHELL—Then there is my difficulty. There is scarcely anything which it may be desirable and beneficial for a Province to deal with locally that might not become at some time or other a matter of Dominion concern and therefore one on which it might be necessary for the Dominion to legislate for the whole Dominion. That deprives the Provincial Legislature of all legislative power.

Lord WATSON—I should like you to deal with the matter in this aspect : supposing that the matter is rightly regarded as not of merely local interest to the Province but as of

Canadian interest, and the Dominion Parliament legislate, and competently legislate, upon that footing, then does it necessarily follow that connected with that very matter there may not be local considerations—considerations which are local in their nature, and with which the Provincial Parliament can still deal, is that possible?

Mr. BLAKE—If there is some other aspect or purpose in which the matter can be viewed.

Lord WATSON—You say that the purpose must not be the same.

Mr. BLAKE—That is so.

Lord WATSON—Then you would deal with the present question in this way: you would say that this legislation is for the purpose of obtaining sobriety, and that so long as you are legislating in that aspect you are within the field already occupied by the Dominion Legislature. But on the other hand may there not be some aspects of that question which are local and require local treatment, and only warrant local treatment?

Mr. BLAKE—I do not know, my Lord; I fail to apprehend why.

Lord HERSCHELL.—It may be necessary for the safety of the Dominion to have at least certain temperance provisions, we will suppose, in operation in the Dominion. Suppose those are necessary for the Dominion. On the other hand there may be Provinces where it would be for the Province's advantage that you should have legislation of an even more stringent character. I do not see any difference between the two. The law was merely local and was not considered necessary, and we will suppose it was not necessary and would be more than was needed for the Dominion. But what is there inconsistent with that, that in the Province something more is needed.

Mr. BLAKE—The subject is the promotion of temperance.

Lord HERSCHELL—No; the promotion of temperance is the intermediate object, the subject is the welfare and well-being of the community, and that they should not be troubled with the results of drunkenness. It is not the morality of the individual or the making of him temperate.

The LORD CHANCELLOR—If that aspect of the case (I designedly use that word) is regarded, it will be necessary I suppose to ascertain whether the facts of the particular Province were such as to justify it. Your contention I quite follow. You say the subject matter itself is one which is for the Dominion.

Mr. BLAKE—In this concrete case I have a decision in which the subject matter has been adjudged to be for the Dominion, but, of course, I am dealing generally at the moment with the principle.

The LORD CHANCELLOR—I was not dealing with that for the moment, but with the hypothesis of a local want. Supposing it is so, in order to justify the legislation it must be the Provincial circumstances which justify Provincial Legislation. If so, those facts ought to be before us.

Mr. BLAKE—Yes, but what I maintain is this, that if you grant the premises that the subject is within the jurisdiction of the Dominion, the Dominion arm is not so shortened, but that it is entitled to look at the condition and circumstances of the people throughout the whole or in any part of the country; and if varying circumstances exist with reference to the evil requiring varying legislation in different parts, it is entitled and is bound to apply the proper legislation for the remedy of the general evil.

Lord HERSCHELL—That I think is a very difficult question—a very difficult question. If there is anything clear, it is that this legislation in sections 91 and 92 was to give the Provincial Legislature power to legislate for things within the Province in so far as it was necessary to keep them to a Provincial Legislature. One cannot shut one's eyes to that because it is exclusively *ex hypothesi* of a merely local character. Now, may not you have a thing which, in a particular aspect, to use your word again, is of general interest to the Dominion Parliament, although the ultimate end is the well being of the community, the same end ?

Mr. BLAKE—Of course it depends upon the kind of aspect, as your Lordship puts the question.

Lord HERSCHELL—Take this very kind of question that we are considering. Supposing that the regulation by whatsoever means of the sale of intoxicating liquors is a thing not intended to be dealt with by any of these Provinces, but that the intention was to leave it as a matter to be dealt with by the Dominion Parliament for the whole of Canada, one has certainly to look at the condition of things before the Confederation when different legislation is passed ; and, looking at the scheme of this Act, one would hesitate a good deal to say that that was the intention of the Legislature. If there was anything to prohibit drinking except under certain restrictions it was not a Provincial matter perhaps, but to say that the Dominion Parliament should undertake it for the whole of Canada, and that the Province could not deal with it for the purpose is a strong proposition.

The Lord CHANCELLOR—But do you admit that the Canadian Parliament could not provide for the particular case of a particular Province ?

Mr. BLAKE—No, my Lord, I do not.

Lord HERSCHELL.—I know you say it could, but that is what strikes me as strange. Looking at the scheme of this legislation— -I am supposing now it is not an enumerated thing of course.

Mr. BLAKE—Quite so.

Lord HERSCHELL—Supposing it is not an enumerated thing, and it is in the particular Province, one would think unless it were thought to be necessary to deal with it elsewhere it was a merely local matter—the restriction of the sale of intoxicating liquors within the Province.

Lord WATSON—But if you carry it to a certain length, the difficulty is to get an enactment within the Province which prohibits any person living in a town (even if he were a Member of Parliament) from getting drunk.

Lord HERSCHELL—If you limit the hours within which

he can get it, it is not merely provincial, and in that sense nothing is merely provincial.

The LORD CHANCELLOR—I do not know about that. Some restrictions with reference to particular hours or places may be quite intelligibly provincial and restrictions not involving general application.

Mr. BLAKE—Quite so.

Lord HERSCHELL.—But still it might affect other Provinces in regard to people who happen, for the time being, to be there.

Mr. BLAKE—Yes, but in dealing with these powers you cannot define too much. You must deal upon broad and general considerations and the mere circumstances that casual visitors, even Members of Parliament, unless, indeed, there is a law providing for their immunities——

Lord WATSON—I do not think it can be seriously suggested that regulations for the benefit of those within the Province, which necessarily affect strangers coming into or passing through it, make it less provincial.

Mr. BLAKE—No, my Lord. It is supposed that when they come they will be amenable to the laws which suit the people who live there all the time.

The LORD CHANCELLOR—You must deal with it from a common sense point of view. Certain persons may be of a very austere nature perhaps, and insist on a fast twice a week and prohibit food, and in that case I should have thought that that interfered with the general right to liberty throughout the whole Dominion, and it would be an infringement of the rights of the rest of the subjects of Canada even if it professed to be applicable to a particular Province.

Mr. BLAKE—Yes, it would tend to depopulation of the Provinces, I fancy.

The LORD CHANCELLOR—I think so, too.

Lord HERSCHELL—This was a matter which had been in every one of these confederated Provinces differently dealt with by the Provinces, and if it was a matter that was intended to be taken from the Provinces and put in the Dominion one would have expected to find it in one of the specifically enumerated classes in clause 91. It is not like a new thing which has arisen. There was legislation in each one of these Provinces.

Mr. BLAKE—Yes, my Lord, but the legislation which existed in each one of these Provinces, speaking of it generally, was of the same character. The general character of the legislation was that which has been described for the regulating of the traffic or trade in connection with licensed houses.

Lord HERSCHELL—One was the very conditions which you say now come in question.

Mr. BLAKE—Yes, one was, but only one. Now I submit that the generally exclusive character of the Provincial power must be recognised and upheld by repudiating the doctrine of double jurisdiction in the sense I have indicated; and, before passing in a moment or two to the decision to which Lord Watson has more than once referred on the incidental powers, I wish to refer to *Parsons'* case. I will not trouble your Lordships with the citation of it, but I point out that it declares that it could not have been the intention that conflict should exist, and it lays down, as I submit, principles of examination and construction, which have been practically followed since that time, and which all go to show that the scheme of the Act is a scheme of mutually exclusive and not of concurrent powers and over-riding powers.

Lord WATSON—You will not take it that it ever was contemplated that the Provincial Legislature should enact one thing and the Dominion Parliament should enact another. I thought that was laid down in *Parsons'* case. I did not think it was intended to deal with the kind of suggestions made in this case that if the field is occupied only to a certain extent by the Dominion Parliament there may not be room for the Provincial Legislature to legislate in.

Lord HERSCHELL—In that case there was a Provincial law which provided that there should be certain implied conditions always in certain circumstances. Now, do you admit or deny that the Dominion Parliament under the power of regulating trade or commerce might prescribe conditions with reference to every trade contract made in the Dominion?

Lord WATSON—It would raise a question of that kind if the Dominion Parliament instead of enacting a Temperance Act for all Canada had enacted that every person who wished it might obtain as much whiskey as he chose, and every person who wished it might purchase as small a quantity as he liked, that would raise a very serious question if a Province had attempted to enact any such thing as is in this section 18.

Lord HERSCHELL—Take the case in *Parsons'* case. If it did not come within section 91 the Province might enact certain things with regard to trade contracts. Now could the Dominion Parliament under the power to regulate trade and commerce generally provide that in every commercial contract there shall be certain conditions applied?

Mr. BLAKE—I will refer to what is said in *Parsons'* case.

Lord DAVEY—Page 278 of 1 Cartwright?

Mr. BLAKE—Yes; page 113, L. R. 7 App. Cas.:

"It is enough for the decision of the present case to say that in their view its authority"

(that is, the authority of the Dominion Parliament)

"to legislate for the regulation of trade and commerce does not comprehend the power to regulate by legislation the contracts of a particular business or trade, such as the business of Fire Insurance in a single Province, and therefore that its legislative authority does not in the present case conflict or compete with the power over property and civil rights assigned to the Legislature of Ontario by No. 13 of section 92."

Lord HERSCHELL—That does not answer my question. That puts it aside. They say it is not within the Dominion Parliament's power to legislate for a contract of insurance in a particular Province. Now I ask you about general legislation over all commercial contracts, of course those amongst others, and I ask is that within the Dominion Parliament's power as a matter of the regulation of trade and commerce?

Lord DAVEY—I think the Judgment on page 275 (of 1 Cartwright and page 111 of 7 App. Cas.) answered that question so far as the decision goes—

"If, however, the narrow construction of the words civil rights contended for by the Appellants were to prevail the Dominion Parliament could under its general power legislate in regard to contracts in all and each of the Provinces, and as a consequence of this the Province of Quebec, though now governed by its own civil code founded on the French law as regards contracts and their incidents would be subject to have its law on that subject altered by the Dominion Legislature * * * ."

Certainly it was the opinion of the Board at that time that the Dominion could not legislate on commercial contracts generally.

Lord HERSCHELL—These words are with reference to the narrow construction of the words " civil rights " being held good.

The LORD CHANCELLOR—Supposing the Dominion Parliament were to enact a Statute with reference to bills of sale for instance——

Mr. BLAKE—I should think they had no power.

Lord DAVEY—Unless they did it specially with reference to banks and lumbermen.

Mr. BLAKE—I hope I shall not be called upon to expound the law in reference to the *Union Bank* v. *Tennant* in addition to the other heavy tasks that are laid upon me.

Lord HERSCHELL—But the regulation of trade and commerce can hardly have been held not to interfere with civil rights.

Mr. BLAKE—Doubtless it must interfere to a certain extent.

Lord HERSCHELL—Therefore it is no answer to say that it would interfere with civil rights. Is it to be said that there is to be no general legislation in reference to commercial contracts ?

Lord WATSON—You could not legislate as to a bill of exchange and so on without interfering with civil rights.

Mr. BLAKE—They are put in and enumerated, my Lord.

Lord HERSCHELL—That is what I wanted to see, whether consistently with what is said in *Parsons'* case it is not possible that there might be Dominion legislation which might override the Provincial legislation although until overridden the Provincial legislation might be good. That is to say : the Province for a particular class or company in the Province might make Provincial legislation with regard to an essential of the contract in the Province, but that would not preclude the Dominion Parliament from making a general provision for the regulation of commerce as to conditions which should be comprehended in all commercial contracts. I do not feel so sure of that.

Mr. BLAKE—Of course that depends largely upon the interpretation of " regulation of trade and commerce," which I was not yet approaching, and perhaps your Lordship will allow me to postpone that.

Lord HERSCHELL—Certainly ; but one is driven to anticipate cases, one cannot go entirely in the air.

Mr. BLAKE—I entirely agree.

Lord WATSON—Take even bills of exchange and promissory notes do you suggest that there being no legislation by the Dominion Parliament the Provincial Legislature could not give any special rights to the holder of a bill of exchange or of a promissory note as against his debtor.

Mr. BLAKE—I do, my Lord.

Lord DAVEY—That would come within the proviso of section 91.

Mr. BLAKE—Certainly.

Lord HERSCHELL—No ; this proviso of section 91 does not apply to that.

Mr. BLAKE—It comes within the head of its section.

Lord HERSCHELL—But not in the tail.

Mr. BLAKE—The sting is in both head and tail here.

The LORD CHANCELLOR—That brings us into a deeper puzzle than we were in before.

Lord WATSON—I am afraid there may be a difficulty which we will have to get out of in that respect.

The LORD CHANCELLOR—For my own part I should have thought a Bill of Exchange and all its incidents was something which was intended to be included in t' e enumerated classes.

Mr. BLAKE—" Notwithstanding anything in the Act contained " they are exclusively within the power of the Parliament of Canada. It happens with regard to this that " property and civil rights " is put into some other part of the Act, but notwithstanding by section 91, bills of exchange are exclusively within the power of the Parliament of Canada. The fundamental law recognises a possible variety of pre-existing Provincial Laws. It recognises the fact that there were different laws in the Provinces, and the fundamental Charter provides that until the Parliament of Canada alter it, the Provincial law shall remain. Then there always was a law; but by whom could that law be changed, by whom could it be repealed, by whom could it be supplemented ? By the Parliament of Canada and by it alone. What I venture to submit is that this theory of construction is not affected by decisions such as that in *Cushing* v. *Dupuy*, and the later insolvency cases. In arguing that case I was asked by your Lordships, and your Lordships in argument expressed a view which is clearly in accordance with the Judgment in the case ; I was asked whether I contended that anything which necessarily came within bankruptcy and insolvency could be the subject of legislation by a Province notwithstanding that there was no Dominion legislation on the subject. I could make no such contention ; I was obliged to acknowledge that whatever really came within bankruptcy and insolvency was exclusively within the power of the Dominion and could not be touched by a Province.

Lord WATSON—You cannot say what may and what may not be incidental to legislation.

Mr. BLAKE—That is the point which your Lordships decided. You said you would not define all that was covered by the words, but you did find what were some essential elements of bankruptcy and insolvency ; and you found that this law did not come within those essential elements. More than these essentials might possibly be embraced as ancillary

N

in a Bankruptcy and Insolvency Act; and therefore there was an elastic margin which might or might not be trenched upon in the exercise of its main power to deal with bankruptcy and insolvency by the Dominion Parliament, thus touching a subject which came within property and civil rights for that other purpose and in that other aspect. In the exercise of this its power to deal with bankruptcy and insolvency what would the Dominion Parliament do? It would cut out for that purpose, and in that aspect some subject which was otherwise within property and civil rights. It would not cut it out altogether, it would not annul for all other purposes and under all other aspects the rights of the Provincial Legislature: the rights of creditors, the rights of contract and the mode of payment and all that would remain.

Lord WATSON—Would it touch the right of creditors except in matters of insolvency?

Mr. BLAKE—No, my Lord; and therefore the subject came to be considered in two aspects, the aspect of the right when insolvency did not exist, and of the right when it did exist. The subject was carved into two—the one was exclusively Provincial and the other exclusively Dominion. There was in one sense an over-riding of the legislation, because in one aspect the subject of the legislation would cease to be Provincial and the legislation would no longer extend to it. It came within bankruptcy and insolvency and ceased to be within local jurisdiction; and for that reason the Provincial law no longer applied to it, but the Provincial law remained applicable to all other cases. That is the principle on which those cases were decided; and it is not inconsistent in the least degree with the view which I present to your Lordships. It is simply this, that if you look to the character of the powers it is impossible by anticipation to define the precise limits of them——

Lord WATSON—There the legislation of the Province to be well exercised would require to be applied to solvents and insolvents alike?

Mr. BLAKE—Yes. If you could find that the legislation of the Province was expressly directed to insolvency.

Lord WATSON—That law might cease to apply to insolvents if not so.

Mr. BLAKE—Yes, it might.

Lord DAVEY—But in some case, the name of which I cannot remember, it was held that a Province could pass a law winding up a particular company.

Mr. MACLAREN—That was the case of *L' Union St. Jacques de Montreal* v. *Belisle,* 1 Cartwright, p. 63.

Mr. BLAKE—The principle of that case was to that effect.

Lord DAVEY—Yes.   The head note says :—

"The Act of the Legislature of Quebec (38 Victoria, c. 58) for the relief of the Appellant Society, then (as appeared on the face of the Act) in a state of extreme financial embarrassment, is within the legislative capacity of that Legislature. The Act was held to relate to ' a matter merely of a local or private nature in the Province,' which by the 92nd section of the British North America Act, 1867, is assigned to the exclusive competency of the Provincial Legislature ; and not to fall within the category of bankruptcy and insolvency ⁂ ⁂ ⁂ ⁂ "

Mr. BLAKE—Yes.

Lord WATSON—It was held that the winding up could prevent the bankrupt becoming insolvent ?

Mr. BLAKE—Yes ; although the stringent method by which that result was accomplished forced the creditors to take a composition. I own to being dull enough not to comprehend that reasoning; but that was the principle of that case. Now I come at last to *Russell's* case, which gives us the concrete question as well as the principle ; and I call your Lordships' attention to the description which is given of the Canada Temperance Act (L. R. 7 App. Cas. p. 835 and 2 Cartwright) p. 17 :—

"The effect of the Act when brought into force in any county or town within the Dominion is, describing it generally, to prohibit the sale of intoxicating liquors, except in wholesale quantities, or for certain specified purposes ; to regulate the traffic in the excepted cases, and to make sales of liquors in violation of the prohibition and regulations contained in the Act criminal offences punishable by fine, and for the third or subsequent offence by imprisonment."

s 2

Then on page 19 there is an approval of the principles of construction given in *Parsons'* case, and they are re-stated :—

> " According to the principle of construction there pointed out, the first question to be determined is, whether the Act now in question falls within any of the classes of subjects enumerated in section 92, and assigned exclusively to the Legislatures of the Provinces ? If it does, then the further question would arise, viz., whether the subject of the Act does not also fall within one of the enumerated classes of subjects in section 91, and so does not still belong to the Dominion Parliament ? But if the Act does not fall within any of the classes of subjects in section 92, no further question will remain, for it cannot be contended, and indeed was not contended at their Lordships' bar, that, if the Act does not come within one of the classes of subjects assigned to the Provincial Legislatures, the Parliament of Canada had not by its general power ' to make laws for the peace, order and good government of Canada,' full legislative authority to pass it."

Then it proceeds to state the sections under which it was suggested that it came within the Provincial power. It deals first with section 9, and points out that this Act is not a fiscal Act—that it is an Act to destroy revenue, not to create it. Then it deals on page 21 in language which is important, with the question of property and civil rights. I say this language is very important, because it gives a character to this particular Act which I design to import into the character of the Acts which your Lordships are asked to determine are within the jurisdiction of the Provincial Legislature. Upon the questions put with reference to prohibition, I ask your Lordships to say that the same observations have got to be made as to the purpose and aspect as are made in this case :—

> " Next, their Lordships cannot think that the Temperance Act in question properly belongs to the class of subjects, ' Property and Civil Rights.' It has in its legal aspect an obvious and close similarity to laws which place restrictions on the sale or custody of poisonous drugs, or of dangerously explosive substances."

And I here advert to the fact that there have been one or two suggestions as to the sale of poisons. Their Lordships in this Judgment indicate that the sale or custody of poisonous drugs, which they instanced as an analogous case, might or would come within the Dominion jurisdiction :—

> " These things, as well as intoxicating liquors, can, of course, be held as property, but a law placing restrictions on their sale, custody or removal, on the ground that the free sale or use of them is dangerous to public safety, and making it a criminal offence punishable by fine or imprisonment to violate these restrictions, cannot properly be deemed a

law in relation to property in the sense in which those words are used
in the 92nd section. What Parliament is dealing with in legislation
of this kind is not a matter in relation to property and its rights, but
one relating to public order and safety. That is the primary matter
dealt with, and though incidentally the free use of things in which men
may have property is interfered with, that incidental interference does
not alter the character of the law. Upon the same considerations, the
Act in question cannot be regarded as legislation in relation to civil
rights. In however large a sense these words are used it could not
have been intended to prevent the Parliament of Canada from declaring
and enacting certain uses of property and certain acts in relation to
property, to be criminal and wrongful. Laws which make it a criminal
offence for a man wilfully to set fire to his own house on the ground
that such an act endangers the public safety, or to overwork his horse
on the ground of cruelty to the animal, though affecting in some sense
property, and the right of a man to do as he pleases with his own, cannot
properly be regarded as legislation in relation to property or to civil
rights. Nor could a law which prohibited or restricted the sale or
exposure of cattle having a contagious disease be so regarded. Laws of
this nature designed for the promotion of public order, safety or morals,
and which subject those who contravene them to criminal procedure
and punishment, belong to the subject of public wrongs rather than to
that of civil rights. They are of a nature which fall within the general
authority of Parliament to make laws for the order and good government of Canada, and have direct relation to Criminal law, which is one
of the enumerated classes of subjects assigned exclusively to the
Parliament of Canada."

Then it goes on to deal with the subject.

Lord HERSCHELL—But is not that true about what we
may call for the moment a local Licensing Act? Might not
every word that is said there be said about it? Its object is
the good order and well being of the community. They may
be punished for doing what is prohibited, if it is within the
power of the Provincial Legislature by fine, penalty or
imprisonment, and why may not all that be said about the
Licensing Act?

Mr. BLAKE—I was going, when I came to the case of
Hodge v. *The Queen*, to point out to your Lordships how your
Lordships thought that it might not be said in the case of
Hodge v. *The Queen*.

The LORD CHANCELLOR—Of course you might at once
say without going into particulars about it, that the selection
of persons fitted to deal in such matters might very well be
properly local.

Mr. BLAKE—Quite so.

The LORD CHANCELLOR—And could only be local.

Mr. BLAKE—That is so.

Lord HERSCHELL.—Take other things mentioned there, because you refer to other things—it does not mention only the liquor question. Supposing that in a particular Province there was a provision that diseased animals, or animals certified to be diseased, should not go to particular markets, do you say then that that would be extra-provincial—beyond the power of the Province ?

Lord DAVEY—You do not say that, do you ?

Mr. BLAKE—I think there is a general law upon that subject if I remember rightly.

Lord DAVEY—But supposing there was not ?

Mr. BLAKE—I do not think so. I do not propose to say that there may not be many of these topics so dealt with within the proper limits of local regulation as to the differences of condition in larger and smaller communities and which yet may not be in all aspects local. I do not say that you may not have the greatest difficulty, when a concrete case arises, in drawing the line, between what is in the view of *Hodge* v. *The Queen* as your Lordships expressed it local and what is not. But what I do say is that there the principle on which the line is to be drawn is to be found. It is to be drawn in each case with reference to the principle laid down in *Hodge* v. *The Queen*, and, when once drawn, you find a purpose and aspect local which gives jurisdiction exclusively to the Province, and beyond that purpose and aspect the subject is within the Dominion jurisdiction only.

Lord HERSCHELL—I have at present a difficulty in seeing a distinction in principle between any amount of fetters which might be put on drink for the well-being of the community and the final fetter which prevents the sale of the intoxicating liquor. The object and aspect appears to me at present to be in both cases the same, namely, the well-being of the community and good order, all of which are supposed to be endangered by excessive indulgence, and all these steps have in view the diminution of what is inconsistent with the well-being and good order of the community.

Mr. BLAKE—I should have thought, in another aspect of this case, as your Lordship and several members of the Board pointed out, that there was the greatest possible fundamental difference between regulation and absolute prohibition.

Lord HERSCHELL.—For some purposes there is a fundamental difference. But as to the purpose and aspect being one thing or another, if you regard the aspect of prohibition, as stated in *Russell* v. *The Queen*, in the words you have just read, namely, the well-being and good order of the community, I do not at present see any difference in aspect between the object of prohibition and the object of restriction.

Mr. BLAKE—My sacred words, I think, read "aspect and purpose" or "purpose and aspect."

Lord HERSCHELL.—"Aspect and purpose." The aspect and purpose is the well-being and good order of the community I think. Is not that the aspect and purpose of the restrictive legislation with regard to liquor? How does the aspect and purpose differ? When you are dealing with such words as regulation and so on, I can understand that there is a distinction between regulation and prohibition.

Mr. BLAKE—I should say that the aspect and purpose with which the local Legislature was adjudged to have a power in *Hodge* v. *The Queen* was in reference to the different local conditions arising in small communities, such as cities, towns and villages, and so forth, for the preservation of local order in minor matters; and although it may be extremely difficult to say that preservation of local order is a minor and minute regulation, and that it is not engrafted upon the same view which is directed to the prevention of drunkenness and the preservation of decency, and which is directed to a keeping up of morality, yet that is the distinction upon which, as I understand in *Russell's* case and *Hodge* v. *The Queen*, the Court held that prohibition was within the Federal power and certain regulations within the local power.

Lord HERSCHELL—I do not think they said that was so.

Mr. BLAKE—The Temperance Act, they said, was within the Federal regulation.

Lord HERSCHELL—But the Canada Temperance Act went beyond what was merely local, because it dealt with it as a matter concerning the whole Dominion.

Mr. BLAKE—Yes.

The LORD CHANCELLOR—I suppose you might put it, as to prohibition, that the fact that you might drink is one thing, but to regulate how often or at what times you are to drink is another thing.

Mr. BLAKE—I do not know about the "often." I do not know whether, if they allowed them to drink at all, they could regulate the time allowed "between drinks," as the saying is. That would depend upon the rapidity of the man's consumption.

Lord HERSCHELL—Supposing it is within the power of the Provincial Legislature, for local order as you call it, to limit the hours, and then they find, perhaps, that what they have done is not enough to accomplish the purpose, and they limit them still more, and even then they find that it does not accomplish the purpose, and they say finally, "now we shall shut the shops up," why is not that the same? It is only now that they are going to the extent that they find necessary, having learned by experience that their first legislation did not go far enough for the purpose. In that case when does it cease to be local order?

Mr. BLAKE—I do not know that I can draw the line, but I am about to point out certain other considerations which I think should be applied to limiting the power, and perhaps it would be most convenient to take it altogether.

Lord HERSCHELL—As you like, only I indicate the difficulties that are present to my mind.

Mr. BLAKE—I am very grateful to your Lordship for indicating them. Then on page 23, in the case of *Russell* v. *The Queen* there is this passage, which is important:—

"It was argued by Mr. Benjamin that if the Act related to criminal law, it was provincial criminal law, and he referred to sub-section 15 of section 92, viz.: ' The imposition of punishment by fine, penalty, or imprisonment for enforcing any law of the province made in relation to any matter coming within any of the classes of subjects enumerated in this section.' No doubt this argument would be well founded if the principal matter of the Act could be brought within any of these classes of subjects ; but as far as they have yet gone, their Lordships fail to see that this has been done."

and then they come (page 24) to sub-section 16 of section 92 : " Generally all matters of a merely local or private nature in the Province "—

> " It was not, of course, contended for the Appellant that the Legislature of New Brunswick could have passed the Act in question, which, embraces in its enactments all the Provinces ; nor was it denied with respect to this last contention, that the Parliament of Canada might have passed an Act of the nature of that under discussion to take effect at the same time throughout the whole Dominion."

Your Lordships see the character of the contentions. Of course it was not contended for the Appellant that the Legislature could have passed an Act which went beyond the legislative limits of the Province, nor, as I understand the whole Judgment, does it proceed simply upon the proposition that the inability of the Legislature to pass an Act which extends beyond the Province confers jurisdiction of itself upon the Dominion if the subject matter of the legislation be in itself local—

> " Their Lordships understand the contention to be that, at least in the absence of a general law of the Parliament of Canada, the provinces might have passed a local law of a like kind, each for its own Province."

Lord HERSCHELL.—That is at least " in the absence," and that seems to indicate the view which was within the mind of the Court.

Mr. BLAKE—I quite concede that there are indications of that being in the mind of the Court in this case. All I ventured to say was that I did not conceive that it had been adjudged, I quite concede that—

> "and that, as the prohibitory and penal parts of the Act in question, were to come into force in those Counties and Cities only in which it was adopted in the manner prescribed, or, as it was said, ' by local option,' the legislation was in effect, and on its face upon a matter of a merely local nature."

Then the Judgment of Chief Justice Allen is quoted, and their Lordships continue :—

"Their Lordships cannot concur in this view. The declared object of Parliament in passing the Act is that there should be uniform legislation in all the provinces respecting the traffic in intoxicating liquors, with a view to promote temperance in the Dominion. Parliament does not treat the promotion of temperance as desirable in one province more than in another, but as desirable everywhere throughout the Dominion. The Act, as soon as it was passed, became a law for the whole Dominion, and the enactments of the first part, relating to the machinery for bringing the second part into force, took effect and might be put in motion at once and everywhere within it. It is true that the prohibitory and penal parts of the Act are only to come into force in any County or City, upon the adoption of a petition to that effect by a majority of electors, but this conditional application of these parts of the Act does not convert the Act itself into legislation in relation to a merely local matter. The objects and scope of the legislation are still general, viz., to promote temperance by means of a uniform law throughout the Dominion. The manner of bringing the prohibitions and penalties of the Act into force, which parliament has thought fit to adopt, does not alter its general and uniform character. Parliament deals with the subject as one of general concern to the Dominion upon which uniformity of legislation is desirable and the Parliament alone can so deal with it."

There again is an indication such as your Lordship has suggested, I quite admit—

"There is no ground or pretence for saying that the evil or vice struck at by the Act in question is local or exists only in one province, and that Parliament under colour of general legislation, is dealing with a provincial matter only. It is, therefore, unnecessary to discuss the considerations which a state of circumstances of this kind might present."

Their Lordships do not therefore intend to decide what would be the result in that state of things—

"The present legislation is clearly meant to apply a remedy to an evil which is assumed to exist throughout the Dominion, and the local option, as it is called, no more localises the subject and scope of the Act than a provision in an Act for the prevention of contagious diseases in cattle that a public officer should proclaim in what districts it should come into effect, would make the Statute itself a mere local law for each of these districts. In Statutes of this kind the legislation is general, and the provision for the special application of it to particular places does not alter its character."

Lord WATSON—The ... ,t favorable words to you in this Judgment which you ha ... just read, as far as I can see, are these, "Matters as to which uniformity of legislation is desirable."

Mr. BLAKE—Yes, my Lord, "uniformity of legislation."

Lord WATSON—There are other passages which tend the other way, but that seems to go in your favor as indicating that that is one of the objects which the Dominion Parliament was entitled to contemplate and act upon.

Mr. BLAKE—Yes.

Lord HERSCHELL—Is it uniformity in any other sense except as a law applicable to the whole Dominion. It might be applicable to the whole, but certainly in relation to temperance its operation was not uniform because it depended upon who took advantage of it.

Lord DAVEY—I suppose you are going to argue at some time or other that the Dominion Parliament having passed the Canada Temperance Act, did as it said occupy the field.

Mr. BLAKE—Yes.

Lord DAVEY—Whatever might be the case if there were no Canada Temperance Act, the Provincial Legislature is thereby debarred from legislating on the same subject.

Mr. BLAKE—It is impossible for the Provincial Legislature, the subject having been competently legislated on, as adjudged by this Board, by the Dominion Parliament, to legislate on it again. That was competently done. It is not merely that it is professed to be done.

The LORD CHANCELLOR—I suppose you would say that the passing of the Act which rendered it competent to them to adopt it or not was an Act which in its purport and effect showed that the Dominion Parliament did not intend that the Provincial Legislature should legislate on that subject against the will of any minority of inhabitants.

Mr. BLAKE—Yes, my Lord.

Lord HERSCHELL—But supposing that the Dominion Parliament has come to the conclusion that it is for the good order and the well being of the whole of Canada that temperance should be at least promoted to a certain extent in a certain way, is it necessarily inconsistent with that that a Provincial Legislature might supplement that legislation by other legislation because it is considered that in some particular Province there was more urgent need ?

Mr. BLAKE—I was about to consider that very point which your Lordship has put to me.

Lord HERSCHELL—Of course they could not legislate inconsistently.

Mr. BLAKE—For one moment, before passing to that, I wish to point out to your Lordship what has been taken out of controversy by these passages of the Judgment which I have just read. First of all, that the law which is passed is a general law—and that it is a general law notwithstanding its adoptive nature ; that the opportunity of uniformity it gives by making a provision under which in various local communities all through Canada it might be put in force is a sufficient generality and a sufficient uniformity, if generality, and if uniformity are required in order to the exercise of the Canadian legislative power, propositions which I respectfully dispute, but if generality and if uniformity are required, this Act is general and uniform : it is general and uniform although it merely provides a machinery by which different localities within the Dominion may at their option and election, evidenced in a particular way, use the provisions and put them into force ; it is adequately general and adequately uniform though *ex facie* it contemplates the probability that it will not be universally applied,—though the particular conditions which it propounds are conditions which indicate in the mind of the Parliament a probability that it will not be universally applied ; and that consequently its actual practical operation will be diversity instead of uniformity,—that at any rate (which is sufficient for my purpose) it is possible there will be diversity instead of uniformity. It is adequately general and adequately uniform although it recognises the view that the condition of things in different parts, not merely in different Provinces but in different parts of each Province of the Dominion, may so differ that the promotion of tempe-

rance, the accomplishment of the objects which the legislature
had at heart and was desirous to promote, would not be
achieved by its being put into operation, that a general
sweeping enactment providing that it should come into force
all over or in any particular locality or over a Province might
be instrumental to the object in view, that is the promotion
of temperance, that unless the test was successfully applied
of a local demand supported by a majority at an election,
there ought not to be this restraint, this prohibition which,
on these conditions, and on these conditions alone, it was
intended should be applied. The Judgment does not indeed
decide that the power of Parliament is limited as possibly
may be the case here. That point is expressly reserved; but
what is decided is that while the power of Parliament to be
competently exercised, should be exercised generally all over
the Dominion, this law whose practical and contemplated
operation was not generality, not uniformity in application
and in operation, was yet a competent exercise of that power.

Lord DAVEY—It is uniform because it gives the same
option to every county in the Dominion.

Mr. BLAKE—Quite so, it is uniform in that sense; it
gives a power to apply it to every place, but its tendency in
fact would be to produce diversity instead of uniformity in
the laws by which the subject is bound in each part.

The LORD CHANCELLOR—I suppose you might say further
that if a Provincial law prevails and it prohibits, it would
come to this that whereas the determination was left to the
Provincial Legislature, according to Canadian legislation each
person has the right to have it one way or the other, the
Provincial Parliament takes away the right.

Mr. BLAKE—Certainly. I say you find Canada divided
into Provinces and of course each Province divided into a lot
of counties, each one of these counties is given a right to
decide whether this law shall come into operation in its
bounds; if the law comes into operation or if it is rejected on
the vote that means that the condition stands for the period
of three years, that it has a rest or a trial. At the end of
three years the inhabitants of that locality may apply for a
repeal, and then a new election takes place and it is decided

whether there shall be a repeal or not. If on the original election they fail to pass the law, or if upon the proposal for repeal they fail to pass the repealing law there is three years rest in that condition and things so remain. If the repeal is passed there can be no further effort to pass the prohibition law for three years. So that the people have an interval of three years under one law or the other. Each locality is given by the machinery which the Dominion Legislature thought best adapted for grappling with that evil, by the provision of those tests which the Dominion Legislature thought the efficient tests for determining whether it was best that total prohibition should take place, ample and adequate provisions to meet the case according to the view of the Legislature which has passed the Act and has provided the means for putting the Act into force, for keeping it in force, for taking it off and putting it on again.

Lord HERSCHELL—That argument of yours would apply to nothing except absolute prohibition would it, because the Legislature has only provided that it is to be enforced where the majority adopts the Act? Does that exclude all right to legislate for anything other than prohibition? In every place that does not adopt the Act, where they do not apply prohibition, is the local Legislature powerless to make stringent regulations?

Lord DAVEY—Mr. Blake says if it did so they would apply only to the majority.

Lord HERSCHELL—The practical case put to us is that you shall not sell except in certain quantities, that is not total prohibition.

The Lord CHANCELLOR—But that is taken from the Canada Temperance Act, as I read it. (I may be wrong.) An altogether different question arises on the subject of prohibition.

Lord HERSCHELL—Take the last one.

Sir RICHARD COUCH—The 18th section prohibits altogether.

Mr. BLAKE—Yes.

Lord HERSCHELL—Only in certain places, that is in shops

and places other than houses of public entertainment. It does not prohibit it altogether in houses of public entertainment. It provides limits as to the quantity that may be sold; that is what it does. It stops short of absolute prohibition.

Sir RICHARD COUCH—It is for prohibiting the sale in certain places.

Lord HERSCHELL—You may not sell, it says, except in certain places, and in those places you may sell it in not less quantity than twelve bottles, but that is not the same prohibition which would come into operation by the adoption of the Act—it is something different.

Mr. BLAKE—For the moment I would ask your Lordship to dispense me from discussing the 7th question.

Lord HERSCHELL—But that is why I put my question—that your argument would only apply, would it not, to the case of absolute prohibition which is provided by the Canada Temperance Act, where the Act is put into operation. What I mean is this: Is your argument this, that the Parliament of Canada having enacted that in any district a certain majority may stop the sale altogether, that precludes any regulation of the traffic short of prohibition in those districts?

Mr. BLAKE—In that general statement of it I would not agree, because there may be minute regulations.

Lord HERSCHELL—But I do not want minute—take big regulations, but short of prohibition. Does the fact that the Parliament of Canada said that wherever people want to prohibit by a certain majority there shall be prohibition, exclude all power of regulation of the traffic short of prohibition in those districts?

Lord WATSON—That depends very much on the way you read the Act. It is one thing to say they have enacted that they shall do so and so, and another to say that these persons shall have the privilege and option of deciding for themselves, and no other person shall say whether this Act is to be adopted.

Lord HERSCHELL—The determining whether the Act is

to be adopted brings in the question of prohibition, and does the adopting of prohibition necessarily exclude all legislation short of prohibition ?

Lord WATSON—The question then arises—and this is one of my numerous difficulties in this case—is not additional legislation or supplemental legislation a practical repeal of the option given by the general law ?, Is it or is it not ? That is only a question. I am not indicating any opinion upon the point, but it seems to raise that question shortly.

Mr. BLAKE—Quite so. I submit that there is here a determination on the part of the Parliament of Canada to take up the question and to legislate upon it.

Lord DAVEY—And they believe that it is a question for the good government of Canada.

Mr. BLAKE—It is a question for the good government of Canada. They have competently dealt with it, as is adjudged. They have decided that on particular conditions and in a particular way——

Lord WATSON—You see that really comes to this. The same difficulty would not have arisen, as far as I am concerned, if, professing to deal with the whole question, the Parliament of Canada had directly enacted that they should be subject to no restriction unless they chose to use this Act. Now, have they in substance done that or have they not ? That is the first question.

Lord HERSCHELL.—Has not *Hodge* v. *The Queen* said that they have not done that, because *Hodge* v. *The Queen* has said that in districts where it has not been adopted and where there is therefore not prohibition, it is still competent for the Provincial Legislature to enact regulations as to times and places within which drink may be supplied.

Mr. BLAKE—Certainly, within certain limits.

Lord HERSCHELL.—I will deal with limits presently ; but the fact that they can do it at all indicates——

Mr. BLAKE—But the Canadian Parliament has not said that there shall be no legislation in reference to it.

Lord WATSON—I rather think the observation made in that case points to regulation as something different from prohibition. No doubt it may involve prohibition, but it points to something which is in substance merely regulation.

Mr. BLAKE—Just consider the point and the observation in *Hodge* v. *The Queen.* They said where the Act had not been locally adopted, and in Toronto that was so, the traffic is still permitted, and is being carried on ; and it would have been absurd to contend that, while the Dominion Parliament had not taken such steps as would effectually prohibit the traffic in the city of Toronto, and had left it a legal traffic, the powers, whatever they may be——

Lord HERSCHELL.—That was precisely my question— whether all powers therefore short of prohibition, which is involved in the Act when adopted, were not consistently with the Act still left to the Provincial Legislature ?

Mr. BLAKE—Nay, my Lord, because I am dealing only with those areas in which the Canada Temperance Act had not been put into operation.

Lord HERSCHELL—Exactly ; that is what I put to you.

Mr. BLAKE—I thought your Lordship was dealing with all the areas.

Lord HERSCHELL—In all the areas where it has been put into operation prohibition exists.

Mr. BLAKE—Nominally.

Lord HERSCHELL—But you must assume that it is on paper or is supposed to exist. The question was directed to those places where it was not adopted, and nothing interfered with it at all, and whether that did not leave open to the Provincial Legislature at all events everything short of prohibition ?

Mr. BLAKE—That may be so within limits as I have before said ; but if your Lordship would permit me to reserve my answer to that till I come to *Hodge's* case, I should be obliged to your Lordship. It is a difficult question which I am not prepared to deal with as fully at this stage of the

т

argument, I say frankly, as I should desire. But I do contend that the Parliament of Canada has done these things as effectively, as Lord Watson suggests, as if it had done what I submit it was not called upon to do, as if it had said there shall be no other interference and no other condition imposed by any other body with reference to this matter. I contend it for one reason which excludes all others; and for a second reason that because the Parliament of Canada had competently delared that this was a general matter, and that, therefore, it was no longer merely local or private. therefore there is no other authority to compete, and if there was authority to compete, I say that when the Parliament of Canada provides conditions under which the thing may be put into force in different localities and kept in force and repealed and so forth—I say that it as exhaustively deals with the whole topic as if it had gone on to say that it shall not be done in any other way. But that was not necessary because the language of the Act itself shows an exhaustive dealing so far as prohibition is concerned.

Lord DAVEY—You say where the Parliament of the Dominion has dealt with the subject, the Provincial Legislature cannot deal with it in the same way?

Mr. BLAKE—Not in the same aspect. Parliament has said this subject of temperance is a subject for the good government of Canada. They are adjudged to have the right to say that, and they have dealt with it as the good government of Canada in their judgment required.

The LORD CHANCELLOR—Shall be subject to local option practically.

Mr. BLAKE—Yes, and the local option which they prescribe is the only local option which can be passed with reference to that subject.

(Adjourned for a short time).

Mr. BLAKE—Then, my Lords, let us consider if your Lordships please for a moment what kind of legislation, what other methods for putting such an Act as the Temperance

Act into force would clearly and obviously be within the power
of the Dominion Parliament, would be good Dominion
legislation having the same effect which, I suggest, follows
from the Dominion being capable of taking up the subject at
all. Of course it could pass an Act providing total prohibition
for the whole country; but it might also provide for prohibition
in each Province at large, and that either by a plebiscite of
the whole Province, the electorate of the whole voting instead
of in bodies, or on condition of a resolution of the local
assembly or on a proclamation of the Lieutenant-Governor,
all local methods for putting the Act into operation, clearly,
on the principle on which this Act is held good, within the
competency of the Canadian Parliament. Or again that Act
might be put into force on a resolution of the House of
Commons, or on a proclamation of the Governor-General—
Dominion powers. Every one of these suggested proposals
would be a less minute and less a local option system than
what is held good; and the conclusion is, as I submit, that if
the Parliament conceives that the peace, order, and good
government of Canada would be served by providing for
prohibition whenever local option favours it, and setting up
conditions on which it should be put into force, it
can so act, and exhaust the subject thus. It can say
therefore we will stop the growing plague where the
conditions in our judgment show that prohibition will stop it.
Then that seems to me to take this particular concrete case
entirely out of "merely local or private." It is adjudged to
have been effectively declared to be an evil general in its
nature, also more or less developed in Canada here and there,
but certainly not on Provincial lines. In parts of any Province
there may be a condition where the Legislature has thought
benefit would result and the evil would be checked by putting
the prohibition into force. In other parts no such results
may arise, and thus enough appears to show, apart from
"merely local or private," that the Provincial jurisdiction is
non-existent, because it has been shown to be in this particular
case a general evil within the jurisdiction of the Dominion.
There are other reasons, as I submit, why it cannot be within
"merely local or private." Take the question of importation.
I think your Lordships rather indicated in the course of the
argument that that must be held to be outside "local or

T 2

private," because it affects the exporter, it affects other Provinces, and also because it affects the revenue. In that connection I have referred to a section, which I shall also have to refer to more at length at another part of the argument, which deals with the free importation of some things. Section 121 of the British North America Act provides that :—

> " All articles of the growth, produce or manufacture of any one of the provinces shall, from and after the Union, be admitted free into each of the other provinces."

Lord WATSON—As to that part of the argument you are passing from ; in *Russell* v. *The Queen* I do not understand this Board put it entirely on the fact that the legislation was within the general and initial clause of section 91.   At the conclusion of their Judgment they state at p. 26 :—

> " Their Lordships having come to the conclusion that the Act in question does not fall within any of the classes of subjects assigned exclusively to the Provincial Legislatures, it becomes unnecessary to discuss the further question whether its provisions also fall within any of the classes of subjects enumerated in section 91.   In abstaining from this discussion they must not be understood as intimating any dissent from the opinion of the Chief Justice of the Supreme Court of Canada and the other Judges, who held that the Act, as a general regulation of the traffic in intoxicating liquors throughout the Dominion, fell within the class of subject ' the regulation of trade and commerce ' enumerated in that section, and was on that ground a valid exercise of the legislative power of the Parliament of Canada."

Lord DAVEY—I understood Mr. Blake was going to deal with the subject of regulation separately.

Mr. BLAKE—Yes, I am going to do so altogether separately; but I was about to observe this much now, that it was not adjudged against us at all even impliedly, and there is no indication of a decision adverse to us in *The Queen* v. *Russell.* As I was saying, it is clear that importation is not merely local or private, and as to articles which are of the growth, manufacture or produce of any Province, there is an express provision—and that was one of the great objects of Federation—to give absolute security for the admission of such articles free into each of the other Provinces.   So the two following sections with reference to customs and excise deal with the free admission as between the Provinces, until the customs laws should be assimilated by providing that any goods imported into one Province should be capable of being imported into the other on paying any additional duty, if any leviable, under the law of the Province of import.

The LORD CHANCELLOR—That would be supposed to be merely fiscal.

Mr. BLAKE—Perhaps; but still there is the provision for importation. The object is as far as possible to make trade and commerce between the Provinces free, and that is the scope and purpose of the enactments. It is in that view only I advert to them. Parliament was convinced it was necessary they should make a general uniform law as to customs duties, because to allow differential laws would have been simply to make one Province the *entrepôt* for the others—then if one considers for a moment the effect of the prohibition of importation into one Province of goods on which customs' duties are laid, that will of course cripple the resources of the Dominion. As to manufacture also I say that it is impossible to call that merely local or private. The intent and object is evidenced by the whole Act and by this 121st section particularly. It is to make the country one for these commercial purposes, and it cannot be declared that one Province is so exclusively interested in the question of the absolute prohibition of the manufacture of articles which it has been in the habit of importing from another Province and consuming, that it becomes a subject merely local. Then as to sale. What is the object of importing? What is the object of manufacturing? Consumption is the object of all these things. The sale is the intermediate step between the importing and manufacturing and the consumption. If you stop sale you stop all the rest. Who will import, who will manufacture if the goods are not to be permitted to be sold afterwards in order to their consumption?

Lord HERSCHELL—Could not the Provincial Legislature prohibit the manufacture of something which could be only noxious?

Mr. BLAKE—Perhaps so.

Lord HERSCHELL—Why, if the manufacture is to be allowed and therefore sale?

Mr. BLAKE—I find it difficult to conjecture as a practical

application of the Act in the mind of Parliament that such a class of manufacture was before their minds, a manufacture wholly noxious, not capable of being used either for commercial, mechanical or other purposes, or in combination for any beneficial purposes to the community.

Lord DAVEY—I suspect that some temperance advocates would put liquor into that category.

Mr. BLAKE—I dare say; but I shall wait a long time before I hear a judicial tribunal decide that.

The LORD CHANCELLOR—I have great difficulty in drawing the distinction. I suppose absolutely noxious could be predicated of nothing.

Mr. BLAKE—That is what I feel.

The LORD CHANCELLOR—It may be of use for some purposes. Take bombs or anything of that sort. One would think that would be a matter that would come within criminal law which is one of the things reserved. It is for the general security of the whole realm which would come within the Dominion power.

Mr. BLAKE—If you prevented the manufacture of something which could be used only for a hurtful purpose it would be a proper and reasonable exercise of the power as to crime to make it a crime to manufacture that article.

Lord HERSCHELL—Because you can make it a crime, I do not see that that has any bearing to my mind on whether it comes within section 92, and the manufacture can be prohibited. You can make anything a crime, but it is quite certain if it comes within section 92, you can make it a crime because the Provincial Legislature can impose the penalty of imprisonment for a violation of their regulation. In that sense you can make it a crime by the Dominion because the same penalty for doing the same is as much criminal law in the one case as the other. Now here it is expressly said not to be criminal if it is for the purpose of enforcing that which is within the jurisdiction of the Provincial Legislature.

Mr. BLAKE—There is an observation in *Russell* v. *The Queen* which I have read, meeting Mr. Benjamin's argument as to Provincial Criminal Law, and pointing out that the power to impose a penalty unquestionably existed, but existed only with reference to the matters which were within the Provincial jurisdiction.

Lord HERSCHELL—That is quite clear, but still that is within a limited area. Criminal law if you can impose imprisonment on a man for doing or not doing a thing——

Mr. BLAKE—The Province has a penal sanction of a high character. But I have always thought it was not the happiest expression to speak of Provincial Criminal Law.

Lord HERSCHELL—What I meant was that you sought to draw the distinction, and I think in one of the cases it was drawn by saying this comes within the criminal law. There is a certain power to legislate—what may be called Criminal Legislation with the view of enforcing something within the Provincial power. That is quite clear.

Mr. BLAKE—Yes, but take the case your Lordship has put. There are things which as the habits of society change, arise from time to time——

Lord HERSCHELL—I believe there are poisons which serve no known medicinal purpose except to destroy life, and would only be useful, if you can so call it, for the purpose of destroying life. Take one of those. Do you say that the Province might not forbid its sale within its borders.

Mr. BLAKE—I should have thought the language which is used in *Russell* v. *The Queen* would have applied to a case of that kind.

Lord HERSCHELL—I only put it in relation to what I understood to be your proposition which seems to be rather a broad one, that the manufacture of everything is lawful and intended to be allowed. You said the object of manufacture was consumption and therefore the sale of everything must be lawful. That is what I understood to be your proposition.

Mr. BLAKE—I admit that that may be open to the exception your Lordship has referred to of some poisons which are not found to have any scientific use at all, and to be wholly noxious, and to the making of bombs which cannot be used

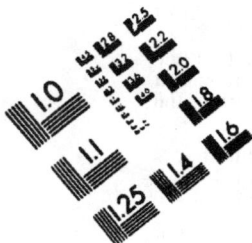

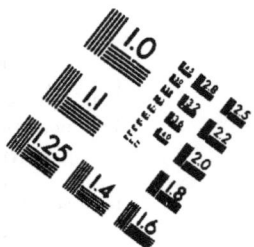

IMAGE EVALUATION
TEST TARGET (MT-3)

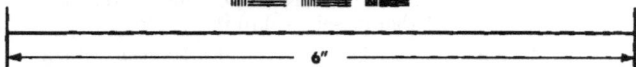

6"

Photographic
Sciences
Corporation

23 WEST MAIN STREET
WEBSTER, N.Y. 14580
(716) 872-4503

for any legitimate or lawful purpose. These were not, I admit, within my mind when I spoke of manufacture. I doubt whether they were in the mind of Parliament. I spoke rather of innocent manufactures.

The LORD CHANCELLOR—The word "innocent," I am afraid, may be subject to a traverse to some minds.

Mr. BLAKE—Quite so : but with reference to such a thing as Lord Herschell has suggested, I should have said those words in *Russell* v. *The Queen* were directly applicable—that the law was of a nature which fell within the general authority of the Parliament to make laws for the order and good government of Canada, and had direct relation to Criminal Law, which is one of the enumerated classes of subjects committed exclusively to the Parliament of Canada.

Lord HERSCHELL—That is only a dictum, and therefore one is not bound to accept it. That seems to me to lose sight of the fact—it is rather *petitio principii*—that there is a Provincial criminal law if the thing comes within the Provincial power. You cannot say everything is assigned to the criminal law. The criminal law means merely punishing what you choose to make offences. Anything that is within the offence making power of the Provincial Legislature it may provide a punishment for. I do not see how you draw any line of distinction and say this must be Dominion because it is within the criminal law. If you can show it to be within one of the enumerated clauses of section 92, then although it is criminal in the sense of its having a penal sanction it is within section 92. If you cannot bring it within any of those classes it cannot be Provincial.

The LORD CHANCELLOR—Section 91 seems to assume there is a particular region of legislation which is to be exclusively within the command of the Dominion.

Mr. BLAKE—Yes, and I have always supposed that the region of legislation was not limited to what the criminal law, as it stood in 1867 in one Province or all the Provinces together was, but that it embraced the power to deal with the subject in the largest sense.

Lord HERSCHELL—It is all the criminal law in the widest

and fullest sense except that part of it which is necessary for the purpose of enforcing, whether by fine, penalty or imprisonment, any of the laws validly made under the sixteen clauses under which laws are to be made by the Provincial Legislature. That is how I should define Dominion power.

Mr. BLAKE—It includes the power of creating new crimes.

Lord HERSCHELL—No doubt, and so have the Provincial Legislatures.

The LORD CHANCELLOR—We will concede that at present.

Mr. BLAKE—I do not admit they have power to create any crime whatever.

Lord HERSCHELL—What is creating a crime except forbidding a thing under the penalty of imprisonment ? What is crime except saying that if you do this the law will punish you for it. One knows there have been distinctions between crimes and offences, but those will not limit criminal law in the Dominion power in that way. The criminal law in the Dominion power will include every form of punishment for every form of act.

Mr. BLAKE—What I should have said is this, that you find a large number of enumerated powers of the Local Legislatures. Those powers include their power to restrain the liberty which the subject would otherwise have in many respects. If within the legitimate exercise of these powers they have proceeded to restrain the liberty, and to impose obligations or restrictions on the subject, they are by the Act given the power of enforcing such laws by sanctions highly penal in their nature, the highest inappropriate in many cases and perhaps in most cases, because the extreme of them come up to the second punishment known to the English and to our own law, namely, imprisonment for life.

Lord HERSCHELL—Criminal law in section 91 would include many similar provisions, would not it ?

Mr. BLAKE—Doubtless.

Lord HERSCHELL—A Dominion Act which said that if you do so and so—even this very temperance thing, if you

infringe this temperance regulation you shall be liable to
imprisonment. That is exactly the same as many Provincial
laws.

Mr. BLAKE—Doubtless.

Lord HERSCHELL—I do not see that you get any light by
saying it comes under "criminal law." There is a branch
of the Criminal law under section 91 exactly corresponding
to something—call it criminal law or whatever you please—
which the Provincial Legislature have power to enact.

Mr. BLAKE—I should have thought that one could say of
certain things which the ingenuity of man has brought into use,
or certain practices in which his depravity induces him to
indulge, that they were naturally things to be declared as
crimes as soon as found out—that the changing exigencies of
Society demanded a new law rendering them crimes, and I should
have thought that was the general sense of the observation I have
read. There are matters which involve no idea of criminality
at all, but which are yet enforced by penal sanction. There
is in my locality the snow by-law for instance under which
you have to clean the snow away from before your door, and
if you break it you are punished for it. That does not involve
the idea which one attaches to criminality.

Lord HERSCHELL—All those are included in Criminal law
in section 91 are not they? If they are not where are they?

Mr. BLAKE—I should have said they fall entirely within
the category of a Provincial law—a local regulation of that
kind enforced by that punishment.

Lord HERSCHELL—It need not be local. There are
certain matters on which you say the Parliament of Canada
has power to legislate for the whole Dominion and impose
penalties. May not this come under the criminal law of
section 91.

Mr. BLAKE—Yes; as shown by the passage I have quoted

Lord HERSCHELL—That does not seem to me to throw
any light on what comes within the Dominion and the
Province; that you must find out elsewhere.

Mr. BLAKE—I had thought that inasmuch as it was a decision of your Lordships' Board in the very case in hand and with reference to the very Act in hand, it had a relevance to the question.

Lord HERSCHELL—I do not say it has not a relevance, only unfortunately to my mind it does not help us to the point we have to solve. It may have relevance but it is not very helpful. That is all I meant. I do not see how to draw the distinction.

Mr. BLAKE—I have been puzzled often as to whether you could find a distinction of which Courts could take notice. I do not know to what fantastic extent the Dominion Parliament might not exercise its power to make some new crime. I do not know what it might not declare to be a crime which yet it would revolt the ideas of any one to regard as a crime.

The LORD CHANCELLOR—There is a very familiar line in English Law which has often been commented on as being an illogical division, namely between crimes and misdemeanours.

Mr. BLAKE—Yes.

The LORD CHANCELLOR—A misdemeanour is a crime.

Mr. BLAKE—We know that new crimes in one sense are legitimately made, but everybody refuses to agree that the stigma of crime attaches to them; and we know that old things which were made crimes have ceased to be crimes. Heresy and witchcraft were crimes not so very long ago in this country, but they have ceased to be crimes.

The LORD CHANCELLOR—I gave you an illustration of one earlier in the day—the exportation of wool.

Mr. BLAKE—I believe that was a crime. I do not know whether that was not mainly an Irish crime.

Lord HERSCHELL—It was a crime until a recent time.

Lord DAVEY—Forestalling and regrating.

Lord WATSON—They ceased to be crimes because they came in the course of time to be incapable of proof.

Mr. BLAKE—I suggest that this question of sale is important, because if you stop sale you stop the rest, and that gives a significance to one of the questions or more than one of the questions, about retail sale; it is suggested that the sale for consumption on the premises—a public house or saloon sale may be prohibited; but I think it is common knowledge that this, after all, looking at it from a venue point of view——

Lord WATSON—There is no absolute prohibition of the trade in liquor when you get beyond the retail.

Mr. BLAKE—There is not absolute prohibition, but there is a practical prohibition, because here and elsewhere the men who can consume at home are but a very small fraction of the community; you must deal with the mass, and the mass take their refreshment in the public house; and, therefore, when you stop that you do in effect in the largest sense prohibit the trade in liquor.

Lord DAVEY—You prohibit any man who cannot afford to buy a dozen bottles.

Mr. BLAKE—Yes, or five gallons.

Lord DAVEY—In a sense everybody is prohibited who has not money to buy.

Mr. BLAKE—Not by the law.

The Lord CHANCELLOR—He has not got the money to buy it with.

Lord HERSCHELL—He is prohibited by law because he cannot get it by law without paying for it.

Lord WATSON—It operates as an absolute prohibition against certain persons situated in a certain way.

Mr. BLAKE—Then if it be the case as it practically is, and I maintain in dealing with a constitution one must look at things as they substantially are without any attempt at refinements, that the wholesale merchant is only a distributor, that the consumer is the end, and that the consumer is, speaking in the large, the man who consumes at the public

house, then the limited prohibition which is suggested in one
of the questions put is really a total prohibition of the trade.

Lord HERSCHELL—Fewer people will drink, that is the
theory of all such regulations, if you close during certain
hours than if you allow them always to be open. In that
way you interfere with the sale.

Mr. BLAKE—Doubtless.

Lord HERSCHELL—Then why is that permissible?

Mr. BLAKE—If your Lordship puts it to me that no
restriction can be made without probably, or possibly, to some
extent, limiting the sale of liquor——

Lord HERSCHELL—Their object being to limit the sale;
because if you do not limit the sale people may get drunk
and then disorderly. That is the very object of the whole
thing.

The LORD CHANCELLOR—With submission to my noble
friend I doubt that. It is very often that the object is to
prevent the sale going on during particular hours, and then
the people will drink twice as much in the next hour; I
doubt very much whether it diminishes the amount actually
consumed.

Lord HERSCHELL—It is to diminish intoxication or it is
supposed to diminish it. I suppose diminished intoxication
will mean less sold.

Mr. BLAKE—Probably, I might say, that is a melancholy
truth, but there may be other considerations and then you
come to the purpose and aspect. If the aspect and purpose
of the legislation is to diminish it is one thing. If it is to
provide for the regulation of a licensed house so as to see
that it is respectably and orderly conducted, that the drinking
however much that may be takes place within reasonable
hours, that people do not drink late at night, and so forth,
that is another thing. That has to do with regulations which
may incidentally diminish the consumption of liquor, but the
object may not be to diminish it.

Lord HERSCHELL—In none of them is the object to

diminish the consumption of liquor. Is not the theory of all
of them to secure good order by diminishing the consumption
because probably you diminish drunkenness. Is not that the
theory of all them ?

Mr. BLAKE—I think, perhaps, that may be said. Then
what I was observing was that that which is effectively and
substantially and largely restrictive and practically prevents
consumption does prevent manufacture and does prevent
importation.

Lord DAVEY—Indirectly.

Mr. BLAKE—It has that effect and has that effect
markedly. It may be that regulations may be made for the
purpose which are indicated in *Hodge* v. *The Queen* which may
not very largely or sensibly affect the total consumption of
liquor, but which tend to a man taking his liquor in a decent
and orderly manner without getting drunk. That may be
their object.

Lord HERSCHELL—Is your contention that no regulation
can be good which interferes with the consumption of liquor ?

Mr. BLAKE—No.

Lord HERSCHELL—Interferes with it sensibly, and enables
a man to take it decently ?

Mr. BLAKE—I acknowledge it passes my capacity to
discharge at present the task which I dare say may come
before this tribunal to decide, how far, under *Hodge* v. *The
Queen* and the principle of that case, the local authority can
go in the way of restriction. That is not one of the questions
that has to be disposed of in this case.

Lord HERSCHELL—I cannot draw the line between the
restrictions in *Hodge* v. *The Queen* and the restrictions in this
Ontario Act. You say it virtually prohibits, but it merely
comes to this, that it creates new obstacles in the way of
obtaining drink ; I do not see how to differentiate that—it is
different in degree, of course—but in principle, and say that
one is regulation and the other is not, the object of both
being the same—to preserve sobriety and order in the
Province.

Mr. BLAKE—I will endeavour to grapple with that legislation in a later part of my argument; and if your Lordships please, I would ask you to take this as applicable to the bulk of the questions which apply to total prohibition and *sub modo*, only subject to the distinction your Lordships suggest as to the 7th question. What I would desire to point out—and I am now upon the question of " merely local or private "—is that this particular trade and commerce was at the time of Confederation and has always since been highly taxed and a large source of revenue to the country.

Now, what appears from the public Statutes ? The trade has been regulated in the fiscal sense. Provisions for license and for bonded warehouses and so forth are arranged. The importation and the manufacture is recognised as lawful. It is regulated in the fiscal sense and for fiscal purposes, and a very substantial portion of the public revenue in the Provinces before Confederation and in the Dominion since Confederation is derived from this source. Canada was given a power to raise money by any mode or system of taxation, and on her was imposed an obligation to pay the interest on the debts and to assume the public debts of the Provinces, and also to pay yearly very considerable subsidies to the Provinces; and this she has to do out of those means of raising revenue which she possesses. Can it be said, then, to be a merely local or private matter within the Province to prohibit the sale or the manufacture or the importation of a subject which is one of the principal elements of taxation and of revenue in Canada, which has been always treated as such, and out of which she has to meet her public obligations, including the obligations to these very Provinces themselves ? I submit that that view, apart from anything else, excludes this particular subject from the general phrase, " a matter of merely local or private importance or interest in the Province." Look at what would happen ; and it is fit to put cases which might very well happen. Supposing this was done in each Province, and supposing it was applied (for it might be applied) to other subjects of taxation and other subjects of revenue as well as intoxicating liquors. The power of the Parliament of Canada to procure its revenue might be fatally crippled. It is true that Canada has the power to raise money by any mode or system of taxation, but it has raised it all heretofore by customs and excise (with the exception for a short period, during which about £40,000 a year was raised from a tax on stamps); and the circumstances of the country are such that no man can foresee the time at which it can be raised otherwise than indirectly—that is, by duties of customs and excise. Then it is of the most serious import to the whole of the fiscal system of Canada; and it cannot be that it is a matter merely local or private within a Province whether the manufacture and the sale or the importation of such a great dutiable or excisable commodity shall be prohibited.

Although, as I have said, I should be very sorry indeed to try to draw the exact line of demarcation which may have to be drawn some day under the principle of *Hodge* v. *The Queen*, yet it seems to me there is all the difference in the world between what we have called a police regulation based on special local conditions which may vary in a town, a city, a village, or a county, or according to local public ideas, and which may be directed to the amelioration of these conditions, and such general and drastic legislation as is proposed. Then in addition I repeat with reference to the question of "merely local or private" the suggestion that in this case there has been a declaration adjudged to be validly made by the Parliament, that this is a general evil and a Dominion question on which the Dominion Parliament has legislated, and that makes the subject no longer capable of being called merely local or private. Then if, contrary to the suggestions which I have made, there be some defeasible power in the Provincial Legislature of dealing with this matter locally, I submit that that power has been defeated; because the Dominion has acted. It has, as I venture to suggest, decided that the proper way and useful extent of legislation is to provide for prohibition, and for a repeal of it, and for a reinactment of it, at the intervals, and on the terms and on the conditions which I have stated. These are the methods for grappling with the general evil which the Legislature adjudged competent to grapple with it, has deemed best. It has not deemed best that greater areas like a whole Province should be by one Act of the Legislature or by a plebiscite subject to total prohibition. It has obviously decided the political question of which it was the sole and sovereign judge, that it would not do to let so large an area dispose in every part of

that area this question.   Probably it thought that there might
be, notwithstanding a majority in the whole Province or a
preponderance of opinion in the whole Province, enormous
majorities adverse in local areas, where a local public opinion
might exist so strongly adverse as to render the Act un-
workable, or worse than useless, as we know has occurred
in the various cases in which such very drastic legislation has
been attempted.   When it has decided to put it in force in
this way and in this way only, it must be presumed, in favour
of the prudent and wise exercise of its powers, that it has
so decided because it had concluded that these were the terms
and conditions upon and the extent to which it might
carefully and ought properly to go in this direction.   It is a
case in which the suggestion that a less rigorous Dominion
law may be supplemented by a more rigorous Provincial law
does not apply.   I may be asked how does it hurt to make
still further and more effective provisions than the Dominion
Parliament has thought proper ?   The answer is that the
competent authority must be taken to have decided that it
will not help but it will hurt to attempt to go further ; that
the attempt will not be effective but mischievous, that it has
gone as far as you can prudently and beneficially go on the
line that it has taken.   Nominal stringency may be as it has
turned out to be, real laxity ; and a more stringent law is
inconsistent with the spirit and with the conditions of that
law which has been passed.   It may be argued that a great
volume and force, and a general diffusion of favourable
public opinion all over the body affected by the law is needed,
in order that the law may be beneficial ; nay, I will say in
order that the law may be otherwise than extremely hurtful ;
because, I suppose, no one can doubt that a law of this kind
evaded or openly violated is not merely not potent for good,
but is very potent for evil.   It teaches habits of evasion, and
habits of breach of the law, and of disregard of the law
which tend generally to the deterioration of the moral and
law abiding and law respecting status of the community, without doing any good, but rather impeding, thus leaving unre-
pressed, unregulated, and unlicensed that trade which might
have been moderated by laws of a different kind.   Well then,
if that be so, in what volume, in what force, and to what
extent diffused shall that public opinion be before the law

v

shall be put into force? This is the question which the
Dominion Parliament has decided. This is the question it
has decided in this case, and that is why it is impossible to
agree that the Local Legislature may apply another set of
tests and say: Well, we do not believe in this area, we do
not believe in these electors, we do not believe in these terms;
we believe that this law ought to be put in force in another
area, and by another set of electors and on other terms. To
say that that is not inconsistent with, and practically thwarting
and interfering with the principle of the law established is to
my mind extremely difficult. All these questions have
been settled by Parliament in the way it thought best.
Then it is said, Are you not going to interfere where the
Prohibition Act is not in operation? I say certainly not,
because the Parliament has decided that the Prohibition Law
shall come into operation provided certain tests indicate that
it ought to come into operation, and is not to come into
operation unless those tests indicate it, and to put it in
operation when the tests are not applied, and the consent of
the majority cannot be obtained for it is to put it in operation
at a time, and under circumstances in which the Parliament,
competent to decide, has in effect decided that it ought not
to be put into operation, and therefore that so far as prohibition is concerned the trade ought to remain free. My
Lords, before passing from this branch of the subject, I have
one word to say with reference to my suggestion that the
general powers of the Parliament of Canada need not be
exercised over the whole area of Canada. If your Lordships
would look at the case of *Dobie* v. *Temporalities Board*, which
is to be found in 1st Cartwright, there was a case in which it
was necessary to decide what the powers of the Parliament
of Canada and of the Local Legislatures respectively were in
reference to a corporation existent before confederation, whose
area and power and property extended over the whole of the
old Province of Canada, afterwards turned into Ontario and
Quebec, two only of the Provinces, and it was determined
that the local legislatures had no power either separately or
by common action to touch or deal with the affairs of that
corporation; and, this being so, that the Parliament of Canada
had that power under the general clause and the general
clause only. That was a bit of legislation which on the face

of it obviously dealt not with the whole of Canada but with that which had been one Province before and became two Provinces after confederation, and in such a case as that the law of course was not extended over the whole country, but the Parliament was held to have power to deal with the more limited area.

The LORD CHANCELLOR—Was not that like the difficulty in our countries where there were difficulties in making regulations applicable to two countries?

Mr. BLAKE—That may be. But I say it establishes this that under the general power to make laws for the peace, order and good government of Canada it is competent to the Parliament of Canada in an appropriate case to deal with a subject which does not extend over the whole of Canada but extends over part of it only.

The LORD CHANCELLOR—Certainly. What I meant was that it would mean that, because there was no power except this that could deal with a subject matter which necessarily extended into two different jurisdictions.

Mr. BLAKE—I think that is true, and I think that was the theory of the decision.

Sir RICHARD COUCH—The ground of the decision was that it extended into two Provinces, and neither Province could legislate for it.

Mr. BLAKE—And therefore they found under that general clause it was swept into the Dominion legislation, and none the less so swept into Dominion legislation than that which applies to the whole of Canada. My Lords, that is the whole of my argument on this head. There have been numerous cases, I do not cite them now because I am not going into them in detail, of Acts ever since confederation on the same theory. I may say that I was instructed by my friend who is with me and who has looked into the Revised Statutes, that there is hardly a subject to be found in which Parliament has not assumed to exercise the power of dealing not uniformly but somewhat separately, and with reference to local conditions as to its powers of legislation. I will take two instances, one the question of restriction on the bearing of arms in particular

v 2

localities by Proclamation, and another a restriction with
reference to this very same drink traffic in public works.
They are notable instances of the same kind, so that on the
whole I submit to your Lordships that it has practically been
adjudicated that this is within the general power of the
Dominion as in *Russell* v. *The Queen*, that it has been adjudged
that the legislation which has taken place does grapple and
deal with this subject, that it obviates local difficulties and
deals with the subject in such an elastic and general manner
that local option and local feeling and wishes can be met as
to the application of the legislation, that it is impossible under
such circumstances to say that either the subject of the
drink traffic dealt with in connection with prohibition and
with the aspect and purpose which are indicated in *Russell* v.
The Queen are " merely local or private " in any one Province,
and that in addition the other considerations I have stated as
to taxation and as to revenue and as to the general interests
of the whole inhabitants of the Dominion in the question
bring it also out of " merely local or private."

　　I now turn to the other enumerated power, namely, the
"regulation of trade and commerce," and I would point out
that what is declared is that " notwithstanding anything in
" the Act, and for greater certainty, but not so as to restrict the
·" generality of the foregoing terms of this section, it is declared
" that the exclusive authority extends to all matters coming
" within the classes of subjects next hereinafter enumerated,"
and in the enumeration is " the regulation of trade and commerce." It is conceded that if the subject we are now dealing
with is to be embraced within this enumeration it is withdrawn
from " merely local or private " by the express terms at the close
of the section. Now the extent of the power of regulation of
trade and commerce is certainly not settled in *Parsons'* case.
It is definitely observed that the attempt is not there made to
settle the extent of the power. What is stated is that the
words do not embrace any minute rule for the regulation of a
particular trade, or for the regulation of contracts in a
particular business or trade in a single Province; but it is
expressly observed that no attempt is made to define the
limits of the authority of Canada beyond the extent of that
exception which is expressly made. It needed not to consider
here the grounds on which the general powers to make

regulations for trade and commerce, when competently exercised, might legally modify or affect property or civil rights or the power of the Provincial Legislature. That is a question I am not troubled with here, because there are the two aspects—the aspect of dealing with property and civil rights, and the aspect of regulating the trade which incidentally may affect property and civil rights, and which comes within the general and rational line of distinction which has been drawn on these subjects. Dealing with these two different aspects, one can understand some so called interlacing or some carving out, to the extent to which the exercise of the Dominion power rendered necessary in that aspect or for that purpose to cut out part of the subject from property and civil rights.

Lord DAVEY—What page are you referring to ?

Mr. BLAKE—I think it is pages 278-9 of 1st Cartwright.

Lord DAVEY—Because there is a very important passage on page 277.

Mr. BLAKE—Yes, my Lord ; I am going to deal with that. I was going to observe, with regard to those passages, that those interpretations—not the one which your Lordship alludes to——

Lord DAVEY—Follow your own course.

Mr. BLAKE—(reading from page 277) :—

> " The words ' regulation of trade and commerce ' in their unlimited sense are sufficiently wide, if uncontrolled by the context and other parts of the Act, to include every regulation of trade ranging from political arrangements in regard to trade with foreign Governments, requiring the sanction of Parliament, down to minute rules for regulating particular trades. But a consideration of the Act shows that the words were not used in this unlimited sense."

I make this observation only for the moment, that it is admitted by the case of the *Bank of Toronto* v. *Lambe* that the words themselves are wide enough to sweep in everything, and that therefore they take everything, except what you find from a consideration of other parts of the Act are to be withdrawn from them. The words are ample enough.

Lord DAVEY—Unless controlled by the context.

Mr. BLAKE—Unless controlled by the context or other parts of the Act. That is where the Judgment begins to indicate what governing considerations may apply :—

> "But a consideration of the Act shows that the words were not used in this unlimited sense. In the first place the collocation of No. 2 with classes of subjects of national and general concern affords an indication that regulations relating to general trade and commerce were in the mind of the Legislature when conferring this power on the Dominion Parliament. If the words had been intended to have the full scope of which in their literal meaning they are susceptible, the specific mention of several of the other classes of subjects enumerated in section 91 would have been unnecessary ; as 15, "Banking "——

Lord WATSON—What is "general trade " ?

Mr. BLAKE—I do not understand.

Lord DAVEY—I suppose they mean regulations relating to trade generally.

Lord HERSCHELL—Not to a particular trade.

The LORD CHANCELLOR—I am afraid it does not go a little deeper than that and that it does not show they exclude mere minute regulation.

Lord WATSON—I think that is what it applies to.

Lord DAVEY—It is explained afterwards in the next passage.

Lord WATSON—Regulations as to loading or unloading in the docks may affect commerce.

Lord HERSCHELL—I think it is open to doubt whether the words, regulation of trade and commerce, do naturally and properly cover regulations which may affect prescribed conditions of a particular trade. It is very broad. It is not " trade or commerce," but it is " trade *and* commerce "—very broad words.

Mr. BLAKE—Yes, of course they are broader.

Lord WATSON—The word " general" was meant to exclude the right to deal with the particular trade and make general regulations for it.

Mr. BLAKE—I do not think there is any word "general' in the Act. It is the regulation of trade and commerce.

Sir RICHARD COUCH—There is no word " general " in the Judgment ?

Mr. BLAKE—I rather think not.

The LORD CHANCELLOR—Yes, the word " general " is in the Judgment.

Lord DAVEY—But it is not in the Act.

Mr. BLAKE—No, my Lord.

The LORD CHANCELLOR—It is in the Judgment but not in the Act.

Lord DAVEY—They explain what they mean if you read on.

Mr. BLAKE—May I, before reading on, just refer as pertinent to the part that I have read to the words in *Parsons'* case ?

> " The words ' regulation of trade and commerce ' in their un-
> limited sense are sufficiently wide if uncontrolled by the context and
> other parts of the Act, to include every regulation of trade ranging from
> political arrangements in regard to trade with foreign governments,
> requiring the sanction of Parliament, down to minute rules for
> regulating particular trades."

The words are very wide. How wide ? What do they mean ? The first suggestion that is made in *Parsons'* case is that the collocation with subjects of national and general concern affords an indication that regulations relating to general trade and commerce were in the mind of the Legislature, but I submit that that is a very far-reaching implication, and that it is hardly likely that the phrase " regulation of trade and commerce " can properly be limited by a suggestion that the enumerations on one side or the other side refer to some general subjects.

Lord WATSON—The definition appears to be almost as indefinite as the text defined.

Lord DAVEY—It is a little more precise afterwards.

Mr. Blake—Yes, on that point and on the connection or collocation, and generally in reference to the probable intent of the Legislature in using the words I venture, to refer, without reading, to the Judgment of Mr. Justice Sedgewick at page 95, and the following pages of the Record, in which he shows the mode in which these words were used in Canadian and Nova Scotian and New Brunswick Legislation for a considerable period before, and at the time of the passing of the Confederation Act, and in which he suggests, I submit with great reason, that it was infinitely more likely that the Canadian framers of this Act or of those Resolutions on which this Act is based had in their minds——

Lord Davey—Is that admissible ?

Mr. Blake—I thought that had already been mentioned in the earlier part of the argument, as to what they had in their minds ; perhaps it may not be admissible ; but it seemed to me that the sense in which the phrases that are used in this Act are found to have been used in Canadian Legisla on generally over the whole area would not be irrelevant in deciding the sense in which they should be held to have been used in the Act itself.

Lord Watson—You might derive some light from previous legislation if it was relevant. It might be relevant. Supposing there had been words in the old Provincial Acts grouped under a particular head and you found that head in this Act, I think such legislation would throw light on that.

Lord Herschell—You do not find " Regulation of Trade and Commerce."

Mr. Blake—In some of them you do.

Lord Herschell—I think it is " Trade and Commerce."

Mr. Blake—You find " Regulation of Trade " in particular cases both in Nova Scotia and New Brunswick.

Lord Herschell—There is the difficulty, if you take it from two Provinces ; are we to suppose they used it in the sense they used it in those two ? If you could show they had used it in all the Provinces or that it was in general use that

would be different. It seems to me rather dangerous to take
the use in two Provinces.

Lord DAVEY—I have read Mr. Justice Sedgewick's
Judgment very carefully and more than once. This passage
I have read more than twice, but I cannot for the life of me
find out what he thinks "trade and commerce" means, because
he says it means one thing in Nova Scotia; and the classes
of subjects to which he attributes it seem to me incapable of
any, I will not say scientific, but any logical meaning. For
instance, he says (Record page 96) in Upper Canada it means :

> "Navigation, inspection laws in relation to lumber, flour, beef,
> ashes, fish, leather, hops, &c., weights and measures, banks, promissory
> notes and bills of exchange, interest, agents, limited partnerships."

Then in Lower Canada it means :

> "The inspection of butter, the measurement and weight of coals,
> hay and straw, partnerships, the limitation of actions in commercial
> cases, and the Statute of frauds."

Will anybody make a scientific classification of subjects out
of that ?

Mr. BLAKE—I do not pretend to be able to do so.

Lord DAVEY—I have referred to these things and have
tried to find out what it was that he thought "trade and
commerce" did mean in the earlier Canadian legislation.

Mr. BLAKE—I suppose the object of the learned judge
was this, to combat the proposition that it meant only in the
view of the Canadians this general regulation of trade and
commerce, that it was shown that in each Province under
"regulation of trade or commerce" there were laws dealing
with particular trades ; and, therefore, that laws dealing with
particular trades must be taken to be within the scope of the
words.

Lord HERSCHELL—Is your proposition this : that no law
can be made dealing with any trade by any Provincial Legislature because that is a regulation of trade and commerce
within the exclusive power of the Dominion under 91 ?

Mr. BLAKE—It depends on the character of the dealing.

Lord HERSCHELL—I say any regulation as to putting
restriction on the mode of carrying on any trade.

M-. BLAKE—I am unable of course to contend that after *Parsons* ase.

Lord HERSCHELL—And after *Hodge's* case. If so I do not quite understand where you draw the line.

Lord WATSON—It is very difficult to understand.

Lord HERSCHELL—I understand the other part of your argument about prohibition, but if you may make regulations for the police, or what you will, which put restrictions and conditions on the carrying on of a particular trade without infringing 2 of 91, then what is the limit of that ?

Lord WATSON—What does trade include ? It is put here along with commerce which may point to this, that it ought to include manufacture, but trade does not necessarily or naturally always include manufacture.

Lord DAVEY—What do you think of inspection of butter which is one of the things the learned ' judge gives. Would not that be a market regulation and within municipal institutions ?

Mr. BLAKE—No, my lord, that is just one of the things which may or may not. Take for instance the question put by his lordship the Lord Chancellor, the other day about flour ; but there are inspection laws as to flour by the Dominion which are of the utmost consequence to the whole Dominion and of the greatest value.

Lord DAVEY—My observation is directed to this, even if it be admissible to look at the way in which the language is used in contemporaneous Acts it does not seem to help us very much.

Mr. BLAKE—The only argument I would draw from it would be this, that it did indicate that under the "regulation of trade," or under "trade and commerce," a power of regulating particular trades in some way, and to some extent, was included ; but it does not make a code of regulation at all.

Lord HERSCHELL—One cannot doubt that great power of regulation of trade must be included in "trade and commerce," but it is another question as to whether the local

Legislature cannot impose any restrictions upon the dealing
in any particular goods without infringing that power of the
Dominion Parliament.

Lord WATSON—And there, remember, in framing that
phrase, they had not the smaller things in view. Take a
dairy in a Province: milk produced at that dairy, unless it is
intended for the market, does not come within the rule as to
market or trade either : it may be intended for home consumption. If it is a local matter to protect that family, I do
not see why the Province should not pass a law for the
inspector to look after that locality, before it is consumed by
the inhabitants. On the other hand, that would not be a
matter affecting more than one Province, one dairy, or two
or half a dozen of them, or all the dairies round a particular
town in the Province.

Mr. BLAKE—The full extent to which I press the facts
stated by Mr. Justice Sedgewick, is this——.

The LORD CHANCELLOR—You see, in each of these cases
the difficulty is suggested to you that there may be something
which is essentially local, there may be something which
cannot be general at all. Take the case my noble friend put :
at this moment suppose it was ascertained by proper analysis
that the washing of butter in a particular stream made it
unfit for human food—surely there is a perfect right to prohibit that.

Mr. BLAKE—I do not deny it ; but I hold that the
Dominion Parliament is not to be deprived of its authority
to legislate at all in larger matters, because it is extremely
difficult to draw the line between local and those larger
matters.

Lord HERSCHELL—Then I do not understand what you
call the larger matters, or how you are to say that because of
the size of the matter it is within their cognisance and the
other is not. To say that nobody shall carry on a particular
trade unless he does it in a house of a particular size or value,
which is a very common thing in these licensing questions,
or within particular hours, or it may be, except on particular
days, that is to say, you may perhaps exclude the Sabbath

and holidays—supposing that you make all those regulations, what are those in one aspect but regulations as to the way in which that trade is to be carried out ? If that makes them " regulations of trade and commerce " within the meaning of 91, no Provincial Legislature could pass them at all. But those are not the small things, those are very big things in the way of a man's trade, and I do not understand where you draw the line, and what are the bigger things which you say would be trade and commerce. I do not mean you should draw the exact line, but if you draw it you must draw it on some principle.

Lord WATSON—Would it be an interference with trade or commerce either if the Provincial Legislature were to enact a law, and penalties for its infraction, as to mixing milk with water—adulteration ?

Mr. BLAKE—I should hardly think so, my Lord.

Lord WATSON—Would that be a regulation regulating commerce and trade ?

Mr. BLAKE—I should hardly think so.

Lord WATSON—I think it would be a law to prevent people selling one thing instead of that which they represented —from selling water-milk under the name of milk.

Lord HERSCHELL—From one point of view it would be a regulation of trade. Everything which says you shall only carry on your trade in a particular way and under particular conditions and restrictions regulates the trade. Then it strikes me as only a question of degree as to how far you carry those restrictions and conditions. I like to get my foot down on some principle ; I do not say I can draw the exact line, but I feel here I am standing with one foot on one side and the other on the other.

Lord DAVEY—The definition in this Judgment which you are going to, whether it can be supported or not, does afford some standpoint.

Mr. BLAKE—Yes ; I propose when I come to *Hodge's* case to read to your Lordships what was the character of the regulation which was thought to be within the power of the

Provincial Legislature, and which answers, as far as I am able to answer them, Lord Herschell's observations. The next suggestion that is made is that "regulation of trade and commerce" may have been used in some such sense as the words "regulation of trade" in the Act of Union between England and Scotland, which is common, and as these words have been used in other Acts of State. *Citizens Insurance Company* v. *Parsons*, L. R. 7 App. Cas. 96 and 1 Cartwright at 277.

> "Article 5 of the Act of Union enacted that all the subjects of the United Kingdom should have 'full freedom and intercourse of trade and navigation' to and from all places in the United Kingdom and the Colonies ; and Article 6 enacted that all parts of the United Kingdom, from and after the Union, should be under the same 'prohibitions, restrictions, and regulations of trade.' Parliament has at various times since the Union passed laws affecting and regulating specific trades in one part of the United Kingdom only, without its being supposed that it thereby infringed the Articles of Union."

Of course it is clear that Parliament had power to deal with the Articles of Union, and legislate contrary to them under any circumstances.

> "Thus the Acts for regulating the sale of intoxicating liquors notoriously vary in the two Kingdoms. So with regard to Acts relating to bankruptcy, and various other matters.
>
> "Construing, therefore, the words 'regulation of trade and commerce' by the various aids to their interpretation above suggested, they would include political arrangements in regard to trade requiring the sanction of Parliament, regulation of trade in matters of inter-provincial concern, and it may be that they would include general regulation of trade affecting the whole Dominion. Their Lordships abstain on the present occasion from any attempt to define the limits of the authority of the Dominion Parliament in this direction. It is enough for the decision of the present case to say that, in their view, its authority to legislate for the regulation of trade and commerce does not comprehend the power to regulate by legislation the contracts of a particular business or trade, such as the business of fire insurance, in a single Province, and therefore that its legislative authority does not in the present case conflict or compete with the power over property and civil rights assigned to the Legislature of Ontario by No. 13 of section 92."

Lord Davey—Consistent with their thinking that it did contain the power to regulate contracts for a particular business in the whole Dominion ?

Mr. Blake—Quite so. There is no doubt that phrase is consistent with that idea.

The LORD CHANCELLOR—Of course one treats those observations with the respect due to them, but I confess it seems to me to employ a good many words without getting very much nearer the proposition.

Lord HENSCHELL—At all events it is a decision for this : that the Provincial Legislature might so far regulate a particular trade as to say that in all its contracts and dealings there should be certain implied conditions, without its being a regulation of trade and commerce within the meaning of 2 of 91.

Mr. BLAKE—I was dealing with the suggested definitions, because I think more than once in the course of the argument they were alluded to by Lord Davey, who asked what was to be the attitude taken with reference to them. Now, what I want to do first is to point out to your Lordships what are the points which it is suggested they would include : First, political arrangements with regard to trade requiring the sanction of Parliament. But then, my Lords, that is provided for expressly by another section. Section 132 deals with that topic. "The Parliament and Government of "Canada shall have all the powers necessary or proper for "performing the obligations of Canada or of any Province "thereof as part of the British Empire, towards foreign "countries arising under treaties between the Empire and "such foreign countries." No political arrangements can be made, excepting through the medium of the supreme authority. The local authority may be, and has been of late years, more recognised in the making of those arrangements by an understanding between the local authority and the supreme authority; but for all that it is always a treaty made by the Supreme Government, which alone is a political arrangement, and which alone can be referred to in the Act; and the Parliament of Canada is given by section 132 express power to make all the arrangements necessary for performing those obligations.

Lord DAVEY—Would it include the making of trade arrangements between Canada and the mother-country which are not covered by section 132 ?

Mr. BLAKE—No, my Lord.

Lord HERSCHELL—Is it very important to inquire what is within 2 of 91 in this relation? What we have to consider is what is either exhaustively defined or to consider what is outside. To find out a number of things within it, is very unimportant is it not? If you can exhaustively define it, no doubt that will show us what may be outside it.

Mr. BLAKE—I think if I disposed of, as settled by other clauses of the Act, all those matters which in *Parsons* v. *The Queen* it was suggested were included in or were the object of trade and commerce——

Lord HERSCHELL—It might be done by saying—"All matters of general regulation of trade within the Dominion." It might include a good deal more than that, but they say distinctly it does not include every particular dealing with the trade.

Mr. BLAKE—Doubtless that is so, and I have no right to ask your Lordships to depart from that. And if your Lordships think that the attempt at a definition or a suggestion, made *obiter* perhaps, and stated in *Lambe's* case to be "thrown out" rather than otherwise, is not important to be discussed, I will not trouble your Lordships.

Lord DAVEY—For the present purposes that would be enough for your opponents would it not—they would say that it has been decided in *Parsons'* case because it does not include interference with the contracts in a particular trade in a particular Province, and they would say it does not interfere with the contracts made in the liquor trade in the Province of Ontario.

Lord HERSCHELL—It does not matter whether it comes within 16 or any other number. We are only now on the question of whether it comes within 2 of 91.

Mr. BLAKE—All that is determined is that it does not comprehend the contracts of a particular trade in a particular Province. Of course this Act which we are dealing with, so far as it may be said to affect contracts in a particular trade in a particular Province—though I find it difficult to see how prohibition of all trade comes within that category—seems to contemplate a trade which is to be generally regulated rather than the extinction of the trade altogether. It is general therefore—it is not within the language of this case. It is a regulatio. generally with reference to the whole Dominion.

Lord DAVEY—But I mean suppose the Legislature of Ontario interferes with the contracts of a particular trade in the particular Province of Ontario ?

Lord WATSON—That seems to be settled by the case of *Parsons* v. *The Queen*, but what would settle in this case ? If none of these questions had arisen and the liquor trade was going on as usual it would have settled this, that if the legislature of Ontario had thought fit to pass a law that when a liquor seller in the Province had contracted to sell a dozen he should sell 13 bottles, it could do so. What then ? I do not see how it illustrates the present case—of course the observations made in the course of it I do not seek to disparage.

LORD HERSCHELL—I take it that it shows at least this, that it is a distinct interference with the mode in which the trade is carried on to say that in every contract you make certain conditions shall be implied. That is an interference which is not a regulation of trade and commerce. Therefore it does say that you may do something in the Province, which interferes with the mode in which a trade is carried on.

Lord WATSON—Although that would refer to the form and shape of a contract between the parties to the trade.

Mr. BLAKE—Yes. It does say you may do something and defines what that something is ; but what other things you may not do——

Lord HERSCHELL—That it leaves open, and then one has to search for the principle. At all events it shows it is not enough to say that this affects the mode in which the trade is carried on ; it is a regulation of trade and commerce, therefore the Provincial Legislature is excluded. You cannot go that length after *Parsons'* case. I do not know that it tells you more than that. You have to find out yourself how far you can go.

Mr. Blake—Yes, my Lord. Then I would just refer, with reference to the other part of this definition without labouring it at all, to the second part—that it may have had to do with matters of inter-provincial trade. I have already quoted section 121 which settles for all time and effectively the inter-provincial trade by providing that it shall be free. There are no regulations of inter-provincial trade that hamper that trade which it would be possible to make.

Lord Herschell—But they have made regulations about the transit from one Province to another?

Mr. Blake—I do not think so, my Lord.

Lord Herschell—It does not mean things shall be carried without charge?

Mr. Blake—No.

Lord Herschell—There might have been regulations made which affected the transit, which means affecting the trade.

Mr. Blake—What it meant, my Lord, was that there should be no legislative hampering of or interference with the free admission of articles of the growth, produce and manufacture of any one of the Provinces into the others.

Lord Herschell—But still that might be a trade regulation which would be quite consistent with freedom in that sense.

Mr. Blake—I thought, my Lord, the object of all regulations was more or less to hamper freedom.

Lord Herschell—But if you use freedom in that wide sense, I doubt whether it is used in that sense here.

Mr. Blake—Perhaps not. Then it states :—

> "Having taken this view of the present case it becomes unnecessary to consider the question how far the general power to make regulations of trade and commerce, when competently exercised by the Dominion Parliament, might legally modify or affect property and civil rights in the Provinces or the legislative power of the Provincial Legislatures in relation to those subjects."

Now with reference to the general regulation of trade affecting the whole Dominion which is suggested : as to this it is difficult to define that definition, and say what it means; but I shall suggest it is enough if the regulation affected more than one Province; and I would suggest also that where trade is concerned you cannot seriously deal with it without affecting it generally—that the ramifications of trade are so wide that it is difficult to say that it is a matter merely local or private; although I quite concede that acting for the other purpose and with the other aspect vindicated and indicated in the cases of *Parsons* and *Hodge*——

Lord WATSON—When you come to curtail trade in liquor you interfere with it. Practically the trade consists of making so much liquor and consuming it, and there and then the transaction is at an end.

Mr. BLAKE—It was suggested that the "regulation of trade and commerce" might not include the prohibition of any one trade, and must mean the continuance of all; but perhaps it is not necessary for me to enter at any length into that proposition after what fell from his Lordship the Lord Chancellor this morning. It seems to me that, whatever inference you might draw, if any one specific trade was named and a power of regulating that trade was given, as to the meaning of regulation in that particular case—supposing you were to draw the inference that it meant not extinction but regulation short of extinction—no such inference could at all arise where the phrase is general. "The regulation of trade and commerce" may involve the prohibition or extinction of some one trade as part of the regulation of the whole subject.

Lord WATSON—It would be rather difficult to decree the absolute prohibition of trade under the word "regulation," unless it were for the purpose of fostering another trade.

Mr. BLAKE—That is precisely our object.

Lord WATSON—That would be regulation.

Mr. BLAKE—Precisely.

Lord DAVEY—There might be prohibition of a particular trade under general regulations.

Mr. BLAKE—That is my argument.   You may prohibit one trade for the benefit of other trades.

Lord WATSON—You might check the production of one kind of trade in order that the products of other trades might sell.

Mr. BLAKE—Yes, as I say, if Parliament thought fit, it could so enact for such a conceivable reason.   " We believe " on the whole a very large trade is injuriously affected by a " small and non-beneficial trade, therefore we will stop the one " for the benefit of the other "—however much that may be opposed to modern notions of political economy, still that would be a regulation of trade, although it did involve that prohibition.

Lord HERSCHELL—Was it or is it within the competence of the Dominion Parliament to contravene section 121 ?

Mr. BLAKE—No, my Lord, I do not think so.   I think that is absolutely binding upon all the powers ; it is a fundamental regulation.

Lord HERSCHELL—That is a provision that all articles shall be admitted into each of the other provinces.

Mr. BLAKE—Yes.   It is very well known to all who know anything of the circumstances that one of the governing objects was to free that trade between the provinces, although they afterwards decided that what was very good as between themselves was very bad as between themselves and the rest of the world.

Lord DAVEY—They pulled down the customs' houses.

Mr. BLAKE—They pulled down the customs' houses between the provinces, but they built them higher as between themselves and the rest of the world.   Then, my Lords, *Parsons'* case and *Hodge's* case do decide the one point, that some things are too minute, and the other that some things are too local, and so do not come within the phrase " regulation of trade " in the sense in which it is to be found in the Act, but although it may be difficult, and Lord Herschell has pressed me very much with that difficulty, to draw the line, what I have to do, as I submit, is to find what has been said,

w 2

and what is the *ratio decidendi* in *Hodge's* case. That case will be found reported at page 161 of Cartwright's Reports, vol. 3 :

> " Their Lordships consider that the powers intended to be conferred by the Act in question when properly understood are to make regulations in the nature of police or municipal regulations of a merely local character for the good government of taverns and so forth, licenses for the sale of liquor by retail——"

Lord HERSCHELL—Will you pause there. They are meant to repress drunkenness. That is the very object that they state. Where do you draw the distinction between one and the other restriction on the liquor traffic which is intended to repress drunkenness ?

Mr. BLAKE—The object may be the same, but the character of the restriction may be entirely different.

Lord HERSCHELL—They do not say anything about the character of the restriction, it is a restriction having that object.

Mr. BLAKE—I think they do say something about the character of the restriction. They say to make regulations "in the nature of police regulations or regulations of a merely local character."

Lord HERSCHELL—Will you take out " police " for the moment. Municipal regulations are of a purely local character : whether they make the restriction on selling more or less those words equally apply, and the object is the same—repressing drunkenness.

Lord WATSON—And the Act is the same in those cases as in those of the Municipal Parliament. The words " municipal " and " police " are introduced, but they convey no more meaning to my mind than this—enacted by the Legislature in order that it may be carried into effect by the municipal and police authorities and confined locally.

Lord HERSCHELL—All that seems to me to apply, however large the restriction is.

Mr. BLAKE—Does your Lordship mean short of prohibition or including prohibition ?

Lord HERSCHELL—On that point as to excepting trade and commerce, I should say whether it goes to prohibition or not. I do not mean to say prohibition may not make a difference because you have the Canadian Legislature dealing with the subject, and there is great force in that part of your argument. That is another point. But apart from that, assuming the field to be clear, I fail to see how you can draw the line ; if you can make all these municipal regulations for the purpose of repressing drunkenness and so on, what is the object ?

Lord WATSON—Assuming the Legislature thought fit not to regulate at all in that direction—assuming that, which is what one means by assuming the field to be clear—what restriction is there upon the Provincial Legislature from passing or imposing such restrictions as they may think fit in the local public interest—mind, it must be local ?

Mr. BLAKE--In so far as *Hodge* v. *The Queen* is a decision, and this is the crucial part of the Judgment, the decision is that their power is to make restrictions in the nature of police and municipal regulations of a merely local character for the good government of taverns licensed for the sale of liquor and so forth.

Lord DAVEY—I have sometimes thought that by section 91, although section 92 is exclusive—that is to say, the jurisdiction of the Provincial Legislature is exclusive—the jurisdiction of the Canadian Parliament is not exclusive. They may make orders for the good government of Canada in any matters not sufficiently reserved to the Provincial Parliament.

Mr. BLAKE—Is not that practically exclusive ? They may make orders in all things in which the local authorities may not.

Lord DAVEY—Yes, but it is quite consistent with this that they may make orders as to the things which are within the jurisdiction of the Canadian Parliament where they are of a merely local character.

Mr. BLAKE—That is what I have argued, my Lord.

Lord DAVEY—I mean as to the subjects.

Mr. BLAKE—That is what I have argued from the beginning; I argue that the power to make rules for the peace, order and good government of Canada, enables the Parliament——

Lord DAVEY—So that the jurisdiction of the Provincial Legislature is exclusive because the Canadian Parliament cannot make laws as to what is of a " merely private or local " character unless it comes within the enumerated subjects.

Mr. BLAKE—Only because the " merely private or local " character is put in amongst the exclusive powers of the Provincial Legislature, but except for that the Parliament of Canada could deal with it.

Lord DAVEY—But the reverse is not said: that Parliament shall have the exclusive power of making laws on matters affecting the good government of Canada.

Mr. BLAKE—But was that needed, my Lord ? because it has the power to make laws respecting the good government of Canada in all matters except those exclusively assigned to the Province, and then you get all the matters affecting the good government of Canada cut into two parts, one a set of enumerations belonging to the Provinces only, and the other all the rest which belongs to the Dominion only. Therefore there is a division. One may be puzzled to find the line in some places, but there is in principle a division.

Lord HERSCHELL.—At all events it seems to come to this that a matter which touches the good order of a particular Province is *primâ facie* a merely local matter on which they have power to legislate, it goes at least that length.

Mr. BLAKE—I should not have supposed it went that far.

Lord HERSCHELL—But does it not ? I mean can it help going that far, because the regulation of public houses there was only in the interest of good order and well being of the Provinces ?

Mr. BLAKE—Regulations in the nature of police and municipal regulations of a merely local character.

Lord WATSON—When you come to the meaning of these words " Municipal and Local " I cannot help thinking that in using those expressions all that is meant is, such matters as are usually in the environs of this Court made the subject of municipal and police regulations. I doubt whether it means anything more than that.

Mr. BLAKE—Your Lordships see what the Court was doing here was declaring what the powers intended to be conferred by the Act in question when properly understood were, and after that declaration saying that they were within the powers of the local Legislature. What they say is that the powers are to make regulations in the nature of police or municipal regulations. It was not a general Act by the Province dealing even with the whole Province but it was an Act remitting to the local authorities of each particular class of municipality certain powers to be exercised locally.

Lord HERSCHELL—Do you rely upon that ? Do you suggest that they could remit what they could not themselves do ?

Mr. BLAKE—Certainly not, my Lord. I am trying to define what this thing was. I believe that they could do directly what they could do indirectly or by delegation; and if they proceeded directly they would be presumed to exercise, and if they did their duty they would be exercising the same discretion with reference to particular local circumstances in each locality for which they acted, which the local authority would be presumed to exercise if it was remitted to it. But it is important as showing what the character of the action was.

Lord HERSCHELL—By " local " there they mean local within the Province, do they not, not local within the locality?

Mr. BLAKE—I should say they mean local within the locality.

Lord HERSCHELL—But can that make any difference. Can they make a Province do that within its locality which it cannot do in all localities. Would it be the less merely local because they did it for all ?

Mr. BLAKE—I think it emphasises the proposition that this was merely local, and purely local. That was recognised because the power was given to the local authorities by which local communities——

Lord HERSCHELL—Is local used in that sense at all in 16. Surely in 16 "local" does not mean local in a spot in a Province, but local in the sense of, confined within the boundaries of the Province.

Lord WATSON—The locality of each Province is the area of which it consists.

Mr. BLAKE—I should say it certainly included the minor locality.

Lord WATSON—Certainly, I quite agree.

Mr. BLAKE—But then when you are speaking of regulations——

Lord WATSON—But I do not think it requires anything more establish their jurisdiction than to define the locality within their Province.

Mr. BLAKE—Look at what was done by the Act. What was authorized? What was authorized was that the Municipal Authorities of a locality should make regulations of a certain character for the good government of taverns in the locality. I should say that, considering that it was a local body in the minor sense in which I am using the term, that was making the regulations; "local" there applies to the character of the regulations which could alone be made by such minor body, and that there is an indication that what the Board was considering was that condition of things, recognising that condition of things which exists in local communities.

Lord WATSON—The only test in the statute is "mere locality," and if you find that there is a power which can be exercised with regard to that, the Provincial Legislature can legislate unless they are excluded by something which is to be found placing the right of the legislation exclusively in the Dominion Parliament.

Mr. BLAKE—Then I point out to your Lordships also as in this definition "for the good government of taverns," and so forth, "licensed for the sale of liquors by retail." It had begun with the question of licenses in respect of which they were given a specific power, they were given the power to license for the purpose of revenue, and it was by this judgment declared that they have the power to remit to local bodies the regulation within certain limits—within the limits here declared of those taverns which are to be licensed for the sale of liquors by retail. It seems to me to be an entirely different proposition to say that that involves necessarily or probably the view that they have the right to give a power of prohibition locally.

Lord WATSON—It does not involve it, I agree, only one has to infer why the one, if it applies just the same way, is more merely local than the other.

Mr. BLAKE—Is it not clear, my Lord, that it more seriously affects those larger considerations to which I have adverted, that it more seriously affects the question of importation, sale, and taxation and so forth; is it not clear that it is a deeper interference with trade and commerce than this local regulation which is for another purpose than interference with trade and commerce? You may say that though this regulation is for another purpose than interference with trade and commerce, yet in effecting that other purpose it still may interfere even by extinction within the locality of the trade. But it seems to me, where you are dealing with "matters of a merely local or private character," it is not an unimportant observation to be made with reference to one not being within while another has been adjudged to be within "merely local or private," that one extinguishes while the other only locally regulates. Then it is adjudged that to deal with and prohibit upon social and moral grounds, grounds of safety, order, and peace is within the Dominion Power in the mode and form in which they have exercised it, and I maintain that that power of dealing for that purpose is within the "regulation of trade and commerce" just as much as it is within the general powers—that there is no reason why you should not regulate trade and commerce with these objects higher than fiscal and economic and political objects, and that when you have a general power of regulating trade and commerce you may regulate for these purposes just as well as for the other. Then there is power of regulating trade and commerce on fiscal grounds as has been already observed.

Lord WATSON—As I read the clause everything that is specified in the first sub-sections—every law made under them —was understood to be a law for the peace, order, and good government of Canada.

Mr. BLAKE—I quite agree.

Lord WATSON—Although there may be other objects.

Mr. BLAKE—Yes, my Lord, I quite agree.

Lord WATSON—The qualification is that there may be others which do not fall within any of these.

Mr. BLAKE—These are stated examples and instances of the power of making laws for the peace, order, and good government of Canada, and it is declared that they come within that power in effect. Then on fiscal grounds you may prohibit production and you may prohibit manufacture : as is shown in the instances of tobacco here, and if I am rightly informed as exists with reference to methylated spirits in Canada, where the Government, I think, is the only producer of that commodity. Of course methylated spirits are permitted to be produced and sold here under very stringent regulations devised to avoid that loss to the revenue which a freer disposition of that article might produce. Then there are so called economic grounds upon which, under the powers of taxation, some imports are pretty well taxed to death ; there is a power to raise money by this method of taxation, and although the power is exercised so as to diminish the return of the possible tax—yet who shall criticize this use of the power of the Dominion Parliament as affecting the law ? There is a conceivable prohibition of a particular trade as has been suggested by Lord Watson on the ground of a greater general interest in fostering something else to which the existence of the particular trade is injurious. The political grounds I have already referred to. I submit, therefore, the regulation of trade and commerce does and must include prohibition ; that there is no inference against the prohibition of a particular trade to be drawn from the use of the word regulation ; that it has been proved and is palpable that "regulation of trade and commerce" generally may legitimately be decided by Parliament, may legitimately require a prohibition of some particular nature, and therefore that it comes within "regulation of trade and commerce." I would invite your Lordships to refer to the observations which are made on this head as to interpretation of the analogous but narrower sentence in the constitution of the United States, because, I think, it cannot be ignored in construing the second example of a great federal constitution, that there have been discussions for a long time, and decisions given, with reference to that analogous power.

Lord WATSON—The power as between the Imperial Government and the State Government is not the same there.

Mr. BLAKE—I quite agree, my Lord.

Lord HERSCHELL.—And the words are not the same.

Mr. BLAKE—No, my Lord, the words are narrower and yet the narrower words are held to include prohibition.

Lord HERSCHELL.—What are the words ? "Trade and commerce"?

Mr. BLAKE—No, my Lord ; it is, I think, to regulate trade between the several states and foreign countries and with reference to Indians.   There are three subjects, the several States, foreign countries, and Indians to which the phrase is limited, but I cannot for the moment remember with certainty what the words are.   But here with what is a mere limited power you find a larger interpretation stated.

Lord DAVEY—How has that been construed ?

Mr. BLAKE—That has been construed to include prohibition, which is what I am dealing with.

Lord HERSCHELL.—Prohibition as to what, trades as between two States or what ?

Mr. BLAKE—I will find the phrase in which it is

described. It is described in two cases, *The City of Fredericton* v. *The Queen* is the first case, I think.

Lord DAVEY—*Fredericton* is the one from which *Russell* was an appeal?

Mr. BLAKE—Yes. In that case *Fredericton* v. *The Queen*, 2 Cartwright, page 35, Chief Justice Ritchie says:—

> "To my mind it seems very clear that the general jurisdiction or sovereignty which is thus conferred emphatically negatives the idea that there is not within the Dominion legislative power or authority to deal with the question of prohibition in respect to the sale or traffic in intoxicating liquors or any other articles of trade or commerce.
>
> "It is said that a power to regulate does not include a power to prohibit. Apart from the general legislative power which I think belongs to the Dominion Parliament, I do not entertain the slightest doubt that the power to prohibit is within the power to regulate. It would be strange indeed that having the sole legislative power over trade and commerce the Dominion Parliament could not prohibit the importation or exportation of any article of trade or commerce, or having that power could not prohibit the sale and traffic if they deemed such prohibition conducive to the peace, order and good government of Canada. There seems to be no doubt on this point in the United States. Mr. Story on the Constitution of the United States with reference to the regulation of foreign commerce which belongs to the National Government (as the regulation of both foreign and internal trade and commerce does to the Dominion Government), says: 'The commercial system of the United States has also been employed sometimes for the purpose of revenue, sometimes for the purpose of prohibition, sometimes for the purpose of retaliation and commercial reciprocity, sometimes to lay embargoes.' "

and so forth. Then I refer also to the case of *The Queen* v. *The Justices of Kings*, to be found in the same volume of Cartwright—2 Cartwright, at page 505—and I refer to it more particularly because when my learned friend who preceded me quoted it, an observation was made which I think is answered by a later passage in that Judgment, that the Judgment conflicted with the subsequent decision of this Board in the matter:—

> "If then the Dominion Parliament authorise the importation of any article of merchandise into the Dominion and places no restriction on its being dealt with in the due course of trade and commerce or on its consumption, but exacts and receive duties thereon on such importation, it would be in direct conflict with such legislation and with the right to raise money by any mode or system of taxation if the local legislature of the province into which the article was so legally imported and on which a revenue was sought to be raised could so legislate as to

prohibit its being bought or sold and to prevent trade or traffic therein and thus destroy its commercial value and with it all trade and commerce in the article so prohibited, and thus render it practically valueless as an article of commerce on which a revenue could be levied. Again, how can the local legislature prohibit or authorise the sessions to prohibit (by arbitrarily refusing to grant any licenses) the sale of spiritnous liquors of all kinds without coming in direct conflict with the Dominion Legislature on the subject of inland revenue involving the right of manufacturing and distilling or making of spirits, &c., as regulated by the Act, 31 Vict., chap. 8."

and so forth. Then he refers to the distinction in this aspect of the United States constitution which is clear, and goes on to say :—

"We by no means wish to be understood that the local legislatures have not the power of making such regulations for the government of saloons, licensed taverns, &c., and the sale of spirituous liquors in public places as would tend to the preservation of good order and prevention of disorderly conduct, rioting or breaches of the peace. In such cases, and possibly others of a similar character, the regulations would have nothing to do with trade or commerce, but with good order and local government, matters of municipal police and not of com-merce, and which municipal institutions are peculiarly competent to manage and regulate."

Lord HERSCHELL—Why would they in that case have nothing to do with trade, why would not they have to do with trade and not with anything else ? Your object is to show in each case a new object—one solely and the other merely——

Mr. BLAKE—The object is good order and good government—matters of police. The incidental interference is with trade and commerce.

Lord WATSON—Although it may be enacted to produce good order and good government, it does not in the least follow that you necessarily deal with that matter. What am I to understand according to your argument by the object of the Statute ?

Lord HERSCHELL—That is my difficulty in the Chief Justice's distinction. The object is the same—you are going the same road to secure that object. You go a little way in one way——

Lord WATSON—There may be a great many objects one behind the other. The first object may be to prohibit the sale of the liquor and prohibition the only object accomplished

by the Act. The second object probably is to diminish
drunkenness; the third object to improve morality and good
behaviour of the citizens; the fourth object to diminish
crime and so on. These are all objects; which is the object
of the Act?

Mr. Blake—I suppose the objects of the legislation were
the latter, and what it did to accomplish the object was first—
the prohibition.

Lord Watson—I should be inclined to take the view
that that which it accomplished, and that which is its main
object to accomplish is the object of the Statute, the others
are mere motives to induce the legislature to take means for
the attainment of it.

Mr. Blake—The immediate purpose of the Statute, so
far as it is enacted, is to prohibit the sale of liquors, the
reasons for which the legislature deemed it prudent and
proper to do, that are the objects. But it seems only a talk
about words.

Lord Herschell—In the other it is to restrict the sale
of liquor within certain hours, but in each case it puts fetters
on the trade more or less, and I do not quite see the difference
between them as local or as being a regulation of trade. I
see many differences between them.

Lord Watson—I think distinction is made there in
calling that the object in one thing which they do not call
the object in another case.

Mr. Blake—The learned Judge goes on to say:—

"But if outside of this and beyond the granting of the licenses
before referred to, in order to raise a revenue for the purposes mentioned,
the legislature undertakes directly or indirectly to prohibit the manufacture or sale, or limit the use of any article of trade or commerce
whether it be spirituous liquors, flour or other articles of merchandise
so as actually and absolutely to interfere with the traffic in such articles
and thereby prevent trade and commerce being carried on with respect
to them, we are clearly of opinion they assume to exercise a legislative
power which pertains exclusively to the Parliament of Canada."

Lord Watson—I think in all those cases as a matter of
fact you will find that legislation does nothing more than

provide the means by which it is expected the object will be attained.

Mr. BLAKE—I suppose so, my Lord. Sometimes in the preamble, although I believe preambles are now gone out of fashion, the object of the legislation is expressed and the reason for doing the thing which it is believed will accomplish the object is found in the preamble. Then I would suggest that it is hardly reasonable to urge that "regulation of trade and commerce" by the Dominion under its local powers does not include prohibition of a trade, but that "merely local or private matters" within a Provincial power does include prohibition of a trade. It does seem to me it is much more reasonable to say that "regulation of trade and commerce" does include a prohibition of a trade, and that if it does "merely local and private" cannot include it, than to say "local and private" does and "regulation of trade and commerce" does not. If the power of regulation by the Dominion does not include prohibition how can the prohibition be local? If you adopt the theory that the Dominion under its power to regulate trade and commerce has not power to prohibit and extinguish, because the trade must be maintained, must not the right of the Dominion to regulate be maintained, and how can it be maintained if another authority has power to extinguish that which is to be the subject of Dominion regulation? How can regulation, which certainly exists in some form or other in the Dominion, because it has got the regulation of trade and commerce, be general, and extinguishment local or private? Now, it is not to be forgotten that your Lordships have got the decision of your Lordships' Board on both sides of the question of jurisdiction for local, police power, and municipal purposes. The decision in *Hodge* v. *The Queen* gave to the Provinces the power that is described there, and as to which the serious difficulty is started of knowing where it stops. Then came the Licenses case, and although we have no Judgment to enlighten us as to the grounds of the decision, yet it seems plain, from the decision in that case, and from the general tone of the discussion, that it was held that the Dominion could not generalise in a matter which was purely local—purely local as had been decided by *Hodge* v. *The Queen*, that

their attempt to deal with that subject, to appropriate it to
themselves, it being a local subject, by acting for the whole
Dominion and appointing their own officers and so forth, did
not alter the character of the matter, or deprive the Provinces
of that power which they had under " merely local or private,"
that it remained a local or private subject, and therefore the
Dominion License Act was void while the Local License Act
was maintained. Here, again, you find another instance of
there being no concurrence. It was the same thing in the
same aspect, and therefore the power did not exist in both.
It had been established by *Hodge* v. *The Queen* to be in the
Province, and therefore it could not be grasped by the
Dominion by an enlargement of the area—local cannot thus
become general. That seems to me to be the reason of the
decision in the License case. I have said that it is difficult—
perhaps it may be impossible, in advance, at any rate—to
draw the exact line where the powers cease to be within
those declared in *Hodge* v. *The Queen.*

Lord WATSON—I think that is a view which has met with
universal acceptation.

Mr. BLAKE—But I can only say they can be no larger
than shall be decided by your Lordships, on some happy day
when that question arises, to be appropriated to that particular
aspect. There must be a point, I should think, when they
cease to be purely local, merely local, merely municipal,
merely adapted to the licensing of taverns and to their
regulation—which point, as I ventured to say a long while
ago——

Lord HERSCHELL—I do not think this Board will draw
the line. I believe it will continue to say from time to time
a number of things are on this side or the other side of the
line, but I do not think you will ever see the day on which
the line will be drawn.

Mr. BLAKE—I am glad to hear your Lordship say that,
because I do not suppose after that your Lordships will ask
me to draw the line again.

Lord HERSCHELL—You may find some foundation on

which you can rest in saying this must be on one side of it and this on the other, though you cannot draw the line.

Lord WATSON—If counsel suggests that there is a line which we have never yet found out, it is a fair question to put to him to explain it according to his view.

Mr. BLAKE—I say it runs a good long way on the hither side of prohibition, but where exactly it runs I could not well argue, save in a concrete case. Then I submit that to treat trade and commerce, as it must be held to be treated, as "merely private or local," would be contrary to the letter and the spirit of the Act. An observation was made, I think in *Lambe* v. *The Bank of Toronto*, where the Court was dealing with the question of the reason why indirect taxation was not left to the Provinces, and that observation has force as directed to this case. It was said that the effect of indirect taxation is necessarily general, it necessarily extends beyond the Province, its ramifications are extra-provincial, and therefore it was that indirect taxation was not permitted to the Provinces as well as to the Dominion; and if the effect of indirect taxation is so general and far-reaching, as I should say it certainly is, must not the effect of prohibition also be *a fortiori* equally general and far-reaching? As I have said, the revenue of the Dominion is wholly indirect, and therefore this subject of prohibition which so seriously affects that indirect taxation must be held to be something more than a merely local and private subject. I have only to trouble your Lordships now with one or two words with reference to the minor questions as I call them. I think as to the second one I said what I have to say when I made the suggestion that where the Canada Temperance Act is said to be not in operation, it is not put in operation because the Dominion Parliament, competently dealing with the subject, has set conditions under which it cannot be put into operation, under which the people do not choose to put it into operation, and therefore it has in these cases its negative operation. The test is supplied for every locality, and the Act has its general effect, either by preventing other interference or by the interference under it in all localities.

Lord WATSON—You say it is equivalent to a positive

x

e.actment that the people of the Provinces shall enjoy an
Act of extended restriction and nothing further ?

Mr. BLAKE—Yes.

Lord HERSCHELL—Do you go as far as that, or do you
take no midway ground, because if it comes to that, they
cannot make any regulations—they cannot m. ke ' 's?

Mr. BLAKE—I have always said from th.. beginning it
was impossible for me to contend——

Lord HERSCHELL—You may perhaps go the length of
saying that if people want prohibition, it is the only way in
which they can get it.

Mr. BLAKE—Yes, and I was applying myself to the case
of prohibition your Lordship sees.

Lord DAVEY—As to manufacture ?

Mr. BLAKE—I hold that almost all the observations that
apply to importation and all that apply to sales——

Lord DAVEY—Not all that apply to importation, because
whatever view you take of trade and commerce, importation
must come within it.

Lord HERSCHELL—And importation cannot be merely
local.

Mr. BLAKE—I agree.

Lord DAVEY—Manufacture is not so strong a case as
importation.

Mr. BLAKE—I said almost all—not all. Here, take this
commodity. It is and was at the time of the Confederation
and has been ever since manufactured in various Provinces
to an enormous extent ; it is manufactured under excise laws
by the Dominion, from it a large quantity of the Revenue of
the Dominion is obtained, it is a trade which the Dominion
has legalized, if it were necessary to legalize it, regulating it
very largely as was necessary for fiscal purposes.

Lord HERSCHELL—And the manufacture can only be
remotely put, speaking generally of municipal police pur-

poses, because if they prohibit the sale everywhere within the Province, of course they prohibit the manufacture. That is going further and seeking to prevent its finding its way to people in other Provinces.

Mr. BLAKE—Quite so.

Lord WATSON—I cannot understand how you say the two things are the same, because to my mind I am not at all satisfied that a trade importation is all the trade. It is a trade either between the Province and some other Province or between the Province and some foreign country.

Mr. BLAKE—Quite so.

Lord WATSON—And the trade consists of both things. That trade is not localised within the Province.

Mr. BLAKE—I suspect it is so general as to include importation from a foreign country.

Lord DAVEY—To prevent importation from one Province into another would be contrary to the section in the Act you read about trade being free.

Mr. BLAKE—Doubtless, so far as it was the manufacture of the Province, that section applies only to those cases.

Lord WATSON—It is very much the same thing as saying there shall not be a sale or barter in a certain commodity between the inhabitants of this Province and the inhabitants of the next.

Mr. BLAKE—That is so. I did not say, I repeat, that manufacture was the same as importation, I said almost. There are important distinctions in favour of importation, but I think manufacture is *a fortiori* beyond sale. To what end do you manufacture? It is in order that you may sell. If sale comes within the powers of the Dominion or its regulation, then manufacture must.

Lord DAVEY—I suppose it might be a matter of local concern to prohibit the manufacture of a noxious drug which is eating the life out of the physical, moral and mental health of the people—putting an extreme view.

Mr. Blake—We come back again to the general question of the manufacture of something from which no good c n come and only evil.

Lord Watson—Strychnine.

Mr. Blake—Strychnine is a very good medicine.

Lord Herschell—There are some trades which are very seriously dangerous to those who carry them on, even with all precautions, and it is conceivable that the local legislature anywhere might think that the advantage gained from the manufacture was not equal to the loss of life and health resulting from its being carried on. What would you say there ?

. Mr. Blake—I have always supposed that these trades were attempted to be dealt with, sometimes a great deal too late, rather by regulation than by absolutely prohibiting.

Lord Herschell—There are some, I believe, where they say that whatever regulations you make there must be a very high mortality.

Mr. Blake—Yes, there are some, unfortunately.

Lord Herschell—Suppose a Provincial Legislature said that the manufacture was not important enough and not worth enough to be allowed to be carried on, would it be within its power ? I suppose you would say it would not.

Mr. Blake—I should have rather thought not.

The Lord Chancellor—You had better not pronounce too positively. You see the difficulties of these questions are they branch out into a great many points. The particular thing we are dealing with is liquor.

Mr. Blake—Yes, I feel that acutely.

Lord Herschell—But still liquor is not a class by itself. You admit this must be tested by some principles which would be applicable to other things.

Mr. Blake—I am not prepared to admit that it should be tested, or that any proposition which may reasonably be advanced should be tested by reference to very extreme and improbable cases. I am rather disposed to think that in framing a constitution which is set down in comparatively few words, what the Legislature had in view were the ordinary concerns and the usual run of things and that they did not provide for or take into contemplation cases of that description.

Lord HERSCHELL—Considering that those who practically framed this Act must have had in their minds the liquor legislation which has been the subject of considerable controversy all over the Provinces, it is a great pity they did not display the bent of their minds more distinctly.

Mr. BLAKE—I agree, my Lord, in which case we should not have been here; though I am not quite so certain of that, for sometimes when they have displayed the bent of their minds it has given trouble to find out what that bent was. The only other thing I have to observe upon is the question of the 18th section.

Lord DAVEY—That is local option because it is there provided the law shall not come into force until the electors wish it.

Mr. BLAKE—Yes, my Lord, but it is in effect prohibition.

Lord DAVEY—It is not absolute prohibition.

Lord HERSCHELL—It is said practically to mean prohibition, because there would be many people who might not be able to get these liquors, but it is not a prohibition of sale because a great many people would buy in quantities of a dozen bottles, which after all is not such a very large quantity. One cannot doubt that they would club together and buy them and distribute them amongst themselves. Therefore it is not a prohibition of sale. There is no doubt it would result in a considerably diminished consumption, or at any rate be very likely to. It is a very stringent regulation, but it is not prohibition.

Mr. BLAKE—It is complete prohibition with regard to sale in shops.

Lord WATSON—No, it is not. It is a sale under conditions which could prevent a thirsty person, who could not buy a certain amount, getting what he wanted.

Lord HERSCHELL.—It is complete prohibition in certain cases, but then you would not deny that it is a regulation so far as it confines the sale to certain places.

Mr. BLAKE—I agree, my Lord.

Lord HERSCHELL—So that it comes to this, that it regulates the places in which it may be sold, and as to those places where it may be sold it no doubt largely tends to diminish the power of purchase and sale.

Lord DAVEY—If you had single bottles in the packages in which they were delivered by the wholesale dealer you might sell a single bottle.

Mr. MACLAREN—It is provided the original package contains not less than a dozen bottles.

The LORD CHANCELLOR—You may by subtle means and devices get round it, but practically it is a prohibition to an ordinary person.

Mr. BLAKE—That is the only observation I was going to make ; that it seems to me to be so according to our common knowledge.

Lord HERSCHELL—Is it a question as to individuals or a prohibition of the sale of these things. If you do not prohibit the selling, a good many people will be able to buy them.

Mr. BLAKE—What I maintain is this, that if the practical effect is that the great masses of the people are disabled from buying, the sale is practically prohibited ; it may not be technically or formally wholly prohibited, but it is practically prohibited.

Lord HERSCHELL—No, the sale is not prohibited.

Mr. BLAKE—Yes, my Lord, the sale is, except in quantities in which it is impossible for most people to buy.

Lord HERSCHELL—That may limit the sale but it does not prohibit it.

Mr. BLAKE—I do not, of course, say that it actually, technically, and formally prohibits it.

Lord WATSON—You mean this, I understand, that as a matter of fact, and as a necessary consequence it will diminish the sale.

Mr. BLAKE—It will, for all those purposes with which the Dominion is concerned, so enormously diminish as to practically prohibit the sale.

Lord DAVEY—You say, I understand, that you have a right to take into account the knowledge of us all that in public houses frequented by persons who buy their glass of beer, or send for a jug of beer, it will be prohibitory.

Mr. BLAKE—Yes, my Lord, and that those persons form the great bulk of the consumers, and that the other class is a mere fleabite compared to the importance of those to whom liquor is sold and dealt with in that way.

Lord HERSCHELL—I think it is extremely probable that if you had this legislation you would have habits altered to a great extent.

Mr. BLAKE—I own that, as far as I can observe, efforts have been made, and not unsuccessfully, to get round, to a large extent, all restrictive provisions affecting deep rooted habits of the masses of the people.

(Adjourned till to-morrow at 11 o'clock).

FOURTH DAY.

Mr. MACLAREN—My Lords, the first observation which I would make in reply is something that applies to a considerable part of the argument of both my learned friends on the other side; and that is where, I think, they have been

applying a wrong test to Provincial Legislation. My learned
friends seem to consider that it is sufficient to destroy the
validity of the Provincial Legislation if it affects or interferes
with Dominion Legislation or Dominion subjects. My friend
Mr. Blake used as one of his expressions against such
legislation as this that it "affects" trade and commerce.
Another expression was that it "more seriously affects" it
than something else. Another expression he used was that
it "interferes with" trade and commerce, that it "interferes
with" customs and excise. Now I respectfully submit that
that is not the test which the Imperial Act has laid down.
Sections 91 and 92, section 91 more particularly—uses the
expressions "in relation to" and "coming within." Those
are the two expressions, and those are the tests. For instance
in section 91 the general power of Legislation is given, and
it is declared in the concluding words of the introduction of
section 91 that the "authority of the Parliament of Canada
extends to all matters coming within the classes of subjects."
Then when we turn to the concluding part of section 91, the
same expression is used.

> "And any matter coming within any of the classes of subjects
> enumerated in this section shall not be deemed to come within the
> class of matters of a local or private nature comprised in the
> enumeration of the classes of subjects by this Act assigned exclusively
> to the Legislatures of the Provinces."

Then when we look at the opening words of section 92 the
same expression is used with the addition of the words "in
relation to."

> "In each Province the Legislature may exclusively make laws in
> relation to matters coming within the classes of subjects next hereinafter
> enumerated."

Now I respectfully submit that a matter might affect something
else, it might interfere with something else, and yet it could not
be said to be Legislation in relation to that matter as coming
within such a class of subjects. To my mind the way in which
this should be looked at is really as a classification. An Act is
put before your Lordships, and you are asked to say whether it
comes within any of the classes of matters assigned to the Local
Legislature. That is the first test—not whether it affects it,
or may affect something else, or interferes with something
else, but, as was said by this Board in *Russell* v. *The Queen*, you

must consider the nature and character of the Legislation. Take the Act, look at it, and where would you classify it? In classification I think this rule is to be observed with reference to the Dominion. We have the list of enumerated subjects in section 91. We have the 28 enumerated subjects. Those are all classes. Then in addition to the 28 the Dominion has a general clause under which *Russell* v. *The Queen* placed the Canada Temperance Act, namely, a law relating to "peace, order and good government." That would be said to be the general clause. So that the Dominion had 28 enumerated subjects and one general subject, that is 29 subjects.

Lord DAVEY—That is not quite accurate. It is a general power of legislation and for greater certainty 28 classes of subjects of legislation.

Mr. MACLAREN—Yes; I wish to put it in this way. I am supposing that a Dominion Act were placed before your Lordships, and it was to be classified if it came within any one of the 28 enumerated subjects and was properly classified under those, the Dominion would have power under the enumerated subjects. It might not come within any of these 28, and yet might be valid Dominion legislation. In tha case I think it would be put under the general power of legislation—the omnibus clause as you may call it.

Lord WATSON—They are two separate questions. I do not say it pervades the whole argument of Mr. Blake, but it appeared to me that the case of the Respondents was put by him mainly on two grounds: in the first place that the Provincial Act deals with the regulation of the liquor traffic within the meaning of sub-section 2 of section 91. The other ground on which I understood him to put his case was this: that assuming the Provincial legislation does not come within sub-section 2, still the Dominion legislation—the Canada Temperance Act—is a competent piece of legislation under the initial words of section 91, and that it not only is competent legislation, but that it is legislation which covers the whole field of prohibition of the liquor traffic, and that prohibition is enacted by a Legislature which is paramount within the limit of its power, and must exclude Provincial legislation on the same subject.

Mr. MACLAREN—I think those are the two grounds.

Lord HERSCHELL.—I think there was a third which was this, that the fact that it had been held that the Dominion Parliament could legislate for the liquor traffic showed that it was not a matter which could be legislated for under section 92, sub-section 16, as a matter of a merely local nature.

Mr. MACLAREN—Yes.

Lord HERSCHELL.—Those were the three main grounds.

Sir RICHARD COUCH—That is really the case.

Mr. MACLAREN—Then to address myself briefly to those in the order named, I would submit this, that it is necessary for the purpose of the argument of the Respondents—I would refer first to a specific Act, the Local Option Act involved in question 7, as an illustration—confining myself to that for the moment, I submit that it would be necessary for the purpose of Mr. Blake's argument, where he takes that Act and asks your Lordships to classify it, that you should classify it under the head of a regulation of trade and commerce. I think that is the first. Now is that a proper classification of that Act? Let us look at the Act. The sale of liquor by retail for the purpose of consumption on the premises is prohibited entirely. It is prohibited in shops, and in places of public entertainment. The sale is not prohibited in the original packets.

Lord WATSON—It is a partial prohibition of the liquor trade and a restriction.

Mr. MACLAREN—It is a restriction and partial prohibition.

Lord WATSON—Prohibition to a certain extent.

Mr. MACLAREN- -Yes. Then look at that Act and let us ask ourselves where we would classify that Act. If we cannot bring it within any of the classes in section 92, then we are out of Court. If we can bring it under any of the classes of section 92, and yet it may also fall within one of the enumerated classes in section 91, we cannot bring it under sub-section 16. That is the position. Now I think it is useful if your Lordships will bear with me for a moment, I am not going to use the argument for the purpose I did in the opening, which I have no desire to repeat, to see that there was similar legislation in Canada before, and Canadian legislation which is classified by the same Legislature that passed the Quebec Resolutions. His Lordship, Mr. Justice Sedgewick, has pointed out the classification, and I wish to point to his Lordship's observation there, in consequence of an observation made by my Lord Davey yesterday, because I think I can show that Mr. Justice Sedgewick is not exact in his statements. Your Lordships will find his observation on page 97 of the Record. He says :—

> " It will be observed that in no case is reference made to the liquor traffic under ' trade and commerce ' or ' the regulation of trade.' In the Canadian Consolidation it is placed under ' revenue and finance ' (sub-head), ' Provincial duty on tavern-keepers.' "

That was the purely fiscal side of the subject.

> " In the Upper Canada Consolidation it is referred to in the Municipal Act (cap. 54, 1866), and in two ways : first, under the head of ' shop ' and ' tavern licenses ' ; and secondly, under the head of ' prohibited sale of spirituous liquors.' "

Then comes the sentence I am going to challenge :—

> " In the Lower Canada Consolidation it is referred to under ' fiscal matters.' "

Now, it is only one very narrow branch of the subject which is referred to in the Lower Canada consolidation under the head of " fiscal matters." Nothing such as the Act which is now before us. We have in the Joint Appendix the very counterpart of the Act which is now before your Lordships passed in Lower Canada, and your Lordships will see it does not come at all where Mr. Justice Sedgewick said, under " fiscal matters," but under an entirely different subject. If your Lordships will turn for a moment to the Statutes of Canada relating to Lower Canada, at page 13 of the Joint Appendix, your Lordships will see there the legislation that was passed in Lower Canada on this subject. It is analogous to the Act we are now considering.

The LORD CHANCELLOR—The Lower Canada Municipal and Road Act of 1855 ?

Mr. MACLAREN—Yes. There your Lordships will see, at

the top of page 13, power was given by section 23 to the municipality for preventing absolutely

" the sale of wine or brandy, or other spirituous liquors, ale or beer, or any of them, by retail, within the Municipality, and the making of such further enactments as may be deemed necessary for giving full effect to any such by-law, and for imposing penalties for the contravention thereof. Provided always that the selling of any wine, brandy, or other spirituous liquors, ale or beer, in the original packages in which the same were received from the importer or manufacturer, and not containing respectively less than five gallons or one dozen bottles, shall not be held to be a selling by retail within the meaning of this Act."

That is almost the counterpart of the legislation we are now considering, because there was the same exc tion of five gallons and one dozen bottles. Now, Mr. Ju   Sedgewick is not correct in saying that this legislation w.. ...aced under " fiscal matters " in Lower Canada. It was placed under the Lower Canada Municipal and Road Act of 1855, as your Lordships will see on page 12, and there was the Amending Act of 1856, 19 and 20 Victoria, on page 13. That is the Lower Canada Municipal and Road Amendment Act, 1856.

Lord WATSON—A very remarkable Statute. I never saw a statute before confer a larger privilege on a body that was in default as to its statutory duty. They had only to commit default and then the statutory regulation entitled them to prohibit.

Mr. MACLAREN—Then there is consolidation in 1861.

Lord WATSON—This argument, I understand, is for the purpose of showing that in the legislation of the respective Provinces prior to the year 1867, the expression " the regulation of trade and commerce " had never been used as including the regulation of the liquor traffic.

Mr. MACLAREN—That is one of the points I wish to make. I say that the classification had taken place and taken place by the authority of the same Parliament that passed the Quebec Resolutions.

The LORD CHANCELLOR—I am not quite certain that I am able to follow that argument. Different Statutes in different parts of the Dominion of Canada, passed with different regulations. What is there in the regulating

Statute, now the Statute of 1867, that appears to adopt any one or more of those as being things that they adopt and re-enact?

Mr. MACLAREN—That opens a slightly further field.

Lord DAVEY—The power of the Legislature is plenary for the division of powers.

Lord HERSCHELL—You are not speaking of these as giving the power?

Mr. MACLAREN—No.

The LORD CHANCELLOR—I follow your argument.

Lord DAVEY—What was the meaning of "Municipal Institutions" at the date of the British North America Act?

Mr. MACLAREN—It goes a little further than that.

Lord HERSCHELL—You mean it had not been included in a Statute dealing with trade and commerce.

The LORD CHANCELLOR—I think I followed your argument, but the difficulty I have is in identifying it. What is the classification where each of the legislatures has ample power. There was no reason why they should classify it.

Mr. MACLAREN—My only reason is that they had classified it.

The LORD CHANCELLOR—That is rather assuming the question. It is not material at all.

Lord WATSON—For instance, take this Act you have referred to at page 13. It is obvious that that restriction of the liquor traffic, though that is dealt with under a Municipal Act, the reason for that appears on the face of the Statute, that it was intended to entrust the duty of administering those regulations for the sale or prohibition of the sale to the body constituted by the Statute.

Sir RICHARD COUCH—To the Municipality.

Mr. MACLAREN—Yes. The present argument is merely as to classification.

The LORD CHANCELLOR—I think I follow what you mean, but I want to see whether I can follow you with more assent than I do at present venture to afford, because I do not see, considering the nature of the body that was then created, and the nature of the legislative body that was then creating it, how one is to deal with that in the same sense that you are now dealing with the Statute, which by virtue of the words themselves created two bodies, one within its powers and one without. I do not see what relevancy there is in the two.

Lord WATSON—Was there any department or authority before this Act, charged with regulation of trade and commerce, created by Statute ? From your statement, all that appears is this, that the regulation of the liquor trade either by partial prohibition or mere regulation of hours, and so forth, had never been classified under any Statute which purported to deal with commerce or trade. On the contrary, the provisions in relation to the particular matter, partial prohibition or regulation or total prohibition, all appear under Statutes affecting municipal and other public bodies entrusted with the administration of law.

Mr. MACLAREN—Yes.

Sir RICHARD COUCH—At that time there was no necessity for any precise classification at all.

Mr. MACLAREN—The necessity did not exist, but the practice was there, and it is merely for the purposes of interpretation or dictionary purposes, as one might say, to define the words that are used.

The LORD CHANCELLOR—I am afraid if you submitted some of our Statutes to a critical examination you would find they deal with a great variety of subjects.

Lord DAVEY—Where I find a difficulty in Mr. Justice Sedgewick's Judgment, is at page 98, line 10 :

> " Where, as in the present case, the Constitutional Act uses a phrase which for years had had a well defined meaning in Canadian legislation ; that is the meaning which should be given to it when used in that Act."

Looking at the examples he gives with reference to trade and commerce, I do not see that the words have any well defined meaning in the legislation of the Provinces generally.

Mr. MACLAREN—I am endeavouring to point out to your Lordships that Mr. Justice Sedgewick was not quite correct in his classification on page 97, which I think destroys the force of part of his argument. I think it would help us a little more than it would appear to on the face of his statement if his classification was correct. I am criticising his classification in order to draw a little more out from the concessions made by him than would appear on the face of it. That is one part of my present argument.

Lord DAVEY—In the Lower Canada Consolidation it is referred to under Municipal Institutions.

Mr. MACLAREN—The same as in Upper Canada, and those were the only Provinces where any classification existed and those were classified under the authority of an Act of Parliament, the same Parliament which passed the Quebec Resolutions.

Lord WATSON—In a General Railway Act in this country—and I think you have the same thing in Canada, you find it dealing with—certainly for the purposes of railways—and altering and amending the law of carriers. It is dealt with no doubt for the purpose of the Act in which it is found.

Mr. MACLAREN—But I submit we have to come back to the rule laid down that you look at every one of those Acts to consider its true nature and character.

The LORD CHANCELLOR—That I entirely agree with.

Mr. MACLAREN—We must fall back on that. We must consider its true nature and character, and that, I think, is the test, and probably the application of the phrase to this particular case is the task that falls to your Lordships. There are a number of Judgments of this Board that I think show that interference and affecting subjects is not the test. In *Tennant v. The Union Bank* on one side there was Dominion Legislation under the head of "Banking," and that was held valid though it interfered with property and civil rights and though it affected property and civil rights; but your Lordships held that it did not come within and it was not legislation in relation to property and civil rights. It was not legislation coming within that class.

The LORD CHANCELLOR—I should a little doubt that to be the exposition of that decision. I should rather think what the decision meant was that those words were not to be understood in their unlimited and unqualified sense.

Mr. MACLAREN—Quite so, I think that is apparent on the face of it. Now I will take the other question about affecting the Customs and Excise. I submit that that is not a proper test. It is not a law with reference to Customs and Excise. It is not a law coming within the class of subjects of Customs and Excise, because it only affects them indirectly. When we come to classification which, I think, is the duty thrown on your Lordships in this case, I say when you have considered its true nature and character to properly classify it, your Lordships would not classify it under the head of taxation. It is not a fiscal law and the fact that it may indirectly interfere with Customs and Excise is no reason for its existence. Take, for illustration, such a case as the *Bank of Toronto* v. *Lambe*. It was held there that although the Dominion had the power of creating the banks and had the regulation of trade and commerce, that did not prevent the local Legislature from taxing. Now could the local Legislature come and say to the Dominion when it is legislating regarding banks and banking we have put a heavy duty on banks, a large part of our revenue is derived from that source, when you make a new Banking Act you must not abolish banks and introduce a national system of banks because that will take away the revenue we are getting from taxing banks. The fact that one authority legislating within its powers may destroy a source of revenue, even a prolific source of revenue, of the other is, I submit, no argument against the legislation.

Lord HERSCHELL—You say to create a state bank and give it a monopoly would destroy all existing banks.

Mr. MACLAREN—Yes.

Lord HERSCHELL—On the other hand, Banking being left to the Dominion Parliament they could do that even

though it effected in that way the destruction of that source
of Provincial Revenue.

Mr. MACLAREN—And I think *Russell* v. *The Queen* is a
strong case. By sub-section 9 the right to issue shop, saloon,
tavern, auctioneer, and other licenses was given to the
Province, as a source of revenue in addition to direct taxation
because it might be thought that this was not direct taxation.
That was given to the Provinces. The Provinces came before
your Lordships' Board in *Russell* v. *The Queen*, and
Mr. Benjamin argued very strongly that the Canada Temperance Act was invalid because it wiped out a source of
revenue, that it destroyed liquor shops and saloons and wiped
out a source of revenue which by section 92, sub-section 9,
was given to the Provinces by the Imperial Act and yet your
Lordships say in *Russell* v. *The Queen* the fact that it has that
effect is no reason against its validity. I come and say that
if this legislation be otherwise within the power of the
Province, the fact that it wipes out a source of revenue which
the Dominion has taken before us to Customs and Excise,
and because it affects that and interferes with it, that is
no test.

My Lords, the next point I would address myself briefly to
is this, that my learned friends claim that the field is occupied,
that the Dominion having occupied the field by the Canadian
Temperance Act it is no longer open to the Provinces to come
in and legislate in addition.

Lord WATSON—The field of prohibition—I do not think
he carries it further.

Mr. MACLAREN—No, my Lord, I meant to apply it to
prohibition.

Lord WATSON—He does not argue—in fact it would be
arguing against some of the Judgments of this Board as
to the right to regulate—only he says regulation must not
involve prohibition.

Mr. MACLAREN—I did not intend to go further in my
expression though my language might perhaps have been
more sweeping. It is that the field of prohibition is occupied.

Y

Prohibition is ambiguous. One needs to define the word to know what is meant by prohibition.

Lord HERSCHELL—You may say practically that it is total under the Canada Temperance Act. The exceptions are so minute that practically you may say it is total.

The LORD CHANCELLOR—Probably for ordinary consumption by human creatures, I think it is total prohibition. The exception is medicine and manufactures and so on.

Mr. MACLAREN—Sacramental and medicinal.

Lord WATSON—Then again it is only prohibition where the Act is applied. In other cases they have a license for selling any quantity.

Lord HERSCHELL—It does not touch it. The only question is this. It is said that anywhere the condition of prohibition shall be a certain plebiscite of the district.

Lord DAVEY—Mr. Justice Sedgewick puts the argument very clearly and concisely at page 105. He says :—

" The Federal Parliament has already seized itself of jurisdiction. It has passed the Scott Act. It has prescribed the method by which in Canada prohibition may be secured, and is not any local enactment purporting to change that method or otherwise secure the desired end for the time being inoperative, overridden by the expression of the controlling legislative will ? "

Lord HERSCHELL—Supposing a place had not adopted the Act, and where the Act therefore was not actively in operation, but where it might be made to operate at any time by the plebiscite. Supposing the Provincial Legislature gave a different local option, giving it to a different number and a different body.

Mr. MACLAREN—Which they have done in a sense.

Lord HERSCHELL—In this particular Act I think there is a different question because there is a question whether that could be regarded as total prohibition, seeing that anyone can buy a dozen bottles, but I am supposing they gave exactly what we have called total prohibition under the Scott Act. Supposing they gave the same power of prohibition, but they gave it to districts differently formed or to a different

majority—a smaller majority so that in fact, exactly the same
prohibition and effect could be brought into operation in the
same district in two different ways by two different sets of
persons. Could it be said that those could stand together ?

Mr. MACLAREN—I hesitate to say that.

Lord HERSCHELL—That is very much the question as to
those districts in which it has not been adopted. It may at
any time be adopted, and if the Local Legislature have full
power to prohibit, it could prohibit on any condition that gave
the prohibitory power to any form of local option. Would it
be consistent with the Dominion legislation that they should
give it to a different majority ?

Mr. MACLAREN—I am going to argue to your Lordships,
and I think I have authority for it, that when this adoptive
or permissive legislation under the Scott Act is not in force,
it is for all practical purposes the same as if it was not on the
Statute Book.

Lord HERSCHELL—If you can make that out. Is that
so, because that is the difficulty. It is so far in existence
and so far effective at this moment in any of these districts
that without any interference of any Legislature the people
in that district can bring it into force.

Mr. MACLAREN—Yes.

Lord HERSCHELL—That is to say, a certain majority in
the district. Now, if the Provincial Legislature enables
another majority in the district to bring exactly the same
prohibition into force, can those two stand together side by
side ? They conflict directly. That seems to be the difficulty
in your way with reference to a total prohibition.

Mr. MACLAREN—It does not apply to what I was considering just now, but I shall have to get to Question No. 7.

Lord HERSCHELL—That, of course, some people would
contend is total prohibition because it prohibits the great
mass of people drinking, but that is another question.
Leaving that Act, that argument would only apply to total
prohibition, because there would be nothing inconsistent in
a certain majority in a district being able to bring about total

Y 2

prohibition, and the Provincial Legislature enabling that or some other body to bring about something less than total prohibition: there would be no inconsistency, and the two might stand together. We are dealing now with the question of total prohibition.

Lord WATSON—Probably we might be obliged to consider that. One of the most important questions in the present case appears to me to be what is the true construction of the Canadian Act for establishing temperance ? How are you to read it ? Is the Act to be read as if it had enacted expressly that the only rule of prohibition in Canada should be that enacted by the Statute ? The enactments of the Statute, reading them in that light, are as I read them, alternative. The Act may have one or two effects within the realm of Canada. In those regions where the inhabitants by a Local majority have elected to adopt and apply the Act the rule is one. It is a rule of prohibition. If the reading of the Statute which I have suggested were to be adopted in those regions where that Act has not been adopted, the rule is, the same license that prevailed at the time the Act passed.

Mr. MACLAREN—That is the construction which I would submit.

Lord WATSON—It appears to me that if that be the true reading of the Dominion Act—I am not deciding in one way or the other—but I do say if that be the true reading of the Dominion Act, a Provincial Act creating prohibition, where according to the Dominion Act they do not exist, would to my mind, be as great an intrusion upon the Dominion of Canada as diminishing prohibition in those regions where the prohibitory provisions of the Act had been applied. They would be equally in collision. There would be the same repugnancy in the one case as in the other case if the Act be of that nature in those districts where it has not been adopted. The law of freedom is as much the law as the law of prohibition in those places where it has been adopted.

Mr. MACLAREN—I most respectfully submit to your Lordships that the proper construction of the Act, and I think the decision on this part of our case at least would lead to the interpretation that where the Canada Temperance Act has not been adopted prohibition more or less extensive, more or less complete may be made by the Provinces——

Lord HERSCHELL—When you say prohibition more or less complete, we are now distinguishing—at least I am—between that which is prohibition and that which falls short of prohibition. What some people would call prohibition I should not call prohibition at all, but something short of it.

Mr. MACLAREN—One would need to define terms to consider it. I submit the full length of the argument of my learned friend as to the field being occupied really goes against *Hodge* v. *The Queen*.

Lord HERSCHELL—No, because what strikes me at present is this as regards prohibition properly so called which you take the Canada Temperance Act to be. The Legislature of Canada has said in every part of Canada this shall be the law, as to prohibition. I am not saying this is so but I am putting it to you—that a certain majority in a district can bring it about. Supposing them to have got that, it may be in the future no Provincial Legislature can say that in any district of the Dominion prohibition shall be brought about in any other way, because if it were you would have at the same time existing over a particular district two laws applicable to prohibition which differ in their nature. But then that would not decide the question whether everything short of prohibition might not still in those districts be within the province of the Provincial Legislature because as to that the Legislature of Canada has done nothing. It certainly has not occupied the field. *Hodge* v. *The Queen* has said that you may regulate and restrict it. That is quite clear. Then to what extent short of prohibition ? It is difficult to see how you can draw any line to say *that* is within *Hodge* v. *The Queen* and *that* is without it. I feel that difficulty at present, but, then, when you are dealing with prohibition you are dealing with a different thing.

Lord DAVEY—*Hodge* v. *The Queen* strikes me as this : Where liquor traffic may be lawfully carried on, it is within the power of the Municipality or the Provincial Legislature to

make the necessary provision for its being carried on in an
orderly manner. That is all that *Hodge* v. *The Queen* says.

Mr. MACLAREN—I submit that it probably goes beyond
that. If your Lordships look at page 160 amongst the powers
when they are considering questions 4 and 5, one of them is
for limiting the number of licenses. Our Courts have held
that the Commissioners may cut the licenses in a Municipality
down to two.

Lord DAVEY—By allowing the traffic to be carried on
where the necessary majority have not voted for prohibition
they do not say that every individual in the place may carry
it on. It is still within the power of the Municipality to say
in a reasonable way there being a traffic which will lead to
disorder : " We will take care it is carried on by respectable
people."

Lord HERSCHELL—And also that it is not carried on by
too many.

Mr. MACLAREN—Yes, and our Courts have held, and I do
not know that it is challenged, that under these limiting
powers they can limit it to two, not to one, because that
would be to create a monopoly, and there is no evidence that
the Legislature meant to give any municipal council the power
to create a monopoly,

Lord HERSCHELL.—It means they may limit the number.

Mr. MACLAREN—Would there be a difference in Toronto
between cutting down the licenses to one and saying there
shall be no retail license at all.

Lord HERSCHELL—There would be all the difference
between the one being prohibition and the other not.

Mr. MACLAREN—There being no retail sales within the
limits.

Lord WATSON—I think it is difficult to define. Even
regulation can be carried out so as to defeat sales altogether.
I do not wish to express any opinion on that point, but my
difficulty is as to this, whether the object of the Dominion law
is not to declare and provide that a rule as to prohibition and

sales is to be a matter depending upon the will of the inhabitants in certain districts expressed in the manner indicated by the Statute. There may be, I quite admit, certain powers of regulation in the way of licensing, because I think it was never contemplated that every person in the country is to sell. The contemplation of all those Acts is that the sale should be restricted, and section 92 gives strong colour to that. It never was intended by the framers of the Act that there should be a selling of liquor at large without license or restriction.

Lord HERSCHELL.—Are there any provisions for clubs in the Province of Ontario ? Are there working men's clubs where they could buy a dozen bottles ?

Mr. MACLAREN--The majority of the clubs in Ontario are registered under a general Act relating to Benevolent Associations, and the License Act has a clause providing that there shall be no liquor sold even to the members of those clubs. There are certain clubs which have charters.

Lord HERSCHELL.—Are those clubs with some particular privileges ?

Mr. MACLAREN—They have special privileges.

Lord HERSCHELL.—Is there anything to prevent a voluntary club being formed asking no particular privileges ? I suppose there are clubs where people may get intoxicating liquors ?

Mr. MACLAREN—There are some clubs, but in the ordinary club it is prohibited.

Lord WATSON—It is made a condition of the statutory privileges they enjoy that they shall not consume liquor ; but the question I understood his Lordship, Lord Herschell, to put to you is this, supposing fifty working men founded an association without going to the Legislature, formed a club and took a room and ordered in their own supplies of liquor, and met there every afternoon and had their drink, would that be prohibited by the law as it stands ?

Mr. MACLAREN—I could refer to the License Law, but my impression is those voluntary associations are included under those clubs. You might go to a county judge and put your rules and regulations before the county judge and he would give a certificate. It is a merely formal matter.

Lord DAVEY—.' re there no social clubs amongst people of the wealthier classes ?

Mr. MACLAREN—There are.

Lord DAVEY—Are they registered under this Act ?

Mr. MACLAREN—No; not under that Act. There are four in the city of Toronto that have special charters. The Royal Yacht Club, the Toronto Club, the National Club, and one political club. There are four clubs in the city of Toronto.

Lord DAVEY—I remember I was invited to dinner at the Montreal Club.

Mr. MACLAREN—That is in Quebec. There is a different law in Quebec, because clubs are licensed.

Lord WATSON—Is there anything in the law of the Province or the law of Canada to prevent twenty miners, supposing this law were in force, purchasing a couple of dozen of whiskey, then to meet together under one roof and consume it at the same time indulging in social intercourse.

Mr. MACLAREN—I presume there is nothing to affect that.

The LORD CHANCELLOR—I can remember on one occasion a remarkable example of that. The town of Cardiff is under a particular law which prohibits the sale of liquor on Sunday absolutely, but the people who desired to have a little entertainment bought by subscription a barrel of whiskey, rolled it into a field and they went there all day on Sunday and indulged in it. The law was found to be powerless to prevent it.

Mr. MACLAREN—The present argument I am addressing myself to is practically this, in answer to Lord Watson I respectfully say that the Canada Temperance Act as construed by *Russell* v. *The Queen* to my mind is not such an Act.

Lord WATSON—I quite understand your argument. It is absolutely necessary to your case. If you were to suggest it was otherwise you would suggest at the same time that the Dominion was paramount.

Lord DAVEY—What is put on the other side is that the Scott Act in effect has two aspects. In the first place it says that prohibition shall take place, subject to the proviso where the necessary majority has voted, and also that there shall be no prohibition unless the necessary majority do vote.

Mr. MACLAREN—I submit that is not a proper construction of the Scott Act for this reason——

Lord DAVEY—I do not think Mr. Blake put it exactly in that way.

Mr. MACLAREN—Not in those words, but I think your Lordship has fairly expressed the idea as I understood Mr. Blake; but I should submit that that is not the true nature of the Canada Temperance Act, and for this reason—your Lordships in *Russell* v. *The Queen* found that good, as being in the nature of Criminal Law. You do not put it under that, but said it was in the nature of Criminal Law. The nature of Criminal Statutes is not permissive but prohibitory. Criminal Law stops at prohibition. The Criminal Law is "Thou shalt not."

Lord HERSCHELL—Putting it under Criminal Law was not necessary to the decision. I must confess, personally, I should hesitate about that because in one sense every law is a Criminal Law. Every law which says that under certain conditions only shall you do this or that, and under certain conditions you shall not do it and imposes a penalty, would be a Criminal Law. In fact in England, it is said, wherever a duty is imposed by Statute and no penalty is imposed, an indictment for misdemeanour could be maintained.

Mr. MACLAREN—The same in the Interpretation Act in Canada.

Lord HERSCHELL—If so, any legislation which imposes a particular duty is based on Criminal Law, which is rather an extravagant proposition.

Mr. MACLAREN—When you are legislating in the nature of Criminal Law——

The LORD CHANCELLOR—What does something in the nature of something else mean ?

Mr. MACLAREN—I am not quoting the precise words, but in *Russell* v. *The Queen* your Lordships speak of it as being in the nature of Criminal Law, and I am saying this—that I think it is in the nature of such laws that they are prohibitory. The object of the law is not to legalize something else, but to forbid.

Sir RICHARD COUCH—We did not in *Russell* v. *The Queen* put it on the ground of Criminal Law at all.

Mr. MACLAREN—But the subject of the legislation is in the nature of Criminal Law, so that I submit the Canada Temperance Act is such an Act that its object is to render something illegal under certain conditions, and this object is not to legalize something and thereby prevent the Provincial Legislature from dealing with it.

Lord DAVEY—Not legalize. It is lawful already to sell liquor. They do not legalize the sale of liquor, but say it shall not be illegal unless the necessary majority vote for it.

Lord HERSCHELL—When a law says in this way you may prohibit it, does not it impliedly say in no other way you shall prohibit it ? That is the question.

Mr. MACLAREN—I do not think the Canada Temperance Act goes so far as that.

The LORD CHANCELLOR—Not in words, but the whole question is, what it means ? It is not a field of legislation of this character.   It does say there shall be no other legislation than that.

Lord WATSON—There are a number of enactments that point very much to that result.   There is a poll to be taken of the inhabitants, and those in favour of adopting the repressive clauses may be in a minority. Then there is a special provision to the effect that no further steps can be taken towards introducing a prohibitory law for three years.

Does not that indicate in the mind of the Legislature that
during those three years there shall be no prohibitory law.

Mr. MACLAREN—It means there shall not be the Canada
Temperance Act at least.

The LORD CHANCELLOR—You are quite right to make
that answer, but whether it is a sound one is another matter.

Lord WATSON—You think it meant to imply that some
other authority might introduce some other law.

Mr. MACLAREN—Some other law. That is the length of
my argument. Then, my Lords, Mr. Blake used this illustration. He said if a matter is local, the fact that it affects
more than one Province does not make it general. I am not
using his exact words, but I think that was the idea. That
was in answer to one of your Lordships, who put this point,
that where a matter remains a local matter affecting one
Province, the Province may deal with it, but if it spreads to
other Provinces to such an extent that the Parliament of
Canada think it is a matter that affects the general welfare of
the Dominion, they may legislate. In answer to that point
of Mr. Blake's, I think one of the cases which he cited and
referred to illustrates that point. That is the case of *Dobie*
v. *The Temporalities Board*.

Lord WATSON—I do not think that that case in the least
degree affects this question. That was a question where, by
a Statute in Canada, a corporate body was appointed, having
its existence equally in both Upper and Lower Canada.
They were severed, and it was held that the Legislature of
neither of the two Provinces into which Old Canada was
divided—Ontario and Quebec—could touch or repeal that law.

Mr. MACLAREN—Nor both together.

Lord WATSON—And that is by reason that the interests
created by the Act were so much one and the same that the
one Province could not deal with its repeal and alteration
without affecting the interests of another Province. I do not
think the present Act would come under that category at all.
I do not think there is a word in that case or anything in the
principle of the decision of that case to the effect that if this

had been a larger Act, applicable to the whole Dominion, that either of the two Provinces could have repealed that, so far as it affected the other Province which was affected by the repeal or alteration which one of the Provinces endeavoured to pass in that case and did pass ineffectually; and in point of fact individual and civil rights in the other Province were affected by this legislation. There is no provision made in the Act for joint legislation.

Mr. MACLAREN—No.

Lord HERSCHELL—I think the point you are on now may be looked at from another point of view. It is the same question. I suppose, if your opponents are right, then the Canada Temperance Act by implication would repeal this Act now in question. It was not in operation at the time, it has been only re-enacted since then.

Mr. MACLAREN—Yes.

Lord HERSCHELL—Supposing that to have been in operation, that is another way of testing it, were the two so inconsistent that the Canada Temperance Act, when passed, by implication repealed it?

Mr. MACLAREN—Yes.

Lord WATSON—Unquestionably, that result would follow if it is an Act of the kind that is represented. It would repeal by mere repugnancy the old Canadian Statute.

Mr. MACLAREN—Yes; but our claim is that the Canada Temperance Act did not repeal the antecedent legislation.

Lord HERSCHELL—I think that is a good way of testing it; if it did you could not re-enact it.

Mr. MACLAREN—Yes; it would be fair to say that *Dobie's* case lays down something that must affect the question of repeal. The head-note states the argument. I am reading it from 1st Cartwright, page 351, and I think the first paragraph of the head-note states the Judgment on that point correctly. It says :—

" The powers conferred by the B. N. A. Act, 1867, s. 129, upon the Provincial Legislatures of Ontario and Quebec, to repeal and alter

the Statutes of the Old Parliament of Canada, are precisely co-extensive
with the powers of direct legislation with which those bodies are
invested by the other clauses of the Act of 1867."

That is an authority that comes up in connection with the
question of repeal.

Lord WATSON—I think that has been recognised again
and again.

Mr. MACLAREN—That I think there is very little doubt
about, and this case of *Dobie* I thought was an authority on
this point.

Lord WATSON—In that case the powers were not co-
extensive.

Mr. MACLAREN—They were not.

Lord WATSON—The power of repeal involved interference
with another Province.

Mr. MACLAREN—To go back for a moment to the power
as to the applicability of the Canada Temperance Act where
not adopted. I refer your Lordships to the expressions used
in *Hodge* v. *The Queen*. It does not go the full length, but I
think it goes a long way towards the interpretation we are
now contending for. After setting out the sections 4 and 5,
those partially prohibitory clauses in 4 and 5, and as to their
nature, your Lordships say, at page 131 of L. R. 9 App. Cas.
and 3 Cartwright, page 161 :—

" As such they cannot be said to interfere with the general regulation of trade and commerce which belongs to the Dominion Parliament,
and do not conflict with the provisions of the Canada Temperance Act,
which does not appear to have as yet been locally adopted."

So that for the purpose of restriction, so far as they were in
question in *Hodge* v. *The Queen* your Lordships have declared
that the Canada Temperance Act, where not adopted, does
not interfere.

Lord HERSCHELL—If it had been adopted it clearly would
have interfered, because there would have been in force in
the particular district one law saying you shall not sell at all,
and the other saying you may sell under certain conditions.

Mr. MACLAREN—So that the more stringent law being
followed would override the less stringent.

Lord WATSON—The *dicta* in that Judgment, or the grounds of that Judgment, I think, aid you very considerably in considering the question whether or not the subject matter of the enactment falls within sub-section 2, but I do not think it throws any light whatever on the question of what is the effect of the Dominion Act, assuming it to be an Act passed under their general powers, because when you come to consider the effect of the Act, it appears to me to be very immaterial whether it falls under sub-section 2 or under the general powers, because either in the one case or the other, to the extent to which it is operative it is paramount, and there is no difference between the effect of a Dominion Statute in these two cases. The effect of the power being within either one or the other may be very different in its extent and very different in its consequences so long as the Dominion Parliament had not legislated, but after they have legislated within the limit assigned to them by the Act, the legislation, whether it is under sub-section 2 simply or whether under their general powers, is equally effective and paramount.

Mr. MACLAREN—I must ask your Lordships to consider this in that connection. To my mind the last clause of section 91 does distinguish between the general powers and the enumerated.

Lord WATSON—There is a clear distinction.

Mr. MACLAREN—So far as refers to sub-section 16.

Lord DAVEY—It has always occurred to me that the Provincial Legislature may legislate in its own Province on a matter on which the Canadian Parliament may also legislate for Canada generally.

Mr. MACLAREN—That I think is clear.

Lord DAVEY—If not within one of the enumerated classes.

Lord WATSON—I would also say this, that I think there is a difference between that which is done entirely in virtue of the general power, and that which is done under a clause and I think that which is done under the general power may be in the same position, or their power to act under the general clause, may be in the same position with their right to legislate incidentally and properly—properly it must be—for the purposes of some of the sections.

Mr. MACLAREN—Your Lordship says " may," and I am glad to observe your Lordship does not say " must," but as to the enumerated powers " must " would be applicable.

Lord WATSON—May or may not. Take the very question which we had in one of the most recent cases where a law was enacted in connection with banks.

Mr. MACLAREN—*Tennant v. The Union Bank.*

Lord WATSON—As to what effect certain documents in the hands of a banker would have. It was held that that was naturally and fairly incidental to the right of legislating as to banking, and was implied ; but in legislating for banking the Dominion might, if they had chosen, have left that to the operation of the existing law, and it did not go the length of saying that under this clause giving them power of dealing with civil rights, the local authority might have regulated that matter (warehouse receipts) and the ground was occupied.

Mr. MACLAREN—In that case the ground was occupied by the Chattel Mortgage provision requiring registration which the Dominion exempted from.

Lord WATSON—That is so. It shows there are some powers of legislation given to the Dominion Parliament incidental to the matters included in some of the classes which may be exactly in the same position as these general powers.

Mr. MACLAREN—"Ancillary" is the word your Lordships used in the Judgment, and, I think it is a very appropriate word. I was going to remark that as to this power of legislation and the right of the Province to legislate, until the Dominion take hold, we have many illustrations. A great many matters were at the time of Confederation and subsequently considered as petty matters to be dealt with by Municipal by-laws, but which the Dominion under its power of Criminal Law has from time to time made statutory offences. I need not trouble your Lordships with an enumeration of them, but perhaps I may mention the classes

under which they would come. There are a great many
matters such as injury to shade trees,—injury to other trees
and crops, and a great many matters which at the time
of Confederation were left to the local legislature to allow
the Municipalities to deal with ; but since that time the
Dominion Parliament under its power of Criminal Law,
finding that these matters were not applicable to one Province
alone but might be made general for the Dominion have put
them as part of the Criminal Law of the Country and made
these offences punishable. In the Act of 1869 there are a
number of illustrations of that kind, but again in the Criminal
Code of 1892 a large number of subjects which had been
previously the subject of legislation by Municipal by-law are
taken and appropriated by the Dominion under the heading
of Criminal Law and put in the Criminal Code and made
punishable offences either by summary conviction or by
indictment. That is, I think, a class of subject in some
respects analogous to the present in which they may be dealt
with locally so long as the Dominion leaves them to the local
Legislature. There are a large number of subjects in that
way the Dominion could take possession of under the head of
Criminal Law by declaring it to be an offence throughout the
Dominion, but the fact that that might come under Criminal
Law does not prevent the Province either by itself or by a
Municipality legislating with reference to it and punishing
infractions of their regulations until there is some over-riding
Dominion legislation.

Lord WATSON—These cases are quite intelligible, but in
those cases I should be apt to say that if the Dominion
Parliament were to occupy what may be called the whole
field, in that case they would trench on the legislative power
of the Province.

Mr. MACLAREN—They might—the whole field. The
emphasis is on " the whole field " in your Lordship's mind.
I do not think the whole field is open to them. Then with
regard to the observation of my learned friend Mr. Blake that
in the United States Constitution the word " Regulation "
has been held to include prohibition I would call attention to
one fact that the well-known law of the United States, what

is known as the Maine Liquor Law, and other prohibitory laws of the United States——

Lord WATSON—I am much disposed to think that these illustrations are not of much weight here because really we are dealing with very general terms and whenever you come to deal with general terms such as " Trade and Commerce " and " the Regulation of Trade and Commerce " it is perfectly obvious you cannot put a general meaning to them, you must refer to the context of the statute to discover what the Legislature meant in employing them.   I do not doubt that the Regulation of Trade and Commerce may very fairly include prohibition.   If the context gave an indication I should not be surprised at its being construed either way in one statute, but then being construed one way in one statute would not lead to its being similarly construed in another.

Mr. MACLAREN—Perhaps not, but the construction in *Parsons'* case as referring to a particular trade goes a long way towards maintaining the position we are claiming in this case.   On these grounds I respectfully ask for a reversal of the Judgment below from your Lordships.

Mr. BLAKE—My Lords, may I be permitted with reference to the question put by Lord Watson as to the voluntary associations to refer your Lordships to the legislation.   In section 53 of chapter 194 of the Revised Statutes of Ontario, 1887, it is to be found ; and it was found that that difficulty which your Lordship suggested existed and the law was amended by providing that proof of consumption or intended consumption of liquor on the premises by any member of the Club would be conclusive evidence of sale, and on proof of consumption would be conclusively presumed to have been sold, and so become liable to the Act.   The whole thing is concluded.

Judgment Reserved.]

z

Judgment

*Of the Lords of the Judicial Committee of the Privy Council
on the Appeal of the*

ATTORNEY-GENERAL FOR ONTARIO

v

THE ATTORNEY-GENERAL FOR THE DOMINION OF CANADA,
and the DISTILLERS' AND BREWERS' ASSOCIATION OF
ONTARIO, from the Supreme Court of Canada ; delivered 9th May,
1896.

Present :

THE LORD CHANCELLOR.
LORD HERSCHELL.
LORD WATSON.
LORD DAVEY.
SIR RICHARD COUCH.

[*Delivered by Lord Watson.*]

Their Lordships think it expedient to deal, in the first
instance, with the seventh question, because it raises a
practical issue, to which the able arguments of Counsel on
both sides of the Bar were chiefly directed, and also because
it involves considerations which have a material bearing upon
the answers to be given to the other six questions submitted
in this appeal. In order to appreciate the merits of the controversy, it is necessary to refer to certain laws for the
restriction or suppression of the liquor traffic, which were
passed by the Legislature of the old Province of Canada
before the Union, or have since been enacted by the Parliament of the Dominion, and by the Legislature of Ontario,
respectively.

At the time when the British North America Act of 1867
came into operation, the statute book of the old Province
contained two sets of enactments applicable to Upper Canada,
which, though differing in expression, were in substance
very similar.

The most recent of these enactments were embodied in the Temperance Act 1864 (27 and 28 Vict. c. 18), which conferred upon the Municipal Council of every county, town, township, or incorporated village, " besides the powers at present conferred on it by law," power at any time to pass a by-law prohibiting the sale of intoxicating liquors, and the issue of licenses therefor, within the limits of the municipality. Such by-law was not to take effect until submitted to and approved by a majority of the qualified electors ; and provision was made for its subsequent repeal, in deference to an adverse vote of the electors.

The previous enactments relating to the same subject, which were in force at the time of the Union, were contained in the Consolidated Municipal Act, 29 and 30 Vict. c. 51. They empowered the Council of every township, town, and incorporated village, and the Commissioners of Police in cities, to make by-laws for prohibiting the sale by retail of spirituous, fermented or other manufactured liquors, in any inn or other house of public entertainment ; and for prohibiting totally the sale thereof in shops and places other than houses of public entertainment ; provided the by-law, before the final passing thereof, had been duly approved by the electors of the Municipality in the manner prescribed by the Act.   After the Union, the Legislature of Ontario inserted these enactments in the Tavern and Shop License Act, 32 Vict. c. 32.   They were purposely omitted from subsequent consolidations of the Municipal and Liquor License Acts ; and, in the year 1886, when the Canada Temperance Act was passed by the Parliament of Canada, there was no Provincial law authorising the prohibition of liquor sales in Ontario, save the Temperance Act 1864.

The Canada Temperance Act of 1886 (Revised Statutes of Canada, 49 Vict. c. 106) is applicable to all the Provinces of the Dominion.   Its general scheme is to give to the electors of every county or city the option of adopting, or declining to adopt, the provisions of the second part of the Act, which make it unlawful for any person " by himself, " his clerk, servant or agent, to expose or keep for sale, or " directly or indirectly, on any pretence or upon any device, to " sell or barter, or in consideration of the purchase of any other " property, give to any other person any intoxicating liquor."

z 2

It expressly declares that no violation of these enactments shall be made lawful by reason of any license of any description whatsoever. Certain relaxations are made in the case of sales of liquor for sacramental or medicinal purposes, or for exclusive use in some art, trade or manufacture. The prohibition does not extend to manufacturers, importers or wholesale traders who sell liquors in quantities above a specified limit, when they have good reason to believe that the purchasers will forthwith carry their purchase beyond the limits of the county or city, or of any adjoining county or city in which the provisions of the Act are in force.

For the purpose of bringing the second part of the Act into operation, an order of the Governor-General of Canada in Council is required. The order must be made on the petition of a county or city, which cannot be granted until it has been put to the vote of the electors of such county or city. When a majority of the votes polled are adverse to the petition, it must be dismissed; and no similar application can be made within the period of three years from the day on which the poll was taken. When the vote is in favour of the petition, and is followed by an Order in Council, one-fourth of the qualified electors of the county or city may apply to the Governor-General in Council for a recall of the Order, which is to be granted, in the event of a majority of the electors voting in favour of the application. Power is given to the Governor-General in Council to issue in the like manner, and after similar procedure, an Order repealing any by-law passed by any Municipal Council for the application of the Temperance Act of 1864.

The Dominion Act also contains an express repeal of the prohibitory clauses of the Provincial Act of 1864, and of the machinery thereby provided for bringing them into operation, (1) as to every municipality within the limits of Ontario in which, at the passing of the Act of 1886, there was no municipal by-law in force, (2) as to every municipality within these limits in which a prohibitive by-law then in force shall be subsequently repealed under the provisions of either Act, and (3) as to every municipality, having a municipal by-law, which is included in the limits of, or has the same limits with, any county or city in which the second part of the Canada Temperance Act is brought into force before the

repeal of the by-law, which by-law, in that event, is declared
to be null and void.

With a view of restoring to municipalities within the
Province, whose powers were affected by that repeal, the
right to make by-laws which they had possessed under the
law of the old Province, the Legislature of Ontario passed
Section 18 of 53 Vict. c. 56, to which the seventh question
in this case relates. The enacting words of the clause are
introduced by a preamble which recites the previous course
of legislation, and the repeal by the Canada Temperance Act
of the Upper Canada Act of 1864 in municipalities where not
in force, and concludes thus,—" it is expedient that munici-
" palities should have the powers by them formerly possessed."
The enacting words of the clause, with the exception of one
or two changes of expression which do not affect its substance,
are a mere reproduction of the provisions, not of the Temperance Act of 1864, but of the kindred provisions of the
Municipal Act 29 & 30 Vict., c. 51, which had been omitted
from the consolidated statutes of the Province. A new proviso
is added, to the effect that, " nothing in this section contained
" shall be construed into an exercise of Jurisdiction by the
" Province of Ontario beyond the revival of provisions of law
" which were in force at the date of the passing of the British
" North America Act, and which the subsequent legislation
" of this Province purported to repeal." The Legislature of
Ontario subsequently passed an Act (54 Vict., c. 46), for the
purpose of explaining that Section 18 was not meant to repeal
by implication certain provisions of the Municipal Act
29 & 30 Vict., c. 51, which limit its application to retail
dealings.

The seventh question raises the issue,—whether, in the
circumstances which have just been detailed, the Provincial
Legislature had authority to enact Section 18 ? In order to
determine that issue, it becomes necessary to consider, in the
first place, whether the Parliament of Canada had jurisdiction
to enact the Canada Temperance Act ; and, if so, to consider
in the second place, whether, after that Act became the law
of each Province of the Dominion, there yet remained power
with the Legislature of Ontario to enact the provisions of
Section 18.

The authority of the Dominion Parliament to make laws

for the suppression of liquor traffic in the Provinces is maintained, in the first place, upon the ground that such legislation deals with matters affecting " the peace, order, and good
" government of Canada," within the meaning of the introductory and general enactments of Section 91 of the British
North America Act; and, in the second place, upon the
ground, that it concerns " the regulation of trade and commerce," being No. 2 of the enumerated classes of subjects
which are placed under the exclusive jurisdiction of the
federal Parliament by that section. These sources of jurisdiction are in themselves distinct; and are to be found in
different enactments.

It was apparently contemplated by the framers of the
Imperial Act of 1867, that the due exercise of the enumerated
powers conferred upon the Parliament of Canada by Section
91 might, occasionally and incidentally, involve legislation
upon matters which are *prima facie* committed exclusively to
the Provincial Legislatures by Section 92. In order to provide against that contingency, the concluding part of Section
91 enacts that " any matter coming within any of the classes
" of subjects enumerated in this section shall not be deemed
" to come within the class of matters of a local or private
" nature comprised in the enumeration of the classes of
" subjects by this Act assigned exclusively to the Legislatures
" of the Provinces." It was observed by this Board in *Citizens
Insurance Company of Canada* v. *Parsons* (7, Ap. Ca. 108), that
the paragraph just quoted " applies in its grammatical con-
" struction only to No. 16 of Section 92." The observation
was not material to the question arising in that case, and it
does not appear to their Lordships to be strictly accurate. It
appears to them that the language of the exception in Section
91 was meant to include, and correctly describes, all the
matters enumerated in the sixteen heads of Section 92, as
being, from a provincial point of view, of a local or private
nature. It also appears to their Lordships that the exception
was not meant to derogate from the legislative authority given
to Provincial Legislatures by these sixteen sub-sections, save
to the extent of enabling the Parliament of Canada to deal
with matters local or private, in those cases where such
legislation is necessarily incidental to the exercise of the
powers conferred upon it by the enumerative heads of Clause

91. That view was stated and illustrated by Sir Montague Smith in *Citizens Insurance Company* v. *Parsons* (7, Ap. Ca. pp. 108, 109), and in *Cushing* v. *Dupuy* (5, Ap. Ca. 415); and it has been recognised by this Board in *Tennant* v. *Union Bank of Canada* (1894, Ap. Ca. 46), and in *Attorney-General of Ontario* v. *Attorney-General of the Dominion* (1894, Ap. Ca. 200).

The general authority given to the Canadian Parliament, by the introductory enactments of Section 91, is, " to make " laws for the peace, order and good government of Canada, " in relation to all matters not coming within the classes of " subjects by this Act assigned exclusively to the Legislatures " of the Provinces " ; and it is declared, but not so as to restrict the generality of these words, that the exclusive authority of the Canadian Parliament extends to all matters coming within the classes of subjects which are enumerated in the clause. There may, therefore, be matters not included in the enumeration, upon which the Parliament of Canada has power to legislate, because they concern the peace, order and good government of the Dominion. But to those matters which are not specified among the enumerated subjects of legislation, the exception from Section 92, which is enacted by the concluding words of Section 91, has no application ; and, in legislating with regard to such matters, the Dominion Parliament has no authority to encroach upon any class of subjects which is exclusively assigned to Provincial Legislatures by Section 92. These enactments appear to their Lordships to indicate, that the exercise of legislative power by the Parliament of Canada, in regard to all matters not enumerated in Section 92, ought to be strictly confined to such matters as are unquestionably of Canadian interest and importance, and ought not to trench upon Provincial legislation, with respect to any of the classes of subjects enumerated in Section 92. To attach any other construction to the general power which, in supplement of its enumerated powers, is conferred upon the Parliament of Canada by Section 91, would, in their Lordships' opinion, not only be contrary to the intendment of the Act, but would practically destroy the autonomy of the Provinces. If it were once conceded that the Parliament of Canada has authority to make laws applicable to the whole Dominion, in relation to matters which in each Province are substantially of local or private interest, upon the assumption that these matters also concern the peace, order and good government of the Dominion, there is hardly a subject enumerated in Section 92 upon which it might not legislate, to the exclusion of the Provincial Legislatures.

In construing the introductory enactments of Section 91, with respect to matters other than those enumerated, which concern the peace, order and good government of Canada, it must be kept in view that Section 94, which empowers the Parliament of Canada to make provision for the uniformity of the laws relative to property and civil rights in Ontario, Nova Scotia, and New Brunswick, does not extend to the Province of Quebec; and also that the Dominion legislation thereby authorised is expressly declared to be of no effect, unless and until it has been adopted and enacted by the provincial legislature. These enactments would be idle and abortive, if it were held that the Parliament of Canada derives jurisdiction from the introductory provisions of Section 91, to deal with any matter which is in substance local or provincial, and does not truly affect the interest of the Dominion as a whole. Their Lordships do not doubt that some matters, in their origin local and provincial, might attain such dimensions as to affect the body politic of the Dominion, and to justify the Canadian Parliament in passing laws for their regulation or abolition, in the interest of the Dominion. But great caution must be observed, in distinguishing between that which is local and provincial, and therefore within the jurisdiction of the provincial legislatures, and that which has ceased to be merely local or provincial, and has become matter of national concern, in such sense as to bring it within the jurisdiction of the Parliament of Canada. An Act restricting the right to carry weapons of offence, or their sale to young persons, within the Province, would be within the authority of the Provincial Legislature. But traffic in arms, or the possession of them under such circumstances as to raise a suspicion that they were to be used for seditious purposes, or against a foreign State, are matters which their Lordships conceive, might be competently dealt with by the Parliament of the Dominion.

The judgment of this Board in *Russell* v. *The Queen* (7 Ap. Ca. 829), has relieved their Lordships from the difficult duty of considering whether the Canada Temperance Act of 1886 relates to the peace, order and good government of Canada, in such sense as to bring its provisions within the competency of the Canadian Parliament. In that case the controversy related to the validity of the Canada Temperance Act of 1878; and neither the Dominion nor the Provinces were represented in the argument. It arose between a private prosecutor and a person who had been convicted, at his instance, of violating the provisions of the Canadian Act, within a district of New Brunswick in which the prohibitory clauses of the Act had been adopted. But the provisions of the Act of 1878 were, in all material respects, the same with those which are now embodied in the Canada Temperance Act of 1886; and the reasons which were assigned for sustaining the validity of the earlier, are, in their Lordships' opinion, equally applicable to the later Act. It therefore appears to them that the decision in *Russell v. The Queen* must be accepted as an authority to the extent to which it goes, namely, that the restrictive provisions of the Act of 1886, when they have been duly brought into operation in any provincial area within the Dominion, must receive effect as valid enactments, relating to the peace, order, and good government of Canada.

That point being settled by decision, it becomes necessary to consider whether the Parliament of Canada had authority to pass the Temperance Act of 1886, as being an Act for the " regulation of trade and commerce " within the meaning of No. 2 of Section 91. If it were so, the Parliament of Canada would, under the exception from Section 92, which has already been noticed, be at liberty to exercise its legislative authority, although in so doing, it should interfere with the jurisdiction of the Provinces. The scope and effect of No. 2 of Section 91 were discussed by this Board at some length, in *Citizens Insurance Company v. Parsons* (7 Ap. Ca. 96), where it was decided that, in the absence of legislation upon the subject by the Canadian Parliament, the legislature of Ontario had authority to impose conditions, as being matters of civil right, upon the business of fire insurance, which was admitted to be a trade, so long as those conditions only affected provincial trade. Their Lordships do not find it necessary to re-open that discussion in the present case. The object of

the Canada Temperance Act of 1886 is, not to regulate retail
transactions between those who trade in liquor and their
customers, but to abolish all such transactions within every
provincial area in which its enactments have been adopted by
a majority of the local electors. A power to regulate, naturally
if not necessarily, assumes, unless it is enlarged by the
context, the conservation of the thing which is to be made
the subject of regulation. In that view, their Lordships
are unable to regard the prohibitive enactments of the
Canadian Statute of 1886 as regulations of trade and
commerce. They see no reason to modify the opinion which
was recently expressed, on their behalf, by Lord Davey, in
Municipal Corporation of the City of Toronto v. *Virgo* (1896, Ap.
Ca. 93), in these terms :—
" Their Lordships think there is marked distinction to be
" drawn between the prohibition or prevention of a trade
" and the regulation or governance of it, and indeed a power
" to regulate and govern seems to imply the continued
" existence of that which is to be regulated or governed."

The authority of the legislature of Ontario to enact
Section 18 of 53 Vict. c. 56 was asserted by the Appellant on
various grounds. The first of these, which was very strongly
insisted on, was to the effect that the power given to each
Province by No. 8, of Section 92, to create municipal
institutions in the Province, necessarily implies the right to
endow these institutions with all the administrative functions
which had been ordinarily possessed and exercised by them
before the time of the Union. Their Lordships can find
nothing to support that contention in the language of
Section 92, No. 8, which, according to its natural meaning,
simply gives provincial legislatures the right to create a legal
body, for the management of municipal affairs. Until confederation the Legislature of each Province as then constituted
could, if it chose, and did in some cases, entrust to a
municipality the execution of powers which now belong
exclusively to the Parliament of Canada. Since its date, a
Provincial Legislature cannot delegate any power which it
does not possess ; and the extent and nature of the functions
which it can commit to a municipal body of its own creation
must depend upon the legislative authority which it derives
from the provisions of Section 92 other than No. 8.

Their Lordships are likewise of opinion that Section 92, No. 9, does not give Provincial Legislatures any right to make laws for the abolition of the liquor traffic. It assigns to them " shop, saloon, tavern, auctioneer and other licenses, in order " to the raising of a revenue for provincial, local or municipal " purposes." It was held by this Board, in *Hodge* v. *The Queen* (9 Ap. Ca. 117), to include the right to impose reasonable conditions upon the licensees, which are in the nature of regulation ; but it cannot, with any show of reason, be construed as authorising the abolition of the sources from which revenue is to be raised.

The only enactments of Section 92 which appear to their Lordships to have any relation to the authority of Provincial Legislatures to make laws for the suppression of the liquor traffic are to be found in Nos. 13 and 16, which assign to their exclusive jurisdiction, (1) " property and civil rights in the Province," and (2) " generally all matters of a " merely local or private nature in the Province.' A law which prohibits retail transactions, and restricts the consumption of liquor within the ambit of the Province, and does not affect transactions in liquor between persons in the Province and persons in other Provinces or in foreign countries, concerns property in the Province which would be the subject matter of the transactions, if they were not prohibited, and also the civil rights of persons in the Province. It is not impossible that the vice of intemperance may prevail in particular localities within a Province, to such an extent as to constitute its cure by restricting or prohibiting the sale of liquor a matter of a merely local or private nature, and therefore falling *prima facie* within No. 16. In that state of matters, it is conceded that the Parliament of Canada could not imperatively enact a prohibitory law adapted and confined to the requirements of localities within the Province, where prohibition was urgently needed.

It is not necessary, for the purposes of the present appeal, to determine whether provincial legislation for the suppression of the liquor traffic, confined to matters which are provincial or local within the meaning of Nos. 13 and 16 is authorised by the one or by the other of these heads. It cannot, in their Lordships' opinion, be logically held to fall within both of them. In Section 92, No. 16 appears to them to have the same office which the general enactment, with respect to matters concerning the peace, order, and good government of Canada so far as supplementary of the enumerated subjects, fulfils in Section 91. It assigns to the provincial legislature all matters in a provincial sense local or private, which have been omitted from the preceding enumeration, and, although its terms are wide enough to cover, they were obviously not meant to include provincial legislation in relation to the classes of subjects already enumerated.

In the able and elaborate argument addressed to their Lordships on behalf of the Respondents, it was practically conceded that a provincial legislature must have power to deal with the restriction of the liquor traffic from a local and provincial point of view, unless it be held that the whole subject of restriction or abolition is exclusively committed to the Parliament of Canada, as being within the regulation of trade and commerce. In that case, the subject, in so far at least, as it had been regulated by Canadian legislation, would by virtue of the concluding enactment of Section 91, be excepted from the matters committed to provincial legislatures by Section 92. Upon the assumption that Section 91 (2) does not embrace the right to suppress a trade, Mr. Blake maintained, that, whilst the restriction of the liquor traffic may be competently made matter of legislation, in a provincial as well as a Canadian aspect, yet the Parliament of Canada has, by enacting the Temperance Act of 1886, occupied the whole possible field of legislation in either aspect, so as completely to exclude legislation by a Province. That appears to their Lordships to be the real point of controversy raised by the question with which they are at present dealing; and, before discussing the point, it may be expedient to consider the relation in which Dominion and provincial legislation stand to each other.

It has been frequently recognised by this Board, and it may now be regarded as settled law, that according to the scheme of the British North America Act, the enactments of the Parliament of Canada, in so far as these are within its competency, must over-ride provincial legislation. But the Dominion Parliament has no authority conferred upon it by the Act to repeal directly any provincial Statute whether it does or does not come within the limits of jurisdiction prescribed by Section 92. The repeal of a Provincial Act by the Parliament of Canada can only be effected by repugnancy between its provisions and the enactments of the Dominion; and if the existence of such repugnancy should become matter of dispute, the controversy cannot be settled by the action either of the Dominion or of the provincial legislature, but must be submitted to the judicial tribunals of the country. In their Lordships' opinion, the express repeal of the old provincial Act of 1864 by the Canada Temperance Act of 1886 was not within the authority of the Parliament of Canada. It is true that the Upper Canada Act of 1864 was continued in force within Ontario, by Section 129 of the British North America Act, " until " repealed, abolished or altered by the Parliament of Canada, " or by the provincial legislature," according to the authority of that Parliament, " or of that legislature." It appears to their Lordships that neither the Parliament of Canada nor the provincial legislatures have authority to repeal Statutes which they could not directly enact. Their Lordships had occasion, in *Dobie v. The Temporalities Board* (7 Ap. Ca. 136) to consider the power of repeal competent to the legislature of a Province. In that case, the Legislature of Quebec had repealed a Statute continued in force after the Union by Section 129, which had this peculiarity, that its provisions applied both to Quebec and to Ontario, and were incapable of being severed so as to make them applicable to one of these Provinces only. Their Lordships held (7 Ap. Ca. 147) that the powers conferred " upon the provincial Legislatures " of Ontario and Quebec to repeal and alter the Statutes of " the old Parliament of the Province of Canada are made " precisely co-extensive with the powers of direct legislation " with which these bodies are invested by the other clauses " of the Act of 1867 "; and that it was beyond the authority of the legislature of Quebec to repeal statutory enactments which affected both Quebec and Ontario. The same principle ought, in the opinion of their Lordships, to be applied to the present case. The old Temperance Act of 1864 was passed for Upper Canada, or in other words for the Province of Ontario; and its provisions, being confined to that Province only, could not have been directly enacted by the Parliament

of Canada. In the present case, the Parliament of Canada
would have no power to pass a prohibitory law for the
Province of Ontario; and could therefore have no authority
to repeal, in express terms, an Act which is limited in its
operation to that Province. In like manner, the express
repeal, in the Canada Temperance Act of 1886, of liquor
prohibitions adopted by a municipality in the Province of
Ontario under the sanction of provincial legislation, does not
appear to their Lordships to be within the authority of the
Dominion Parliament.

The question must next be considered, whether the
provincial enactments of Section 18, to any, and if so to
what extent, come into collision with the provisions of the
Canadian Act of 1886? In so far as they do, provincial
must yield to Dominion legislation, and must remain in
abeyance unless and until the Act of 1886 is repealed by the
Parliament which passed it.

The prohibitions of the Dominion Act have in some
respects an effect which may extend beyond the limits of a
Province; and they are all of a very stringent character.
They draw an arbitrary line, at 8 gallons in the case of beer,
and at 10 gallons in the case of other intoxicating liquors,
with the view of discriminating between wholesale and retail
transactions. Below the limit, sales within a district which
has adopted the Act are absolutely forbidden, except to the
two nominees of the Lieutenant-Governor of the Province.
who are only allowed to dispose of their purchases in small
quantities, for medicinal and other specified purposes. In
the case of sales above the limit, the rule is different. The
manufacturers of pure native wines, from grapes grown in
Canada have special favour shown them. Manufacturers of
other liquors within the district, as also merchants duly
licensed, who carry on an exclusively wholesale business, may
sell for delivery anywhere beyond the district unless such
delivery is to be made in an adjoining district where the Act
is in force. If the adjoining district happened to be in a
different Province, it appears to their Lordships to be doubtful, whether, even in the absence of Dominion legislation, a
restriction of that kind could be enacted by a Provincial
Legislature.

On the other hand, the prohibitions which Section 18

authorises municipalities to impose within their respective limits do not appear to their Lordships to affect any transactions in liquor which have not their beginning and their end within the Province of Ontario. The first branch of its prohibitory enactments strikes against sales of liquor by retail in any tavern, or other house or other place of public entertainment. The second extends to sales in shops and places other than houses of public entertainment; but the context indicates that it is only meant to apply to retail transactions; and that intention is made clear by the terms of the explanatory Act 54 Vict. c. 46, which fixes the line between wholesale and retail at one dozen of liquor in bottles, and five gallons if sold in other receptacles. The importer or manufacturer can sell any quantity above that limit; and any retail trader may do the same, provided that he sells the liquor in the original packages in which it was received by him from the importer or manufacturer.

It thus appears that, in their local application within the Province of Ontario, there would be considerable difference between the two laws; but it is obvious that their provisions could not be in force within the same district or province at one and the same time. In the opinion of their Lordships, the question of conflict between their provisions which arises in this case does not depend upon their identity or non-identity, but upon a feature which is common to both. Neither statute is imperative, their prohibitions being of no force or effect until they have been voluntarily adopted and applied by the vote of a majority of the electors in a district or municipality. In *Russell* v. *The Queen* (7 Ap. Ca. 841), it was observed by this Board, with reference to the Canada Temperance Act of 1878, "The Act as soon as it was passed "became a law for the whole Dominion, and the enactments "of the first part, relating to the machinery for bringing the "second part into force, took effect and might be put in "motion at once and everywhere within it." No fault can be found with the accuracy of that statement. *Mutatis mutandis*, it is equally true as a description of the provisions of Section 18. But in neither case can the statement mean more than this, that on the passing of the Act, each district or municipality within the Dominion or the Province as the case might be, became vested with a right to adopt and enforce certain prohibitions, if it thought fit to do so. But the prohibitions of these Acts, which constitute their object and their essence, cannot with the least degree of accuracy be said to be in force anywhere, until they have been locally adopted.

If the prohibitions of the Canada Temperance Act had been made imperative throughout the Dominion, their Lordships might have been constrained by previous authority to hold that the jurisdiction of the Legislature of Ontario to pass Section 18, or any similar law, had been superseded. In that case no provincial prohibitions such as are sanctioned by Section 18 could have been enforced by a municipality without coming into conflict with the paramount law of Canada. For the same reason, provincial prohibitions in force within a particular district will necessarily become inoperative whenever the prohibitory clauses of the Act of 1886 have been adopted by that district. But their Lordships can discover no adequate grounds for holding that there exists repugnancy between the two laws in districts of the Province of Ontario where the prohibitions of the Canadian Act are not, and may never be in force. In a district which has, by the votes of its electors, rejected the second part of the Canadian Act, the option is abolished for three years from the date of the poll; and it hardly admits of doubt, that there could be no repugnancy whilst the option given by the Canadian Act was suspended. The Parliament of Canada has not, either expressly or by implication, enacted, that so long as any district delays or refuses to accept the prohibitions which it has authorised, the Provincial Parliament is to be debarred from exercising the legislative authority given it by Section 92, for the suppression of the drink traffic as a local evil. Any such legislation would be unexampled ; and it is a grave question whether it would be lawful. Even if the provisions of Section 18 had been imperative, they would not have taken away or impaired the right of any district in Ontario to adopt, and thereby bring into force the prohibitions of the Canadian Act.

Their Lordships, for these reasons, give a general answer to the seventh question in the affirmative. They are of opinion that the Ontario Legislature had jurisdiction to enact

Section 18, subject to this necessary qualification, that its provisions are, or will become inoperative in any district of the Province which has already adopted, or may subsequently adopt the second part of the Canada Temperance Act of 1886.

Their Lordships will now answer briefly, in their order, the other questions submitted by the Governor-General of Canada. So far as they can ascertain from the Record, these differ from the question which has already been answered, in this respect, that they relate to matters which may possibly become litigious in the future, but have not as yet given rise to any real and present controversy. Their Lordships must further observe that these questions, being in their nature academic rather than judicial, are better fitted for the consideration of the officers of the Crown, than of a court of law. The replies to be given to them will necessarily depend upon the circumstances in which they may arise for decision; and these circumstances are in this case left to speculation. It must therefore be understood that the answers which follow are not meant to have, and cannot have, the weight of a judicial determination, except in so far as their Lordships may have occasion to refer to the opinions which they have already expressed in discussing the seventh question.

Answers to Questions I and II.—Their Lordships think it sufficient to refer to the opinions expressed by them in disposing of the seventh question.

Answer to Question III.—In the absence of conflicting legislation by the Parliament of Canada, their Lordships are opinion that the Provincial legislatures would have jurisdiction to that effect, if it were shown that the manufacture was carried on under such circumstances and conditions as to make its prohibition a merely local matter in the Province.

Answer to Question IV.—Their Lordships answer this question in the negative. It appears to them that the exercise by the Provincial legislature of such jurisdiction, in the wide and general terms in which it is expressed, would probably trench upon the exclusive authority of the Dominion Parliament.

AA

Answers to Questions V. and VI.—Their Lordships consider it unnecessary to give a categorical reply to either of these questions. Their opinion upon the points which the questions involve has been sufficiently explained in their answer to the seventh question.

Their Lordships will humbly advise Her Majesty to discharge the Order of the Supreme Court of Canada, dated the 15th January 1895; and to substitute therefor the several answers to the seven Questions submitted by the Governor-General of Canada, which have been already indicated. There will be no costs of this Appeal.

William Brown & Co. Limited, Printers, &c., London, E.C.

www.ingramcontent.com/pod-product-compliance
Lightning Source LLC
Chambersburg PA
CBHW030906270326
41929CB00008B/598